Children's Literature
Volume 23

Volume 23

Annual of
The Modern Language Association
Division on Children's Literature
and The Children's Literature
Association

Yale University Press

New Haven and London

1995

Children's Literature

The editors gratefully acknowledge support from Hollins College.

Editorial correspondence should be addressed to The Editors, *Children's Literature,* Department of English, Hollins College, Roanoke, Virginia 24020.

Manuscripts submitted should conform to the style in this issue. An original on non-erasable bond with two copies, a self-addressed envelope, and return postage are requested. Yale University Press does not accept dot-matrix printouts, and it requires double-spacing throughout text and notes. Unjustified margins are preferred. Writers of accepted manuscripts should be prepared to submit final versions of their essays on computer disk in XyWrite, Nota Bene, or Word Perfect.

Volumes 1–7 of *Children's Literature* can be obtained directly from John C. Wandell, The Children's Literature Foundation, P.O. Box 370, Windham Center, Conn. 06280. Volumes 8–22 can be obtained from Yale University Press, P.O. Box 209040, New Haven, Conn. 06520-9040, or from Yale University Press, 23 Pond Street, Hampstead, London NW3 2PN, England.

Library of Congress catalog card number: 79-66588
ISBN: 0-300-06235-4 (cloth), 0-300-06236-2 (paper); ISSN: 0092-8208

Set in Baskerville type by Tseng Information Systems, Inc., Durham, N.C.
Printed in the United States of America by Vail-Ballou Press, Binghamton, N.Y.

A catalogue record for this book is available from the British Library.

The paper in this book meets the guidelines for permanence and durability of the Committee on Production Guidelines for Book Longevity of the Council on Library Resources.

10   9   8   7   6   5   4   3   2   1

Contents

Reviews

From the Editor

Putting together a volume of *Children's Literature* is like devising a final exam for a course: one is startled to find how selections deserving of inclusion on their own merits have further justified their inclusion by forming connections with others. For example, when I heard Naomi Wood's paper on Barbara Follett at the 1993 MLA, I was immediately struck by the parallel between Barbara as a child writer and Marjory Fleming, whose writings Mitzi Myers discusses in her essay on Maria Edgeworth's "Madame de Fleury." A few weeks after I received Wood's revised conference paper, Jean Marsden submitted her essay on Mary Lamb, whose *Mrs. Leicester's School* was published a year after Edgeworth's novel. All three essays, which I have placed in a Forum modeled on recent issues of *PMLA*, deal with the female child's acquisition of language, the mother or mother surrogate's role in this acquisition, and the degree to and conditions under which this acquisition proves empowering. Although Myers presents the education of one generation of women by another in a positive light, both Marsden and Wood question, at least implicitly, whether such an education can succeed in a world still governed by men. Nonetheless, all three essays subvert the notion of the "natural" child, an idealization that has denied children, even as similar essentialist notions have denied women, agency in constructing their selves and their lives.

As I began organizing the remaining essays, I began to see that many, like the Forum essays, reflected the new "paradigm for the sociology of childhood" presented in Allison James and Alan Prout's collection *Constructing and Reconstructing Childhood* (London, 1990). This new paradigm regards "children as people to be studied in their own right and not just as receptacles of adult teaching." It also calls for a reassessment of John Holt's "mythic 'walled garden' of 'Happy, Safe, Protected, Innocent Childhood.'" In "Dwarf, Small World, Shrinking Child," Caroline Hunt demonstrates how these three variations on the miniature in children's books reflect the child's sense of vulnerability and insignificance as well as her strategies for coping with it. Tim Wolf, Reuben Sánchez, and Eva-Maria Metcalf discuss how Dr. Seuss, Sandra Cisneros, and Astrid

Lindgren portray children as confronting psychological, sociological, and existential problems, respectively. Seuss's protagonists are
rejected by distracted and depressed parents; Cisneros's heroine
battles poverty, homelessness, and urban violence; and Lindgren's
protagonist copes with the loss of loved ones, disease, and death.
Roberta Trites depicts Patricia MacLachlan's heroines struggling
with epistemological and related emotional problems, which they
resolve by synthesizing apparent opposites. Wolf, Sánchez, and
Trites each explore how in the texts they discuss access to language,
especially written language, both creates dilemmas for children
and provides solutions. For Cisneros's Esperanza and MacLachlan's
Cassie Binegar, writing promises empowerment rather than the
eventual loss of self suffered by Mary Lamb's Ann Withers and by
Barbara Follett. And although the protagonist of Seuss's *Mulberry
Street* is silenced by his parent, the hero of *Green Eggs and Ham* con-
vinces hers to share her imaginative vision, and Lindgren's Jonathan
Lionheart's fantasy world proves a rich legacy to his dying brother.
Just as the protagonists of these works create tales and texts meaningful to themselves and others, so, according to the contributors,
the works themselves meet needs of child readers that may overlap
with but often diverge from those of adults.

The essays of Miller, Franson, and Nodelman cannot be so neatly
tied together, but each in its way deals with the adult writer's translation of his or her own reading experience into a text intelligible
to a child or younger adult. Miller's essay relates to those discussed
earlier in that it deals with language and the way it can impede or
impel a child's engagement with the world, specifically the world of
the Middle Ages. Franson is less concerned with the child reader of
Baum than with Baum's reading of *Pilgrim's Progress* and how that
reading affects almost every major episode, as well as myriad details,
in *The Wonderful Wizard of Oz*. Franson's important source study
tends to support those Baum critics who see the book not as a satire
on religion but as a story of spiritual adventure. Finally, Nodelman's
essay on Ursula Le Guin's Earthsea trilogy and its belated sequel,
Tehanu, takes as its point of departure critic Len Hatfield's reading of the four novels (*Children's Literature* 21) and revisits his own
reading of the trilogy prior to the publication of *Tehanu*. His essay
relates to those in the Forum as well as to those by Wolf, Trites,
and Sánchez in its concern with gender. Although Nodelman does
not share Hatfield's view that Le Guin's feminism is implicit in the

trilogy, he does see *Tehanu* as offering a corrective to the unexamined assumptions about gender embedded in the earlier works.

That gender issues and the nature of the adult-child relationship, especially the relationship between adults and child readers and adult and children's texts, continue to dominate these pages attests to their continuing importance to literary scholars. Readers are encouraged to respond to the essays in this volume, as Nodelman has responded to Hatfield and Myers has to Wood. They are also invited to submit essays and Varia (no, that feature has not been abandoned) for *Children's Literature* 25 (1997) to be guest-edited by Mitzi Myers (UCLA) and U. C. Knoepflmacher (Princeton University), a special issue on what Myers has called "cross-writing—authors and works which transgress the usual demarcations separating children's from adult literature" and thus "focus attention on issues central to contemporary critical theory and cultural studies." For further information, or to submit an essay for consideration, please write directly to the guest editors. But I cannot imagine any special topic attracting a more interrelated group of essays than it has been my pleasure to edit this year.

Elizabeth Lennox Keyser

Children's Literature

Volume 23

Articles

The Erotics of Pedagogy:
Historical Intervention, Literary Representation, the "Gift of Education," and the Agency of Children

Mitzi Myers

> *I know that pedagogy is a depressing subject to all persons of sensibility, and yet I shall not apologize for touching upon it.*
>
> Lionel Trilling

> *In these times of wonderful revolution, and incalculable, & sudden changes in the fate of empires and the fortunes of individuals, the only good things of which we can feel absolutely secure are the possession of our minds, & of the esteem & affection of our friends.*
>
> Maria Edgeworth to Etienne Dumont, 12 August 1815

> *Works of art exist simultaneously in two 'economies,' a market economy and a gift economy. . . . with gifts that are agents of change, it is only when the gift has worked in us, only when we have come up to its level . . . that we can give it away again. . . . the end of the labor of gratitude is similarity with the gift or with its donor.*
>
> Lewis Hyde

Literary childhood, the representation of children for both juvenile and adult audiences, begins to play a significant part within the Anglo-American cultural tradition in a Revolutionary era. The global backdrop of the child's domestic debut is transnational change: the American, French, and industrial revolutions and the Napoleonic wars.[1] But how do children and their literary history relate to what historians think of as "big" history—the macropoli-

Children's Literature 23, ed. Francelia Butler, R. H. W. Dillard, and Elizabeth Lennox Keyser (Yale University Press, © 1995 Hollins College).

tics and institutional events that identify and dominate the "masculine" public sphere?[2] Literary critics are mostly content to say that this period's tales teach, without specifying precisely *what* they teach, *whom* they reach, or, most important, *how* they carry out their pedagogical agenda. For example, Claudia Nelson's study of late nineteenth-century children's literature packages its prehistory as an unproblematic narrative of obedience: "The stress in such stories is on the world as it is. Secure in the knowledge that adult civilization was daily going from good to better, eighteenth-century rationalist writers felt no urge to portray their young protagonists as in any way more powerful morally than their adult preceptors. . . . [T]he goal of overweening obedience forbids the implication that children may in any way positively affect their environment; their world neither asks nor needs any help from them."[3]

Neither the rationalist educator's own experience nor the stories she tells about her world seem quite so secure on closer inspection. Nor, for that matter, can Enlightenment education be equated with Wordsworth's reasoning little monster of the *Prelude*'s Book 5, though few literary historians can resist the temptation (ll. 296–363). Maria Edgeworth (1768–1849), the Anglo-Irish writer who is my subject, lived through all the cataclysmic events which mark the beginning of "modern" history and witnessed many of them at first hand. She saw Revolutionary Paris, fled for her life when the French invaded Ireland in 1798, and lived amid Irish upheaval. She coped with events ranging from murderous local marauders like the Defenders of the 1790s to the nationwide calamity of the Great Famine in the 1840s. Her public writing and its interplay with her world, her readers, and her life as a feeling daughter and a rational female writer solicit critical attention as exemplary of literary terrain we have not yet explored, not ground we know so well that we can dismiss it with a label. How, then, can historical contextualization and contemporary theory help us to specify what we mean when we say that a story from the literary past is "didactic"?

Despite the theoretical bombardment to which the academy has long been subjected, despite the recognition that all texts (and interpretations) are historically and ideologically conditioned, despite the preoccupation with Difference, the Other, the Colonized, the Repressed, and the Marginal, it still does not seem to have occurred to the critical world at large that works for, about, and/or by children are ideal investigatory sites for trying out just about any contemporary theory that elicits one's curiosity, be it gender, games, or gifts, subjectivity or psychoanalysis. Those who work with children's literature know better.[4] Yet, as I've indicated, thus far critical investigation of earlier fiction usually elides the thorny questions that contemporary theory raises about how past representations of the child can be read. Viewed backward through the Romantic configurations that have conditioned subsequent thinking about childhood, children's literature in the example above from Nelson is constructed as a closed world, bracketed off from what really counts, and children themselves are simultaneously generalized and transparent. "Childhood" is read as at once an unspecified abstraction and the name of (or sign for) an apprehensible entity, a something really out there instead of a historically constituted locale within a complex web of power relationships and signifying practices, a something we have to come at through words written by somebody at a particular moment for a particular purpose.

Habit makes us wince if asked to exchange the satisfyingly familiar "historical" child of Wordsworthian or sentimental fantasy for a shifty sign or discursive space. Habit makes it hard to think of earlier child and adult readers as inhabitants of one literary world, or at least of parallel reading worlds with more permeable boundaries than those we are accustomed to. Habit also makes it difficult to think back past aestheticized Romantic notions of Literature to pragmatic notions of literature doing useful cultural work in the everyday world. Nostalgia and memory play their seductive parts as well: we are all familiar with the generic interview in which author X tells us s/he just writes for the child within, the staple gambit of innumerable collections.[5] Nevertheless, I want to read with the child as historically constituted signifier in mind—an evocative, contradictory, and ideologically weighted verbal image—and to think about what it means to write under the sign of the child, to author a work *about, for,* and *as* a child—how doing so might constitute a radical gesture, an intervention in public history as much as a nostalgic personal regression.

My title surveys the ground this essay maps. Using one story by one writer, a tale both representing women and children and read by adult and child audiences, I employ current theory on gender and gifts to suggest how "didacticism" functions within stories and within the lives of readers and writers. I argue also that pedagogy unites domestic education and public event, that it legitimates

the female writer's agency as well as that of the child protagonist. The "gift of education" is Maria Edgeworth's own term from
"Madame de Fleury," the 1809 tale I discuss. Wonderfully evocative,
the phrase calls up the pupil's gratitude and labor to change the
world in consequence of the teacher's gift. Edgeworth's story does
not just state a moral, but embodies the subject, modeling for adult
and child readers a utopian pedagogy to cope with Revolutionary
times. Thus I use the term "erotics" to stress the affiliative nature of
so-called "rationalist" cultural transmission, for Edgeworth's story
works through love. The "gift of education" evokes the "didactic"
female writer's relationship with her imagined audiences outside
the story as well as her theme within it. Publicly resonant, "Madame
de Fleury" offers a woman's way of bridging private and public
spheres of human endeavor and thus participating in the reconstitution of British cultural identity occasioned by Revolutionary
conflict.[6]

Edgeworth's tale of French trauma is dense with covert allusions
to Ireland's perilous situation, too, and its answers are home truths
as much as French solutions to the problem of "revolutionary education," a heading in the unpublished notebook Edgeworth kept
while abroad. It is not fortuitous that Maria and Richard Lovell
Edgeworth's innovative manual for parents, *Practical Education*, was
published in 1798, the year of the Irish Rebellion, nor that Maria
Edgeworth's letters of the 1790s recurrently link the representation
of literary childhood and political insurrection, her own "wee-wee
stories" and the "dreadful disturbances" of French invaders and
Catholic rebels: "I am going on in the old way, writing stories. I
cannot be a captain of dragoons, and sitting with my hands before
me would not make any of us one degree safer." Spare us, "Oh,
rebels, oh, French!" her 1798 letter continues: "We have never injured you, and all we wish is to see everybody as happy as ourselves"
(Edgeworth *Memoir* 1: 83–84). Writing stories that reconceptualize
the child and her education is the woman writer's way of realizing
that wish.

But Edgeworth's story has an even more personal subtext than
its submerged Irish provenance: she received and refused the only
marriage proposal of her life during her French visit. Already
thirty-four, plain, and (as the wit Sydney Smith put it) "extremely
deformed—diminutive almost to invisibility," she knew that another
offer was unlikely and that she would remain her father's child-sized

daughter in a crowded household.[7] "Madame de Fleury" is not just a thank-you note to Madame de Pastoret, the real-life French friend whose "gift of education" it fictionalizes. It is also a present for the father who had educated his daughter in estate management and "manly" subjects like philosophy, economics, and political theory, a love letter reciprocating his continuing paternal affection and care. The notion of the literary work as useful gift is as important for Edgeworth's emotional life as it is for what she likes to call her public "authorship self." In thus exploring pedagogic transactions as affective gifts with multiple cultural implications, I draw on the work of Lewis Hyde and other theorists of the gift. Particularly illuminating on teachings as transformative gifts, Hyde emphasizes gift exchange as an "'erotic' commerce, opposing *eros* (the principle of attraction, union, involvement which binds together)" to the market economy which is an emanation of *logos* (reason, logic, differentiation rather than incorporation).[8] Linking pupil and teacher, child and adult, such work helps us to comprehend fictional pedagogy as relational and rehabilitative, to imagine it as other than the imperialistic thought police of both conventional and more recent psychoanalytic and Marxist children's literary history.[9]

As preface to my argument that texts produced under the sign of the child are peculiarly political, peculiarly relational, peculiarly liminal works—generated by, written about, structured to produce cultural mediation and negotiation—I want to take as emblematic prologue a real little girl's writing and its historical and interpretive frames. Marjory Fleming's inimitable journals, poems, and letters were written in early-nineteenth-century Scotland by a child of six to eight, largely in response to the assignments of her beloved and beleaguered cousin Isa, a teenager herself: "Isabella teaches me everything I know and I am much indebted to her," the first journal begins. Marjory (1803–1811) was a handful—a warm lover, a good hater, a wide reader. She threw temper tantrums, vowed to be good, fantasized about being a "heroin," slept at Isa's feet, and wrote passionate verses to her patient, pretty, and sorely tried teacher: "I love in Isas bed to lie / O such a joy and luxury / The botton of the bed I sleep / And with great care I myself keep / Oft I embrace her feet of lillys / But she has goton all the pillies / Her neck I never can embrace / But I do hug her feet in place." Marjory also, so the family legend says, enchanted her countryman Sir Walter Scott, who gave her copies of Maria Edgeworth's *Rosamond* and *Harry and Lucy*. Flirt, moral commentator, charming romper, and penitent pupil, Marjory is easy to glamorize as the quintessential child, easy to sentimentalize because of her early death (from measles). Mark Twain thought her a free spirit whose pieties were all sham; gushy Victorians cuddled her as "Pet" and "rosy, little wifie" (Fleming 23, 183, vi).

As Twain's and the Victorians' contradictory appropriations imply, Marjory's work is a touchstone of great interest not just for itself but also for what it reveals about post-Romantic Western culture's pervasive framing of the child image as rebel or locus of nostalgia.[10] Marjory is neither, nor can she be considered in isolation. Rather, her work emerges within a pedagogical relationship; it is an apprentice's gift that pays tribute to a cherished instructor by striving, however fitfully, to incorporate her teachings. Inscribed literally between the ruled lines of adult discourse, Marjory's remarkable writings exemplify a coming to language and literature, a child's entrance into and commentary upon British culture in a Revolutionary era.[11] They show off, dramatizing achievement, autonomy, naughtiness; simultaneously, they ingratiate Marjory with Isa and the mother back home for whom the journals are visible signs of educational progress. Littered with non sequiturs and hilarious spellings, Marjory's compositions are bricolage, a collage of cultural tags, the topoi of contemporary reading, the mores of contemporary culture. Neither contained by adult usages nor cordoned from them, Marjory imaginatively assembles clichés and conventions to shape her own subjectivity. Embodying in her journalizing what it means to write under the sign of the child, Marjory is a living trope for the terms of my title. The social negotiations and literary techniques Marjory deploys *as* a child in her journal, Maria Edgeworth as Enlightened adult author uses child characters to embody in her fictions—and, as is often the case in Edgeworth's life and career, the rational author as feeling daughter uses those pedagogical fictions in her relations with a beloved teacher, too.[12]

I suggested above that works concerning juvenile characters and experience (whether or not they are officially designated as children's literature) are labile, given to addressing basic representational and cultural issues and therefore as amenable to contemporary theorizing as they are neglected by it. People who write about children's literature are mainly read by other people who write about it, even though their insights could also illuminate adult lit-

erature. Marjory's work bears witness to the impossibility of brack-
eting off the image of the child and of children's reading from the
world at large; it equally implies the reverse difficulty of elucidating
child characters in adult literature without reference to traditions
of juvenile representation. Marjory did not limit her reading to
children's literature alone, nor did she confine her commentary to
juvenile issues; politics, mores, sexuality, and sin are on her agenda,
too. Marjory's jackdaw journal is a marvelously informative docu-
ment for countering rarefied images of the juvenile mind—she had
a voracious appetite for cultural knowledge as well as imaginative
delight. Here is a typical page from the first journal, written in
spring and early summer 1810 (I have not reproduced Isa's under-
linings for misspellings): "Climbing is a talent which the bear excels
in and so does monkeys apes & baboons.—I have been washing my
dools cloths today & I like it very much people who have a good
concience is alwa happy but those who have a bad one is always unhappy & discontented There is a dog that yels continualy & I pity
him to the bottom of my heart indeed I do. Tales of fashionable life
ar very good storys Isabella campels me to sit down & not to rise till
this page is done but it is very near finished only one line to write."
The third journal, in spring 1811, returns again to Marjory's enjoyment of "Miss Egwards tails," which she pronounces "very good,
particulay some that are very much adopted for youth" (Fleming
4, 104).

Marjory's 1810 reference is to the three-volume set of five stories
which make up the first series of Maria Edgeworth's *Tales of Fashionable Life* (1809). There was a second three-volume set in 1812,
but Marjory did not live to read it. She certainly had read Edgeworth's stories for children and probably also her *Moral Tales for
Young People* of 1801 and her *Popular Tales* of 1804 for the middling
classes; for Marjory, unlike modern critics, a good "tail" is a good
tale, and the instructive is as welcome as the imaginative. I want to
look at one story that she read: of course I think I know which one
she especially enjoyed: "Madame de Fleury," the only fiction in the
1809 *Tales of Fashionable Life* which gives children a starring role.

Tales of Fashionable Life begins with "Ennui," one of Edgeworth's
national tales of masculine Irish life, and includes two shorter stories, "Almeria" and "The Dun," as well as "Madame de Fleury," in the
second volume. The third volume is an adult feminine fiction, "Ma-
noeuvering," in which the antiheroic English mother is a female

politician whose grown-up children are wiser than she. Interestingly, the second three-volume set (published in 1812), which concludes with "The Absentee" (another Irish tale with a male hero),
also features a story foregrounding a brave adolescent heroine,
"Emilie de Coulanges" (a French émigrée, like Madame de Fleury),
along with another antiheroic adult tale called "Vivian." One of
Edgeworth's many psychological studies of weak "feminized" males,
"Vivian" depicts an Englishman whose subsequent life is shaped
and spoiled by a bad early education. Interestingly also, "The Absentee," one of Maria Edgeworth's most successful adult tales, began as a children's play for a home audience of siblings and their
visiting cousins. The 1809 and 1812 series were frequently packaged
as a set, so that the arrangement makes an emblematic point about
the way that Edgeworth's work democratizes representation as to
gender, generation, and nation, an emphasis I mean my own essay
to suggest. Within the brackets of the two Anglo-Irish stories, Edgeworth purposefully integrates child and adult, male and female,
English, Irish, and French. All belong to the same fashionable, that
is, contemporary world; Edgeworth's term signals not coterie fiction, but stories about the dominant types and attitudes who construct the contemporary culture that everyone, regardless of age,
gender, class, or nationality inhabits.

Always writing within and for a family audience, Edgeworth regularly has children play major parts in adult tales (as in *Belinda* and
Ormond), and she pioneers the psychological analysis of early childhood in adult fiction, as in *Harrington,* where she draws on the
psychic life of her half-brother Henry, who was her special charge
when she was a teenager. All of Edgeworth's work is enriched
by the observations on child thought and talk that she undertook
in the early 1790s for *Practical Education,* the Edgeworth's progressive parental guide. Education is always her central theme,
although, as this essay argues, it assumes a more complex form
than the extractable moral lesson that literary histories presuppose. Maria Edgeworth's correspondence is full of letters from
children who, like Marjory, do not differentiate their enjoyment
of her adult material from her juvenile fiction, and her children's
stories were read and critically remarked on not just by parents, but
also by such men of letters as Sir Walter Scott, John Gibson Lock-
hart, and John Ruskin.[13] In those pre–Sir Walter Scott, pre–Jane

Austen days, Edgeworth was the top draw in fiction, garnering extraordinary public attention and large royalties. Even then, though, "Madame de Fleury" was upstaged by the Irish tales largely responsible for Edgeworth's niche in conventional literary history—which has never quite known what to do with the tale or *conte* as genre, how to talk about mixes of fact and fiction, or where to situate any work starring children, for that matter. Predictably, male reviewers for the powerful new shapers of literary opinion like the *Edinburgh Review* and the *Quarterly Review* usually prefer to read about men instead of women or youngsters. Singling out Edgeworth's most masculine tales for praise, they anticipate Henry James and later influential critics of the novel, who increasingly disparaged works that could be generationally cross-read; the dual audience work representing and read by women and children could not be high art.[14]

But then Maria Edgeworth always thought of herself as an educator, not an aesthete; her art always concerns what is going on in the world. When the Peace of Amiens provided a brief lull in the lengthy wars against Napoleonic France in 1802, she, her father, his fourth wife, Frances, and Maria's half-sister Charlotte set out— like many other Britons—to see the new France for themselves.[15] The Edgeworths met many notables in Paris (including the Pastorets, whose adventures are the factual basis for the story I discuss), talked, listened, and took notes. Maria Edgeworth's unpublished papers include the tiny notebook which details Monsieur Pastoret's flight during the Terror and includes the noteworthy rubric, "revolutionary education."[16] How the young should be prepared to face a world in tumult is the topic of "Madame de Fleury," and Madame de Pastoret's post-Revolutionary role as the national founder of the French infant school is pushed back to the days of the Terror and amalgamated with her earlier incarceration and the seizure of the family's estates. Edgeworth's rearrangement of chronology, her melding of fact and fiction, and her creation of the child heroine Victoire as Madame's savior cast education and juvenile agency as performative answers to the dilemma of Revolutionary violence. Edgeworth's narrative enactment of the recent past is a history, so to speak, of what the future should be. For some contemporary interpreters, the guillotine and the Terror were the legacy of the French Enlightenment, the inevitable result of rationalist philosophy, not an interruption of it. Edgeworth writes otherwise, but she also reshapes and revises the rationalist Enlightenment patrimony she inherited from her father as a woman's family politics, a cultural renovation which spreads outward from domestic affection.[17]

Rooted in historical facts—real teachers, real schoolchildren, real hairbreadth escapes—even begun on the scene in Paris in 1803 where the action had just taken place, "Madame de Fleury" has elicited amusingly contradictory responses from reviewers and critics when it has been noticed at all. Marjory's avid interest in contemporary culture, her pedagogic situation (away from home, desirous of pleasing her teacher, Isa), and her yearning to be a "heroin" can help us here. In fact (much as a bat's wing and a mouse's foreleg are biological homologies), considering Marjory, the child heroine Victoire, and Maria Edgeworth herself as homologous actors in an historical erotics of pedagogy has implications not only for reassessing the image of the child but also the characteristic genres and themes that contain her. How might a child like Marjory have construed such a story and why might girl readers have felt particularly drawn to an "adult" tale like "Madame de Fleury"? It begins with a vivid image of child imprisonment and rescue—satisfyingly cheeky children saved from the bloody consequences of their naughtiness by a fairy godmother who forces open a locked door and heals the injured. Despite the wordy protests of her servant François, Madame de Fleury insists that her carriage stop so she can discover the cause of the shrieks she hears in passing through a slum. Her "bright vision" literally as well as metaphorically brings enlightenment, as she wrenches free the door of the smelly, dark room where three little children have been confined by their working mother. They are, in modern parlance, latchkey children. To keep them from consorting with pickpockets and vagabonds on the streets, their struggling single parent locks them up while she hunts out the menial work that is an uneducated woman's only resource. Eight-year-old Maurice is soaked in blood from a cut, the still younger Victoire has a broken arm, and the baby, Babet, has narrowly escaped burning to death while making dirt pies from the fire's ashes. Separating the realistically squabbling children—"She screams that way for nothing often. . . . Her arm is no more broke than mine"—Madame gives more than momentary charity. Madame de Fleury's "gift of education"—the opening of a school for latchkey children—confers child power, the agency of children which ultimately reconstitutes community at both the personal and the national level.[18] She changes the children's lives, and her own, by founding a school for twelve little girls, to be headed by another surrogate mother, good Sister Frances (2:182, 184, 194).[19]

The story develops the consequences of Madame's gift and the children's gratitude. "Madame de Fleury" provides vividly detailed images of children doing what Marjory did—being bratty, being good, learning lessons, negotiating the tremendous changes going on during the Revolutionary decade. The tale furnishes comforting mother images in Madame and Sister Frances, the little community's artist and teacher. It flatters child agency with its use of the familiar fables of the mouse and the lion, and the old man, his sons, and the bundle of sticks. Everybody has names that are amusing to decode—Victoire for the heroine, Tracassier for the mischief-maker. Even real names like Fleury obligingly denote thriving and blossoming: Madame de Pastoret's country home was really named Fleury, which also means "flowering." The tale is filled with children's gardens and games, with gifts of flowers and fruit. Wicked villains threaten and little girls who are tempted fall; Victoire's naughty cousin and opposite number is named Manon, after the courtesan heroine of a celebrated French novel. The tale delivers mysterious helper figures, bizarre reversals, and equally marvelous restorations of fortune. Its contrasting images are the uncertainties of life under the Revolution—"And may not the wheel turn?"—and the reciprocity of gifts and affection which bond the good characters together, as in the children's communal feast of roasted chestnuts to celebrate the miniature stoves they have earned by their "united industry" (2:304, 221).

The lowly turn mighty by the aid of the guillotine, as when Manon becomes a rich kept woman in a victim's fine hotel. No longer a benefactor, Madame finds herself "a close prisoner in her own house" like the children she had rescued. But she is miraculously redeemed from execution, spirited to England, and saved from penury there by the mental skills and monetary gifts of the "indefatigable" Victoire, the mastermind of the little school (2:262, 275). Ogres and drunken mobs threaten the destruction of the Château de Fleury, but Madame's mythically resonant country home is preserved by odd coincidences and the female bravery of Sister Frances and Victoire, who dares to interrupt the raging mob and remind the leader that he owes his life to the Sister's nursing: "By my faith you are a brave girl, and a fine girl, and know how to speak to the heart" (2:293). He too is capable of gratitude, so that Madame's original gift has ever widening (and amusingly interconnected) consequences and duplications. Gradually moving from the adult's generous action to the child's perspective, the tale invites us to identify with the juvenile protagonist Victoire, a "heroin" who would satisfy even Marjory's energetic standards, and to feel what education and reciprocated affection mean in her life. Victoire changes from the passionate "little rebel" who defies all authority (and gravity) to ride down the banister with her whip (2:210). She learns to work with and command others, so that eventually she is Madame's rescuer: "Though but a girl of fourteen, Victoire showed . . . all the sense and prudence of a woman of thirty. Gratitude seemed at once to develop all the powers of her mind. . . . She had invented, she had foreseen, she had arranged every thing." In striking contrast, her hysterical mother—her mind undeveloped and her health broken by hard work—collapses when the dreaded "domiciliary visitors" arrive; only a timely swoon prevents her from betraying the hidden Madame and sending them all to certain death (2:273, 270). Through her own intelligence and the communal network of friendship that radiates from Madame's school, Victoire sustains Madame de Fleury while she is abroad, saves her château from destruction, gets her name taken off the list of prescribed persons, and restores her benefactor to her country, her home, and her friends. The tale is rooted in recognizable fact, yet it conjures all the conventions of fantasy and is richly indebted to literary resources.

Even more allusive than Edgeworth's always culturally referential fiction, "Madame de Fleury" is as packed with literary echoes as it is with real people, events, and places. Every chapter starts with a literary epigraph, most of them from standard teaching texts that children as well as adults would be likely to know—Pope on "infant wo," Goldsmith on the demise of pastoral life, Anna Laetitia Barbauld and Thomas Gray on youngsters at school. The story highlights two familiar fables too. Aesop's allegory of the old man, his sons, and the bundle of sticks, which can be snapped one by one but are unbreakable together, is both a resonant image for family (and national) unity and a validation of the part that even the smallest twig plays in making up a strong whole. La Fontaine's retelling of the Lion and the Mouse fable makes Edgeworth's case for the powers of the weak still more vividly. When the noble lion lets the humble mouse go instead of crushing it, he never thinks that the mouse could return the good deed. But when the lions are entrapped in nets, the rodent's sharp teeth save the day. The apologue that Madame tells Victoire comes alive as the written tale unfolds. As recent work on fables, pedagogy, and eighteenth-century political life suggests, Edgeworth's use of seemingly innocuous stories is freighted with meaning: British writers habitually employed fables as a way for the politically powerless to have their say. "Madame de Fleury" shows fables first in dialogue and then in action. They do not just encapsulate the theme, but show, like the story as a whole, how the transmission process works. They are affective lessons transmitted through oral dialogue and carried out through love. For adult readers of the story, they also underline the tale's querying of French educational and political solutions, because Rousseau's notorious hostility to fables—his notion that children are not savvy enough to get the metaphoric point—is delicately subverted. Edgeworth's tale is what we might call metatextual or meta-pedagogic; that is, it is about how to transmit cultural knowledge, as well as a dramatic picture of what happens when child agency is empowered.[20]

The story works at multiple levels politically and personally, just as it does pedagogically. It's full of exciting real life details, from the stench and squalor of latchkey children's lives to the noisy mobs and bloody guillotine that Madame de Fleury (like the real Madame de Pastoret) is compelled to watch from the windows of her own town house. The rioting mobs and the grateful few who pay back their teachers' gifts are as Irish as they are French. The seemingly fantastic features of "Madame de Fleury"—the children's schoolroom invaded by armed rioters, the malicious arrest and near deportation of the enlightened father who dares to protest against French barbarity, and the family mansion saved by the mob leader who recalls the owner's good deeds and wards off fiery destruction—are real facts from the Edgeworths' experiences in Ireland and France. Obsessed by the mob that had stoned her father and threatened her life and home, Edgeworth no doubt vicariously enjoyed Victoire's triumph as much as her juvenile readers would.

Apprehending the narrative from the naif's perspective as well as the adult author's dignifies the agency of children and foregrounds the crucial relation between cultural authority and the female author's narration which simultaneously describes and lays claim to it. Edgeworth's narrative appropriates real facts to promote a female

educator's representation of history as it ought to work out. By empowering, in turn, adult and child characters, she gives her female
readers models with whom they can identify, and she suggests that
the answer to men's wars and the masculinist Terror of the guillotine is women's affectively grounded family politics. The adult
female audience of "Madame de Fleury" would of course bring to
the tale more complex resources of allusion and cultural knowledge
than a child reader would. They would notice, for example, that although Victoire is a teenager by the time the "public disturbances"
begin, Edgeworth gives her heroine an emblematic name which
marks her role as the author's utopian image for a rehabilitated
France (and Ireland), as well as the representative of real working-
class French childhood (2:248). Hers is a specifically "Revolutionary" name, the vogue of the early 1790s, for the French Revolution
changed private life as much as public politics. Edgeworth's coded
names belong to her repertoire of symbolic characterization.[21] If
Victoire is Edgeworth's figure for the schooled and redeemed child
of possibility, juvenile France not as she is but as she might be, her
naughty cousin Manon calls up the associations of the past.

The product of a bad education, Manon is a juvenile liar and thief
and an adolescent mistress whose name identifies her with *Manon
Lescaut,* the immoral heroine of Abbé Prévost's famous 1731 novel,
who pays her bills with her body. Although Manon fancies herself
an advocate of the "rights of woman" and brags of her inside political knowledge, she achieves her fleeting wealth and power only
through her person (2:249). She's not the new Revolutionary *ci-
toyenne,* just a debased edition of the old aristocratic feminine mode
of political intrigue as seduction. Unlike Victoire and her school-
mates, who become independent working women, Manon has no
occupation and cannot support herself. She is dependent on men,
exchanging sexual favors for temporary triumph as a republican
mistress. When her lover is guillotined, she ends up dying young in
a hospital, the victim of bodily politics. Victoire makes visible the
child as potential rescuer of a nation gone bad; Manon is doubly
the abandoned child, the unfamilied prostitute who threatens the
social body. Never one for sentimental deathbed scenes, Edgeworth
kills her off briskly to focus on Victoire's emblematic marriage to
Basile, which represents the hope for a regenerated nation based on
regenerated children.[22] The union of Basile—the son of Madame's
old steward, who has become the right-hand man to an illiterate

general of the Directory's army—and Victoire—the resolute new working girl, as different from her ineffectual and childlike mother as Madame is from the usual fine lady—concludes the narrative.[23] The fête at Madame's country château, which reunites the newly returned Madame with her grateful former pupils, updates the "custom of the country," for the French pastoral festival appropriated by the masculinist state during the Terror is resacralized as a celebration of family and community, as a coming together of the tale's characters and themes. The "singing and dancing" mark the birth of a new order predicated on Enlightened values, a hope for the future that "the feeling and intelligent reader," whether child or adult, must help bring into being (2:326–27).[24]

The strategic interdependence of child and adult inside the narrative mirrors the book's dual readership. It also mirrors the dual position of the children's author toward her text, as in Edgeworth's simultaneous alignment with the victorious child heroine who saves the parent and with the adult teacher who bestows the "gift of education." In appropriating Madame de Pastoret's factual history for her own narrative, Maria Edgeworth *and* her book tell the story of the good daughter who can save her country. The politicians who chopped off the head of the father king created the French Revolution as a family romance in the Gothic mode; Edgeworth rewrites the thriller as a different family romance, a tale of domestic education.[25] Edgeworth's story is ambitious, and so are the claims advanced by her representation of the working-class Victoire's energy, intelligence, and determination. What girl wouldn't want to engineer a prison rescue, stop a rampaging mob, save a castle, and restore her former benefactor's château and citizenship? What daughter-author wouldn't envision her work as educating a nation and protecting her father and family? Under the sign of the child, within the slippery category of the tale (which can slide from fact to faerie), Edgeworth can write a story which both documents "truth" and aspires to cultural mythology, which is both a public political statement—an educative present for a warring world— and a personal gift—a present made to her father and teacher ratifying her allegiance and her love. Conceptualizing the reader and the story of reading via the child and the daughter helps us make sense of what initially may seem to be warring elements in Edgeworth's tale, which nevertheless do inhabit the same fictional universe: fact versus history, wish-fulfilling narrative structures versus utterly natural dialogue, characterization, and domestic detail. "Madame de Fleury" is a marvelous example of Edgeworth's sophisticated deployment of the child image—and yet, as I indicate later with a brief sample of prior assessments, that is precisely what's been erased from adult-oriented interpretations.[26]

Only when we look through a Marjory's eyes, only when we factor Edgeworth's multivalent child image into the context, can we make any headway. Even given this essay's brief summation, we can see that the story assumes, transvalues, and reconstitutes the child-adult relationship at the heart of "didactic" children's literature and that its doing so is instinct with historical, literary, and personal resonances. The tale's embodied pedagogy is more than the ideological author's power trip. The utopian images of restoration and renewal that conclude the book—the pastoral fête and dance which celebrate Madame's return to the Château de Fleury and the wedding of Victoire—invite us to imagine and to join Victoire in working toward the healing of division, to use the "gift of education" that the story bestows and to pay it back by becoming like the gift and giver. Gratitude, the story insists over and over through its figuration of gifts, obligations, thefts, and manipulations of property, acquires meaning when it is transformed to action, when Victoire has thoroughly manifested what enabled Madame to brave the slums and save a shrieking child. "Female resolution and presence of mind are indispensably requisite," the reader learns early: "Safety, health, and life, often depend upon the fortitude of women"—and, so the story shows, of girls who can become like them.[27] "The lion was not too proud to be served by the poor little mouse," says Victoire as she in turn rescues Madame (2:185, 269). The tale's play with the familiar mouse and lion fable exemplifies Victoire's gratitude and heroism—and by extension the cultural reconfiguration that can change the world—as, literally, mousework, heroic agency available to the lowliest, available to us all.[28]

Through its historical framework and densely allusive technique, the story re-presents the Revolution that it represents; using the modality of the child, it intervenes in history with a dual system of representation, each kind of narrative claiming a distinctive authority. Both kinds of narrative authority are necessary if what has become "true" in the story is to become "true" in a wider world. The story is solidly grounded by innumerable details of actual experience both personal and historical, hence its continuous referentiality. Its factuality, far from being adversary to the story's faerie, is the fantasy's necessary precondition; if the tale is grounded in things that can be proved, that narrative authority validates the truth of feeling that brings the restorative conclusion into being.[29] The story's dual conceptualization of narrative authority says we need both knowledge and feeling to make the world different. The story uses conventions as conveyers for the emotive that must accompany the cognitive, just as the children not only acquire knowledge from Madame but also learn to be like her, to be united with her in affective sympathy. In the name of childhood feeling and agency, Edgeworth's practice eludes the utilitarian clichés that dog her reputation, for the tale's most striking departure from truth was to put the founding of the actual school before the Revolution and to make the children the saviors and restorers. The escape and restoration and school were all real, but the school was not founded until 1801. To conflate the facts in this way is to use facts to change what counts *as* fact. Facts are used to create feelings that will make different facts "true"—and the mediatory child image is thematically central to this redefinition and reconstitution of cultural fact.

But how have adult critics interpreted the story? What have they defined as its context? During the French travels that led to the story, Edgeworth wrote of the period's "cheek-by-jowl-ism of power and literature" (*ME in France and Switzerland* 54). Yet the child image through which power operates in "Madame de Fleury" is continually erased or misaligned by adult critics lacking Edgeworth's vivid sense of the ethical content, of the cultural mattering, of women's and children's lives. Only the *Tales of Fashionable Life* with male heroes got the early reviewers' attention.[30] The critic for the *Monthly Review* wonders why the children are here and seems romantically to assume that the juvenile and the pathetic are one: "The juvenile anecdotes in the tale of Madame de Fleury are extremely touching: but this story seems better calculated for insertion among the 'Moral Tales,' than in the present set" (Barbauld 97). The more politically conservative *Quarterly Review* made short shrift of Edgeworth's insistence on child agency: "The story of *'Madame de Fleury'* is of a very unambitious kind. Its chief object, is to convey several minute practical lessons to charitable females of rank. . . . It is also intended to shew that the rich and the great may in their turn be sometimes indebted to the objects of their benevolent care . . . a moral not very important" because lions are unlikely to need mice (Stephen and

Gifford 153).[31] The *Quarterly's* assumption that Edgeworth's narrative is contained by her expository educational writing persists after almost two centuries.[32]

In an even odder take on the customary equation of Edgeworthian story and rational information, Marilyn Butler, Edgeworth's biographer, attempts to read the tale, not as the outgrowth of the Edgeworths' *Practical Education* for children, but as the result of the reading on masculine professions that Maria did in order to write *Professional Education,* a guide to choosing a bourgeois boy's career which was published under her father's name. As there is no masculine professional education in "Madame de Fleury" and the few male characters are not central, such an origin fails to convince.[33] The children are not mentioned in Butler's very brief assessment, and their experience is dismissed as irrelevant in a recent French Marxist analysis: "We have excluded from our investigation the aspect directly linked with education which takes up about one third of the book, and dealt with it only in relation to social levels and social change as Maria Edgeworth saw them" (Paratte 71). Because Edgeworth represents the social via the educational and the juvenile, a story of reading that eliminates its own ground is not likely to win acquiescence. The critic's "one third" must refer to actual classroom scenes, since few of Edgeworth's plots are more focused on the ever widening ramifications of one educational act than "Madame de Fleury." Critics who fail to factor the child image into their interpretations fare no better when they consider Edgeworth's dual conceptualization of narrative, some praising her extraordinary naturalness and truth to everyday life and talk, others discovering only "fairy tales that refuse to confess" what they are (Newby 59). Neither and both are right, for Edgeworth's pedagogic fiction is heuristic and utopian, a narrative enactment that needs both fact and fantasy. That multilayeredness is what makes her moral tales so peculiarly appealing, once we step aside from later presuppositions about child representation and recognize the allusive referentiality of the conventions through which she operates. Ambitious rational teacher and empathetic daughter, Edgeworth never writes a paragraph that is not alive with cultural, literary, and personal allusions; her many references to her period's facts and fictions constitute her stories as cultural narratives and oblique autobiographies as well as teaching texts.[34]

My essay argues for decoding this "thick description" and "local detail" to help us answer the question of how past scripts for children work: how juvenile representations earn the allegiance of girl and women readers, as well as the distrust of male critics, how child portraits simultaneously serve authorial and audience needs, and how fictions are agents of cultural and social change—not just mirrors of alterations but complex ideological forces fostering and legitimating them.[35] Although conventional literary history has conditioned us to assume otherwise, pedagogic texts are anything but inert; they register the two-way traffic between producer and consumer, adult and child, public and private, rational and affective. To reconceptualize the didactic as an erotics of pedagogy thus situates the image of the child within multiple intersecting *relationships:* the implicitly political dimension of educational writing that I sketch at this essay's start, women's pedagogic texts encoding public intervention via educational writing and child agency; a highly charged personal relationship in which the text enacts the gift of education bestowed by a beloved teacher, as meaningful for the author outside the story as for the protagonist within; an empathetic compact between author and reader which facilitates the text's representation of the cultural politics which are bringing it into being: teaching texts can't work unless they engage and flatter their readers, unless those readers help the author make the story come true. Finally, there is the past text's relation to current thinking about what people do when they write narratives that is part of this century's revolution in literary and cultural theory.[36]

Sensitized to our own interpretive location as well as to the historical location of the story's contemporary readers, we know that no interpretation can achieve total truth or final validity, but we can hope that our images of historical pedagogy are liberatory, rather than banking metaphors depicting teaching as the passive deposit of information.[37] Knowing that writing only acquires force in historically specifiable situations, we can try to make our interpretive acts as much a space for the erotic and relational—for caring about the text and why it took this shape—as a site for ideological struggle and dominance. The story of reading that we construct around fictions of the past depends largely on what we know of conventions and what we define as context.[38] That is why seeing "Madame de Fleury" through Maria Edgeworth's *and* Marjory Fleming's eyes is helpful. Like the child-identified author, Marjory surely enjoyed the tale's obvious foregrounding of child agency, and she would have had no trouble in becoming the sympathetic reader able to meld factual and wishful narrativizing that the story requires for the fictional gift to enter the referential world. I think Marjory would have understood.

Notes

I should like to thank the American Philosophical Society, the American Council of Learned Societies, and the John Simon Guggenheim Memorial Foundation for their support of my research.

Notes to epigraphs: Beyond Culture: Essays on Literature and Learning (New York: Viking Press, 1965), 3.

I am grateful to the Bibliothèque for permission to quote from its materials. A few of Edgeworth's many letters to Dumont, the French popularizer of Jeremy Bentham, were printed in much garbled form by Rowland Grey in 1909. Grey sought to discover a nonexistent romance, but the archive's importance is its delineation of how a woman writer thinks politically, of how a daughter and an author connects her domestic affections with her clearsighted analysis of public events. See Rowland Grey, "Maria Edgeworth and Étienne Dumont," *Dublin Review* 145 (1909): 239–65.

The Gift: Imagination and the Erotic Life of Property (New York: Random House, Vintage Books, 1983), xi, 47.

1. There are, of course, many portrayals of children in more distant cultures and locales, just as there is abundant evidence of warm family feelings well before the late-eighteenth-century period that is usually described by social historians as a new age for the child and the family. Without venturing into the debates that enliven family history and the history of childhood, it is safe to say that literary representations of the juvenile first become a major commodity in this period. One material reason may be that, thanks to what economic historians call the "demographic revolution," many more children began to survive toward the end of the eighteenth century than had formerly been the case.

2. Contemporaneous changes in thinking about literacy, education, class, race, and gender may well deserve to be considered revolutions, too. For an interesting example of how such "fractional" histories might be integrated with traditionally androcentric academic history, see Dorinda Outram's *The Body and the French Revolution: Sex, Class, and Political Culture*.

3. Nelson 6, 8. It is troubling to find so important a study as Nelson's *Boys Will Be Girls: The Feminine Ethic and British Children's Fiction, 1857–1917,* failing to discriminate between rigorous Evangelicals and writers like Maria Edgeworth, who later came to be stigmatized for being thoroughly irreligious. Nelson remarks that eighteenth-century writers inculcate " 'feminine' decorousness" rather than " 'masculine' inventiveness," but Edgeworth and other Enlightenment writers insist that children should be taught to think for themselves; one of Edgeworth's recurrent themes is "teaching to invent," a topic on which she projected an entire work. Rosamond (whom Nelson calls Rosamund) doesn't learn obedience by not pressing her mother for a stone plum (not a crystal pear); she's given a choice about her future by her mother, and she must *"think for yourself, my dear"* (Nelson 7; Edgeworth *Rosamond* 17). Nelson certainly has a point about differences between earlier and later portrayals of gender, but she does her interesting case a disservice by worrisome overgeneralizing. Nancy Armstrong, whose influential *Desire and Domestic Fiction* Nelson cites, doesn't discuss children's books at all and apparently considers Maria and Richard

Lovell (whom she calls Robert) Edgeworth's *Practical Education* a conduct book, when it is a very different kind of work. My point is not to carp at small errors, but rather to gesture toward the amount of archival work that needs to be done before we are in a position to reconceptualize children's literary history.

4. Or so I thought until I read Peter Hunt's *Criticism, Theory, and Children's Literature,* which seems less postmodern than one might expect of a book on theory. A British writer, Hunt may have missed recent American scholarship which seeks to meld critical theory with the study of children's literature, such as Perry Nodelman's essay on "The Other: Orientalism, Colonialism, and Children's Literature" and Margaret R. Higonnet's work, as in her review essay "Critical Apertures." Peter Hollindale's "Ideology and the Children's Book" is an interesting British example; for a clever anatomy of "big" literary criticism's neglect of children's literature, see Beverly Lyon Clark's "Thirteen Ways of Thumbing Your Nose at Children's Literature." However, most studies informed by theory don't address early texts. Although it analyzes eighteenth-century child portraits rather than writings with child characters, Marcia Pointon's essay on decoding "The State of a Child" provides some useful ways of thinking about the complex webs of signifying practices and power relationships within which child representations achieve their meanings (see chapter 7); for a problematizing of "the child" from a sociological perspective, see Anna Davin's "When Is A Child Not A Child?" Important instances of growing recognition that writing about children can illuminate larger cultural issues are Ruth B. Bottigheimer's "Review Essay: Recent Scholarship in Children's Literature, 1980 to the Present" in the adultstream *Eighteenth-Century Life* and the 1992 special issue of *Poetics Today,* edited by Zohar Shavit.

5. Jack Zipes has recently remarked that "no longer is the child considered the repository of innocence, truth, and untarnished nature, symbolical of an idyllic past that we are nostalgically urged to recover" (8). This death announcement for the child constructed by Romantic ideology seems to me premature; the infant philosopher is very much alive and kicking, even in several of the books which Zipes is discussing. Geoffrey Summerfield's *Fantasy and Reason: Children's Literature in the Eighteenth Century* is a striking example.

6. Jürgen Habermas's influential notion of the eighteenth century's enlightened bourgeois public sphere, an explanation of the transition from absolutist states to those governed by informed public opinion, is currently being rethought by feminist theorists, who seek to factor gender into Habermas's model. Such work is especially important to the study of women educators and their audiences because it demonstrates that women's "private" sphere is interdependent with "public" life and because it foregrounds the development and transmission of enlightened knowledge—in other words, the work of education—as central to modern cultural and political authority. See, for example, Nancy Fraser's "What's Critical about Critical Theory? The Case of Habermas and Gender" and Iris Marion Young's "Impartiality and the Civic Public: Some Implications of Feminist Critiques of Moral and Political Theory," as well as Habermas's *The Structural Transformation of the Public Sphere: An Inquiry into a Category of Bourgeois Society.* Keith Michael Baker's discussion of Mary Wollstonecraft's appropriation of rational discourse is also relevant to Edgeworth's arguments for woman's right to reason and literature; see Baker's "Defining the Public Sphere in Eighteenth-Century France." For an interesting adaptation of Habermas's ideas to eighteenth-century adult fiction, see John Richetti's "The Public Sphere and the Eighteenth-Century Novel: Social Criticism and Narrative Enactment." For useful readings of foreign pedagogic literature focusing on *how* texts teach (and not just their extractable didactic moral), see Janie Vanpée's "Rousseau's *Émile ou de l'éducation:* A Resistance to Reading"; Dorothea E. von Mücke's *Virtue and*

the *Veil of Illusion: Generic Innovation and the Pedagogical Project in Eighteenth-Century Literature;* and Margaret R. Higonnet's "Civility Books, Child Citizens, and Uncivil Antics."

7. I am grateful to the Pierpont Morgan Library for permission to quote from Sydney Smith's unpublished letter of 1 April 1803 (to Mrs. Hickes Beach MA 4500). He does not mean that Edgeworth is crippled, only that she is dwarfish; she was about four feet, seven inches, in youth. (On their way back from France, the Edgeworths stopped off in Edinburgh, where a son was at university, and met Smith and other Scottish Enlightenment notables.) Although Richard Lovell Edgeworth differed from his daughter in thinking that her lover did care enough to make her happy, he let her decide for herself. As his means were moderate and his large family still increasing (twenty-two children before his death), he might well have pressured his eldest daughter to provide for herself. She seems later to have felt that he was right in his evaluation of her Swedish diplomat suitor, but it does not seem likely that one so devoted to domestic happiness would have relished life in a foreign court. Her pretty young half-sister Charlotte wrote to a recently married sister a few years later that Maria "is in much fear I think at present that she has little chance of being ever in *the happy state which you enjoy at present*" (my thanks to the National Library of Scotland for permission to cite this manuscript letter to Emmeline Edgeworth King).

8. See *The Gift: Imagination and the Erotic Life of Property* (xiv, 40–55). Other useful excursions in gift-exchange theory include Marcel Mauss's *The Gift* and Ronald A. Sharp's chapter on "Friendship as Gift Exchange" in *Friendship and Literature: Spirit and Form* (82–117).

9. See Jack Zipes's essay for an overview of recent trends. I imagine that most critics now discussing children's literature would agree that it is inherently "ideological," that there is no innocent, merely amusing addressing of the child. But this assumption does not tell us very much about how specific texts by specific writers work. Writers for and about children do not express a monovocal ideology any more than writers for and about adults do.

10. Marjory has been a cult figure since the mid-nineteenth century, four editions of her oeuvre appearing within a few years. John Brown's and Mark Twain's essays gave her a wide fame and perpetuated myths about her which are still being recapitulated. For an interesting discussion of Marjory from this point of view, see Judith Plotz's "The Pet of Letters: Marjorie [*sic*] Fleming's Juvenilia." Carolyn Steedman's ch. 3, "Domestic Education and the Reading Public: The Historical Uses of Children's Writing," in *The Tidy House* places the sentimentalizing of girl writers in context.

11. Precisely because Isa is a newcomer to adult culture, she takes her socializing role to heart; she is ultimately responsible to Marjory's family for educating their visiting daughter. The interplay between preceptor and pupil is fruitful for gender analysis as well as nostalgic mythologizing; for an interesting essay from this perspective, see Alexandra Johnson, "The Drama of Imagination: Marjory Fleming and Her Journals." I am grateful to the author for having made her work available to me in manuscript.

12. As my longer study of Maria Edgeworth's fictional techniques indicates, bricolage—the mix of pastiche, parody, and allusion with abundant fact—is as fitting a label for the very sophisticated work of Edgeworth the adult author as it is for Marjory's journals. In neither case should we misread or condescend to the seemingly naive.

13. Edgeworth's letters to child correspondents are numerous and invariably charming. With twenty younger brothers and sisters, she had had plenty of practice in talking with children. She does not condescend and is never cute or sentimental;

she always assumes that children have something interesting to tell her. When young readers remark on adult work, she simply tells them not to read anything that bores them or that they don't understand. Edgeworth's own young brothers and sisters were always included in the nightly family readings and urged to voice their opinions on adult works, including their sister's fiction in progress. They were, of course, the original audience for her juvenile stories. Edgeworth also makes an ideological point of democratizing literary response in her introduction to the Edgeworths' 1816 *Readings on Poetry*, where children (and women) are explicitly urged not to be intimidated from voicing their own aesthetic assessments even when male authors' canonical masterpieces are involved.

14. For Henry James's scorn of what might be called the bi-textual work, the story that could be enjoyed by both mothers and daughters, see Mitzi Myers, "Little Girls Lost: Rewriting Romantic Childhood, Righting Gender and Genre." Earlier authors of children's literature and cross-writers fare little better in conventional literary histories specially devoted to children. One might expect Peter Hunt's call to theory to include historical revisionism too, but instead he erases children's literary history from theoretical consideration, downgrading all pre-twentieth-century writers in the process: "It is only in twentieth century [*sic*] that the most notable talents have directed themselves towards children's literature" (62).

15. Although the Anglo-Irish novelist, educator, and children's author had not yet achieved the remarkable fame she enjoyed in the first two decades of the nineteenth century, she was already well known in France as a progressive educational thinker. Much of her early juvenile work was abridged and lavishly praised by important French journalists, and she had two briskly selling adult fictions just out as well. Maria Edgeworth's growing literary reputation made her a welcome addition to French cultural circles. In addition, her father was a scientist with French connections of his own; he had lived in France decades before, enjoying access to noted *philosophes* like D'Alembert, Diderot, and Rousseau.

16. Edgeworth's notebook also records visiting Pestalozzi, many of whose methods the Edgeworths anticipate. The family letters from France describe several visits to schools and further mention of educators who were applying the Edgeworths' *Practical Education* in their work.

17. Edgeworth describes a woman's coming to political thinking at some length in the letters to Dumont cited in the epigraph; she also exemplified this kind of politics by indirection in her years of work as estate manager at Edgeworthstown. She emphasizes that she began to write out of affection for her father, not abstract public spirit, and "by degrees, enlarged my views—one circle succeeded to another,— larger & larger." The "beauteous circles" depend on the daughter's connected ways of knowing and feeling (Maria Edgeworth to Étienne Dumont, 18 September 1813, Bibliothèque Publique et Universitaire, Geneva). Michael Hurst's *Maria Edgeworth and the Public Scene*, based on unpublished papers, is an invaluable account of Edgeworth's handling of the Irish family estate after her father's death.

18. Madame's scheme and the domestic details through which Sister Frances realizes it create a family environment much like *The Schoolhome* that educator Jane Roland Martin is developing in her updating and reconceptualization of Montessori.

19. François (the name given to Madame's servant) is a private joke as well as a class portrayal, for his name and speech habits are based on the Edgeworths' actual employee during their French visit. The character Sister Frances, who runs the little girls' school on a day-to-day basis, is simultaneously a teacher whom Maria Edgeworth met and a compliment to Frances Ann Beaufort, the last of her father's four wives, who had become Maria's "mother" in 1798. Like Sister Frances, she was a talented artist as well as an agent of domestic harmony and union. Her marriage,

which initiates a new stage in the Edgeworth ménage, contrasts ironically with the flight, mobs, and bloody slaughters of the Irish Rebellion that year, just as "Madame de Fleury" juxtaposes domestic pastoral with the urban Terror.

20. For the political argument implicit in early fables, see Annabel Patterson's *Fables of Power: Aesopian Writing and Political History;* for queries about Patterson's methodology, see the review by Jacob Fuchs in *Eighteenth-Century Studies* 25.3 (Spring 1992): 369–72. Neither writer investigates how children's association with the genre affects the political environment in which the fable operates. Dorothea E. von Mücke and Janie Vanpée explore the theoretical reasoning behind Rousseau's hostility to fables in *Émile*. British writers usually make more of the capacities of juvenile and lower-class characters than do the French, and, as my essay argues, there is an implicit political revaluation in thus conferring cognitive and affective capacities on the "lower orders." It is much easier to recognize the class bias of the past, which certainly exists, than it is to recognize writers' attempts to reconceptualize stereotyped images.

21. See Lynn Hunt, "The Unstable Boundaries of the French Revolution," in *A History of Private Life,* for the connotations of such names; Hunt also underlines the historical interplay of public and private life that Edgeworth is fictionally recreating. Carolyn Steedman argues in *Childhood, Culture, and Class in Britain: Margaret McMillan, 1860–1931,* that McMillan's much later portrayals of the working-class child are the first to embody that child as simultaneously literary figure and realistic image for cultural reform. There are certainly important differences between early-nineteenth-century work and that at the turn of this century, but Steedman's otherwise valuable analysis erases a prior women's tradition of juvenile portrayal that anticipates later writers in important ways.

22. In her 1974 life of Mary Wollstonecraft, Claire Tomalin tries to identify Edgeworth's portrait of Manon with Madame Roland, a moderate who was guillotined for her role in her husband's political life (243). Roland's family nickname was Manon, but her given name was Marie-Jeanne, and the public knew her through her *Memoirs* as Madame. Tomalin's attempt to read women writers of the past through the feminism of the 1970s not only dehistoricizes Edgeworth's portrayal of the generation victimized by Revolutionary politics, but it also misreads Madame Roland. Roland professes herself a follower of Rousseau and no advocate for the rights of woman as Tomalin understands that term. Like many enlightened women of her period, Roland argues that the "common felicity" depends on "domestic happiness" (*Private Memoirs* 282). Edgeworth in fact admired Roland and her book, though she always endorses imaginative rationality over romantic or Stoic republican posturing. She calls Roland's memoirs "beautifully written, and like Rousseau: she was a great woman and died heroically, but I don't think she became . . . more happy by meddling with politics; *for*—her head is cut off, and her husband has shot himself" (Edgeworth *Memoir* 1:70). For current readings of Roland's conflicted position toward the public role into which events thrust her, see Gita May's biography and essay; Chantal Thomas's essay; and Dorinda Outram's analyses of the gendered language of republican masculine virtue in "'Le Langage Mâle De La Vertu'" and of Roland in *The Body and the French Revolution* (129–51). Jean H. Bloch's "Women and the Reform of the Nation" situates French thinkers' arguments for the social usefulness of girls' education within the context of their time.

23. The Directory followed the bloody Reign of Terror, followed in turn by Napoleon Bonaparte's leadership as consul and then as emperor. The Edgeworths' visit to France, where the story was begun in early 1803, occurred in the brief lull between lengthy wars, just before Napoleon became emperor. By the time the tale was published in 1809, it was even more of an anticipatory fantasy than when it had

originally been conceived. The wars and Napoleon's dictatorship would continue until Waterloo in 1815.

24. *Blood Sisters,* Marilyn Yalom's recent study of cross-class gender commonalities among French women of the Revolutionary period, gives factual weight to the imaginative interdependence Edgeworth's tale embodies. Camille Naish's "Dame Guillotine," in *Death Comes to the Maiden,* makes the same point from another perspective.

25. For a lively reading of French politics as family drama, see Lynn Hunt, *The Family Romance of the French Revolution,* which could make use of children's literature but does not.

26. What Jill Paton Walsh in "The Rainbow Surface" calls the "simplicity-significance problem" of children's literature inheres in the moral-philosophical tale as genre, whether for children, adolescents, or adults. The problem is "that of making a fully serious adult statement . . . and making it utterly simple and transparent," which imposes "an emotional obliqueness, an indirectness of approach." Philosophical tales derive their force as much from their allusive variations upon known conventions as upon direct statement. For a discussion of *The Idea of Difficulty in Literature,* which is useful for children's literature as a field and the conte as genre, see the collection edited by Alan C. Purves.

27. What Francis Jeffrey writes of Edgeworth's *Popular Tales* in the *Edinburgh Review* also applies to her child heroines generally: "We could not help smiling at the partiality which has led Miss Edgeworth to represent almost all her female characters in so amiable and respectable a light. There is not a tale, we believe, in which there is not some wife or daughter who is generous and gentle, and prudent and cheerful: and almost all the men who behave properly, owe most of their good actions to the influence and suggestions of these lovely monitresses. If the pride of our sex would permit us, we might perhaps confess, after all, that this representation is not very far from the truth" (337). It is important to notice that the wives and daughters make their impact through work in the world, not merely via sentimental influence.

28. From youth to old age, Edgeworth playfully images her writing as a little mouse. Gratitude, the idea of paying back the gift received, is a recurrent theme in Edgeworth's tales and letters, particularly in periods of stress, such as the aftermath of refusing the proposal. One of the last letters of the French tour, for example, exclaims: "How few people in this world are so rich in friends! When I reflect upon the kindness that has been shewn us abroad and upon the affection that awaits us at home, I feel afraid that I shall never be able to deserve my share of all this happiness—that I shall never be sufficiently grateful" (*Maria Edgeworth in France and Switzerland* 95). Both classic fables that Edgeworth dramatizes in the tale stress interdependence: the contribution that everybody makes to the whole. "The Old Man and His Children" makes the point that single twigs break, but a bundle of them won't; "The Lion and the Rat" emphasizes that "One often needs the help of smaller fry" (31): see number 47 in *Aesop's Fables*; and *The Best Fables of La Fontaine.* Most printed versions of the latter still retain the original "rat," but the more appealing and childlike "mouse" seems to have been generally used for versions presented to juvenile readers.

29. Relevant recent studies of the eighteenth-century fact/fiction debate (which also involves the status of history writing) include Davis, McKeon, and Ray. McCormack considers the historical referentiality of two of Edgeworth's adult novels.

30. More impressed than the reviewers, visitors to France who had read Edgeworth's story of Madame de Pastoret frequently visited her and heard the facts behind the tale from the real-life heroine. Harvard professor George Ticknor visited

her twice, first in 1818, when she impressed him with her intellect and eloquence and told him the horrors of the guillotine rattling outside during her imprisonment, and again in 1837, when she had just stepped down as "Lady President" of French infant schools: "She had lived long enough to see the grandchildren of her first objects of charity coming daily to receive its benefits" (Ticknor 1:255–56; 2:119). Another distinguished traveler impressed by the "substantially true" tale was Charles Kendal Bushe, the future chief justice of Ireland. Bushe's account is especially apposite because he vividly captures the interpenetration of public politics and private domesticity that the story embodies. The garden of Fleury fronted the king's palace and an immense wood on one side, "tho from the hall door you have a Panoramic view of Paris" a few miles away (Sommerville and Ross 229).

31. The Edgeworths tend to explain masculine reviewers' negative responses in terms of fact and fiction, but gender plays a large and hitherto insufficiently explored role in the reviewers' formation of the early-nineteenth-century reading public's taste. Edgeworth's stories about men are discussed in a different way from those about women and the young, but being overtly political in a man's world is dangerous, too, as the negative response to her ambitious 1814 political novel, *Patronage*, indicates.

32. Discussing Edgeworth's "art of prose fiction" with the inappropriate tools of a naive New Critical formalism, Harden's 1971 study concludes unsurprisingly that "Madame de Fleury" is "essentially a teaching on how to teach. . . . All activities are based on the principle of utility, and the principles and practices of *Practical Education* are enforced"; thus, "the tale is only a trifle which cannot be classified as fiction. Madame De [*sic*] Fleury is a lifeless creation, and her pupils are all lifeless models of perfection. Virtue is rewarded and vice punished at the greatest sacrifice of realism. . . . The tale lacks narrative interest, the machinery is awkward and clumsy, and the events falter throughout their progression. The tale is one of the worst specimens of Miss Edgeworth's composition" (184). Like most of that period's discussion of fiction, Harden's assessment assumes that all fiction aspires to a post-Jamesian kind of art and that there is an unproblematic relation between fiction and the reality it purports to represent.

33. Butler's story of Edgeworth's career reads Richard Lovell Edgeworth's much-disputed influence on his daughter as the positive factor enabling Maria Edgeworth to write the manly Irish tales which Butler believes her strong suit. This pattern necessarily reduces Edgeworth's earlier writings about women and children to apprentice work. Since "Madame de Fleury," a work about women, children, and education, inconveniently cuts across the before and after *Professional Education* break, Butler must find in the story the traces of the daughter's reading for the father's book; "it is startling to see how faithfully the plots . . . repeat its double message" (331). Revealingly, Butler, usually a careful scholar, misreads a letter in which Maria Edgeworth describes the real-life Madame de Fleury, Madame de Pastoret: "She thought Mme de Pastoret resembled Edgeworth himself " (190). What Maria Edgeworth wrote was that the husband, not the wife, "resembles my father in character" (*Maria Edgeworth in France and Switzerland* 39).

34. Most juvenile readers would notice Edgeworth's factual references and foot-noted recipes for making things like rush candles, rabbit traps, and sugar crystal candy, but few authors, even in that allusive period, are more so than she is. Like her adult fictions, her explicitly juvenile works are structured by her tongue-in-cheek rewriting of conventional plot elements from fairy tale and romance. They are also alive with all kinds of local references, a kind of compendium of cultural literacy. At the same time, they play a secret game with family and kin, encoding many Edgeworth names, sayings, and doings with the fictional material.

35. These now-classic phrases in recent historicist writing originally derive from

Clifford Geertz's work in cultural anthropology. See ch. 1, "Thick Description: Toward an Interpretive Theory of Culture," in *The Interpretation of Cultures*. Also helpful for empathetic entry into historical child signification is ch. 2, "Found in Translation: On the Social History of the Moral Imagination," in Geertz's *Local Knowledge*. More interesting still, the notions of imaginative reason that Edgeworth adapted from Scottish Enlightenment thinking have been reactivated in Mark Johnson's *Moral Imagination: Implications of Cognitive Science for Ethics*, which belongs to the growing body of transdisciplinary thinking using narrative patterns to elucidate complex cultural and ethical issues.

36. No longer limited to literature and critical theory, narrative is rapidly being institutionalized as the basic mode of human cognition and self-fashioning. This development is very important for those interested in countering the canonical marginality of children's literature.

37. I am borrowing the trademark phrases of the Brazilian educator Paulo Freire, although (like most feminist teachers) I am bothered by his failure to factor gender into the educational process. For an influential description of teaching as transformative dialogue rather than as transfer of information, see Freire's *Pedagogy of the Oppressed*. Freire reminds us that educational talk entails action *in* the world.

38. Useful studies historicizing reader response theory include those by Robert Morgan and Jane P. Tompkins. Because it emphasizes that texts are produced by the knowledge of contexts and conventions that readers bring to them, Peter Rabinowitz's *Before Reading* is also helpful in historical interpretation.

Works Cited

Aesop. *Aesop's Fables*. Told by Valerius Babrius. Trans. Denison B. Hull. Chicago: U. of Chicago P., 1968.

Armstrong, Nancy. *Desire and Domestic Fiction: A Political History of the Novel*. Oxford: Oxford U.P., 1987.

Baker, Keith Michael. "Defining the Public Sphere in Eighteenth-Century France: Variations on a Theme by Habermas." In *Habermas and the Public Sphere*. Ed. Craig Calhoun. Cambridge: MIT P., 1992. 181–211.

[Barbauld, Anna Laetitia.] Review of *Tales of Fashionable Life*, by Maria Edgeworth. *Monthly Review* 2nd ser. 62 (May 1810): 96–97.

Bloch, Jean H. "Women and the Reform of the Nation." In *Woman and Society in Eighteenth-Century France*. Ed. Eva Jacobs, et al. London: Athlone P., 1979. 3–18.

Bottigheimer, Ruth B. "Review Essay: Recent Scholarship in Children's Literature, 1980 to the Present." *Eighteenth-Century Life* 17.ns3 (November 1993): 89–103.

Brown, John. "Marjorie Fleming." In *Rab and His Friends and Other Papers*. London: Dent; New York: Dutton, n.d. 85–111.

Butler, Marilyn. *Maria Edgeworth: A Literary Biography*. Oxford: Clarendon, 1972.

Clark, Beverly Lyon. "Thirteen Ways of Thumbing Your Nose at Children's Literature." *Lion and the Unicorn* 16.2 (December 1992): 240–44.

Davin, Anna. "When Is A Child Not A Child?" In *Politics of Everyday Life: Continuity and Change in Work and the Family*. Ed. Helen Corr and Lynn Jamieson. New York: St. Martin's, 1990. 37–61.

Davis, Lennard J. *Factual Fictions: The Origins of the English Novel*. New York: Columbia U.P., 1983.

Edgeworth, Maria. "Madame de Fleury." In *Tales of Fashionable Life*. 3rd ed. 3 vols. London: J. Johnson, 1809. 2: 178–328.

———. *Maria Edgeworth in France and Switzerland: Selections from the Edgeworth Family Letters*. Ed. Christina Colvin. Oxford: Clarendon, 1979.

―――. *A Memoir of Maria Edgeworth, with A Selection from Her Letters by the Late Mrs. [Frances] Edgeworth.* Ed. by Her Children. 3 vols. London: Privately printed Joseph Masters and Son, 1867.

―――. *Rosamond: With Other Tales.* New York: Harper, n.d.

Edgeworth, Richard Lovell, and Maria Edgeworth. *Readings on Poetry.* 2d ed. London: R. Hunter, 1816.

Fleming, Marjory. *The Complete Marjory Fleming: Her Journals, Letters and Verses.* Ed. Frank Sidgwick. London: Sidgwick and Jackson, 1934.

Fraser, Nancy. "What's Critical about Critical Theory? The Case of Habermas and Gender." In *Feminism as Critique: On the Politics of Gender.* Ed. Seyla Benhabib and Drucilla Cornell. Minneapolis: U. of Minnesota P., 1987. 31–56.

Freire, Paulo. *Pedagogy of the Oppressed.* Trans. Myra Bergman Ramos. 1970. New York: Continuum, 1986.

Fuchs, Jacob. Review of *Fables of Power,* by Annabel Patterson. *Eighteenth-Century Studies* 25.3 (Spring 1992): 369–72.

Geertz, Clifford. *The Interpretation of Cultures: Selected Essays.* New York: Basic Books, 1973.

―――. *Local Knowledge: Further Essays in Interpretive Anthropology.* New York: Basic Books, 1983.

Grey, Rowland. "Maria Edgeworth and Étienne Dumont." *Dublin Review* 145 (1909): 239–65.

Habermas, Jürgen. *The Structural Transformation of the Public Sphere: An Inquiry into a Category of Bourgeois Society.* Trans. Thomas Burger. 1962. Cambridge: MIT P., 1992.

Harden, O[leta] Elizabeth McWhorter. *Maria Edgeworth's Art of Prose Fiction.* The Hague and Paris: Mouton, 1971.

Higonnet, Margaret R. "Civility Books, Child Citizens, and Uncivil Antics." *Poetics Today* 13.1 (Spring 1992): 123–40.

―――. "Critical Apertures." In *Children's Literature* 17 (1989): 143–50.

Hollindale, Peter. "Ideology and the Children's Book." *Signal* 55 (January 1988): 3–22.

Hunt, Lynn. *The Family Romance of the French Revolution.* Berkeley: U. of California P., 1992.

―――. "The Unstable Boundaries of the French Revolution." In *A History of Private Life.* Vol. 4, *From the Fires of Revolution to the Great War.* Ed. Michelle Perrot. Cambridge: Belknap P. of Harvard U.P., 1990. 13–45.

Hunt, Peter. *Criticism, Theory, and Children's Literature.* Oxford: Basil Blackwell, 1991.

Hurst, Michael. *Maria Edgeworth and the Public Scene: Intellect, Fine Feeling, and Landlordism in the Age of Reform.* Coral Gables, FL: U. of Miami P., 1969.

Hyde, Lewis. *The Gift: Imagination and the Erotic Life of Property.* New York: Random House, Vintage Books, 1983.

[Jeffrey, Francis.] Review of *Popular Tales,* by Maria Edgeworth. *Edinburgh Review* 4.8 (July 1804): 329–37.

Johnson, Alexandra. "The Drama of Imagination: Marjory Fleming and Her Journals." In *Infant Tongues: The Voice of the Child in Literature.* Ed. Elizabeth Goodenough, Mark Heberle, and Naomi Sokoloff. Detroit: Wayne State U.P., 1994. 80–109.

Johnson, Mark. *Moral Imagination: Implications of Cognitive Science for Ethics.* Chicago: U. of Chicago P., 1993.

La Fontaine, Jean de. *The Best Fables of La Fontaine.* Trans. Francis Duke. Charlottesville: U.P. of Virginia, 1965.

Martin, Jane Roland. "Romanticism Domesticated: Maria Montessori and the Casa dei Bambini." In *The Educational Legacy of Romanticism.* Ed. John Willinsky. Waterloo, Canada: Wilfrid Laurier U.P. for Calgary Institute for the Humanities, 1990. 159–74.

———. *The Schoolhome: Rethinking Schools for Changing Families.* Cambridge: Harvard U.P., 1992.

Mauss, Marcel. *The Gift: The Form and Reason for Exchange in Archaic Societies.* 1950. Trans. W. D. Halls. New York and London: W. W. Norton, 1990.

McCormack, W. J. *Ascendancy and Tradition in Anglo-Irish Literary History from 1789 to 1939.* Oxford: Clarendon, 1985.

McKeon, Michael. *The Origins of the English Novel 1600–1740.* Baltimore and London: Johns Hopkins U.P., 1987.

May, Gita. *Madame Roland and the Age of Revolution.* New York: Columbia U.P., 1970.

———. "Rousseau's 'Antifeminism' Reconsidered." In *French Women and the Age of Enlightenment.* Ed. Samnia Spencer. Bloomington: Indiana U.P., 1984. 309–17.

Morgan, Robert. "Reading as Discursive Practice: The Politics and History of Reading." In *Beyond Communication: Reading Comprehension and Criticism.* Ed. Deanne Bogdan and Stanley B. Straw. Portsmouth, NH: Boynton/Cook, Heinemann, 1990. 319–36.

Myers, Mitzi. "Little Girls Lost: Rewriting Romantic Childhood, Righting Gender and Genre." In *Teaching Children's Literature: Issues, Pedagogy, Resources.* Ed. Glenn Edward Sadler. New York: Modern Language Association, 1992. 131–42.

Naish, Camille. *Death Comes to the Maiden: Sex and Execution 1431–1933.* London: Routledge, 1991.

Nelson, Claudia. *Boys Will Be Girls: The Feminine Ethic and British Children's Fiction, 1857–1917.* New Brunswick: Rutgers U.P., 1991.

Newby, P. H. *Maria Edgeworth.* English Novelists Series. London: Arthur Barker, 1950.

Nodelman, Perry. "The Other: Orientalism, Colonialism, and Children's Literature." *Children's Literature Association Quarterly* 17.1 (Spring 1992): 29–35.

Outram, Dorinda. *The Body and the French Revolution: Sex, Class, and Political Culture.* New Haven: Yale U.P., 1989.

———. "'Le Langage Mâle De La Vertu': Women and the Discourse of the French Revolution." In *The Social History of Language.* Ed. Peter Burke and Roy Porter. Cambridge: Cambridge U.P., 1987. 120–35.

Paratte, Henri-Dominique. "Maria Edgeworth's 'Madame de Fleury,' An Anglo-Irish View of the French Revolution." *Cahiers irlandais* 2–3 (1974): 69–82.

Patterson, Anabel. *Fables of Power: Aesopian Writing and Political History.* Durham: Duke U.P., 1991.

Pointon, Marcia. *Hanging the Head: Portraiture and Social Formation in Eighteenth-Century England.* New Haven: Yale U.P., 1993.

Prévost, Antoine François. *Manon Lescaut.* 1731. Trans. Helen Waddell. 1935. Westport, CT: Hyperion P., 1978.

Purves, Alan C., ed. *The Idea of Difficulty in Literature.* Albany: State U. of New York P., 1991.

Rabinowitz, Peter. *Before Reading: Narrative Conventions and the Politics of Interpretation.* Ithaca and London: Cornell U.P., 1987.

Ray, William. *Story and History: Narrative Authority and Social Identity in the Eighteenth-Century French and English Novel.* Oxford: Basil Blackwell, 1990.

Richetti, John. "The Public Sphere and the Eighteenth-Century Novel: Social Criticism and Narrative Enactment." *Eighteenth-Century Life* 16.ns3 (November 1992): 114–29.

Roland, [Marie-Jeanne Phlipon]. *The Private Memoirs of Madame Roland.* Ed. Edward
    Gilpin Johnson. 3d ed. Chicago: McClurg, 1901.
Sharp, Ronald A. *Friendship and Literature: Spirit and Form.* Durham: Duke U.P., 1986.
Shavit, Zohar, ed. *Poetics Today.* Special issue on Children's Literature. 13.1 (Spring
    1992).
Somerville, E[dith] Œ., and Martin Ross. *An Incorruptible Irishman.* London: Nichol-
    son and Watson, 1932.
Steedman, Carolyn. *Childhood, Culture, and Class in Britain: Margaret McMillan, 1860–
    1931.* New Brunswick: Rutgers U.P., 1990.
————. *The Tidy House: Little Girls Writing.* 1982. London: Virago, 1987.
[Stephen, Henry John, and William Gifford.] Review of *Tales of Fashionable Life,* by
    Maria Edgeworth. *Quarterly Review* 2.3 (August 1809): 146–54.
Summerfield, Geoffrey. *Fantasy and Reason: Children's Literature in the Eighteenth Cen-
    tury.* Athens: U. of Georgia P., 1985.
Thomas, Chantal. "Heroism in the Feminine: The Examples of Charlotte Corday
    and Madame Roland." In *The French Revolution 1789–1989: Two Hundred Years
    of Rethinking.* Ed. Sandy Petrey. *The Eighteenth Century: Theory and Interpretation*
    (1989): 67–82.
Ticknor, George. *Life, Letters, and Journals of George Ticknor.* 6th ed. 2 vols. Boston:
    James R. Osgood, 1877.
Tomalin, Claire. *The Life and Death of Mary Wollstonecraft.* New York: Harcourt Brace
    Jovanovich, 1974.
Tompkins, Jane P. "The Reader in History: The Changing Shape of Literary Re-
    sponse." In *Reader-Response Criticism: From Formalism to Post-Structuralism.* Ed. Jane
    P. Tompkins. Baltimore and London: Johns Hopkins U.P., 1980. 201–32.
Trilling, Lionel. *Beyond Culture: Essays on Literature and Learning.* New York: Viking P.,
    1965.
Twain, Mark [Clemens, Samuel Langhorne]. "Marjorie Fleming, The Wonder
    Child." In *Europe and Elsewhere.* Stormfield ed. New York: Harper, 1929.
Vanpée, Janie. "Rousseau's *Émile ou de l'éducation:* A Resistance to Reading." In *Read-
    ing the Archive: On Texts and Institutions.* Ed. E. S. Burt and Janie Vanpée. *Yale French
    Studies* 77 (1990): 156–76.
von Mücke, Dorothea E. *Virtue and the Veil of Illusion: Generic Innovation and the Peda-
    gogical Project in Eighteenth-Century Literature.* Stanford: Stanford U.P., 1991.
Walsh, Jill Paton. "The Rainbow Surface." In *The Cool Web: The Pattern of Chil-
    dren's Reading.* Ed. Margaret Meek, Aidan Warlow, and Griselda Barton. London:
    Bodley Head, 1977. 192–95.
Yalom, Marilyn. *Blood Sisters: The French Revolution in Women's Memory.* New York:
    Basic Books, 1993.
Young, Iris Marion. "Impartiality and the Civic Public: Some Implications of Femi-
    nist Critiques of Moral and Political Theory." In *Feminism as Critique: On the Politics
    of Gender.* Ed. Seyla Benhabib and Drucilla Cornell. Minneapolis: U. of Minne-
    sota P., 1987. 57–76.
Zipes, Jack. "Taking Political Stock: New Theoretical and Critical Approaches to
    Anglo-American Children's Literature in the 1980s." *Lion and the Unicorn* 14.1
    (June 1990): 7–22.

Letters on a Tombstone:
Mothers and Literacy in Mary Lamb's
Mrs. Leicester's School

Jean I. Marsden

The gift of education represented so vividly in Maria Edgeworth's "Madame de Fleury" stands in contrast to a more problematic vision of education published within a year of Edgeworth's work. In Edgeworth's tale, unlike the work by Mary Lamb that is the subject for this essay, formal schooling is the gift of a benevolent maternal figure who enriches a child's life and in so doing reiterates a cultural expectation linking mothers, or mother surrogates, and education.[1] Mothers, writes Hannah More, are responsible for, and even empowered through, educating their children:

> The great object to which YOU, who are or may be mothers, are more especially called, is the education of your children. If we are responsible for the use of influence in the case of those over whom we have no immediate control, in the case of our children we are responsible for the exercise of acknowledged *power;* a power wide in its extent, indefinite in its effects, and inestimable in its importance. On YOU depend in no small degree the principles of the whole rising generation. To your direction the daughters are almost exclusively committed. (I.322)

In their stress on the mother's central role in the education of her children, and in particular her daughters, More's comments express the ideal of the solicitous and pedagogically involved mother popular in the late eighteenth and early nineteenth century. Moralists as divergent as Mary Wollstonecraft and Rousseau cited mothers as the proper instructors of moral edification, but even more so of basic rudiments of reading and writing.[2] Although mothers had for a time the "mighty privilege of forming the hearts and minds" of their sons (More, I.322), it was the education of their daughters to which they were more "exclusively committed." It was their daughters whose characters they were to shape even as they were teaching

Children's Literature 23, ed. Francelia Butler, R. H. W. Dillard, and Elizabeth Lennox Keyser (Yale University Press, © 1995 Hollins College).

them to shape their letters. Neglect of this "bounden duty" could have dire consequences, More warns; neglectful mothers contribute to "expel Christianity from her last citadel" (I.322).

When such natural education was not possible, a maternal substitute became necessary. Even Wollstonecraft, who believed that mothers could best educate their own daughters, admits that "many family reasons render it necessary sometimes to send them from home" (57). Concern over the education of girls extended to these boarding schools,[3] and this concern with the form of female education fuels the rise of a new subgenre: the girls' school narrative. Beginning with *The Governess* by Sarah Fielding in 1749, children's literature features portraits of firm but benevolent maternal teachers, mother surrogates who educate girls to become morally upright, self-reliant, and well read. Mitzi Myers charts the rise of the "new educating heroine" (36), the mother-teachers who dominate so much of Georgian children's literature, finding in these works "a resilient and purposeful maternal discourse, a female mode of cultural reform directed toward improvement of both self and community" (55).[4]

A striking exception to this tide of edification appears in Mary Lamb's second book of tales for children, *Mrs. Leicester's School*. Published in 1808 and containing seven tales by Mary Lamb and three by Charles Lamb, this short book of supposed children's narratives follows the general pattern of Fielding's *Governess* as each little scholar repeats the story of her life when asked to relate "whatever happened to make a great impression on [her] when [she was] very young" (4). Although *The Governess* and *Mrs. Leicester's School* share a similar structure, the two books differ radically in focus and in tone. Despite the title, Mrs. Leicester never appears, nor do we hear accounts of life—or education—at her school: the guiding maternal influence is absent. Instead, the book's dedication describes a forlorn little group of girls with "traces of tears" on every cheek (2). They report their stories not to Mrs. Leicester, but to a young teacher who is more akin to the girls themselves than to the school's headmistress. Commenting on the children's tears, the unnamed narrator remarks: "I also was sad; for I, like you, had parted from my friends, and the duties of my profession were new to me" (2). After the dedication, even this voice effectively vanishes, reentering the book only three times to comment briefly on the girls' responses to their classmates' stories.

Lacking the embracing frame provided by a motherly guide, the tales themselves reiterate this maternal absence, detailing a series of imperfect mothers. Each tale involves a mother who in some way fails to fulfil what More terms her "bounden duty" through death, abandonment, or neglect. Three of the children lost their mothers in infancy, three found themselves temporarily or permanently abandoned, one was ignored, and one was forced to give up life with the only mother she knew. (Only in one of Charles Lamb's contributions does a girl tell of a stable life with her natural mother.) Even when these failures are reversed, the bond between mother or mother surrogate and daughter is ultimately broken, resulting in the child's tearful presence at Mrs. Leicester's school. That the book focuses on the girls' tales of their early life and education rather than on the schooling they receive from Mrs. Leicester emphasizes the impression of maternal indifference and of daughters forced to find education through other means.

In each case, the absence of the mother results in incomplete, inadequate, or incorrect learning. The school seems populated almost entirely by daughters whose reading and writing has been directly affected by their absent mothers, and the incidents of female reading they relate are inevitably tinged with death and loss. One child learns to read from her mother's tombstone, another is taught to read in her dead mother's room, while a third, by writing the secret story of her own birth, is reunited with her real mother while losing the only mother she has ever known. Each tale not only relates a story of maternal loss, literal or symbolic, but directly links this loss to the child's literacy. The girls are driven by their own desires to read and to write so that the tales represent literacy as both dangerous and necessary.

One way to interpret this duality is to link the tales' disturbing pictures of maternity to Mary Lamb's own ambivalence toward the mother who had curtailed Mary's education and whom Mary killed in a fit of insanity. Mary's formal education was limited; she attended school for a very short time and never learned to spell. We have no way of knowing whether her own mother accepted Mary's education as a "great object," but what records we have suggest not. Charles Lamb comments sorrowfully to Samuel Taylor Coleridge that his mother "would always love my brother [John Lamb, Charles and Mary's older brother] above Mary, who was not worthy of one tenth of that affection, which Mary had the right to claim"

(*Letters*, I.52), and it is evident she saw Mary's education as a secondary concern. Duty to family came first, and Mary worked as a seamstress to support her younger brother and ailing parents.[5] Yet the pressures of her position as breadwinner eventually exacerbated the manic-depressive illness which plagued her all her life and erupted in a deadly attack on her mother. Not surprisingly, Mary could never escape thoughts of her mother, commenting to her friend Sarah Stoddart that "my dear Mother (who though you do not know it, is always in my poor head and heart)" (*Letters*, II.124).[6]

Mary's pictures of absent mothers and garbled reading also suggest a traumatic induction into a Lacanian symbolic order, where reading and writing (in Lacan's terms the "Name of the Father") quite literally involve the loss of the mother. Yet, unlike the Lacanian model, this transition is expressly linked with women and leads the girls ultimately, though unhappily, to the matriarchy of Mrs. Leicester's school, where their stories end abruptly. Literacy, then, is both a necessary rite of passage for the female child and a paradigm of loss. A girl's connection with this symbolic order is deeply important; as depicted by Lamb, it represents the primal experience of childhood.

Of the seven tales Mary Lamb contributed to *Mrs. Leicester's School,* four directly address the link between schooling and literally or figuratively dead mothers. A fifth story, "Charlotte Wilmot: the Merchant's Daughter," connects a girl's failure to learn simple tasks with absentee parenting.[7] Charlotte, the daughter of rich parents who overspent their income, was a spoiled child whose mother never taught her to look after herself; she cannot even dress herself without assistance because she had "a woman servant whose sole business it was to attend on me" (71). When her parents go bankrupt, they flee England, leaving Charlotte behind where she must be instructed by a school friend in these basic accomplishments. Charlotte's formal education has been more than adequate: "My parents spared no cost for masters to instruct me; I had a French governess" (71). Yet her lack of knowledge of "useful works and employments" (74), or such rudiments as dressing herself, results in her humiliation, and she must be instructed in these arts by the daughter of her father's clerk. Charlotte's father eventually regains some wealth, but sends her away to school "to retrench his expenses" (75), perpetuating the cycle of abandonment which began with Charlotte's inadequate personal and social education.

Ironically, the dead mothers of two of the other girls at the school are more directly linked with their education than Charlotte's absent mother. In the first story of the volume, "Elizabeth Villiers: The Sailor Uncle," Elizabeth's mother dies when she is very young. Her father, a country curate, teaches the child to read from her mother's tombstone. Following the teacher/narrator's injunction to "tell us the first thing you can remember," Elizabeth recounts: "The first thing I can remember was my father teaching me the alphabet from the letters on a tombstone that stood at the head of my mother's grave. . . . Many times in the day would my father lay aside his books and his papers to lead me to this spot, and make me point to the letters, and then set me to spell syllables and words: in this manner, the epitaph on my mother's tomb being my primer and my spelling-book, I learned to read" (5). Even though the mother herself is not present, she is the means by which Elizabeth learns to read. This identification of mother and reading is so immediate that when asked by her uncle who taught her to spell, she replies, "Mamma." Driven by this association of symbols ("Mamma's pretty letters") and the maternal figure, Elizabeth's early experience of her mother is almost purely textual. Her visualization of her mother consists entirely of the tombstone and its epitaph. "I never made out any figure of mamma" (7) except the tombstone, she relates, and when her long-lost uncle reappears and asks her to lead him to her mother, she takes him directly to the tombstone, proclaiming "Here is mamma!" (6).

Actually as well as symbolically, mother and daughter are bound together through the medium of letters. Even so, Lamb reveals that this bond is ultimately inadequate. Not only does the morbid obsession with the mother's grave exacerbate Elizabeth's father's grief and prevent Elizabeth from knowing anything about the woman who was her mother, but it also limits the scope of her reading to the context of the graveyard. When presented with real books, she cannot make out the letters, "they were so much smaller than I had been accustomed to; they were like Greek characters to me; I could make nothing at all of them" (10). Reading this maternal text, then, is ultimately void, a literal dead end. In the end, the uncle becomes a mother surrogate, taking the place of his dead sister, recreating her memory and teaching his niece to read. His love for his sister and her daughter enables him to replace the pedagogically inadequate mother (and even more inadequate father). Properly educated by the end of the story, Elizabeth gains an image of her mother as well as a sense of her loss and can read texts other than tombstones.

A more positive linking of dead mothers and reading appears in the fourth story, "Elinor Forester: The Father's Wedding." Elinor, like Elizabeth, loses her mother, but her mother's name is not rehearsed; she remembers that "from the time of her death no one had ever spoken to me of my mamma" (43). Elinor's father remarries, and her confusion between her old and new mothers is resolved and her grief healed only when her stepmother, a school friend of her mother, first takes her into the room in which her mother died and then teaches her to read at the site of her mother's deathbed so that the mother's room becomes Elinor's schoolroom.

> Here my new mamma taught me to read. I was a sad little dunce, and scarcely knew my letters. My own mamma had often said, when she got better she would hear me read every day, but as she never got better, it was not her fault. I now began to learn very fast, for when I said my lesson well, I was always rewarded with some pretty story of my mother's childhood; and these stories generally contained some little hints that were instructive to me, and which I greatly stood in want of for, between improper indulgence and neglect, I had many faulty ways. (45–46)

As with Elizabeth Villiers, education through the mother is inadequate; Elizabeth can read only tombstones and Elinor is a "sad little dunce." Again, a mother surrogate must remedy the lack, here the mother's school friend rather than the mother's sibling. (Elinor's father, like Elizabeth's, is rarely mentioned as Lamb ignores the possibility of paternal intervention.) Although Elizabeth actually read her mother, physically tracing the letters of her name in stone, Elinor's mother becomes a moral text; anecdotes of her life become the guidebook for remedying Elinor's "many faulty ways." Thus, learning to read via the mother becomes a complex nexus of death, education, and loss that each child presents as the defining moment of her life.

A more unsettling vision of the link between mothers and literacy appears in "Ann Withers: The Changeling." Ann is an older child, and her story involves not the process of learning, but the deployment of this education through writing. Ann's loss comprises not death but displacement, which she brings upon herself by the unselfconscious writing of her own story. The focus of this story is the deed of a mother she barely knows, and in her attempt to manipulate language, Ann loses both her real and foster mothers. Born to the nurse of an aristocratic family, Ann was substituted for the infant heiress by her mother and raised as a lady. The cheat is only discovered when the nurse, overwhelmed by guilt, confesses to her supposed daughter, who in turn tells Ann the secret in strict confidence.[8] Not realizing the potential ramifications of her actions, Ann uses the story as the basis for a play which she writes and in which she performs the principal role. The little drama is performed for her "parents"—and her real mother. The nurse cries out that the story is "all true," and, as Ann comments, "in the catastrophe I lost not only the name I personated in the piece, but with it my own name also" (30). What was to be a "scene of triumph" for the young dramatist becomes a devastating denouement as the spectators see a "strict poetical justice done" when Ann is returned to a mother she barely knows.

In this story, the relationship of child, mother, and the written word is more subtly entwined than in the tales focusing on a child's reading, and the consequence of the bond is catastrophic. As the story suggests, learning to write, or more properly to compose, is a more complex process and requires more self-awareness than learning to read. Ann's experience reveals that she has not fully grasped the power of language. For her, writing the play is a chance to display her talents and make amends for the "injury" a friend (the real heiress, Miss Lesley) had suffered, but she is unable to invent a new story, and thus tells her own, a failure of both thought and creativity. In her treatise on the education of daughters, Mary Wollstonecraft comments that "writing well is of great consequence in life as to our temporal interest, and of still more to the mind; as it teaches a person to arrange their thoughts, and digest them" (46). Wollstonecraft cautions, however, that, in such pursuits of knowledge, improvement rather than admiration must be sought, "for those seldom make observation who are full of themselves" (47). "Full of" her desire for admiration, Ann is unable to understand the larger implications of the words she pens, and her writing results in self-revelation rather than self-knowledge. She thus writes herself and destroys that self at the same instant.

As Lamb relates, the most devastating effect of Ann's playwriting is the immediate loss of the only mother she has ever known. By contrast, the new Miss Lesley engrosses the attention of *both* mothers; as Ann comments unhappily, "to have in a manner two mothers, and Miss Lesley to engross them both, was too much indeed" (40). The form this maternal affection/rejection takes is education. With a new daughter as the focus of their attention, Sir Edward and in particular Lady Harriot devote themselves to her education: "The whole house was, as I may say, in requisition for her instruction" (39). Even Ann is asked to assist in the process, and, with governesses and masters hired to supplement parental instruction, Miss Lesley makes rapid progress. In contrast, Ann reports that "I was not remarkably forward in my education. . . . I spoke French very correctly, and I had made some progress in Italian; but I had had the instruction of masters only during the few months of the year we usually passed in London" (39). Worst of all, Lady Harriot discovers Miss Lesley's musical abilities and "gave up all company and devoted her whole time to instructing her daughter in this science" (40). This allocation of talents reiterates class hierarchies—the child to the manor born seems inherently ready to learn, although this argument for the ascendancy of nature over nurture is undercut by Ann's suggestion that her own education had never excited such interest, being left to the "few months" the family spent in London. In the end, Ann's experiment in writing results in maternal loss, made all the more traumatic by the scenes of successful maternal education Ann is forced to watch. Her sense of exclusion from this world becomes so painful that Ann is sent off to school, away from both her mothers, a circumstance she refers to as "my hard fate" (42). In this dark tale, the link between maternity and language brings pain, suggesting that the danger of writing is the loss of the mother.[9]

Thus far my comments have been addressed only to those tales written by Mary Lamb. Charles Lamb's three tales do not depict an intimate connection between mothering and reading or writing and in general lack the darker quality of many of Mary's tales, where daughters struggle with maternal absence or neglect.[10] The children in his tales seem to fit more neatly into the conventional views of girls during the early nineteenth century; they are "timid," "weak," "foolish" (terms they use to describe themselves) and more religious than the girls in Mary's tales. These differences can be most clearly seen in two parallel tales, Charles's "Maria Howe: The Witch Aunt" and Mary's "Margaret Green: The Young Mahometan." Both tales involve girls who read without supervision and end up terrifying themselves, but Charles's account of the young girl who thinks, for a time, that her aunt is a witch is much gentler in tone than Mary's tale of a girl who thinks that her neglectful mother will go to hell because she does not believe in Mahomet.

In their accounts of how reading can fire an overheated imagination, both Lambs stand in stark contrast to John Ruskin, who later in the century would advocate that girls be allowed to wander, "like fawns," through a library.[11] In "The Witch Aunt," Charles relates the difficulties that befall a young reader of "unrational" or "unsprightly" texts. Maria Howe's parents, finding her too serious, frequently leave her home with her elderly aunt. When left alone, she likes to explore the book closet outside her mother's dressing room. There she pulls down any books she pleases and reads them, "no matter whether they were fit for my years or no, or whether I understood them" (64). Among her favorite "reading" ("I was too ignorant to make out many words," 65) we find Fox's *Book of Martyrs,* Stackhouse's *History of the Bible,* and *Glanvil on Witches;* the stories of witches so terrified her that she cannot sleep at night and eventually comes to believe that her dearly loved aunt is a witch. Maria, who narrates the tale when older, blames her own foolishness for this error, adding, "I was let grow up like a wild weed, and thrived accordingly" (69). The terror which had so frightened Maria over the witch who was not a witch was finally resolved when Maria is taken away by a friend of her mother "and soon found the grand effects of a change of scene. Instead of melancholy closets and lonely avenues of trees, I saw lightsome rooms and cheerful faces; I had companions of my own age; no books were allowed me but what were rational and sprightly; that gave me mirth or gave me instruction" (70). The effect of this change of scene and change of reading matter is electrifying. Maria comes back cured of her fear of her aunt, and her relations with her parents improve. In this idyllic fable, proper reading, both instructive and entertaining, creates a harmonious family.

Charles's story lacks the maternal conflict that makes Mary's stories so distinctive. Maria's parents begin by paying little attention to their daughter because of her somber temperament, but by the end of the story Maria has become sociable and companionable, commenting, "I impute almost all that I had to complain of in their neglect to my having been a little, unsociable, uncompanionable mortal" (71). She never questions that the trouble was all of her own making. A very different picture appears in Mary's story, "Margaret Green: The Young Mahomentan," which, like "The Witch Aunt," deals with the perils of improper reading. Margaret, like Maria, is a solitary child ignored by the adults around her—she lacks even the sometimes comforting presence of an elderly aunt. In her case, however, the neglect is specifically maternal. After the death of Margaret's father, Margaret's mother accepts a position as companion to an elderly lady. Under the influence of her patroness, Margaret's mother begins to ignore her daughter, speaking to her rarely and focusing her attention instead on a large piece of needlework. "My mother, following the example of her patroness, had almost wholly discontinued talking to me. I scarcely ever heard a word addressed to me from morning to night. If it were not for the old servants saying 'Good morning to you, Miss Margaret!' as they passed me in the long passages, I should have been the greatest part of the day in as perfect a solitude as Robinson Crusoe" (50). As Mary Lamb relates, this maternal neglect is the direct cause of the problems that befall Margaret. Left without an adult guide, she soon fails to distinguish between right and wrong.

These blurred moral sensibilities appear most noticeably in Margaret's reading. She begins each day by reading aloud from a large-print family Bible to her mother and the elderly lady. When she is finished with the reading and with her daily allotment of needlework, she is free to roam throughout the house—she is not supposed to do more reading or needlework because her eyes are weak. In her wanderings, she finds her way into the library, and, once there, spends hours searching for interesting books. Her great discovery is a well-worn volume entitled *Mahometanism Explained.* Many of its pages have been torn out, but enough remains for her to read sketchily the story of Ishmael (her favorite biblical character) and of Mahomet himself. Her troubles begin when she mistakes the stories in *Mahometanism Explained* for truth—"I concluded that I must be a Mahometan, for I believed every word I read" (51)—and begins to fear that her mother and the elderly lady will be damned to fall into a bottomless gulf because they are not Mahometans.

These fears increase, but Margaret finds it difficult to express them: "But it wanted more courage than I possessed to break the matter to my intended converts; I must acknowledge that I had been reading without leave; and the habit of never speaking, or being spoken to, considerably increased the difficulty" (51). The result of this anxiety is a dangerous fever during which Margaret confesses incoherently to her mother and begs her to "be so kind as to be a Mahometan" (52). Margaret is saved from her mistaken views, not by her mother, but by a kindly doctor and his wife who take Margaret home and amuse her so well that *Mahometanism Explained* "vanished out of my head in an instant" (53). In addition to meeting other girls of her own age, she is taken to a fair where the doctor and his wife buy her a variety of different items, including her workbasket, pincushion, and needlecase—and a geographical game,[12] which the doctor's wife (yet another mother surrogate) plays with her all evening long, a distinct change from the silent treatment she had received from her mother.

Unlike Charles's treatment of Maria Howe, Mary Lamb does not allow Margaret Green to voice much condemnation of her own conduct. The blame instead lies largely elsewhere; Margaret's trauma can be linked to the neglect she suffers from her mother and an earlier reader's censorship of *Mahometanism Explained*. Not only does she lack a guide for her reading—or for any other activity— but the book she reads is incomplete. Many pages have been ripped out, giving Margaret an incorrect idea of the text's purpose: "If the leaves of my favourite book had not been torn out, I should have read that the author of it did not mean to give the fabulous stories here related as true, but only wrote it as giving a history of the Turks" and their beliefs (53). Although the lack of supervision under which Margaret reads suggests that girls cannot be trusted to read on their own, the damaged state of the book suggests that censoring those texts that girls do read is equally dangerous. Margaret needs a solicitous mother who would help her find appropriate readings, as the doctor and his wife do. Her story illustrates the lack of "sprightly and rational" reading for girls, a lack which the Lambs hoped *Mrs. Leicester's School* and their earlier children's book, *Tales from Shakespeare*, would fill.[13]

In contrast to those written by her brother Charles, Mary's tales evince a deep suspicion of the maternal transmission of culture. Her tales refute the happy vision of maternally guided education voiced by Hannah More and portrayed by Maria Edgeworth. The mothers mentioned in *Mrs. Leicester's School* are emphatically *not* involved in their daughters' education—instead they are absent, dead, or neglectful. The committed mother More describes is nowhere to be seen, and nowhere do we see a mother exercise the "acknowledged *power*" of which More writes. These are mothers who intentionally or unintentionally relinquish power over their daughters. As a result, the daughters are left adrift, their struggles symbolized by their difficult entrance into the world of language. Lamb presents the achievement and deployment of literacy as a defining moment in the female acquisition of culture, and, in her tales, girls confront a gulf where traditional guides fail them. Nearly two hundred years later, Nancy Chodorow writes that "women mediate between the social and cultural categories which men have defined; they bridge the gap and make transitions—especially in their role as socializer and mother—between nature and culture" (180). In these stories, however, this bridge is absent and the socializing role must be taken over by nonfamily members or by a series of surrogate mothers like Elizabeth Villiers's kindly uncle and Elinor Forester's stepmother, whom Lamb presents as the girls' most positive links to literacy.

In the end, Mary Lamb's tales suggest that for the intelligent girl (like Lamb herself) there is little hope of proper education in the home. Her mother will not support her, and the girl's unsupervised instincts may lead her astray. Presenting an often melancholy picture of a solitary child, these tales begin in fractured or single-parent families and end with the sorrowing child at Mrs. Leicester's School, "eyes red with weeping" (2). Although the girls' presence at the school suggests that the problem will be resolved, Lamb leaves the ending open and the schooling unfinished. The matriarch of this little sisterhood is absent, her pedagogical role as yet unfulfilled. Haunted by her own experience, Lamb stands apart from her contemporaries in her stark portrayal of girls' acquisition of culture. In her depictions of girlhood, surrogates provide parental care and the only hope for a girl's schooling lies away from home. Providing no comfortable monitory vision of proper education, Lamb leaves her readers with a purely female dilemma in which literacy and the mother are set in seemingly inescapable conflict. Represented by Lamb as both necessary and painful, this primal experience marks a harsh transition into the world of language.

Notes

1. In Edgeworth's tale, it is Madame de Fleury rather than the children's actual mother who fills this role.

2. See Wollstonecraft, *Thoughts on the Education of Daughters,* and Rousseau, *The New Heloise.*

3. See, for example, Erasmus Darwin, *A Plan for the Conduct of Female Education in Boarding Schools* (1797), in which Darwin creates an extensive blueprint for running a school, providing numerous details from the size of the desks to specific foods in the boarders' diet.

4. Not all pictures of girls' schools are so benevolent. In *Moral Instruction and Fiction for Children, 1749–1820,* Samuel F. Pickering describes a range of works in which schools are portrayed as irreligious and immoral, a trend that seems to have been particularly common during the later eighteenth century (see especially pp. 102–106).

5. Charles even refers to her lack of education in the autobiographical essay "Mackery End, in Hertfordshire." In contrast, Charles, like his older brother, attended Christ's Hospital School, a school "commonly attended by the children of middle rank, but financially distressed, families" (Aaron, 58).

6. For a more detailed account of how Mary's act of matricide may have affected her life, see Jane Aaron, *A Double Singleness.* Aaron sees *Mrs. Leicester's School* as closely linked to Mary's relation with her mother. See especially chapter 4, "A Modern Electra," pp. 115–132.

7. One of the remaining tales describes a child's visit to her grandmother ("Louisa Manners: The Farmhouse"), and the second describes yet another example of parental absence; in this case a child is left, unhappily, with her cousins until her parents reappear after a year-long absence ("Emily Barton: A Visit to the Cousins").

8. The "real" Miss Lesley seems somewhat hypocritical. Not only does she take care to inform Ann of the swap, but she stresses the affection that Ann's mother feels for her: "On the Sundays, when she used to bring me here, it was more pleasure to her to see me in my own father's house, than it was to see you, her real child" (29). Ann herself comments on Miss Lesley's behavior: "I thought at last she seemed to make a parade about [her affection for her foster mother], and affect to be more glad to see her than she really was after a time" (38).

9. For another representation of the relationship between the writing child and her mother, see Naomi Wood's essay in this volume. In this account of a real child writer, writing does not break the bond—however destructive—between mother and daughter.

10. The two tales by Charles not discussed in this essay are distinctly more sentimental than those by his sister. One describes a child's first trip to church, and the second a sea voyage during which a young girl is befriended by a gentle sailor who dies before the ship reaches England.

11. See Ruskin's influential essay "Of Queens Gardens," in *Sesame and Lilies.*

12. Mary's views on the benefits of geography obviously differ considerably from those of Charles, who in a letter to Coleridge complained about the unimaginative education children received: "Think what you would have been now, if instead of being fed with Tales and old wives fables in childhood, you had been crammed with Geography and Natural History" (*Letters,* II.82).

13. For more on Mary Lamb and the purpose of *Tales from Shakespeare,* see Marsden, "Shakespeare for Girls."

Works Cited

Aaron, Jane. *A Double Singleness: Gender and the Writings of Charles and Mary Lamb.* Oxford: Clarendon Press, 1991.

Chodorow, Nancy. *The Reproduction of Mothering.* Berkeley: University of California Press, 1978.

Darwin, Erasmus. *A Plan for the Conduct of Female Education in Boarding Schools* (1797).

Fielding, Sarah. *The Governess* (1749).

Lamb, Charles and Mary. *The Letters of Charles and Mary Lamb,* ed. Edwin W. Marrs, Jr. Ithaca: Cornell University Press, 1975. 3 vols.

——. *Mrs. Leicester's School.* (1809) In *Mrs. Leicester's School and Other Writings in Prose and Verse.* New York: A. C. Armstrong and Son, 1900.

Marsden, Jean I. "Shakespeare for Girls: Charles and Mary Lamb's *Tales from Shakespeare.*" *Children's Literature* 17 (1989), 47–63.

More, Hannah. *Strictures on the Modern System of Female Education.* In *The Works of Hannah More,* vol. 1. New York: Harper and Brothers, 1836.

Myers, Mitzi. "Impeccable Governesses, Rational Dames, and Moral Mothers: Mary Wollstonecraft and the Female Tradition in Georgian Children's Books." *Children's Literature* 14 (1986), 31–59.

Pickering, Samuel F. *Moral Education and Fiction for Children, 1749–1820.* Athens: University of Georgia Press, 1993.

Rousseau, Jean Jacques. *The New Heloise* (1761).

Ruskin, John. "Of Queens' Gardens." In *Sesame and Lilies* (1864).

Wollstonecraft, Mary. *Thoughts on the Education of Daughters: With Reflections on Female Conduct, in the more important Duties of Life* (1787).

Who Writes and Who Is Written?
Barbara Newhall Follett and
Typing the Natural Child

Naomi J. Wood

When children become authors, they cease to be children in our thought.
Anne Carroll Moore

She is normal childhood. Wilson Follett

In 1923, eight-year-old Barbara Newhall Follett began writing *The House Without Windows* as a birthday present for her mother on the small portable typewriter she had been using since she was four years old. Though later that year her manuscript burned in a house fire, she rewrote the entire story and her father, Wilson Follett, an editor at Knopf, supervised its publication in 1927. In this extended fantasy, a young girl, Eepersip, runs away from home to live in idyllic Nature (successively, a meadow, the sea, and, finally, the mountains). She eats only berries and roots and wears dresses woven of ferns and crowns of flowers; her playmates are butterflies and deer. When her parents try to capture her and bring her back home, she evades them. Eventually, Eepersip's body transforms into something more elemental than human, and she disappears: "She would be invisible for ever to all mortals, save those few who have minds to believe, eyes to see. To these she is ever present, the spirit of Nature—a sprite of the meadow, a naiad of lakes, a nymph of the woods."[1]

The book was greeted rapturously by reviewers all along the Atlantic seaboard. Here was evidence of a natural child's imagination, authentic, rich, and accessible to any reader. Critics seized upon this accessibility as the book's chief value; it seemed to provide a conduit to the natural child's mind—the archetypal Child, removed from the materialistic concerns of humankind. Paradoxically, however, Follett's *House Without Windows* was made possible by a machine; this natural child's reliance on technology bemused

Children's Literature 23, ed. Francelia Butler, R. H. W. Dillard, and Elizabeth Lennox Keyser (Yale University Press, © 1995 Hollins College).

her reviewers. Indeed, Barbara's reviewers show themselves to be as fascinated with the way in which the text was produced as they were with the product.[2] Following the lead of Barbara's father, they agreed that the typewriter was crucial in generating the phenomenon of Barbara Newhall Follett. However, they interpreted the significance of Barbara, her machine, and her book differently in ways that reveal, tellingly, the era's ideological matrices of language, technology, and gender. In their reactions, most adults made use of the established ideal of the child as fundamentally separate from the adult, as representing a kind of metaphysical presence, or plenitude, associated with innocence before the Fall. Made to represent this prelapsarian presence, the child became paradoxically absent from the day-to-day concerns of civilization. A return to this childhood state, even a fictional return, was desired by the adults who felt this loss of innocence all the more strongly because they were reminded of it—even promised its possibility—by the phenomenon of Barbara and her book. Barbara's text reassured those who feared the increasing mechanization of the world that escape from capitalism and the marketplace was possible, if only for a little while. Barbara's text, and by implication her language, seemed to close the anxiety-producing gap between word and thing, between ideal and reality. In short, Barbara's text delivered what adults desired: an opportunity to fantasize that there was no contradiction between writing and being.

In the "Historical Note" appended to *The House Without Windows* (at her request), Barbara's father insisted upon the ordinariness of his exceptional child. Denying the precociousness of his daughter's work, he described it as "the full expression . . . of what is in a normal, healthy child's mind and heart during that mysterious phase when butterflies, flowers, winging swallows, and white-capped waves are twice as real as even a quite bearable parent, and incomparably more important—the phase before there is any unshakable Tyranny of Things" (164). Positing a mythology of "normal, healthy" childhood development, before the inevitable fall into the "Tyranny of Things" to which all adults must succumb, Wilson anticipated the critical accolades the book received, and laid the foundation for the discussion which ensued. Barbara's book offered marketable innocence, which appeared to belie the power of the marketplace and promised, by its purported authenticity, satisfaction that eluded purchasers elsewhere.

Reviewers of Barbara's book sought and found nostalgic confirmation of the child, uncorrupted by society and intimately linked with Nature, and a kind of originary authenticity. Along with other primitives (like the Savage, the Woman, and the Neurotic), the natural child was enviously regarded by middle-class white men as free from the corruptions and inauthenticities of civilization.[3] After all, this era of modernity was also an era of nostalgic retreat into child-worship. (For example, Peter Pan, the boy who wouldn't grow up, was "born" only 12 years before Barbara Follett.) The 1920s witnessed a vogue for publishing children's writing; David Sadler points out that Barbara Follett's book "epitomized the quality of innocence which many adults seemed to be searching for in books by child authors."[4] She was represented as a living confirmation of the possibility of a natural child. Her writing was celebrated because it enabled adults to enter into an unalienated consciousness. Her natural wisdom, garnered not from human books but from the text of nature, offered adults both pleasure and a return to Eden.

More than one review portrayed Barbara Follett as a charmingly naïve nymphet, inviting adult readers into lost childhood territory. According to a review published in the *Boston Transcript:*

> No sophistication taints [*The House Without Windows*]. It is as purely crystalline as the singing brooks that share with her the secrets the winds and the leaves have told them. Nor is this story, shimmering with the iridescence of a rarely delicate fancy, for children only. Every lover of children, every student of their mental processes should read it, not only for the psychological nuances it unconsciously reveals, but even more that for a little happy space they may escape with Eepersip into the Land of Heart's Desire, and themselves "become as a little child."[5]

According to this reviewer, *The House Without Windows* was a transparent expression of a natural child's mind. Barbara was an Aeolian harp singing childhood—and the essence of originary Nature—to her readers. Students of psychology could learn from this book about the subtleties of a child's mind, explicitly linked to ideal Nature and fundamentally separate from adulthood. This review valued the text primarily because it offered adults the natural child's mind and self. Barbara's "delicate fancy" revealed a paradisiacal interiority that promised a return to the Source, the Origin which adult compromises had foregone.[6] Though the story's heroine supposedly escapes the adult world altogether, this review, pruriently following Barbara/Eepersip into her garden, found that the book was valuable because in it the "lover" of children could feast on psychological sweets, escape "into the Land of Heart's Desire," and traverse the landscape of the idealized child's mind.

This theme was echoed by nearly all the male reviewers of the book. Lee Wilson Dodd agreed that the book's significance lay in its ability to convey nature-as-paradise transparently to the adult reader. Although "it is the contention of Barbara's parents that she is not precocious," and that "her extraordinary ability to record her imaginings in artistic prose [is] due to the system of home-education which they devised for her . . . I am not at all convinced that 'The House Without Windows' can be attributed to any system but the mysterious system of Nature."[7] While Dodd acknowledged the artistry of the text (he praised Barbara's description of a "daisied fawn," for example),[8] he focused on the product and could authenticate its art only by erasing the process. In so doing, he offered adults the prospect of escaping "from the tiresome world of grown-up mechanisms and compromises." He concluded: "Weary middle-age and the clear delicacy of a dawn-Utopia beckoning . . . The contrast sharpens to pain. One closes the book and shuffles about doggedly till one finds the evening paper and smudges down to one's element—that smudged machine-record of what man has made of man."[9] Dodd's language ("mechanism," "smudge," "machine-record") echoed and elaborated Wilson Follett's "Tyranny of Things." The gross machinery of modern life dirties and corrodes the natural paradise the child inhabits; Barbara's fantasy offers temporary redemption to adults who read it. Dodd neglected to mention at this point that Barbara's text was made possible by one of the very machines that "smudge" out records of life: the typewriter. In the hands of the natural child, he implied, this typewriter disappears as only a means to an end, allowing true Nature to express itself authentically and fully.

The ambiguous relationship between natural child and typewriter, and the interpretation male critics gave it, was perfectly enunciated by Henry Longan Stuart in his *New York Times* review, entitled "A Mirror of the Child Mind." Like many others, Stuart saw Barbara's work as an opportunity to enter into the Eden of an inno-cent child's mind, suggesting again that it lay altogether outside the realm of the social: "There can be few who have not at one time or another coveted the secret, innocent and wild at the same time, of a child's heart. And here is little Miss Barbara Follett, holding the long-defended gate wide open and letting us enter and roam at our will over enchanted ground. And a typewriter did all this!"[10] His conventional response stressed again the secret territory of child-hood; Stuart envied Barbara the paradise he had lost and sexual-ized the invitation he received from the pre(co)cious "little Miss" who opened her gate. Stuart's last sentence, however, undercut Barbara's creative role and, instead of seeing a "system of nature," credited the mechanical device with generative, nearly authorial, responsibility. Barbara was not an author for Stuart; rather, she, together with her typewriter, was a conduit for something else.

Barbara's use of technology to produce this remarkable text elicited varying reactions from the critics. Male critics tended to see the typewriter as a tool that transcribed (without contamination) Barbara's authentic and authenticating impulses. In fact, some, like Stuart, almost erased Barbara herself by suggesting that she was im-portant chiefly as a conduit for the voice of Nature, thereby allow-ing the desiring reader full access to her plenty. Reading the type-writer as transparent was more possible for male critics because of their gendered relationship to production. Accustomed to a social matrix in which men dictate and women take dictation, not surpris-ingly they assumed that the typewriter meant no more than simple transcription of thought or impulse onto page. Secure in their own subject positions, male critics tended to admire the product without considering the ramifications of the process.

Operating from a different cultural matrix, female writers, al-though still subscribing to the ideology of the natural child, tended to express more interest in Barbara as a subject who produced; they wondered about her future and what her precipitation into the world of professional writing might mean. Under no illusions about what would be Barbara's treatment in the marketplace, they were concerned about the standardization this free spirit might undergo, though often equally lyrical about the rejuvenating aspects of the story. Leonore St. John Power celebrated Barbara as artist: "That a child should record such experiences as these is not strange in

itself. . . . The strange thing is that a child should have the words
and the workmanship in which to set it all down in such incredibly
good form as Barbara Newhall Follett has done." [11] Naomi Royde-
Smith in the *New Statesman* complimented Barbara by reviewing her
book with three other books by adults. Not linking artistry to age,
her two-paragraph reaction ended: "[*The House Without Windows*]
affords grounds for an expectation that a lady who can compose
a tale of this calibre at the rate of 1,200 words an hour (using a
typewriter) before she is ten, will by the time she is as old as Miss
[Sylvia Townsend] Warner be able, at a slightly reduced speed let us
hope, to write another island fantasy." [12] Far from being infatuated
by Barbara's uniqueness, Royde-Smith hoped that Barbara would
slow down so that she could realize her future potential. Without
fetishizing Barbara or her product, Royde-Smith wished her the
best of luck. Anne Carroll Moore, on the other hand, doubted any
child prodigy's chances for success in later life. In her column, "The
Three Owls," in the *New York Herald Tribune,* Moore wrote: "I can
conceive of no greater handicap for the writer between the ages of
nineteen and thirty-nine, than to have published a successful book
between the ages of nine and twelve" (8). Couching her reservations
in conventional rhetoric of the cult of childhood, she believed the
publishing world too corrupt and unsafe for children's innocence;
she feared that child prodigies' "sensibilities are . . . unduly excited
or prematurely deadened by such experience in childhood and
early adolescence" (8). Arguing that children pay with their childhood for the questionable gains of early professionalism, Moore
posited that, rather than protecting Barbara from the marketplace
and the "Tyranny of Things," her father had precipitated her entrance into it.

> What price will Barbara Follett have to pay for her "big days"
> at the typewriter. . . . As the work of a nine-year-old whose
> manuscript was destroyed by fire and who rewrote it by a feat
> of memory, I think it raises rather a grave question rather
> than a justification of a homegrown system of education. That
> a child should carry so well defined a professional attitude
> toward writing between the ages of nine and twelve, seems to
> me less a matter for congratulation than for keen regret over
> certain inalienable rights of childhood which she is bound to
> have forfeited by that same token. (8)

To Moore, nothing was free in the marketplace, so Barbara's professionalism at this early age would cost her as human subject and as artist. Moore believed that because Barbara had been isolated, she was at risk in ways that her father seemed not to have recognized; though home-schooling may effect an outstanding product, it cannot substitute for the "variety of social relationships" available in school, the "companionship of other children" (8). While Moore's reservations about Barbara's accomplishments shared assumptions with her male counterparts about what constitutes the ideal childhood, she was more consistent than they in insisting that childhood ought to have nothing to do with the marketplace—that childhood ought to be for children rather than for adults. According to Moore, children had a "right" to childhood; appropriating Barbara's childhood as commodity foreshortened the very experience deemed valuable for its nonmarket, nonadult, nonsocialized qualities.

This natural child was, ironically, isolated from other children in a world carefully constructed by her parents. Wilson claimed that the story would not have been told if Barbara had not been "free" of childhood encumbrances such as school and had not been expert at the typewriter. However, he still insisted that Barbara was nothing if not normal: "The fact is, [the story] was conceived and written at the end of a phase which could not return—that phase of *normal* childhood in which nature means nearly everything and civilization nearly nothing. The whole purport of Eepersip's existence is *simply a healthy nine-year-old consciousness* made articulate" (160-61, emphasis mine). Here Wilson imputed to Barbara a spontaneous desire to express herself as any normal, healthy child would if given the chance, in that idyllic time before innocence must change to experience. He acknowledged that Barbara was unusually articulate, but insisted that Barbara's tale was all her own—no corrosive, civilizing hand had touched it, marred it.[13] However, Wilson also revealed that Barbara had been protected from the tainting effects of social interaction (with, presumably, abnormal, unhealthy, children): "The author of the story never had (and never has) experienced any school system, public or private, her education having been exclusively the home-made one devised by her mother" (157). According to Wilson, because Barbara never interacted on a regular basis with adults other than her parents or with children (other than in her books), she had had the freedom to be her own authentic self: "nothing has standardized her" (164). He overlooked, however, how the civilized and artificial media of both books and typewriter did, indeed, standardize his daughter, and set her up for even more standardization in the workplace.

While dilating on Barbara's self-sufficiency as a writer in his historical note to her book, Wilson wrote, "Barbara's vocabulary at nine was, of course, a stratified arrangement of deposits from Walter de la Mare and George Macdonald, W. H. Hudson and Mark Twain, Shelley and Scott" (160). To authenticate Barbara, Wilson separated vocabulary and idea, implying that Barbara learned words but not concepts from her reading. Though later in the note he complained briefly of Barbara's "annoying . . . preference for Oxford spelling," he argued that her spelling habits were really proof that she had not been overly influenced by her parents, again trying to disconnect Barbara from all but natural influences and development (166).

However her father protested otherwise, Barbara's favorite books clearly reveal more than simple orthographic influences. Although Barbara may not have been standardized by her peers, she was certainly standardized by the fin-de-siècle fantasies that embodied and produced the ideology of the natural child. In a footnote, Wilson explained, "No books meant more to her, between the ages of six and ten, than *The Three Mulla-Mulgars, A Little Boy Lost,* and *The Princess and the Goblin*" (HWW 160n). De la Mare, Hudson, and MacDonald all wrote fantasies intended as much for adults as for children. They created somber portrayals of idealized children who, because they are one with Nature, must inevitably be either compromised or destroyed by human greed; death is frequently liberation in their books.[14] Though each book involves a quest, the goal in each is ambiguous: in *The Princess and the Goblin,* it is belief in the transcendent goddess-grandmother, the Princess Irene; in *The Three Mulla-Mulgars,* the valley of Tishnar;[15] in *A Little Boy Lost,* the book which most influenced Barbara's writing, the end is beauty itself.

In *The House Without Windows,* Eepersip's quest is likewise provoked by a desire for the ineffable—a search for an undefined answer in Nature. But no one setting satisfies her; she leaves each place lured by as-yet-unknown beauty. Having gained her independence from her parents (who attempt for several seasons to capture and bring her back home) and living blissfully for some time in a meadow, Eepersip is undone by the sight of the ocean:

She loved the meadow so much that [leaving] would be almost impossible for her. Yet she knew that, in spite of her love for the meadow, her longing for the sea would grow, and that one day she must leave her present home. . . . One night Eepersip woke up to find the full moon as if hanging in the sky. A few faint stars could be seen. She tried to go to sleep, but could not. . . . All entranced with the beauty of the night, she ran lightly over to the spot where she often had a view of the sea. And she beheld it with the full moon reflected in it—a globe of soft silver, shimmering and quivering in the unstill waters. This time it was too much for Eepersip. She could stand it no longer—her heart gave way. She decided that the next morning she would satisfy her longing. . . . She kissed the ground of the meadow, and she wept to think that she was leaving it; but she knew that her love for the sea had become greater than her love for the meadow. (HWW 58–59)

Such descriptions of natural beauty typify Barbara's luxuriant style. We eventually learn that for Eepersip, beauty alone is sufficient for life, and by the book's end beauty substitutes even for food: Eepersip subsists finally on icicles and snow. As with her literary precursors (Curdie and Irene in MacDonald, the Mulla Mulgars in de la Mare, and Martin in Hudson), Eepersip transcends the human/mortal sphere altogether. Transformed into an invisible force (a "sprite . . . a naiad . . . a nymph" [HWW 153]), she will sing and dance her way through ever-increasing natural beauty and ever-decreasing interaction with living creatures.

Barbara Newhall Follett shared with W. H. Hudson an aesthetic sensibility that saw both specificity and transcendence in nature. Both were amateur naturalists with a keen eye both for beauty and for authentic detail. Barbara, for example, had a butterfly "collection" which consisted of typed descriptions of every detail of the butterflies' bodies as she caught them in a sieve and then released them back into the air.[16] She also had a written "flower diary" (McCurdy, 25). Similarly,

Hudson's nature essays convey his passionate love of nature and demonstrate his intimate knowledge of wildlife. Intellectually, he was influenced by Charles Darwin and Herbert Spencer, but he disagreed with their attempts to explain nature in terms of scientific theories with no regard for the beauty of nature. Instead, he advocated an approach to nature that combined both

intellectual and spiritual understanding. . . . Hudson idealized
nature, and although his descriptions are accurate, they are
characterized by a tone of admiration and wonder.[17]

As consummate romantics, Follett and Hudson both embrace Nature as redemptive, especially when separated from the grubby
world of civilization and market value.

As it exhibits the ethos of *A Little Boy Lost, The House Without
Windows* also recapitulates the details and the plot of W. H. Hudson's novel.[18] On first wandering away from home, both Martin and
Eepersip throw away their shoes, symbolizing their independence
from the parental roof and their identification with Nature (LBL
23; HWW 7). Both Martin and Eepersip satisfy hunger with the
white, sweet roots of plants (LBL 44; HWW 10). Both encounter
parental figures who wish to possess the children and to compromise their freedom, either as exploitable labor or as love objects in
Hudson, and simply from an unexplained possessiveness in Follett.
Both prefer natural forces, such as the sea, to humans and even
animals: Martin finds in the sea a "companion and playmate" (LBL
176), whereas Eepersip discovers it to be both friend and protector:
at her request, the waves save her from being captured by an adult
(HWW 94). In addition, both Martin and Eepersip go out to sea on
a raft, which carries them far out of sight of land, though the first
book ends with this event, while the second uses it as a bridge to
another episode. Like Eepersip, Martin lives an isolated life with his
parents in a beautiful natural setting where he plays with birds and
butterflies instead of other children. Martin "loses" himself when
he chases a lovely mirage which beckons him to follow. Eepersip
leaves home in search of a "joy" that can only be satisfied by wild,
natural beauty. Both Martin and Eepersip seek sources of natural
beauty but move on when another untraveled landscape lures them.
Martin moves from the plains to the mountains to the sea. Eepersip
moves from the meadow to the sea to the mountains.

Both books end without closure: Martin, swept out to sea on a
raft, wakes, lonely, to a drifting ship that has been lost for months.
Although the sailors take his presence as a sign of civilization and
signal for him to come aboard, Martin simply smiles and goes back
to sleep on his raft and the men fear he is dead. "But he was only
sleeping" (LBL 183)—end of story. Our record of Eepersip's adven-

tures concludes in the mountains. Clad only in a dress of ferns and a crown of flowers, and living on ice, she gradually loses materiality. She notices that "[a]s she danced she seemed to float through the air, her feet almost motionless. . . . She seemed to have no weight at all, and a breeze would almost lift her off the ground and hold her up in the air" (HWW 149–50). The book ends as Eepersip vanishes.

W. H. Hudson's and Barbara Follett's books do not end with the kind of closure children's books traditionally exhibit—the "home/ away/home" plot trajectory is not of primary concern to these authors. Instead, they refuse the closure that would imply accommodation to civilization, suggesting that children need not be reconciled to the reality principle. There is no reason why Martin and Eepersip can not live happily by themselves in worlds uninhabited by other humans—especially adults.

To see the affinities between *A Little Boy Lost* and *The House Without Windows* is not to diminish Barbara's work as merely derivative. But clearly, Barbara had her context as artist and as reader, and the literary, "artificial" antecedents of *The House Without Windows* put into perspective the lavish claims Wilson, and other male critics, made for the book's nature-only etiology. Rather than being a child produced directly from nature, who unconsciously expressed the secrets nature pressed upon her, Barbara was working within the literary tradition of the books she grew up reading: the pastoral fantasy of Edenic childhood innocence. That her own expression of this fantasy, along similar lines as books she read, was presented as "natural" actually defines the artificiality—the standardization, if you will—of the very ideology of childhood that adult male reviewers found so compelling because of the ways it mirrored their own nostalgia. Barbara's text was valorized for the ways in which it offered back to them something—paradise—that they were conscious of having lost.

When Barbara ceased to cater to adult desires for natural innocence, her work was concomitantly viewed as less important. Barbara's second book, *The Voyage of the Norman D,* published only a year after *The House Without Windows,* did not receive anything like the interest and praise her first book elicited. In this epistolary travelogue, written in an entirely different tone, about a trip Barbara took from New Haven to Nova Scotia on a schooner, Barbara's voice is confident, even superior. She is already conscious of the differences class and education make in the world. "I went about, in my old blue shirt with a sailor collar and my old black pants, very gaily indeed, feeling sailorly and wanting to show the crew that I didn't put on airs or try to be superior to them" (*Voyage*, 109). It does not seem to occur to her that they might not instinctively respond to her superiority. At thirteen, she believes that she can learn whatever she needs to know from her books. She rather scorns the relatively unlettered seamen with whom she travels, condescendingly relishing their rough grammar and way of life—she laments that the captain should change to go to shore: "I was rather sorry . . . to see the old fellow dressed up" (*Voyage* 21–22)—she learns the names of sea-faring terms out of Webster's before she even sets foot on a schooner, and she memorizes the points of the compass "after about fifteen minutes of hard studying" (*Voyage* 4, 39–40). Throughout the voyage she derides the obtuseness of the only other teenager on board the vessel[19] and flaunts her knowledge and initiative to the crew. No wonder that this book, the original and lively record of a caustic and unsubmissive teenager, did not resonate particularly well with the adult establishment.[20] *The Voyage of the Norman D* was written in the distinctive voice of its writer, yet, when Barbara ceased to deliver the voice of the natural child, she ceased to be of general interest. *The House Without Windows* mirrored without significant alteration the contemporary ideology of the natural child and was praised as unique, whereas *The Voyage of the Norman D* demonstrated the results of a professionalized childhood and a highly individualized education in its increased confidence, unusual articulacy, and presumptions of superiority. Barbara's writing perhaps was already tainted by the sophistication that adult critics deplored in writings of the young,[21] and her move to a new genre and voice served only to expose the stake adults had in her standardization as a natural child whose maturation must inevitably be a disappointment.

In marked contrast to the valorization of Barbara's so-called natural status, Helen Thomas Follett, Barbara's mother, wrote about her daughter's accomplishments as if they were machine-made. As the author and overseer of Barbara's home education, Helen saw the typewriter rather than Nature as Barbara's chief influence. She celebrated the novel standardization this offered parents and educators. Apparently influenced by contemporary trends in progressive, child-centered education,[22] Helen argued that traditional schooling caused children to become blasé about knowledge.[23] Educated and literate herself, she had collaborated with her English-professor husband on a series of articles in the *Atlantic Monthly* and the *Yale Review* (which culminated in 1919 in the book *Some Modern Novelists: Appreciations and Estimates*). She resisted a limiting definition of motherhood and vested herself in raising a superior kind of child, in having a modern and improved relationship with it. In 1929, only two years after reviewers acclaimed her child's natural genius, she wrote more coolly: "Being a parent is not such a bad thing, after all, if you can be something more than a parent as that word is commonly used. I can see very well now that I should never have been content to limit my relationship with the child to that of nurse, social secretary, cook, or general adviser. I wanted something more permanent and lasting than any of these things; I wanted a friend and intellectual companion" ("Education à la Carte" 2). Helen Follett's public discussion of her educational program de-emphasized Barbara's genius and stressed the hard work both mother and daughter had put into learning. As Helen recounted, when three-year-old Barbara expressed interest in the noises the typewriter made, Helen allowed her not only to touch the keys, but encouraged her to begin making words. The immediate satisfaction offered by adult-looking, standardized writing encouraged Barbara to continue, with plenty of coaching from her mother.

Barbara's first written product was a typewritten thank-you to a cousin. As more letters followed, Barbara gradually began to express her own thoughts and feelings through the typewriter. At eighteen, Barbara recalled that "[typewriting] seemed to me a very efficient, logical, and delightful way of getting things said" ("Butterflies" 24). The tone here is strikingly different from her reviewers' effusions. Although Barbara elsewhere described the typewriter as "magical," she also lauded the typewriter's "efficiency"—a conduit for her creativity, but not responsible for it. She continues: "At that time I was beginning to find a good deal that I wanted to talk about. When I discovered beauty in bird-songs, apple-blossoms, music, sunsets (but chiefly butterflies), I yearned to put it into tangible form so that I could keep it, hold it, understand it. I wrote masses of stuff, about everything under the sun, just for the pleasure and relief it gave me. This relief I could not have had in any other way." Barbara's need to capture these impressions in words, to fill

reams of paper, are not simply the natural responses of a natural
child.[24] After all, if Barbara were truly a child of nature, she would
have no need to represent it: she would simply *be* it, as her heroine
Eepersip is. The "pleasure and relief" of writing, the "relief" she
"could not have had in any other way," suggest other, more social
constrictions. To imprison words on a page, to capture her impressions, implies that she recognized the fleeting status of all natural
beauty. She could best "keep" Nature, "hold," and ultimately understand it only when it was abstracted into ink on paper, a deep irony
for this supposedly natural child. Prevented from having childhood
friends, eighteen-year-old Barbara writes that her "little battered
typewriter [was] . . . my best friend" ("Butterflies" 25), the friend
to which, through which, she could stabilize nature and create the
ideal child world already written out for her by the authors she was
given to read, as a matter of course, by her parents.

Thus, while Wilson Follett insisted that Barbara—and her writing—were uniquely valuable because she had never been standardized by association with other children in schools, Barbara's own
recollections of that time suggest that she felt lonely and isolated.[25]
Ironically, it was not her normal, healthy status as a natural child
that drove her to write *The House Without Windows* but her surrogate
"best friend" the typewriter that facilitated her explorations of her
own mind. Most significant, Barbara originally conceived the book
as a gift for her mother, the first contribution the child Barbara
would make as her mother's "friend and intellectual companion."[26]
Adults' needs and desires—those of her parents, of the writers of
her books—influenced Barbara's drive to produce.

According to Helen Follett, the typewriter itself was both agency
and benevolent influence upon Barbara. In a 1932 article, "Education via the Typewriter," she implied that the typewriter first
opened Barbara's eyes to the outside world:

> All the doors and windows of this five-year-old's world were
> wide open. The typewriter had helped to open them, and
> it would help to keep them open. As soon as it imprisoned
> in words one fact from her world, one scrap of imaginative
> beauty, one echo of laughter or of a dream, it asked for more
> and still more. Where she went, what she did, what she saw—
> the typewriter enticed her, by urging its own simple magic
> upon her, to tell in her own words. . . . With the typewriter

giving a clear sight of each word as it came to life, words couldn't help falling into sentences, and sentences arranging themselves in paragraphs. . . . [As Barbara wrote her first story,] the typewriter was in the midst of all that was going on; it caught in simple fact or colorful detail the whole story of the clock idea . . . and it urged us to continue our way, joyfully and without regret. (24)

If one accepts Helen's argument, then any child, given a typewriter, can become an author, a self-expressive prodigy. The machine itself generates the interest, perhaps even generates the self that is being expressed. In contrast to the freedom Barbara imagined as a "house without windows," the typewriter here "imprisons" words and facts upon the page, abstracting them. Continuing, Helen suggests that the freedom the typewriter seems to grant is not without benefits to commercial interests: "There was growing out of her adventure an educational scheme that was proving as practically sound as it was romantically adventurous. An inquiring person could have found in it . . . the approved habits of a commercially-minded world—accuracy, efficiency, neatness, mechanical dexterity" ("Education via the Typewriter" 54).

Sadly, the same mechanical and artificial aspects of Barbara's education that enabled her to produce a book at so young an age overwhelmed her in later years. Although Helen voiced a sanguine hope that adventurousness and commercial use might not be at odds, both mother and daughter recognized in the 1930s that the real relationship between a typewriter and a girl-woman was determined by gender.[27] Wilson Follett left his family for another woman in 1928, and Helen and Barbara began to write frantically to make ends meet. Helen Follett attempted to market her educational system by describing it for the readers of *Good Housekeeping* and *Parents' Magazine*. At the height of the Great Depression in 1932, Helen advocated purchasing typewriters for public schools, as a spur to a better-educated society. Writing alone, however, could not sustain them, and in 1930, Barbara (at sixteen) began to work as a stenographer—or, in the parlance of that era, a typewriter. In a letter from this period Barbara writes that she is "hardly a person right now—I am more like a machine. Typewriting, typewriting, editing, editing, cooking, sweeping, mopping."[28] Tellingly, these are all the invisible though labor-intensive activities that support literary achievement

but tend not to be credited on the title page. What the male reviewers had overlooked in their celebrations of Barbara's natural
childhood expression was that the ability to type in a woman "naturally" resulted not in authorship—in paying someone else, perhaps,
to type one's words—but in becoming oneself a typewriter.

Thus, although they were both female and writers, Barbara and
her mother occupied different places within the male-dominated
matrix of gender, technology, and language; perhaps because they
were so intimately involved with the process, they expressed a more
mechanistic view of the typewriter's role. For them, the typewriter
became the director of thought and of fate, a sign of women's labor
and its co-optation by the market. As Barbara grew older and no
longer fit the cultural script of natural child, she was imprinted by
the next culturally scripted role for women: that of amanuensis.
These various representations of the child, the book, and the typewriter help us understand how language, technology, and gender
constructed Barbara, predicting, perhaps, the inglorious conclusion
of Barbara's career as an author. Barbara never broke into the adult
publishing market, though she had another semi-autobiographical
novel in progress during her late teens. Instead, she took various
jobs as a stenographer helping to support first her family and then
her husband during the Great Depression.

When Barbara was twenty-five years old, after nine years as a
stenographer and in the wake of a failing marriage, she left her
Boston apartment on December 7, 1939, with some money and the
scraps of shorthand she had recorded that day. No one ever saw her
again.[29] Tragically, after having typed herself so successfully as a
natural child, Barbara could not type her way to successful authorship as an adult. Instead, her skill erased her own voice, given the
constraints of a marketplace that will pay for dexterous fingers, but
not the mind. The same cultural imperatives that typed Barbara
Newhall Follett first as natural child, who incidentally used a typewriter, went on to write her as stenographer. Ultimately, then, the
typewriter both wrote and erased her.

Barbara's parents tried to locate her after her disappearance. Her
father attempted contact in May 1941 through an open letter in
the *Atlantic Monthly,* in which he laments her disappearance, theorizes that she is trying to rewrite herself into another existence, and
rather ironically blames the failure of her marriage on her inability

to let go of her self. As late as the 1960s, her mother was still trying to make sense of her daughter's disappearance and to justify the choices she had made in educating her. Collaborating with Harold Grier McCurdy, a psychologist who specialized in the "childhood problem of genius," Helen co-authored *Barbara: The Unconscious Autobiography of a Child Genius* (1966). Helen insists upon Barbara's lack of agency and self-consciousness, even in the title of the book. Unlike her ex-husband's and even her own writings from the 1920s and 1930s, Helen concentrates on Barbara's precociousness and uniqueness. At Helen's death, her obituary mentions that she was organizing Barbara's papers, still worrying at the problem of her disappearing daughter.

McCurdy wanted to read all of Barbara's life as a fulfillment of the prediction of her text. "Is *The House Without Windows* to be read prophetically? Barbara never lived far from the bright country of her imagination, even when apparently subdued to the drabness of a civilization she never quite accepted. Her outward life in some measure followed the plot of her stories. . . . Can we be far wrong in substituting Barbara's name for Eepersip's in the closing scenes of that book?" (146). McCurdy, even more than his predecessors Wilson Follett, Lee Wilson Dodd, and Henry Longan Stuart, fetishizes Barbara as the disappearing child who teaches us all about lost desire. Barbara for him is the child who disappears.[30]

Though Barbara's story (both life and work) is a story about a typewriter, other factors—her family, her class privilege, the larger contexts of the Great Depression—unquestionably influenced Barbara's production. Her story raises many important questions about education, socialization, and the cultural context in which children's artistic productions (alongside the childlike avant-garde work of Klee, Miró, Picasso, Matisse, Chagall, and Joyce) were objects of interest and desire. Further investigations of the reasons for the fetishization of childhood that the reception of Barbara's work implies are needed for that era, and, indeed for our own. We do not know how much Barbara wished to cooperate, exhibitionistically, with adults' voyeuristic desires, and how much she used the tools she was given to serve a subversive agenda. Certainly the appeal of Barbara's story is in part the seeming symmetry between her life and text, its uncanny aptness in satisfying our own narrative desires. Barbara Newhall Follett's disappearance at the cultural moment when clerical work was being feminized and proletarianized is important not as the romantic extinction of a frustrated child genius, but as the market-driven erasure of the typewriting child growing into a woman typewriter.

Notes

I thank Carol Franko, Alison Wheatley, Carolyn Sigler, Craig Stroupe, Linda Brigham, Anne Phillips, and Dean Hall for their useful responses and suggestions during the writing of this essay. All inaccuracies and infelicities are mine alone. This is an expanded version of a paper delivered at the 1993 MLA in Toronto.

Notes to Epigraphs: Moore, "When Children Become Authors," 8; "Notes on a Junior Author with a Glance at Precocity," *Horn Book* 4.2 (1928), 11.

1. Follett, *The House Without Windows, and Eepersip's Life There,* 153. Subsequently cited in text as HWW.

2. Because I discuss three different members of the Follett family, I will refer to them by their first names, except in my discussion of W. H. Hudson and Barbara Follett, where I will refer to her as "Follett" to preserve symmetry.

3. For more details, see the exhaustive treatment of George Boas, *The Cult of Childhood.* The linking of Child, Savage, Woman, Neurotic is Boas's.

4. Sadler, "Innocent Hearts," 25.

5. February 23, 1927, 4. Although this reviewer is not identified, the quotation is typical of the kind of desire expressed by all of the identifiably male reviewers of the book. Although the reviewer notes that "the child Barbara's fancies, expressed with a facility which at least phophesies [*sic*] a notable literary future, are exquisitely beautiful," he or she is not as concerned with Barbara's future as with what this particular fantasy offers adult readers.

6. The move recalls Jacqueline Rose's treatment of *Peter Pan* and complicates it, for here the child makes a gift to the adult of her self as the adults would wish to see it. For nostalgia and interiority, see Susan Stewart's treatment in *On Longing,* particularly the chapter on "The Miniature."

7. Dodd, 592.

8. Barbara was so pleased that he noticed, that she wrote him a thank-you note (McCurdy with Follett), 84–85.

9. Ellipsis in original. Dodd, 592.

10. *New York Times Review of Books,* February 6, 1927, 5.

11. *New York Herald Tribune,* March 27, 1927, 8.

12. Naomi Royde-Smith, "New Novels," *The New Statesman* (London) May 21, 1927, 184. Wilson had written in his "Historical Note": "On her big days the small typist clicked off fresh copy to the extent of from four to five thousand words. . . . Having used a typewriter as a plaything from a time that she can't remember, she was able to rattle off an easy 1200 words an hour, without any awareness of the physical process" (HWW 157, 165).

13. "In short, what the reader is here given is an articulate eight- and nine-year-old child's outpouring of her own dreams and longings in a fanciful tale, superficially revised by the hand of a twelve-year-old girl whose life on its more artificial side is made up principally of books and music" (HWW 162).

14. See, for example, my analysis of Diamond and other children in "'Suffer the Children': The Problem of the Loving Father in *At the Back of the North Wind.*" Hudson's preoccupations with children-of-nature and death can be seen both in *A Little Boy Lost* and *Green Mansions.* On de la Mare, and his fascination with children

and their affinities with nature, solitude, and death, see Bremser, "The Voice of Solitude."

15. "Tishnar is a very ancient word in Munza, and means that which cannot be thought about in words, or told, or expressed" (de la Mare, *The Three Mulla-Mulgars*, 5).

16. B. Follett, "In Defense of Butterflies," 24.

17. *Twentieth-Century Literature Criticism* 29: 134, Introductory notes.

18. Hudson, *A Little Boy Lost*, cited in the text as LBL, followed by the page number.

19. See, for example, p. 125. Here, she draws out and agrees with the mate about Richardson's stupidity.

20. Reviewers tended to link the book with Barbara's earlier work rather than her later work. See Jordan, "Seafaring," 3–5, and Bianco, "New Horizons," 943–44.

21. Nathalia Crane, another child writer, "was attacked . . . because she was not childlike enough. She had the effrontery to write about sophisticated subjects using an adult vocabulary. She was throwing away all the advantages of childhood and choosing instead to enter the adult world" (Sadler 27).

22. See Cuban, "Teaching at the Turn of the Century," in *How Teachers Taught*.

23. H. Follett, "Education à la Carte."

24. Barbara's intense interest in the beauty of nature was reflected in her writing, and also in her outdoors activities. An avid hiker and camper, she (with her father) took many mountain and canoe trips that allowed her to observe, and to record her observations firsthand.

25. From a letter in 1938: "My sister . . . gets to be more and more of a corker every day. She is fifteen now, and getting a kick out of being just in between, neither a child nor an adult, so that she can, as she says, get away with anything at all. When I contrast her with myself at fifteen, I am likely to weep and gnash my teeth in envy. She is happy, well poised, gets along well with everybody, a good sport, and a grand person. . . . She gets invited everywhere, goes to lots of parties, and gets fun out of every situation" (quoted in McCurdy, 140–41).

26. In her teens, Barbara collaborated with her mother on a travel book, *Magic Portholes* (Macmillan, 1932), about their trip to the West Indies (the title was Barbara's suggestion). Her essay "In Defense of Butterflies" (1933) also echoes eerily her parents' diction: "I after [the butterfly], net in hand, with all the energy of any healthy nine-year-old who wants very badly to capture a large, black and orange butterfly" (24); "I have often wondered what would happen if every child of four were given a typewriter to work and play with" (27).

27. Helen writes: "It was a piece of machinery—the indispensable tool of business and commerce—that was turning the education of one child into a grand adventure" ("Education via the Typewriter" 54). Wilson had parodied the standardization implied by a girl learning to type in an essay published in *Horn Book* after *The Voyage of the Norman D* was reviewed there. "When she wanted to typewrite, no one said, 'Oh no, you have to learn to write first,' or 'Oh no, you have to learn to read first,' or 'Oh no, you aren't going to be a stenographer,' or 'Oh no, the motions of typewriting are against the laws of eurhythmy.'" He presumes here that choice is free and that outside forces can be circumvented if one is truly, authentically, "normal." "Notes on a Junior Author" 11.

28. Letter of April 28, 1930. McCurdy, 103.

29. McCurdy, 144–45.

30. James Kincaid has argued persuasively that this is precisely what we like most about our culture's conception of "childhood" and "the child": "Pure energy, nature, love—pure nothingness. . . . Childhood can be made a wonderfully hollow cate-

gory, able to be filled up with anyone's overflowing emotions, not least overflowing passion" (*Child-Loving* 12).

Works Cited

Bianco, Margery Williams. "New Horizons." Review of *The Voyage of the Norman D*, by Barbara Newhall Follett. *Saturday Review of Literature*, 9 June 1928: 943–44.

Boas, George. *The Cult of Childhood*. London: Warburg Institute, 1966.

Bremser, Martha. "The Voice of Solitude: The Children's Verse of Walter de la Mare." *Children's Literature* 21 (1993): 66–91.

Cuban, Larry. *How Teachers Taught: Constancy and Change in American Classrooms 1890–1980*. New York: Longman, 1984.

De la Mare, Walter. *The Three Mulla-Mulgars*. London: Duckworth, 1910.

Dodd, Lee Wilson. "In Arcady." Review of *The House Without Windows*, by Barbara Newhall Follett. *Saturday Review of Literature*, 19 February 1927: 592.

Follett, Barbara Newhall. "In Defense of Butterflies." *Horn Book* 9.1 (1933): 24–28.

———. *The House Without Windows, and Eepersip's Life There*. New York: Alfred A. Knopf, 1927.

———. *The Voyage of the Norman D, as told by the cabin-boy*. New York: Alfred A. Knopf, 1928.

Follett, Helen Thomas. "Education à la Carte." *Pictorial Review*, July 1929: 2+.

———. "Education Via the Typewriter." *Parents' Magazine*, September 1932: 22+.

———. "Questions! Questions! Questions!" *Good Housekeeping*, December 1932: 36+.

Follett, Wilson. "Notes on a Junior Author, With a Glance at Precocity." *Horn Book* 4.2 (1928): 6–13.

———. "Schooling Without the School." *Harper's Monthly Magazine* 139 (1919): 700–708.

———. "To a Daughter, One Year Lost, From Her Father." *Atlantic Monthly* 167 (May 1941): 564–571.

"The House Without Windows." Review of *The House Without Windows, and Eepersip's Life There*, by Barbara Newhall Follett. *Boston Evening Transcript*, February 23, 1927, sec. 3:4.

Hudson, W. H. *A Little Boy Lost*. 1905. New York: Knopf, 1920.

"Hudson, W. H." Introduction. *Twentieth-Century Literary Criticism*, Dennis Poupard and Paula Kepos, eds. Vol. 29. Detroit: Gale Research, 1988.

Jordan, Alice M. "Seafaring." Review of *The Voyage of the Norman D*, by Barbara Newhall Follett. *Horn Book* 4.3 (May 1928): 3–5.

Kincaid, James. *Child-Loving: The Erotic Child and Victorian Culture*. New York: Routledge, 1992.

McCurdy, Harold Grier, with Helen Thomas Follett. *Barbara: The Unconscious Autobiography of a Child Genius*. Chapel Hill: University of North Carolina Press, 1966.

Moore, Anne Carroll. "When Children Become Authors." *New York Herald Tribune Books*, 27 March 1927: 8.

Rose, Jacqueline. *The Case of Peter Pan, Or, The Impossibility of Children's Fiction*. London: Macmillan, 1984.

Royde-Smith, Naomi. "New Novels." Review of *The Magic Formula and Other Stories*, by L. P. Jacks; *Mr. Fortune's Maggot*, by Sylvia Townsend Warner; *The House Without Windows*, by Barbara Newhall Follett; *Knock Four Times*, by Margaret Irwin. *New Statesman*, 21 May 1927: 184–85.

Sadler, David. "Innocent Hearts: The Child Authors of the 1920s." *Children's Literature Association Quarterly* 17.4 (1992–93): 24–30.

St. John Power, Leonore. "Eepersip's Escape." Review of *The House Without Windows*, and *Eepersip's Life There*. The Three Owls (column), *New York Herald Tribune Books*, 27 March 1927: 8.

Stewart, Susan. *On Longing: Narratives of the Miniature, the Gigantic, the Souvenir, the Collection*. Baltimore: Johns Hopkins University Press, 1984.

Stuart, Henry Longan. "A Mirror of the Child Mind." Review of *The House Without Windows, and Eepersip's Life There*, by Barbara Newhall Follett. *New York Times Book Review*, 6 February 1927: 5.

Wood, Naomi J. "'Suffer the Children': The Problem of the Loving Father in *At the Back of the North Wind*." *Children's Literature Association Quarterly* 18 (Fall 1993): 112–19.

Of Mimicry and (Wo)Man:
Infans *or Forked Tongue?*

Mitzi Myers

> *Mimicry reveals something in so far as it is distinct from what might be called an* itself *that is behind. The effect of mimicry is camouflage. . . .*
> *It is not a question of harmonizing with the background but, against a mottled background, of becoming mottled.*   Jacques Lacan

Lacan here aligns mimicry with the technique of camouflage as "practised in human warfare"; he lists travesty and intimidation as the other "major dimensions" in which the mimetic activity is employed. Organisms don't take on the coloration of other organisms just as an adaptive mechanism, he suggests: imitation and mockery are ways of talking back. If we can't grab the originary "itself," we can decode the mimetic mottling that a particular milieu generates. Lacan's remarks on crustaceans have been borrowed to good effect in discussing the language systems of colonial subjects, as the title I've appropriated from Homi K. Bhabha indicates.[1] Keeping in mind Barbara Newhall Follett, Marjory Fleming, and authors like Maria Edgeworth who started writing as girls, I should like to "kidnap" some recent "adult" theorizing about language and cross-cultural translation and about the social construction of subjectivity to discuss the ways that some critics do—and more could—talk about child writers and readers. Even though the juvenile literary subject hasn't much interested French masculinist high theory (or, for that matter, pragmatic American feminist theory), the mimicry of child readers and writers is surely as wily and inventive as that of crustaceans or persons of color. Yet as long as the only metanarrative we have is the tired Romantic tale of wise child philosophers interfered with and suppressed by adult culture, we can't tell the story of the juvenile passage from *infans* (literally, the being before language) to forked tongue (the being who moves easily among multiple languages, *making* a self from what's available, rather than uttering the intuitive).

Like the recent *Children's Literature Association Quarterly*'s special

Children's Literature 23, ed. Francelia Butler, R. H. W. Dillard, and Elizabeth Lennox Keyser (Yale University Press, © 1995 Hollins College).

issue on juvenilia, Naomi Wood's discussion of Barbara Newhall
Follett is moving, troubling, and most of all, provocative: interesting as much for the questions it raises about the child self and the
child's language as about the binary opposition it discusses.[2] The
implicit dualism of "who writes" (a Romantic agentic self, organic,
coherent, unified, natural) and "who is written" (the modernist self
as produced by technology, the reproducer of somebody else's languages, the mechanized self that is the appropriate emblem of late
capitalist society) still structures our thinking about children and
their culture. Recent work across a range of disciplines—medi-
cal, historical, ethnographic, theoretic—suggests that this either-or
framework of individualism versus determinism prevents us from
seeing the dialogic nature of juvenile linguistic and literary acquisition. Just as often as they have been typed as victims, children,
like colonial subjects, have been figured as somehow free of culture
(Diderot was not the only eighteenth-century philosophe to align
the savage and the juvenile), but not by Rousseau who, despite his
phony reputation, watches his pupil with a surveillance that would
put Jeremy Bentham's Panopticon to shame. Despite his demerits
as a sexist educator and his dither about the noble savage, Rousseau
demonstrates that without the tutor's acculturation, there would be
no natural child; if Emile were really home alone, there would be
nobody home.

Follett's and Fleming's (and Edgeworth's) mentors, like Emile's
tutor, can be read in multiple ways, but they cannot be left out of the
picture: it is they who provide the cultural capital which the child
uses and abuses. The Brontës are the sole juvenile authors I have
discovered so far who did not keep a shrewd eye on handy adult
readers, imitating them, offering them gifts, wanting to please and
to be read. When we invoke the Romantic child genius voicing a
primal self or when we lament adult intervention, we are probably
giving children both too much and too little credit, but most of all
we are telling the same old story. I cannot help wondering if that
solipsistic Romantic mythology had anything to do with Follett's
sad end: was the privileged daughter of highly literate parents the
victim of a literary and class daydream rather than a gendered typewriter (or a casual murderer)? And what do we make of a daughter
whose fantasy erases the dedicated parents whose textual conventions of Romantic liberation she is borrowing? Follett's is doubly a
strange gift.

As Wood's overview of Follett's male adulators and Judith Plotz's

of Marjory Fleming's demonstrate, it is difficult to free discussion
from escapist voyeurs who lust both to possess the child and to be
her: indeed, if James R. Kincaid's *Child-Loving* is right, our discipline is a dirty subject.[3] I prefer to think that it has as much to
teach us about the reproduction of culture and the formation of
subjectivity as about our own secret desires. Among all the other
cultural work they perform which adultist critics haven't yet espied,
children's literacy and literature (with their layered meanings of
by, for, of, as, and *to*) provide, as Scottish Enlightenment thinkers
noticed, the originary ground of human knowledge. From pioneering Enlightened psychology to trendy postmodern cultural studies,
children reading and writing instruct adults about community—not
tales of lone souls grown anorexic on icicles, but narratives about
how human subjects create themselves and their cultures through
storytelling, through collage. Michel de Certeau's *Practice of Everyday Life* makes a compelling case for the devious creativities of ordinary living, the ways in which we evade being "always already" written by our culture: playing games, giving gifts, inventing figurative
language, and, most important of all, telling stories.[4] In his sce-
nario, strategic resistance is *bricolage,* an enabling self and story we
put together from and in resistance to the culture that surrounds
us: an ongoing conversation rather than a mythology of solitary
authorship. Marjory Fleming was not, as has recently been claimed,
the "only notable child romantic poet," unless we use that word to
refer to period alone (Plotz 4). Instead, she (like Maria Edgeworth)
is very much a product of Scottish Enlightenment sociality, inter-
subjectivity, and insatiable curiosity about the human condition.
Measles may have done her in, but she would never have wasted
into immateriality or run away from home. Were she alive today,
very likely she would be reading Certeau with as much avidity as he
would study her: he discusses what she—and most bright, literate
children—practice in everyday life. Their mimicry is both taking
in and talking back; paradoxically, they look a lot more natural
without that Romantic halo and plot line.

Notes

Note to epigraph: Readers of postcolonial theory will recognize my title's gendered theft from Homi K. Bhabha's now classic essay, "Of Mimicry and Man," most
recently reprinted in *The Location of Culture.* The epigraph comes from chapter 8
of Lacan's section "Of the Gaze" in *The Four Fundamental Concepts of Psycho-Analysis,*

99. Although current research on childhood language acquisition questions Lacan's theories of human entry into language, his discussions of mimicry and the gaze remain provocative for students of children's literature.

1. The burgeoning field of postcolonial language and literary studies opens out exciting possibilities for studying how children (and women) simultaneously learn and subvert a hegemonic "master" discourse. Especially useful and relevant are the studies by Bhabha; Bill Ashcroft, Gareth Griffiths, and Helen Tiffin; François Lionnet; Lisa Lowe; and Mary Louise Pratt. Exploring subject populations' use of the master's tools to restructure the supposed prisonhouse of language, they variously complicate Edward W. Said's monovocal construction of the "other" in *Orientalism*.

2. The essays by Judith Plotz and David Sadler and the editor's comments by Gillian Adams in this issue—17.4 (Winter 1992–93)—are the most relevant to the conceptualization of the "Romantic" child writer. Sadler situates Follett in the 1920s milieu of other young writers, but does not interrogate the notions of gender and "innocence" which produced her and her work.

3. Plotz's useful analysis unfortunately perpetuates the misspelling of Marjory's name and some of the resilient myths about her. It only strengthens Plotz's case for men's valorizing of little girls to recognize that there's no solid evidence for the romanticized tales of Marjory's instructing Sir Walter Scott. John Brown, whose fanciful account captivated Mark Twain and others, apparently elaborated some old family legends into a cultural myth that strikingly anticipates Follett's twentieth-century sanctification. Scott's and Marjory's papers don't refer to one another, and the cute anecdotes that delighted late Victorians don't have a lot to do with Scott's plentiful recorded comments by and for children. A single surviving letter (from a relative a half-century after Marjory's death) says only that the families were acquainted and that Scott gave Marjory copies of Maria Edgeworth's children's tales. The most reliable and least sentimental record of Marjory Fleming's work is Frank Sidgwick's edition.

4. See especially part 1 and chapter 12 in part 4 ("Reading as Poaching").

Works Cited

Adams, Gillian. "Speaking for Lions." *Children's Literature Association Quarterly* 17.4 (Winter 1992–93): 2–3.

Ashcroft, Bill, Gareth Griffiths, and Helen Tiffin. *The Empire Writes Back: Theory and Practice in Post-Colonial Literatures*. London and New York: Routledge, 1989.

Bhabha, Homi K. *The Location of Culture*. London and New York: Routledge, 1994.

Brown, John. "Marjorie Fleming." In *Rab and His Friends and Other Papers*. London: Dent; New York: Dutton, n.d. 85–111.

Certeau, Michel de. *The Practice of Everyday Life*. Trans. Steven Rendall. 1984. Berkeley: U. of California P., 1988.

Fleming, Marjory. *The Complete Marjory Fleming: Her Journals, Letters, and Verses*. Ed. Frank Sidgwick. London: Sidgwick and Jackson, 1934.

Kincaid, James R. *Child-Loving: The Erotic Child and Victorian Culture*. New York and London: Routledge, 1992.

Lacan, Jacques. *The Four Fundamental Concepts of Psycho-Analysis*. Ed. Jacques-Alain Miller. Trans. Alan Sheridan. 1973. New York: Norton, 1978.

Lionnet, François. *Autobiographical Voices: Race, Gender, Self-Portraiture*. 1989. Ithaca and London: Cornell U.P., 1991.

Lowe, Lisa. *Critical Terrains: French and British Orientalisms*. Ithaca: Cornell U.P., 1991.

Plotz, Judith. "The Pet of Letters: Marjorie Fleming's Juvenilia." *Children's Literature Association Quarterly* 17.4 (Winter, 1992–93): 4–9.

Pratt, Mary Louise. "Arts of the Contact Zone." *Profession 91*. New York: Modern
    Language Association, 1991. 33–40.
Sadler, David. "Innocent Hearts: The Child Authors of the 1920s." *Children's Litera-
    ture Association Quarterly* 17.4 (Winter, 1992–93): 24–30.
Said, Edward W. *Orientalism*. 1978. New York: Vintage, 1979.

"Thy Speech Is Strange and Uncouth": Language in the Children's Historical Novel of the Middle Ages

Miriam Youngerman Miller

I began, some years ago, to look at images of the Middle Ages in children's literature to find materials which would at least make comprehensible to my son my enthrallment by the medieval world. Although my son found my collection of "medieval" books less than compelling, I discovered a substantial body of literature treating the Middle Ages from a wide variety of perspectives. I also found that, although there is considerable commentary on individual authors of medieval historical fiction (including Howard Pyle, Rosemary Sutcliff, and Geoffrey Trease) and on the children's historical novel in general, there has been no extended study of what these works, as a body and individually, convey to their young readers about the Middle Ages.[1]

Although there are many possible ways to analyze the view(s) of the Middle Ages presented individually and collectively by these novels (including the treatment of gender roles, religion, and social hierarchy), this study will deal solely with medieval language. I will explore the techniques—successful and less than successful—employed by historical novelists to indicate to contemporary children in ways they can comprehend that just as the material culture and social institutions of the Middle Ages differed from what prevails today, so too did language. To ignore linguistic difference is to compromise accuracy, and I will argue that the historical novel, whether intended for children or adults, must come to terms with historical accuracy, however slippery that concept may be. Yet to attempt to imitate medieval speech directly, to stud the dialogue with archaisms and—worse—pseudo-archaisms, is to risk losing the young audience entirely. Although some novelists fail to acknowledge linguistic change and diversity in the medieval world and others succumb to pedantry and fustian, the best (at least from this point of view) find imaginative ways to convey to children the linguistic

Children's Literature 23, ed. Francelia Butler, R. H. W. Dillard, and Elizabeth Lennox Keyser (Yale University Press, © 1995 Hollins College).

reality of the Middle Ages without resorting to arcane vocabulary and tortured syntax.

Because children's historical novels about the Middle Ages have not previously been discussed as a body, I would first like to give some idea of the scope of this category. Carnegie and Newbery medalists and honor books include the following historical novels with medieval settings: Cynthia Harnett's *The Wool-Pack* (1952) and *The Load of Unicorn* (1960), Robert Welch's *Knight Crusader* (1955), Barbara Leonie Picard's *Ransom for a Knight* (1957), Rosemary Sutcliff's *The Shield Ring* (1957), C. Walter Hodges's *The Namesake* (1964), Eric P. Kelly's *The Trumpeter of Krakow* (1929), Elizabeth Janet Gray's *Adam of the Road* (1943), Eleanore Myers Jewett's *The Hidden Treasure of Glaston* (1947), and Marguerite De Angeli's *The Door in the Wall* (1950) and *Black Fox of Lorne* (1957). In addition to these, many other important authors, past and present, like Robert Louis Stevenson, Howard Pyle, Charlotte M. Yonge, Geoffrey Trease, Henry Treece, Barbara Willard, and Jill Paton Walsh have chosen medieval settings for their historical novels written for children.

Indeed it is possible to marvel with Sheila A. Egoff at the "sheer power of talent" that has devoted itself to the children's historical novel in general and the medieval period in particular. In Egoff's judgment these authors "have produced fiction that is every bit as convincing as the modern realistic novel, at the same time describing past societies with the knowledge and integrity of the scholar" (160).

Egoff's concern draws attention to the crucial issue of whether historical accuracy is necessary, desirable, or even possible in historical fiction. What is the relationship, if any, between historiography and the historical novel? Avrom Fleishman concedes that although "historical fiction, like all art, tells some kind of truth, it clearly does not tell it straight," but "by the same token, history itself does not tell truths that are unambiguous or absolute; even the nature of historical fact is problematic." Yet he continues, "the value and . . . the meaning of a historical novel will stand in some relation to the habitual demand for truth." The historical novelist, then, "provokes or conveys, by imaginative sympathy, the *sentiment de l'existence*, the feeling of how it was to be alive in another age" (4). "In the historical novel," as Fleishman sees it, "the generic properties of plot, character, setting, thought, and *diction* . . . operate on the materials of history to lend esthetic form to historical men's experience" (8, emphasis added).

Geoffrey Trease, the well-known and prolific author of children's historical novels, also stresses the importance of accuracy in this genre. He asks, "Is it really essential to distort the truth in order to produce an exciting plot? . . . To do so seems a confession of deficiency, since the more truly imaginative an author is, the more colour and drama he can reveal in things-as-they-were" (*Tales* 98). Although language, not plot, is at issue here, the point holds. Trease illustrates his thesis with a reference to his own work: "a whole chapter . . . had to be rewritten when I discovered by chance that a certain morning at Versailles in May, 1789, had been grey and drizzly, not sunny as I first pictured it. What does it matter, a pedantic detail like that? Just as much, or as little, as the workmanship which old-time sculptors and carvers put into figures so far from the ground that no human eye would ever appreciate it" (*Tales* 99). Trease's comparison of the contemporary historical novelist to the artists and craftsmen who embellished the Gothic cathedrals is apt. It is the sum total of accurate details, none of which may be all that important in its own right, that conveys the sentiment de l'existence to the reader of the historical novel, just as, paradoxically, it was the sheer mass (and collective beauty) of ornament, incomprehensible in its detail, that enabled medieval worshipers to transcend the material world in their quest for the spiritual.

Fleishman's and Trease's comments seem particularly appropriate in evaluating novels about the Middle Ages because the profound changes which western civilization has undergone since 1500 make it especially difficult to recreate convincingly the medieval world view and way of life. A writer who sets a novel during the American Revolution, for example, can count on an audience that shares certain fundamental social and political assumptions with the revolutionaries—the desirability of representative government, the possibility of social mobility, separation of church and state, anti-colonialism, and so forth—and which finds the language of the American colonies more or less understandable. A writer who chooses to portray accurately the Middle Ages for children, on the other hand, must deal with such issues as feudalism, chivalry, a rigid social hierarchy, and the permeation of religion into all areas of life—which are not only unfamiliar to contemporary children, but which are completely antithetical to the values of the Enlighten-

ment on which contemporary society rests. The task of conveying
the sentiment de l'existence of the Middle Ages to contemporary
children in ways that they can understand is formidable indeed,
but to do less is to do a substantial disservice to an audience that
deserves better. As George Orwell put it, "The fact is only unim-
portant if one believes that what is read in childhood leaves no
impression behind" (quoted in Trease, *Tales* 14).

A sense of language is especially difficult to convey accurately in
an historical setting, while still appealing to young readers who as
yet have limited control over contemporary written English. Depending on the exact time and place of the story, a novel set in
the British Isles during the Middle Ages, for example, may involve
characters speaking Latin, the various medieval Celtic languages,
Old or Middle English, Scots, Danish, several varieties of French
and Occitan, and the languages of the Low Countries. Novels set
elsewhere, such as on crusade, may include characters speaking
Byzantine Greek, Arabic, various forms of medieval Spanish, Italian, and Slavic, and Old and Middle German (High and Low). Any
author who attempts to render one or more of these languages in
modern English, differentiating among them and between them
and modern English, has undertaken a very difficult, and perhaps
unrewarding, task.

Trease blames children's bias against historical fiction on problems of language: "Many children will not read historical stories. It
seems a matter of prejudice [because] . . . an historical novel almost
invariably uses a richer vocabulary than its modern counterpart
and can hardly avoid an element of description" (95).[2]

Edith Nesbit's delicious parody of the nineteenth-century "medieval" romance in *Five Children and It* illustrates two of the dreadful
possibilities for handling medieval languages—pseudo-archaicisms
and ultra-contemporary youthful slang—neither of which is accurate or appealing to children. In the chapter "A Castle and No
Dinner," the children's wish to inhabit a castle under siege has been
fulfilled by the Psammead (sand fairy), and one of the children
(Robert) finds himself in conversation with Sir Wulfric de Talbot,
the commander of the besieging forces:

> The only difficulty was that he knew he could never remember
> enough "quothas" and "beshrew me's," and things like that,
> to make his talk sound like the talk of a boy in a historical

romance. However, he began boldly enough with a sentence straight out of *Ralph de Courcy; or, The Boy Crusader.* He said:

"Grammercy for thy courtesy, fair sir knight. The fact is, it's like this—and I hope you're not in a hurry, because the story's rather a breather. . . .

"Thy speech is strange and uncouth," said Sir Wulfric de Talbot. "Repeat thy words—what hadst thou?"

"A ripping—I mean a jolly—no—we were contented with our lot—that's what I mean; only, after that we got into an awful fix." (154–55)

An awful fix, indeed. It is possible to give an accurate sense of medieval language without resorting to either of Robert's extremes, but it is not easy, and even novelists of distinction are sometimes less than successful.

Margery Fisher, writing of this problem of the spoken word in the historical novel, agrees with Nesbit that approximating period language "at its worst . . . degenerates into a ludicrous pishtushery," but nonetheless sees a place for "archaic or antique" idiom "as supremely well suited to moments of lofty importance" (207), a view far from universal. Fisher also points out that a "neutral style, with a sprinkling of period words" can be effective, as it is in her example of Sir Walter Scott (228).

Scott, writing as Laurence Templeton in the preface to *Ivanhoe,* defended his own methods: "It is necessary, for exciting interest of any kind, that the subject assumed should be . . . translated into . . . the language of the age we live in," but "it is one thing to make use of the language and sentiments which are common to ourselves and our forefathers, and it is another to invest them with the sentiments and dialect exclusively proper to their descendants" (quoted in Fleishman 25). Thus, while Scott rejected antiquarianism "which detail[s] and embellish[es] the past for its own sake and without reference to the present" (Fleishman 25), he was, in large measure, successful in avoiding the glaring anachronism, as Fisher and Fleishman point out.

Geoffrey Trease, who set his groundbreaking first novel, *Bows Against the Barons,* and many of his subsequent novels in the Middle Ages, credits Naomi Mitchison with eschewing "the varlet-and-halidom type of language" in favor of "natural, modern but not anachronistic dialogue" (*Tales* 96). Trease, feeling that "archaic dia-

logue had strangled the life out of the historical story," claims
to have accelerated the movement toward "natural living speech"
begun by Mitchison:

> Today it seems self-evident that, if the reader accepts the con-
> vention of Arabs, Eskimos and even Martians conversing in
> modern English, Robin Hood and Friar Tuck should be per-
> mitted to do the same. After all, if we were to set down their
> actual thirteenth-century speech, it would be almost as unin-
> telligible as Arabic. . . . But there was never any suggestion that
> the Sherwood outlaws should use an authentic medieval dic-
> tion. . . . What was expected was a bogus sort of Wardour Street
> jargon which was supposed to "convey period atmosphere," but
> which some of us would have said, more simply, stank. (*Tales*
> 96–97)

Trease perhaps exaggerates the difficulty of Middle English, but
his Sherwood outlaws do speak a modern, almost featureless, dialect. In the interest of accuracy (which, as noted above, he sees as
necessary) and of his Marxist theme of class struggle, he makes several passing references to the trilingual state of affairs in thirteenth-
century England, all of which emphasize the oppression of the
English-speaking peasantry by those who speak French or Latin:

> This was no forester, Dickon realized. Most of them were
> French, but this man spoke in the local dialect. (22)

> "It's a cunning trick of theirs."
> "An old one," put in a young scholar from Oxford. *"Divide et
> impera."*
> "What the devil's that?" growled the bridle-smith.
> "It means 'divide—and rule'," said the scholar proudly. "It's
> Latin."
> "Latin won't solve our troubles—or open the door to the
> jail." (38)

> There were six of them, sallow Gascons all of them, specially
> brought from the forests across the sea. They hardly under-
> stood the English speech, and they were not likely to show any
> favor to peasants. (53)

> Then the harper began to sing in the broadest Nottingham-
> shire dialect, which hardly a Southern Englishman, let alone a

Gascon could understand. It was the speech of Dickon's own people, and he pricked up his ears. (56)

Other than these references, the only indications that the characters in *Bows Against the Barons* speak something other than modern English are very occasional substitutions of nonstandard or archaic forms, like *ye* for *you:* an apprentice asks Dickon, "What d'ye lack?" (clearly a conventional peddler's cry), and when Dickon answers, "Er—nothing," the apprentice pointedly responds, "Anyone with half an eye can see *you* couldn't afford beef, anyhow" (33).

Thus, with Trease's "worst of both worlds"—illustrated by a quote from Carola Oman, "I am not in a great hurry, if you truly desire aught, but I think I ought to be turning home now" (*Tales* 96)—as one extreme, and his own solution of unadorned modern dialogue as the other, let us look at a variety of specific stylistic devices used, more or less successfully, to give the effect of medieval language.[3]

Marguerite De Angeli, in *The Door in the Wall,* demonstrates a knowledge of the muddled linguistic situation in medieval England and refers with some frequency to the language or dialect spoken by her characters. For example, the noble mother of the protagonist, Robin, is said to speak with a "pleasant mixture of Norman French and good English words that were becoming the fashion" (10), and Robin's nurse, Ellen, has "Cockney speech." However, such linguistic distinctions are not carried through successfully in the dialogue itself. Robin's mother's speech is written in straightforward style with particularly simple syntax and no unusual vocabulary to indicate an admixture of French and English. In any case, the mixture of French and English "became the fashion" around 1250, a good century before the setting of this novel in the England of Edward III, presumably from the many references to the plague, during the pandemic of 1348–49. By 1350, the nobility of England spoke English, their French being maintained as a second language in which many of them, like Chaucer's Prioress, were none too adept.[4]

The nurse's speech, likewise, has no sign of Cockney (the modern characteristics of Cockney have their roots in the speech of medieval Londoners)[5] but is simply archaic: "Scarce able to stand have I been this day, yet have I been faithful. . . . Just wait and see when more victuals are brought thee!" (11). Note the inverted syntax and use of the second person singular pronoun, with which adult characters address Robin throughout the novel, while he properly addresses his elders in the second person plural, an appropriate distinction, but one which makes the dialogue seem fusty and archaic.

Toward the end of the novel, Robin is challenged by a Welsh sentry, "Art tha' but a shepherd boy, then? . . . And hast fallen into the river? Come, then, lad, and warm tha'self by the fire. Be not frightened. We'll not fright thee" (94). Robin delays his response, "trying to think what he must say and *how he must speak*" (emphasis added). Finally his answer comes: "Nay," he began, trying to appear stupid, " 'tis na far to the cottage" (94).

Although evidence of fourteenth-century Anglo-Welsh speech patterns is not readily available, it is clear from later documentation that the most obvious feature of Anglo-Welsh is the "confusion" of consonants, in particular initial consonants, due to the lenition of initial consonants in the Celtic language family.[6] Thus, De Angeli's Welsh sentry would be better characterized by speech similar to that of Fluellen, Shakespeare's stage Welshman in *Henry V*, who says *pridge* for *bridge*, *cheshu* for *Jesu*, *athversary* for *adversary*, *falorous* for *valorous*, and so on, rather than by the substitution of *tha* for both *thou* and *thy* and the use of nonstandard syntax and morphology which simply serves as a generalized marker of "dialect" speech. Robin clearly takes care to reply in what he mistakenly hopes will be passable Anglo-Welsh, substituting *na* for *not* (rather like a lowland Scot).

Robin associates stupidity with the use of dialects other than his own, and there is some evidence to support Robin's dialect snobbery in Middle English literature. Chaucer's Parson, for example, expresses in the prologue to his tale a southerner's disdain for the "rum, ram, ruf" of northern England, and one of the shepherds in *The Second Shepherds' Play* of the Wakefield cycle (Wakefield being in the north of England) responds to Mak the trickster's "pseudo-posh" accent by telling him to stick his southern tooth in a turd (a line which is often woefully bowdlerized in translation). Thus, this aspect of De Angeli's representation of language in medieval England is apparently authentic. However, if De Angeli can in general be praised for her awareness of language diversity in the England of Edward III, her handling of specific dialect features leaves much to be desired.

Elizabeth Janet Gray takes an unusual approach to depicting medieval language in *Adam of the Road*, the story of a minstrel's son in late thirteenth-century England in search of his lost father. In general, Gray's style is exceptionally plain and transparent: a predominance of simple subject-verb-object syntax, standard modern morphology, and a minimum of "medieval" vocabulary. Appropriate to the thematic stress on minstrelsy and storytelling, however, Gray peppers her text with numerous references to Middle English literature—sometimes passing allusions, often substantial quotations or entire retellings—and it is these references that give the reader a sense of medieval language.

The linguistic context of Adam's life is made clear early on. He speaks a northern dialect of English, having grown up "in the shadow of York Minster," which is a source of amusement to his schoolfellows in the midland Abbey of St. Alban (15). This amusement dies down when Adam demonstrates his knowledge of French, for "not many of these sons of franklins and burgesses knew the language of the Court folk" (16). Finally, Adam must also learn Latin, for "all their talk in school was in Latin, which was hard for Adam at first" (17). Adam's linguistic situation is then placed in an even broader context when he attends the great St. Giles's Fair at Winchester: "He heard northern voices and midland voices and southern voices; he heard Welshmen speak; he heard Norman French and French from France; he heard tongues he had never heard before" (200). Although it is thus made clear that Adam, like many thirteenth-century Englishmen, is more or less trilingual, the dialogue does not demonstrate any switching from one language to another, nor is there any differentiation between his northern speech and the midland speech of his friend Perkin. All dialogue is in a modern, colloquial (but not slangy) style which is so straightforward as to seem almost featureless.

One method Gray uses to add medieval color to her otherwise colorless prose is to allude throughout the novel to the *Canterbury Tales*. Strictly speaking, such allusion is anachronistic: Adam's adventures take place in 1294–95, and Chaucer will be creating his immortal pilgrims and their tales exactly a century later. Nonetheless, Gray skillfully uses Chaucer's language, characters, and incidents to create a credible late thirteenth-century world. Gray quotes (in modern English) well-known lines from the General Prologue and the tales. For example, a village widow calls Adam "as pert as a pie" (30), a phrase the Reeve applies near the beginning of his tale to the Miller's proud wife. Adam's father arrives "all hot" from France (31), like the Pardoner's wallet full of pardons all hot from Rome. When gaily dressed Roger the minstrel sees his son, he "wouldn't give a pulled hen" (38) for Adam's clothes, just as the Monk does not give a pulled hen for the rule of St. Benedict by which he has sworn to live. Adam sings, "Come hither, love, to me" for a group of aristocratic children, recalling to mind (the mind of the adult reader, at least) the less savory rendition of the same lyrics by the Pardoner and the Summoner. The affected lisp of a steward (90) parallels Friar Huberd, lisping for his wantonness (that is, out of affectation), a linguistic fashion in Chaucer's day, if not before. Like the Prioress's dogs, Adam is fed with "milk and wastell bread" (218). Many of the proper names, too, can be found in the *Canterbury Tales:* Jankin, Oswald, Emilie, Perkin, Malkin, Walter, Hubert, Gervase, Harry, and Alison, to name a few.

Another way in which Gray uses the *Canterbury Tales* to provide authenticity to her story is to sprinkle references to Chaucerian characters and incidents throughout the novel. We see Adam at Dame Malkin's cottage, this widow being almost identical to the poor widow possibly of the same name in the Nun's Priest's tale, right down to owning the same number of chickens (26). Adam travels the Pilgrims' Way (132) albeit toward Winchester instead of Canterbury, and at various times encounters a fluting squire (64), men at law conducting business at St. Paul's (99), a knight, squire, and yeomen traveling together (169), a parson (218), a merchant (164), a sailor (198) with a ship called Magdalen (and gap-toothed like the Wife of Bath), a parish clerk (222), friars and a hunting monk (238), a fox with a chicken in its mouth (253), a plowman (295), a miller blowing on his bagpipe (301), and a clerk of Oxford (309).

Although the *Canterbury Tales* is the principal source of authenticity (social as well as linguistic), Gray also uses direct quotations from retellings of, and allusions to, a host of other Middle English literary works—creating in some sense a mini-anthology of medieval literature. Early in the novel, for example, Adam sings the famous cuckoo song:

> "Summer is i-cumen in," he sang in his high, clear voice, "Loude sing cuckoo!" . . .
>
> "Groweth seed and bloweth mead, and springeth the wude nu—" . . .
>
> "Sing cuckoo, sing cuckoo, nu!" he finished. (29)

This text is given in the original Middle English albeit with normal-
ized spelling. Later Roger the minstrel tells a group of aristocratic
children the Breton lai of *Sir Orfeo* "in French that rippled along in
short rhymed lines" (58)—Gray's text, unlike the poetic original, is
discursive prose (58–63).

Among the other literary works quoted, told, or alluded to are
the *Proverbs of Alfred* (70, 115), *The Squire of Low Degree* (84), *King
Horn* (119), the mystery play of the fall of Adam (210), *Havelock
the Dane* (252), and *The Second Shepherds' Play* (271). Use of familiar
rhymes like "London Bridge" (79–80) and "Oranges and Lemons"
(274) reminds modern children that much of the common lore of
childhood has its roots in the medieval world.

In addition to this innovative use of literary language which permits children (whose reading skills may not be advanced) to get
some of the linguistic flavor of the medieval world without stumbling over unfamiliar syntax or morphology, Gray employs another
technique to introduce difficult lexicon: the child protagonist is instructed in the specialized vocabulary pertaining to his culture, and
the child reader learns simultaneously both the vocabulary words
and the new concepts for which they stand. Thus, Perkin, a more
advanced student, instructs Adam on heraldry:

> "There's one of the Cliffords—checky gold and azure with a
> fesse gules," said Perkin, pointing to a shield painted with gold
> and blue checks and a wide red stripe across the center. . . .
> "It's the de Lisle leopard I'm looking for," said Adam.
> "Gules a leopard silver crowned gold," said Perkin, showing
> off. The heraldic terms were almost another language. . . .
> A knight rode past with the silver leopard on the red ground
> blazoned on his shield. (35–36)

The reader is introduced rather painlessly both to the new terms
(although *silver* and *gold* should probably be replaced by their he-
raldic equivalents, *argent* and *or*) and to the use of heraldry for
purposes of identification.

Another medieval concept, falconry, is likewise explained to both
Adam and the reader:

> Adam was pleased to know the word lanneret. Some words
> were like pets to him, and especially the new words that Simon
> was teaching him. A lanneret was a kind of falcon that a squire

was permitted to own. A king had a gerfalcon, a lady . . . a mer-
lin, and a yeoman a goshawk. Simon had taught Adam, too,
the right words for flocks of different kinds of birds. If you
saw, for instance, a number of swallows together, you spoke of
a *flight* of swallows, but you said a *walk* of snipe, and a *gaggle* of
geese. (71)

This passage also contains a subtle lesson in the medieval sense of
hierarchy.

Like Gray, Cynthia Harnett also uses the technique of instructing the characters and the reader simultaneously. In *The Sign of
the Green Falcon,* Master Richard Whittington answers a young girl's
question about her brother's future:

> "What happens next?" she inquired. "I mean, when Dickon
> has finished his seven years as apprentice?"
> "Then he will be admitted as a freemen of the Mercers' Com-
> pany and have the right to serve any master he wishes as a
> journeyman; that is, a man who works by the day, a *journee*
> man; the French call him *homme de journee*." (46)

Frequently, however, Harnett simply provides a running gloss:

> so many bales of chipped wool, called *"Sarplers,"* and so many
> sheep skins, called *"wool-fells."* (*The Merchant's Mark* 4)

> Bendy tiptoed along the full length of the ambulatory, the long
> aisle which ran right round the outside of the choir. (*The Cargo
> of the Madalena* 39)

> thirteen aged men could end their days in peace, their only
> duty being to offer bedes, or prayers, in the church. (*The Writing
> on the Hearth* 12)

Harnett relies primarily on medieval lexicon to depict medieval
speech, although when unfamiliar medieval terms are integrated
into the dialogue, Harnett handles this technique less smoothly and
more pedantically than does Gray. Often, Harnett simply incorporates the medieval lexicon and accompanying glosses into lengthy
expository passages in which fact after fact about medieval history
and culture is heaped upon the child reader's plate, creating an
effect about as appetizing as lumpy porridge: "The first treasure
was a small book bound in vellum. It was a Prymer, a prayer-book,
in Latin, containing the Little Office of Our Lady, the penitential

psalms, and all the other usual things. What made it so precious was that it was *printed*. To possess a printed Prymer was a feather in his cap at school. His father had given it to him on St. Benedict's day, the feast of his name saint, his patron" (*The Cargo of the Madalena* 23). Although her techniques for depicting medieval language are overwhelmingly lexical, Harnett does use the contraction '*tis* and occasional inverted syntax (in particular commands like *come you* and *get you*) to flavor her dialogue.

All of the novels examined so far are set in England and convey, in one way or another, the prevailing linguistic situation during the time in which each novel is set. In other novels the child protagonists find themselves far from home, surrounded by speakers of alien tongues, and must adapt to their altered circumstances. Novelists who choose this type of plot must develop a means to allow their young characters to communicate—credibly—with the strangers around them, to permit young readers to understand that more than one language is being spoken without taxing their own reading skills.

Bruce Clements's *Prison Window, Jerusalem Blue* tells the story of two ninth-century Anglo-Saxon children who are seized in a Viking raid and carried off to Denmark as slaves. They, of course, speak Old English, a West Germanic language, and their captors speak the Danish variety of Old Norse, a North Germanic language. The two languages are linguistically related, but not so closely as to be mutually intelligible. Clements clearly indicates this when Sydne, the girl captive, listens to the Vikings playing dice on the long-ship taking her to Denmark:

> Every so often, somebody would say something—a short sentence or a word—and each time she felt as if she could almost understand it, and that if the man would say the same thing again, slower, she *would* understand it. It was like listening to people talking around your bed when you're half asleep or have a fever. You can't understand exactly what they're saying or what they mean, but it's not a foreign language they're talking either. (40–41)

As the voyage continues on their second day of captivity, Sydne and her brother Juls learn to understand Old Norse:

> they listened to the Vikyngr talk and yell. Slowly they began to get used to the sounds they made, and to understand them

better and better. It was like listening to English spoken by dogs. Half the words sounded like barks. . . . Their ancestors and Juls's and Sydne's ancestors had once spoken the same language, and yet the sounds they made were terrible.

Still, their language had a lot of English in it, and once you got to know how they changed certain sounds, you began to understand them. More, even, than the English, they liked to put two words together and make a third word. Sydne heard the word "arm-craft" three or four times before she realized that it was a way of saying "work," and when she told Juls that he didn't believe her until he listened for it himself. (51–52)

If we place any stock in the notion of accuracy in the historical novel, this passage presents several problems. Old English and Old Norse are not so closely related that anyone who is a native speaker of one, even the linguistically flexible young, can pick up the other in a few hours' time. The two languages share many roots (Sydne notes that Old Norse "had a lot of English in it"), but their inflections are markedly different.[7]

The two children are described as instant comparative Germanic philologists, intuiting systematic sound changes so that they can easily convert Old English to Old Norse. While there are such sound changes (for example, *skirt* and *shirt, dike* and *ditch, egg* and *ey,* and *hale* and *whole* are all exact cognates, the first of each pair being of Old Norse derivation), knowledge of them would still not allow the children to surmount the grammatical barrier. And, since the children are kidnapped from the south of England in 831 A.D., well before the Danelaw was established in northeast England by the Treaty of Wedmore in 878, there can be no question of familiarity with the Danicized English that developed there in the tenth and eleventh centuries.[8]

Curious also is the reference to putting two words together to make a third, a process which is characterized as being more common in Norse than in English. If what is meant is the creation of self-explaining compounds (words like *blackbird* or *toothache*), then that process is common to all Germanic languages, including English, and there is certainly no reason for Juls to find it surprising. If what is meant is the kenning (and the example *arm-craft* for *work* would seem to so indicate), then there is no reason for Juls to be surprised. The kenning is a form of poetic diction (unlikely to be heard during a casual shipboard dice game) in which a simple noun is replaced by a compound noun. The two elements of the compound constitute a sort of riddle, the answer to which is the simple noun which has been replaced. The kenning can be either metaphorical—as when one of the Vikings calls the ship a "wave-goat" (18)—or nonmetaphorical, as in the *arm-craft* example. In any case, the kenning is an ornament of both Old English and Old Norse poetry and should be no surprise to either of the children.

Does any of this matter? Even if the young audience has no way of knowing about kennings and sound changes, nonetheless they are likely to find the notion of acquiring fluency in a foreign language in the space of an afternoon unconvincing, rendering the "evocation of time and space" in this novel less than "brilliant" (as the jacket blurb would have it). An author more concerned about accuracy and perhaps more imaginative could well have made the difficulty of communication between captors and captives an important thematic element.

This is precisely what Jill Paton Walsh does in *The Emperor's Winding Sheet*. Walsh's protagonist, Piers Barber, is shipwrecked on a trading voyage from his home in Bristol to the Holy Land, is rescued by pirates, and escapes to a Greek province of the Byzantine Empire. Because of a prophetic dream, Piers is forced to serve as a living talisman, his constant presence at the emperor's side presumed to protect Constantinople and its imperiled ruler. But the year is 1453, and Piers is fated to witness the fall of Constantinople to the Turks.

Because not even the most linguistically naive young reader would believe that English-speaking Piers could learn Byzantine Greek in an afternoon, Clements's solution to the communication problem, however inadequate, is not available to Walsh. Instead, Walsh uses Latin as the means of communication, a solution in keeping with the fifteenth-century setting. When the famished Piers is first fed by the Byzantines, he thanks them in English. They fail to understand, and he ventures, "Gratias ago":

> Someone . . . began . . . talking rapidly in Latin, asking questions. But the boy scarcely understood. In the first place he was eating . . . and that took his attention off case endings and parts of speech; in the second place, though he had spent a good part of his childhood in the new grammar school, being beaten for mistakes in Latin, and beaten again for speaking English in the play hour to his friends, all that was both long ago and far

away, and the man who questioned him spoke very elaborate Latin, and with a heavy unfamiliar accent. (7)

Piers (renamed Vrethiki, "lucky find" in Greek) struggles to improve his school Latin (32), "Latin so barbarous it would torment the ear of a saint" (48). Finally, with time Vrethiki's Latin becomes so "well practiced" that he can "nearly . . . but not quite understand" the Italian of the Genoese who are helping to defend the great city (196).

Walsh also uses understanding (and failing to understand) language thematically. The novel begins with Piers fainting with hunger at the feet of a purple-robed stranger. When the boy regains consciousness, he finds himself a witness to a strange ritual (the coronation of the Despot Constantine as the latest—and last—Byzantine emperor): "The boy did not understand. But he knew that he had tumbled into something far out of his scope" (11). At the end of the ceremony, an old man pronounces a prophesy. Constantine's advisors discuss its implications at length—all in Greek and beyond Piers's ken—and decide that this boy must remain with the emperor as his "lucky charm": "Thus the boy's fate was settled, and he had not understood a word of it" (14).

The rest of the novel records Piers's efforts to understand the moral complexities of the world beyond childhood, a quest symbolized by his struggle to understand the foreign tongues whose inscrutable sounds surround him. First he must learn where he is:

> "But if he's a *Roman* emperor . . . why does he not speak Latin?"
> "Greek is the language of the Romans, and has been since the time of the Emperor Heraclius." . . .
> "And this land is Greece?"
> "It is the Morea; a province of the Empire."
> "Of the *Roman* Empire?" The boy strove to find his feet among these mind-boggling answers. (19)

When he reaches Constantinople, Vrethiki sees it only as a fraud, a place "all faked and painted" (68), where he himself is imprisoned like a caged bird (72–73). He must learn from Stephanos Bulgaricus, Eunuch of the Emperor's Bedchamber, who serves as his Latin translator, and from John Inglis, the English-speaking captain of the Varangian Guard, that his captivity is illusory, that he is free to struggle against his fate—or to embrace it.

That the young boy from Bristol has learned this lesson is, significantly, signaled linguistically in the emotional climax of the novel. When it becomes apparent that the city cannot hold against the Turks, Constantine arranges a place for his young companion on the last ship out. "Shattered and confused," Vrethiki responds, "It's true, I did want to go home. . . . But to leave now! And the Emperor . . . and you, Stephanos . . . stay here still, and I am to go, and have no share in what is to happen! Let me stay!" Stephanos tells him that there is nothing to stay for but death. The emperor asks, "What is he saying?" and Stephanos translates from Latin, "He says he will die for the Empire."

But for once the translation is not accurate:

> Vrethiki had been hearing Greek for a long time now, and the sentence was simple, made up of familiar words. He understood it.
>
> "No," he said. "To die for the Empire is the Emperor's privilege—but lesser folk may dare for lesser things." . . .
>
> "Let him stay, then," said the Emperor to Stephanos. "And out of all possible lesser things, what is it, I wonder, that keeps him?"
>
> As though for an answer, the boy fell on his knees . . . and managing at last to get his tongue round two words of Greek, he said, "*Affendi mou!*—My true Lord."
>
> "If I had a son, you know, Stephanos . . ." said the Emperor.
>
> "Yes, Sire, I know," said Stephanos. (188–89)

And so Piers/Vrethiki completes his journey from ignorance of both his fate and the words in which it is expressed to knowledge that there is something worth the willing sacrifice of one's life—and the words to name it.

A survivor of the sack of Constantinople, Piers has another journey to make—home to Bristol:

> He knew he would never be able to explain to his family at home. How could such a distance be bridged with a handful of words? Why, he would probably stumble speaking English, just at first. "I shall be like that bird Stephanos gave me . . . that fluttered in its wicker cage. But when I let it go free it

beat from without on the bars, as though it would fain enter in again. In the very house that I was born in, I shall carry an exile's heart, thinking of that immortal City, and how it passed away. And nothing will be simple for me, ever again." (272)

To return to Trease's question, "Is it really necessary to distort the truth to produce an exciting plot?" a comparison of *Prison Window, Jerusalem Blue* and *The Emperor's Winding Sheet* supports Trease's answer that the "more truly imaginative an author is, the more colour and drama he can reveal in things-as-they-were" (*Tales* 98). Walsh's accurate handling of language adds to the texture of her novel, enriching it far beyond Clements's.

Although the works examined here are merely representative of the large body of historical novels for children set in medieval times, they demonstrate that it is possible to convey the linguistic realities of the Middle Ages while appealing to the young reader. Imaginative authors like Gray and Walsh use their knowledge of historical linguistics to enhance both the style and content of their works. On the other hand, inaccuracies such as can be found in the novels of De Angeli and Clements only render their stories less credible and less nuanced. Although Harnett cannot be faulted for inaccuracy, her pedantic running glosses can hardly enchant her youthful audience. Trease, by opting almost entirely for what he calls "natural living speech" (*Tales* 96), misses the opportunity to enrich the sentiment de l'existence of his novel by depicting medieval language more creatively. Gray and Walsh demonstrate that this can be done without lapsing into the strangling archaicism Trease so rightly deplores.

Notes

1. But see Suzanne Rahn's survey of children's historical fiction, "An Evolving Past: The Story of Historical Fiction and Nonfiction for Children," for a good overview of historical fiction for children in general and for her comments on the impact of nineteenth-century medievalism on such authors as Charlotte Yonge and Howard Pyle. I am currently examining what the massive body of children's literature with medieval subject matter conveys to its audience about the Middle Ages.

2. For a defense of the children's historical novel against the prejudices of both children and adults, see David Self's recent article, "A Lost Asset? The Historical Novel in the Classroom."

3. An interesting technique for the accurate representation of language in historical novels is described by John and Patricia Beatty. In their novels (set in the age of Samuel Johnson and the English Civil War), they painstakingly avoid using any

words which could not be documented in the writings of the period in question. This extreme regard for linguistic historical accuracy would be appropriate only for works set in English-speaking milieus from the Renaissance forward, not, of course, to novels set in the Middle Ages (114–121, *passim*).

Although Alan Garner's *Owl Service*, set in modern Wales, is not directly germane to this study of language in historical novels about the Middle Ages, it does incorporate material from medieval Welsh literature. Michael Lockwood's article, " 'A Sense of the Spoken': Language in *The Owl Service*," discusses in detail Garner's "use of language varieties: different languages, dialects, accents, and registers" to illuminate "the novel's meanings both at the simple level of plot and at the levels of wider social and psychological significance" (84). Those who wish to pursue the study of literary dialect in children's literature should find Lockwood's article helpful.

4. See Albert C. Baugh and Thomas Cable's standard treatment of the reestablishment of English after 1200 (126–157).

5. Documentation of Cockney is not available before the late fifteenth and early sixteenth centuries. (Chaucer the Londoner is the first author known to make specific use of regional dialect speech, but his example is the northern speech of the Cambridge students in the Reeve's Tale, not the speech of those denizens of lower-class London, Harry Bailly and Roger Ware the Cook.) When Cockney begins to appear in written records, familiar features such as dropping the initial *h* are already in place. Thus, an author who wishes to depict a fourteenth-century Cockney would be on reasonably safe ground to include a sprinkling of the phonological features associated with that dialect from the end of the fifteenth century on. For a discussion of Cockney, see William Matthews's *Cockney Past and Present*.

6. Inhabitants of the Welsh marches in the fourteenth century were bilingual in Welsh and English. For a brief discussion of this issue, see Jeffrey Huntsman's "The Celtic Heritage of *Sir Gawain and the Green Knight*" (178).

7. In addition to Old English, I have studied Old Norse intensively, and I can personally testify that, because of its many irregularities, Old Norse grammar is far more difficult than that of Old English.

8. For more information about Scandinavian influence on Old English, see Baugh and Cable, 90–104. For a far more sophisticated treatment of Scandinavian influence in England, see Rosemary Sutcliff's *The Shield Ring*, set in the Lake District in the years immediately following the Norman Conquest. To demonstrate the immersion of her heroine, Frytha, in an Anglo-Norse world, Sutcliff describes Jarlstead by mixing archaic Anglo-Saxon words (*bower, byres*) with Norse (*foreganger, kale-garth, bee-skeps*) (23). Sutcliff is, in my mind, the outstanding practitioner of the children's historical novel. For an examination of her use of literary dialect, see my article, " 'The Rhythm Of a Tongue': Literary Dialect in Rosemary Sutcliff's Novels of the Middle Ages for Children."

Works Cited

Baugh, Albert C., and Thomas Cable. *A History of the English Language*. 3d ed. Englewood Cliffs, N.J.: Prentice-Hall, 1978.

Beatty, John, and Patricia Beatty. " 'Watch Your Language—You're Writing for Young People!' " *Horn Book Reflections: On Children's Books and Reading*. Boston: Horn Book, 1969. 114–121.

Clements, Bruce. *Prison Window, Jerusalem Blue*. New York: Farrar, Straus & Giroux, 1977.

De Angeli, Marguerite. *Black Fox of Lorne*. Garden City, N.Y.: Doubleday, 1956.

———. *The Door in the Wall*. Garden City, N.Y.: Doubleday, 1949.

Egoff, Sheila A. *Thursday's Child: Trends and Patterns in Contemporary Children's Literature*. Chicago: American Library Association, 1981.

Fisher, Margery. *Intent upon Reading: A Critical Appraisal of Modern Fiction for Children*. 1961. New York: Franklin Watts, 1962.

Fleishman, Avrom. *The English Historical Novel: Walter Scott to Virginia Woolf*. Baltimore and London: Johns Hopkins U.P., 1971.

Gray, Elizabeth Janet. *Adam of the Road*. New York: Viking, 1942.

Harnett, Cynthia. *The Cargo of the Madalena*. Minneapolis: Lerner, 1984. Originally published as *The Load of Unicorn*. London: Methuen, 1959.

————. *The Merchant's Mark*. Minneapolis: Lerner, 1984. Originally published as *The Wool-Pack*. London: Methuen, 1951.

————. *The Sign of the Green Falcon*. Minneapolis: Lerner, 1984. Originally published as *Ring Out, Bow Bells!* London: Methuen, 1953.

————. *The Writing on the Hearth*. 1971. New York: Viking, 1973.

Hodges, C. Walter. *The Namesake*. New York: Coward-McCann, 1964.

Huntsman, Jeffrey. "The Celtic Heritage of *Sir Gawain and the Green Knight*." *Approaches to Teaching* Sir Gawain and the Green Knight. Ed. Miriam Youngerman Miller and Jane Chauce. New York: Modern Language Association, 1986. 177–181.

Jewett, Eleanore Myers. *The Hidden Treasure of Glaston*. 1946. 4th ptg. New York: Scholastic, 1963.

Kelly, Eric P. *The Trumpeter of Krakow*. New York: Macmillan, 1928.

Lockwood, Michael. "'A Sense of the Spoken': Language in *The Owl Service*." *Children's Literature in Education* 23 (1992): 83–92.

Matthews, William. *Cockney Past and Present: A Short History of the Dialect of London*. 1938. London and Boston: Routledge and Kegan Paul, 1972.

Miller, Miriam Youngerman. "'The Rhythm of a Tongue': Literary Dialect in Rosemary Sutcliff's Novels of the Middle Ages for Children." *Children's Literature Association Quarterly* 19 (1994): 25–31.

Nesbit, E. [Edith Nesbit Bland]. "A Castle and No Dinner." *Five Children and It*. 1902. New York: Coward-McCann, n.d. 145–166.

Picard, Barbara Leonie. *Ransom for a Knight*. New York: Walck, 1956.

Rahn, Suzanne. "An Evolving Past: The Story of Historical Fiction and Nonfiction for Children." *Lion and the Unicorn* 15 (1991): 1–26.

Self, David. "A Lost Asset? The Historical Novel in the Classroom." *Children's Literature in Education* 22 (1991): 45–49.

Sutcliff, Rosemary. *The Shield Ring*. 1955. New York: Dell, 1966.

Trease, Geoffrey. *Bows Against the Barons*. 1934. Rev. ed. London: Hodder and Stoughton, 1966.

————. *Tales out of School*. 2d ed. London: Heineman, 1964.

Walsh, Jill Paton. *The Emperor's Winding Sheet*. New York: Farrar, Straus & Giroux, 1974.

Welch, Ronald [Ronald Oliver Felton]. *Knight Crusader*. London: Oxford U.P., 1954.

From Vanity Fair to Emerald City:
Baum's Debt to Bunyan

J. Karl Franson

My interest in a possible "confluence of reminiscences" affecting the creation of L. Frank Baum's *Wonderful Wizard of Oz* (1900) began (like the curiosity of Lowes regarding Coleridge's imaginative vision) with "a strange footprint caught sight of accidentally just off the beaten track" that became "an absorbing adventure along the ways which the imagination follows in dealing with its multifarious materials" (Lowes 180, 3). It was the beaten track itself, the Road of Yellow Brick, that led me to a major source of Baum's classic tale and ultimately a new perspective from which to read it.[1]

On the original map of Oz, Baum envisioned the road leading to the Emerald City in a straight line.[2] It resembles the famous road to the Celestial City in John Bunyan's *Pilgrim's Progress* (1678, 1684), which is "straight as a Rule can make it" to enable pilgrims to stay on course.[3] In addition, both roads are associated with the color yellow: the road through Oz is paved with yellow brick (27), and the road to the Celestial City becomes paved with gold inside the City itself (162).[4] Additional similarities between the books convinced me that Baum's supposedly original tale is simply a recasting of Bunyan's. Doubtless Baum was familiar with Bunyan's book, the most famous allegorical journey in Western literature. The work of a creative genius, *Progress* is a colorful, imaginative, and suspenseful story often claimed, in past generations, by children although not written originally for them (Georgiou 31), and is thus a logical source of inspiration for Baum's book.[5]

No extensive inquiry has been made into what influenced or inspired Baum's story, even though a variety of sources have been suggested for several of Baum's other books.[6] Greene and Martin propose that parts of *Oz* came from stories Baum had made up for his sons (10; see also Mannix 36–37). Perhaps warded off by the widely held view that *Oz* is a uniquely American fairy tale and hence original and experimental, commentators generally have ignored

Children's Literature 23, ed. Francelia Butler, R. H. W. Dillard, and Elizabeth Lennox Keyser (Yale University Press, © 1995 Hollins College).

the possibility that Dorothy's adventures might be modeled directly upon stories Baum had read.[7] Baum himself acknowledged no direct literary influences, claiming that *Oz* was "pure inspiration . . . right out of the blue" from the Great Author Himself.[8] His introduction to *Oz* alludes to European fairy tales by Grimm and Andersen but purports to be presenting a new kind of tale without the horrible and bloodcurdling incidents, the heartaches and nightmares of traditional tales.[9]

In the first published essay on Baum's book, Wagenknecht records his suspicion that the author used quite freely whatever suited his purposes from older literatures (*UA* 23), and that in *Mother Goose in Prose* (1897), Baum's fancy "plays about and transforms not things that he has seen but things that he has read about" (*UA* 19). Nye later expresses the same view, that the Oz books are far more derivative than even Baum realized (2). *The Pilgrim's Progress,* in particular, has come to the minds of many who have written about *Oz,* but none has recognized it as a direct Baum source.[10] Nevertheless, strong empirical evidence that Baum relied heavily on *Progress* calls into question his own claim to having been inspired when composing *Oz.* His likely purpose in rewriting Bunyan gradually emerges as the extent and nature of his borrowing become apparent.

A close comparison between *Oz* and *Progress* reveals that Baum drew heavily upon the earlier book for narrative structure, episodes, visual imagery, and diction. The nature of his appropriation suggests that it depends upon a vivid recollection of *Progress* rather than a direct copying of Bunyan's text. Baum combines parts 1 and 2 of *Progress,* the former depicting Christian's journey to the City, and the latter, the journey of his wife, Christiana, accompanied by their four boys and a friend named Mercy. He omits overtly religious elements, transporting the tale to the American prairie and to a mythical, secular Land of Oz. Also omitted are episodes Baum presumably considered unsuitable for children.[11]

Not every aspect of *Oz,* however, derives from the cornucopia one finds in *Progress.* The Munchkins, the Winged Monkeys, and the Hammer-Heads have no obvious counterparts in Bunyan and probably are Baum's own creations or derive from other sources he used. Nor does Baum replicate every major Bunyan episode and character. Missing, for instance, is the man in an iron cage at Interpreter's House, the Arbor where possessions are often lost, the notable Mr. Talkative, Faithful's trial by jury, a fearful mastiff, and the bottle of tears. Nearly all Baum's borrowings from *Progress* appear in the first three-quarters of *Oz*, or until Dorothy and her companions leave the Emerald City for the second time. The final chapters of *Oz*, which contain fewer similarities to Bunyan, have less narrative appeal, as evidenced by their being omitted from the classic 1939 film of the book.[12]

A major consequence of this discovery is to locate *Oz* more clearly within the tradition of religious allegory, thus corroborating the two book-length studies of *Oz*, both of which read the book allegorically. Moore views *Oz* as an allegory of self-reliance (135), and Nathanson identifies its strong religious elements (*Rainbow* 13–14), observing in a recent address to the American Academy of Religion that Dorothy's adventures tap into religious themes deeply embedded in American culture (*"The Wizard of Oz"* A16). Like *Progress*, Baum's book is more than a voyage imaginative or a psychological journey: it depicts a Grail-like quest during which each traveler seeks to conquer an inner emptiness or deficiency (Downing 29).

Because allegories seek to communicate on two levels, those of outward events and of ideas they convey, we are led while reading *Progress* to place ourselves in the roles of Christian and Christiana. So is it with *Oz*, wherein Dorothy (Littlefield 52), or the four protagonists together, also typify each of us. Baum's intent was to delineate aspects of spiritual growth, not through promotion of organized religion or established creed, which he rejected, but through creation of protagonists whose inward journeys toward spiritual fulfillment the reader follows as they progress toward the Emerald City and beyond. Always a religious man, Baum was raised a Protestant but drifted into Theosophy and Buddhism. As his friend Rev. Ryland put it, Baum clearly had a religion of his own, and "he lived and wrote by it" (Potter 12). His concern for spiritual well-being and moral values is apparent in his belief that our "earthly journey [is] but a step in our spiritual evolution."[13]

Why Baum's substantial indebtedness to Bunyan has gone virtually unnoticed may be owing to a twentieth-century lack of familiarity with Bunyan's allegory, in particular the less popular part 2, which captured Baum's imagination the most.[14] Examples of Baum's use of Bunyan that follow are arranged from the first chapter of *Oz* to the last: episodes preceding Dorothy's departure for the Emerald City, during her journey to the City, and following her arrival. The

study makes no pretense at being comprehensive, nor does it consider illustrations to various nineteenth-century editions of *Progress*
that may have influenced Baum's book.

Similarities between the initial settings of *Oz* and *Progress* are
readily apparent. Kansas as depicted by Baum is a foreboding
wasteland: Dorothy's one-room farmhouse epitomizes the family's
poverty and is surrounded by a great gray prairie, the plowed
ground baked by the sun "into a gray mass, with little cracks running through it" (12). Dorothy is an orphan taken in by a taciturn
uncle who is a stranger to joy and a thin, gaunt aunt who never
smiles.[15] Dorothy's guardians consider her odd because she is cheerful. Aunt Em is astonished Dorothy can find anything to laugh at
(12–13), leading one commentator to describe her situation accurately as "a home environment of spiritual death" (Barasch 56).

Dorothy's extreme poverty causes Scarecrow, as well as many
readers, to wonder why, once in the verdant Land of Oz, she wishes
to return to Kansas (44). Baum's narrative emphasizes Dorothy's
love and concern for Em and Henry, locating it symmetrically at
the beginning, middle, and end. Arriving in the Land of Oz, she
says, "I am anxious to get back to my Aunt and Uncle, for I am sure
they will worry about me" (25), a concern she repeats at the Emerald City (128), then again at the palace of Glinda the Good Witch
(254). In *The Emerald City of Oz* (1910), Baum brings Dorothy's concern for Em and Henry to a happy resolution when Princess Ozma
rescues the couple from physical and spiritual dissolution by transporting them to live with Dorothy in Oz permanently.[16] Bunyan
does the same in his own sequel: supernatural intervention brings
Christian's wife and children to the Holy City to be reunited with
him forever.

This opening scene of *Oz* closely resembles that of *Progress*, part 1.
Christian appears in rags (8), evidence of his poverty. A wide field
or plain extends from his house into the distance (10), and although
neither the sun nor drought is mentioned, Bunyan does depict a
spiritual drought that reappears in the Kansas farmhouse. Christian and his family must escape the City of Destruction (11) to avoid
being burned with fire from Heaven (8). When he proposes fleeing, like Dorothy he is considered mentally imbalanced, his family
concluding that "some frenzy distemper" affects him (9), and none
will accompany him. After his pilgrimage and death, his wife an-

nounces that she and her children are fleeing the city, whereupon she too is treated as if she were mentally ill (182). Both Baum's and Bunyan's books, therefore, open on scenes of physical and spiritual poverty amid vast, empty fields threatened by the sun or fire from heaven, and both portray unsympathetic relatives who, while agreeing circumstances are dreadful, consider it madness to leave.

Rereading Baum with these similarities in mind, we must consider Dorothy's grim circumstances to be representative of America as Baum saw it at the turn of the century, focused more on temporal than spiritual matters. Dorothy's aunt and uncle reflect despair, and we cannot imagine their finding security and happiness on their own. Only the intervention of a cyclone, ironically, opens the way for them to escape the dissolution, both physical and spiritual, that threatens them.

Dorothy's adventures in the Land of Oz are not depicted as a dream, but as real-life experience in an isolated land somewhere on earth.[17] When Dorothy returns to Kansas, Uncle Henry has built a new farmhouse (259), thus precluding a dream experience. Nevertheless, because she falls asleep while transported by the cyclone (16), and because the Land of Oz is fantastical, the implication of dream fantasy is strong. This element is important because both Bunyan title pages specify the accounts are offered "under the Similitude of a Dream." In addition, Bunyan claims to have dreamed part 1 while imprisoned in "a Denn" or jail (8), which bears similarity to Dorothy's falling asleep in the one-room, cell-like farmhouse while being carried off by the cyclone. Bunyan begins part 2 by stating that his vision of Christiana's journey also came to him in a dream (174). Within these dream frameworks in Bunyan are yet other dreams (156, 178, 222), emphasizing this aspect of his allegory.

Dorothy is supposed to be five or six years old, but she appears more mature than this.[18] Bunyan describes only one young girl, Much-afraid (282), who is timorous and so vaguely delineated it is impossible to imagine Dorothy being modeled after her. Baum's young heroine more closely resembles Christian and Christiana, despite their difference in age and purity. All three are optimistic, determined, resourceful, and compassionate; all are essentially alone, Dorothy orphaned, Christian separated from his family, and Christiana widowed; and both Christiana and Dorothy lead a band of travelers to a city. Whereas her adult counterparts possess spiri-

tual weaknesses typical of adults who have grown up in the City of
Destruction, Dorothy is an innocent and untainted child.

Dorothy's arrival in Munchkin Country suggests two representative groups of correspondences with Bunyan: the narrator's description of the Land of Oz, and Dorothy's encounter with three men and a witch. When Dorothy arrives in Oz, the sights and people appear "strange" to her (20, 26), as does the Land of the Winkies, where she is later held captive (155). The entire country, in fact, is described as a "strange land" (33). Baum's basic idea of transporting a young girl to a country alien to her, and describing it repeatedly as "strange," may have come to him from Giant Maull's false accusation of Great-heart: "Thou practises the craft of a Kidnapper, thou gatherest up Women and Children, and carriest them into a strange Country" (244). Both Bunyan and Baum consider the regions through which their travelers pass to be odd, unfamiliar, and often hostile country in which they can never be entirely at ease. This view of the world is taught by most religious faiths, and Dorothy's eventual move to Oz with her aunt and uncle must be understood in this light: it is ever so much better than Kansas, truly "a family-style Utopia" (Nye 12), but not their eternal destination.

Landing in the Munchkin countryside, Dorothy is approached by three Munchkin men and a small old woman wearing a white hat and a gown sprinkled with little stars that glisten like diamonds (20). She tells Dorothy of the four witches in Oz: the Wicked Witch of the East, killed by Dorothy's falling house; the Wicked Witch of the West, a midget with an eye-patch and pigtails who later captures Dorothy; Glinda, the lovely Good Witch of the South, who later assists Dorothy in returning home; and herself, the Good Witch of the North. While she and Dorothy converse, the body of the East Witch disappears beneath the farmhouse: she was so old, says the North Witch, she dried up quickly in the sun. Only her silver shoes with pointed toes remain, so after shaking the dust from them, the witch presents them to Dorothy (22, 25). Baum's good witches are attractively dressed, whether old and wrinkled (like North), or young and beautiful (like Glinda). Both bad witches are old, repulsive, and tyrannical, the West Witch later forcing Dorothy to work in her kitchen as a slave (150–51). All these aspects are noteworthy, for they can be traced to the single Bunyan passage about a witch.

Bunyan's witch, named Madam Bubble, is associated with the Enchanted Ground, a dangerous region she has cursed (123, 301).

Portrayed as tall and comely, Madam Bubble appears to pilgrims beautifully dressed, enticing them with her body and her purse. Sometimes she casts goldlike dust from her purse to tempt them. Despite her appearance, she is old and has brought many to bondage, the gallows, or Hell (300, 302). Baum's witches are similar: a contrast between youth and old age, the wearing of beautiful garments, an association with dust, the ground, and enslavement. Madam Bubble's positive and negative features may have given Baum the notion of creating good as well as bad witches, a feature of *Oz* that continues to provoke criticism. Such a reaction, in light of Baum's modeling *Oz* on a Christian allegory and its strong strain of moralism (Nye 5), now seems largely unjustified.[19]

The North Witch informs Dorothy that a charm is connected with the silver shoes, although she does not know what it is (25). Dorothy decides to wear them, her own being worn thin (32). Much later, she loses a shoe temporarily to the West Witch (153), and finally she is instructed how to use the charm of the shoes to return home, for they can carry her anywhere in the world (257). While she is being transported back to Kansas, the shoes fall off and are lost forever in the desert (259). Several Bunyan passages may have inspired these magical silver shoes. The armory at House Beautiful contains pairs of shoes that never wear out (54) and, like Dorothy's, will carry a person anywhere. Also, a Mr. By-ends boasts of being most zealous "when Religion goes in his Silver Slippers," or when ostentatious (99).[20] Finally, when Christiana's company passes through the region cursed by Madam Bubble, some of her grandchildren lose their shoes in the mire (296), just as Dorothy loses hers over the desert.

Dorothy begins to comprehend the extent of her predicament when the North Witch offers her no hope of returning home, so she begins to cry, causing the Munchkin men to weep also (26). This prompts the witch to balance her cap upon her nose and count to three, whereupon the cap changes into a slate with the message "LET DOROTHY GO TO THE CITY OF EMERALDS." Determined to visit the city and ask the Wizard for help, Dorothy pleads with the witch to accompany her because the way promises to be dark and fearful at times, but she is gently refused (26–27). Yet the witch gives her a protective kiss on the forehead, assuring her that no one will dare injure a person who has been kissed by the Witch of the North, and her lips leave a "round, shining mark" (27). The Munchkins depart, and the witch whirls about on her left heel three times, then disappears (28).

This imagery comes from Bunyan, much of it associated with Hill Calvary and the Crucifixion. Beyond the Wicket Gate and Interpreter's House, Christian is observed weeping at the summit of Calvary (38). Earlier, Evangelist had given him a parchment roll (appearing in *Oz* as the invitation on the slate) enjoining him to flee the city (10) and return home to his heavenly Father. At Calvary he receives another roll that comforts and reassures him (38), which functions as a certificate when he arrives at the City (163). Evangelist had instructed him where to begin his journey (10), then after departing, reappeared to give him a kiss (24). On Calvary, Christian is approached by three "shining ones," angels sent to prepare him for the journey, their raiment bright like the North Witch's glistening white gown. One of them places a mark on his forehead, like Dorothy's, to identify him as a pilgrim (38). When the angels depart, Christian takes three leaps for joy, similar to the witch's three revolutions, then proceeds to the bottom of the hill and discovers three sleeping men bound with irons on their heels. He then encounters two men who tumble over a nearby wall on the left side of the narrow path (39). Presumably these disparate references to the heel and the left side reappear as Baum's image of the witch's left heel. Bunyan's three "shining ones," Christian's three leaps, and the three sleeping men possibly gave Baum the notion of using the number three, three times in the same scene.

Part 2 of *Progress* also contains images that pertain to *Oz*. Christiana's invitation to the City, although not on a slate like Dorothy's or a roll like Christian's, is similar in being delivered by an elderly, supernatural person, a heavenly messenger named Mr. Secret. He presents a letter inviting Christiana to the City, whereupon she (like Dorothy) begs to be accompanied but is refused (179–80). Shortly after embarking, Christiana, her children, and Mercy are kissed by the Keeper of the Wicket Gate (190), and at the Interpreter's House they each receive a sacred mark on their foreheads that makes them appear like angels (208), an image reinforced when Christiana and her granddaughters later have jewels placed on their foreheads (288).

The sacred or magic tokens (the forehead mark, scrolls, and letter of invitation in Bunyan; the silver shoes, forehead mark, and slate invitation in Baum) have four major symbolic functions: protection, reassurance, certification, and liberation. In *Progress,* the forehead mark, the roll, and the letter represent God's protection (50, 180). They comfort and reassure pilgrims, and the roll and letter certify the bearers at the City gate after their liberation from the world. Dorothy's shoes and forehead mark are protective, for when she is captured by the Winged Monkeys and the West Witch, the shoes and mark prevent them from harming her (148, 150). Dorothy is reassured by these charms, and only because of them is she allowed to speak with the Wizard (126). The slate also functions as a certificate, giving her an official invitation to the City, and the shoes eventually liberate her from the Land of Oz (258).

Departing for the City at last, Baum's "little girl" (19) follows the road through Munchkin farmland, "walking briskly [with] her silver shoes tinkling merrily on the hard, yellow roadbed" (33), an image that may owe its inspiration to Bunyan's prefatory allusion (part 2) to "little Tripping [nimbly stepping] Maidens [who] follow God" (172). The depiction of Dorothy may also have been influenced by Bunyan's observation that "a little Child might lead them" (281), meaning a group with two disabled pilgrims. Bunyan's allusion is to Isaiah 11:6, which depicts a child leading animals, including a lion.[21] Dorothy leads a small band of travelers, including a lion, each claiming to have a disability, either of mind (Scarecrow), of body (Tin Man), or of spirit (Lion). The value of Dorothy's kindhearted assistance to them is made clear at book's end when each one attributes his progress and good fortune to the girl. Without her, Scarecrow would still be hanging on a pole in the cornfield, Tin Man still rusting in the forest, and Lion still fearing the forest creatures (257).

Scarecrow, Tin Man, and Lion owe many elements of their creation to Bunyan. Dorothy encounters Scarecrow high on a pole in a cornfield, his arms outstretched, his body stuffed with straw. He complains of not feeling well and tells Dorothy he yearns for some brains (36–38). As he accompanies her, he often stumbles because of holes in the road, requiring Dorothy to pick him up (43); later in the story he is pulled apart by the Winged Monkeys (148). Later still, Scarecrow reveals that the Wizard has appointed him ruler of the Emerald City, where he is already loved by the inhabitants (255).

This straw man appears to originate in several characters and situations in *Progress.* A pilgrim, Mr. Fearing, stumbled at "every

Straw" that anybody cast in his way (249).[22] A scarecrow on a pole
calls to mind the image of the Crucifixion, particularly in a work,
like *Oz*, based on a Christian allegory. Like Jesus, Scarecrow suffers
on the pole and is a model of humility, compassion, and leadership, eventually ruling the City when the Wizard departs. Further,
Dorothy encounters Scarecrow at a point in the story analogous to
Christian's encounter with the Cross at Hill Calvary. Scarecrow's
supposed lack of intelligence may derive from Mrs. Know-nothing
or Mr. Feeble-mind (184, 266), the latter being one of seven major
figures Christiana encounters on her pilgrimage (172–73). Scarecrow's being picked apart by flying monkeys bears a similarity to
Mr. Feeble-mind's being threatened by a giant who intends "to pick
his Bones" (266). In addition, Scarecrow's need of assistance is like
that of Mr. Feeble-mind, a man of no strength at all who must be
helped along the road (266–67).

After Scarecrow joins her, Dorothy enters a dense forest where a
rusting Tin Man is encountered near his cottage. He explains that
while enchanted by the East Witch he had chopped off his own legs
and head, but when he had chopped himself in half, his heart had
been lost forever (57–58).[23] Notwithstanding, he shows himself to
be tenderhearted and joins the group as an axe-toting protector.
Soon he is clearing the road where the trees and branches grow so
thick nobody can pass (57). A Bunyan character with many of these
traits is Mr. Great-heart, who also is associated with a house (being
a servant to the Interpreter) and whose name describes Tin Man's
essential nature. Like Tin Man, he is associated with metal, having
a sword, helmet, and shield (208). He, too, cuts off arms and heads
(of giants, 219, 245, 267, 282), guards women and children who
are on pilgrimage, and leads travelers through a region overgrown
with grass (218), analogous to Tin Man's clearing the Yellow Road.
His association with the heart is also explicit, not only in his name,
but also in his alluding to a character named No-heart (213).

Baum's Lion, while claiming to be king of beasts, admits he is
a coward (68). When confronted by a ball of fire in the Wizard's
Throne Room, he creeps "tremblingly" to a place near the door
(134). Nevertheless, he roars on occasion (e.g., 66) and near the end
of the narrative has gained the courage to kill an elephant-sized spider (239–41). Also, he loves flowers, "always did like flowers, they
seem so helpless and frail," and soon he is lying fast asleep in a field
of poppies, overcome by their scent (93, 95). Cowardly Lion may

derive, in part, from two lions encountered near House Beautiful that are harmless because they are chained (45–46, 218). Mercy spies another ineffectual lion following the pilgrims that promptly retreats when confronted by Great-heart (242).

In all likelihood, however, Baum's major source for Cowardly Lion is the insecure Mr. Fearing, Mr. Feeble-mind's nephew described at great length in part 2. His chief trait is cowardice, for everything "that had the least appearance of Opposition in it" frightened him, and Bunyan labels him "Chickin-hearted" (249–50). At the Wicket Gate he knocks timidly, but when the Keeper opens and asks, "Thou trembling one, what wantest thou?" he falls to the ground in fear (250). Bunyan associates Mr. Fearing with lions, another reason to believe Cowardly Lion is modeled after him: at the Slough of Despond he is heard "roaring" for more than a month before venturing across (249); Bunyan notes that he did not fear lions, as his fear was merely about his acceptance at the City (251, 254). When he anticipates rejection, Mr. Fearing weeps (251), just as Cowardly Lion weeps when Dorothy slaps him for threatening Toto (67). Finally, there is Mr. Fearing's love of flowers, a memorable correlation with Baum's beast in the field of poppies: while in the Valley of Humiliation, "he would lie down, embrace the Ground, and kiss the very Flowers" (252).

Dorothy and her companions next encounter two ditches. The road is disrupted by a "great ditch" that Baum describes as "very wide" and "very deep," with many jagged rocks at the bottom and steep sides. With the travelers, one at a time, on his back, Lion leaps the chasm (77–78). They next confront a second ditch, which they find too wide for Lion to leap, so Tin Man fells a tree across it. While crossing, the party is startled by "a sharp growl" and discovers two Kalidahs, beasts with the bodies of bears and heads of tigers, bounding after them (80). Lion fears that the Kalidahs are apt to "tear us to pieces," but he manages a mighty roar that causes the Kalidahs to pause, Dorothy to scream, and Scarecrow to fall over backward. Tin Man saves the day by chopping loose the tree-bridge on which the Kalidahs are crossing the wide ditch, sending the snarling beasts to their deaths, "dashed to pieces" on the sharp rocks below (81).

Approximately at this juncture in *Progress,* pilgrims encounter the Valley of Humiliation and the Valley of the Shadow of Death. The sides of the first valley are precipitous (55–56, 236), and the second valley is deeper than the first, both details retained by Baum. Within the second valley, writes Bunyan, lies a "very deep Ditch" (62), most likely the source of Baum's depiction of the first chasm. The path through the second valley is "exceeding narrow," and with the ditch on one side and a quagmire on the other, the way is hazardous, particularly since the valley is quite dark (62). This narrow pathway reappears as Baum's narrow tree-bridge across the second ditch. As Christian passes through the valley, he often fears he will "tip over into the mire," perhaps Baum's source of Scarecrow's falling over backward when Lion roars.

In the first valley, Christian is attacked by Apollyon, a beast with wings of a dragon, feet of a bear, and mouth of a lion that makes a "hideous roaring" (56, 60). Doubtless Apollyon was Baum's impulse for the fearful, growling Kalidahs; his roar may be the origin of Cowardly Lion's roar. In addition, the Kalidahs may owe something to the group of Fiends Christian hears coming after him, "nearer and nearer," in the second valley. At this same location, Bunyan's pilgrim fears "he should be torn in pieces" by creatures he cannot see in the dark, a description echoed in Cowardly Lion's fear the Kalidahs will "tear us to pieces." When the fiends are nearly upon him, Christian cries out with a "most vehement voice," much like the threatening roar of Cowardly Lion that causes the Kalidahs to retreat (63). Finally, at the end of the second valley Christian sees blood, bones, ashes, and the "mangled bodies of men" (65), and Christiana's group sees a man cast into the ditch "with his flesh all rent and torn" (243–44), images resurfacing in Baum as the bodies of the Kalidahs on the jagged rocks in the second ditch. Baum's phrase "dashed to pieces" also occurs in Bunyan with reference to the fall of Vain-Confidence into a deep pit (112). Like Bunyan's valleys, Baum's ditches present travelers with frightening obstacles threatening them with death.

After the episodes at the ditches, Baum's travelers arrive at a river. Scarecrow has found only nuts in the forest for Dorothy (76), but at the swift, deep river (88) Dorothy finds plenty to eat. The perennially green meadows are dotted with bright flowers, and the road is "bordered with trees hanging full of delicious fruits" (82). After a night by the river, Dorothy breakfasts on fruit, including plums (87). Each of these images has a counterpart in Bunyan. After Vanity Fair, Christian and his companion Hopeful arrive at the River of Life, where they discover green trees bearing all kinds of fruit on both sides of the river (rather than the road, as in Baum), and a meadow verdant all year long and beautified with flowers (110–11). Children eating nuts and fruit do not appear at this juncture, but they appear later in part 2 at Graius's Inn where Christiana's group is presented a dish of nuts; someone observes that nuts are especially harmful to children's teeth, prompting the innkeeper to recite a poem about nuts (263). The narrator recommends fruit as wholesome (280), and one of the boys relates an illness he suffered from eating green plums (194, 230, 263), probably Baum's source for Dorothy's plum breakfast.

The *Oz* travelers attempt to cross the river on a raft they have made, but they are carried swiftly downstream far from the Yellow Road, and Scarecrow becomes stranded on a pole midstream. When they manage to reach the opposite shore, they must pass through a dangerous region to regain the road. The river constitutes the only juncture at which they become sidetracked on their journey. Similarly, Christian detours only once, at a river where he and Hopeful turn aside onto a soft path that soon leads them astray. A thunderstorm swells the streams they had crossed, preventing their return to the road (112–13); they soon find themselves prisoners at Doubting Castle, an episode Baum re-creates as Dorothy's imprisonment at the castle of the West Witch.

Following Scarecrow's rescue from the river, the travelers seek to return to the road. Passing through a pleasant area near the Emerald City, they hear the singing of brightly colored birds and marvel at the flowers, eventually coming upon "great clusters of scarlet poppies." Their way leads them through a large meadow of poppies so brilliant they dazzle Dorothy's eyes. Baum describes their "spicy scent" as poisonous and deadly (93–96). When Dorothy succumbs to the oppressive odor, Lion exclaims, "If we leave [her] here she will die" (92–93), but Lion and Toto are also overcome, so it remains for the nonmortals, unaffected by the flowers, to rescue the party. Scarecrow and Tin Man fashion a chair, with their hands as the seat, to carry Dorothy and her pet to a lovely place beside the river with soft grass and a fresh breeze (95–96). On a cart made by Tin Man, Lion is dragged from the field by thousands of mice.

The primary Bunyan source of these gardenlike scenes, excluding the field of poppies, appears to be the Land of Beulah through which pilgrims pass shortly before reaching the City. In this pleasant country, pilgrims hear the singing of birds, see a multitude of flowers, and find the air sweet and pleasant (154), the images (birds, flowers, air) re-created by Baum in the same order. The region of scarlet poppies seems to come from a Bunyan location immediately before the Land of Beulah and the City, the Enchanted Ground cursed by Madam Bubble. Although no flowers are mentioned growing in the area, the air "naturally tended to make one drowsy." Christian warns his companion that if they fall asleep in the area, they will never awake because the air produces a state approximating death (136), so their strategy is to keep talking while they walk.

Even the lengthy religious discourse between Christian and Hopeful as they cross the Enchanted Ground appears to have impressed itself upon Baum. Hopeful alludes to Christ "upon a mercy-seat" (141), most likely the source of the chair and seat fashioned by Dorothy's friends to save her. Hopeful proclaims fervently, "Had I now a thousand gallons of blood in my body, I could spill it all for the sake of the Lord Jesus" (144), probably the origin of Baum's image of the field of red poppies (93). Bunyan's reference to vast quantities of blood and Baum's to vast quantities of scarlet poppies both connote death. The general import of Baum's poppy scene is similar to that of Bunyan's at Doubting Castle, namely, when travelers leave the "strait and narrow way," as both groups do at a river, they risk being diverted permanently from their goal. Christian and Hopeful are imprisoned and threatened with death, and Dorothy and Lion are threatened with death without the aid of their friends.

After regaining the road, Dorothy's group spends a night with a poor farmer who has injured his leg (112). He tells the travelers the Wizard keeps "a great pot of courage in his throne room which he has covered with a golden plate, to keep it from running over" (114). The farmer is modeled, it would seem, after Bunyan's Mr. Ready-to-halt, a crippled pilgrim Christiana meets, also near the City, making his way on crutches. The Wizard's pot and the adjective "golden" probably come from this scene as well, for the angel who invites Mr. Ready-to-halt to the Celestial City says, "I have broken thy golden Bowl" (307); "broken" perhaps reappears as the broken leg of the Oz farmer.

Approaching the City of Emeralds, Dorothy's group is astonished at its brightness, which dazzles even the painted eyes of Scarecrow

(115). To protect their eyes, the Gate Guardian places upon them green spectacles like those worn by all the City's inhabitants (117). Then he warns that if they are "on an idle or foolish errand," the Wizard might destroy them, for he is quite terrible to dishonest persons (116–17). They discover the City to be studded with sparkling emeralds, the inhabitants seemingly dressed in green and having greenish skin (121–22). The atmosphere is distinctly fairlike, its many shops offering such commodities as candy, popcorn, and lemonade. Dorothy and her friends cause quite a stir in the streets (122). The City's magistrate, the Wizard, rules by benevolent deception; later, he departs in a balloon (207–08). Baum's metropolis, in short, is glorious, colorful, and festive, but to Dorothy it represents only bitter disappointment (211), for the Wizard fails to help her return to Kansas.

The striking appearance of Baum's Emerald City derives from Bunyan's Celestial City. The reflections of the sun render Zion so "extreamly glorious" that approaching pilgrims cannot look upon it without "an Instrument made for that purpose" (156, 223), presumably spectacles of tinted glass. Like the Emerald City, Zion is ornamented with precious stones (155). The matter of honesty at the City gate is raised in *Progress* (parts 1 and 2), as it is in *Oz*, in the following ways. Christian meets a young man named Ignorance near the gate who attempts to enter without credentials (162); in part 2, he is called "green-headed Ignorance" (294), a memorable description that may have led to the greenish skins of the Emerald City inhabitants, and a reaffirmation of the ignorance of the Oz citizens that has been fostered by the Wizard. When Christiana prepares to enter the City, she meets a pilgrim named Mr. Honest (308–09).

The Emerald City's festive atmosphere, however, derives from Bunyan's Vanity Fair, with its rows of streets where worldly commodities are sold (88). Pilgrims entering the town are questioned (90), just as Dorothy's group is, and they too cause a hubbub while passing through the streets (89). The magistrate of the Fair, Beelzebub, grants citizens whatever they desire, deceiving them into complacency with worldly pleasures. Although Beelzebub does not ascend into the sky like the Wizard, Faithful's soul ascends in a chariot from Vanity Fair to the Celestial City (97). In appearance, the Emerald City is based upon the Celestial City, but its atmosphere and its deceptive, fraudulent nature comes from Vanity Fair, that worldly and iniquitous town offering pilgrims no hope, as long as they remain, of completing their journey to their heavenly home.[24]

Eventually Dorothy and her friends are admitted, one at a time, to the Throne Room at the Wizard's palace, where Dorothy meets a giant head, Scarecrow a lady with wings, Tin Man a grotesque beast, and Lion a ball of fire—each a mechanical trick performed by the Wizard (126–36). All but the last have counterparts in Bunyan. The giant head is reminiscent of the severed heads of giants slain by Great-heart, three of which are erected as warnings to pilgrims (245, 267, 283). The winged lady resembles winged spirits in the Celestial City (162). The beast, large as an elephant and having the head of a rhinoceros, five eyes, five arms, and five legs, is similar to Bunyan's dragonlike monster with seven heads and ten horns (277) that derives, in turn, from one of the Beasts of Revelation 17:3.

Having been promised assistance by the Wizard if they destroy the West Witch, Dorothy's disappointed party departs to find her. Seeing them approach her castle, the witch dispatches a wolf pack to "tear them to pieces," but Tin Man kills the beasts and piles them in a heap (141–42). She sends a flock of crows to peck out their eyes and tear them to pieces, but these are likewise killed and piled up (143–44). When her enslaved Winkies reveal their fear of Lion, she beats them for cowardice (145). Only with the aid of the Winged Monkeys is she able to capture Dorothy, Toto, and Lion. When the latter proves incorrigible, she threatens him with starvation (151). She threatens to beat Dorothy with an umbrella, an article representing her fear of water, and she actually strikes Toto with it, causing him to bite her leg (151–52). She fears water because her blood has dried up many years before, rendering her only dry skin and bones (152). Consequently, when she robs Dorothy of a silver shoe and the girl throws a bucket of water on her, the liquid causes her to melt away, turning her into "a brown, melted, shapeless mass" that spreads over the floor and obliging Dorothy to throw another bucket of water over the mess in order to sweep it out the door (154).

These scenes at the witch's castle seem to have their origin in two episodes from *Progress*. The first occurs at Doubting Castle where Christian and Hopeful, after being benighted by a rainstorm, are imprisoned by Giant Despair. His wife Diffidence is probably

Baum's model for the midget-sized West Witch, although opposite in size. Diffidence urges her husband to beat the pilgrims, which he does with a cudgel after berating them as though "they were dogs" (114), an incident that corresponds to the witch's threatening Dorothy and striking Toto. Christian and Hopeful, like Lion, are threatened with starvation (114). Many prisoners have their eyes put out by the giant (121), which probably prompted Baum to create a one-eyed witch who sends birds to peck out the eyes of Dorothy and her friends. Christian and Hopeful are shown piles of bones and skulls of prisoners (117), corresponding to Baum's heaps of dead wolves and crows. Diffidence urges Despair to tell the pilgrims he will "tear them in pieces" (117), a threat repeated by Baum's witch in sending wolves and crows to attack the travelers. Bunyan's thunderstorm probably inspired the witch's umbrella.

The melting of the witch, however, appears to have its genesis in an episode at Interpreter's House in which Christian is shown a parlor that is full of dust because it is never swept. A man called in to sweep it succeeds only in stirring up the dust, so a girl is directed to sprinkle the floor with water, enabling it to be swept and cleaned properly. The dust represents sin and corruption, and the sprinkling of water represents goodness and religious truth (29–30), Bunyan's point being that humankind cannot remove the effects of sin without divine assistance. Because Bunyan's dust becomes Baum's melted witch, and his girl becomes Dorothy, the Wizard must embody the ineffectual man who cannot clean the room alone; indeed, the Wizard admits he has lived in deadly fear of the wicked witches for many years and been unable to rid the Land of Oz of them (188).

Back at the Emerald City to report the death of the witch, the travelers discover that although the Wizard is thought to be immortal (27), omnipotent (114), and omniscient (182), he is actually none of these. When Toto knocks over a "screen" in the Throne Room, the Wizard is discovered to be merely a little old man with a bald head and wrinkled face (183). Dorothy later calls him the Great and Terrible Humbug (191). The Wizard's concealment behind the screen associates him with Bunyan's Mr. Fearing, who also hides behind a "Screen" at House Beautiful to take in conversation, being too ashamed and insecure to show himself (251). The Wizard, nevertheless, is a good man who tries to help Dorothy's company, but his incompetence is most apparent when he inadver-

tently leaves her behind when he departs in a balloon. That Baum
conceived the Wizard as a parody of God seems unlikely, because
he is shown to have no supernatural attributes at all. Nor can he
closely represent Beelzebub, Lord of Vanity Fair, for he is not inherently evil, only deceptive and impotent, as males in the Oz series
invariably are.[25] He cannot represent traditional Christian clergy, as
Downing implies (28), because clergy make no claims of divinity as
he does. Rather, he appears to represent the kindhearted men of
the world as Baum perceived them: benevolent, patient, mechani-
cally minded, yet, when confronted by evil, fearful, dissembling,
and powerless.

When Dorothy and her friends leave the City for the last time,
Baum's reliance on *Progress* dwindles, but he does include a final
episode from Bunyan, that of the Fighting Trees.[26] En route to the
palace of Glinda for help in returning Dorothy to Kansas, the company encounters a thick forest in which a tree grabs Scarecrow and
flings him to the ground. Tin Man chops off the offending branch,
allowing all to pass except Toto, who is caught by another branch
and shaken until he howls (222–23). In a similarly chaotic scene
at the Enchanted Ground, in an area overgrown with briers and
thornbushes, one of Christiana's party tumbles over a bush, then
a grandchild cries, "I am down," and another child cries, "The
Bushes have got such a fast hold on me, I think I cannot get away
from them" (296).

Following four chapters of charming but tangential episodes unrelated to *Progress,* Baum's "bright and joyous" book draws to a
close.[27] At the castle of the beautiful Glinda, Witch of the South,
Dorothy learns how to activate the magic silver shoes. After bidding
her friends farewell, she clicks her magic heels together three times
and repeats the words "Take me home to Aunt Em!" (258). Baum's
focus on returning home continues to the end, for when she is once
again in the arms of her aunt, she exclaims, "I'm so glad to be at
home again!" Unlike Christian and Christiana, however, Dorothy
has only just begun her journey through life.

Despite Baum's considerable indebtedness to Bunyan and his attempt to replicate *Progress*'s spiritual power, *Oz* displays a quite
different independent style, mood, and character. It is addressed
to children, particularly girls, and presents a distinctly matriarchal
society.[28] It introduces automatons and benevolent witches who in-

termix with mortals, and it replaces the supernatural powers of God and Satan with that of good and bad witches. Yet Baum seems to have consciously tapped into the inherent power of Bunyan's myth to activate his own imagination. The number and nature of similarities between *Oz* and *Progress* suggests that Baum's imaginative faculties were so indelibly affected by *Progress* that he was continually predisposed to draw upon its episodes, characters, images, and diction, as though he sensed in them a power to bring his own creation to life. Plainly, the mythical land depicted in *Oz* owes much of its creation to the "strange blendings and fusings" (Lowes 55) of many elements of *Progress* that took place in his imagination. Baum's reliance upon Bunyan continues even beyond *Oz*, but much less extensively.[29]

The essence of *Oz* thus lies close to religious allegory, which casts additional light upon Nathanson's assertion that the book exhibits signs of being ambiguously related to both religion and secularism (*Rainbow* 14). Baum began with a series of overtly religious episodes, removed the obtrusive religious trappings, and recast them. Inevitably many religious elements in addition to imagery remain: idealism, humility, morality, compassion, and the necessity of supernatural aid in human progress (the latter finding embodiment in Glinda the Good, Baum's substitute for a traditional male Deity).[30] Like religion, the book deals with the most fundamental problems of human existence, including origin, destiny, and identity (Nathanson, *Rainbow* 13–14). Baum's concerns, therefore, are more than psychological, and *Oz* is more than a juvenile story about "the power of positive thinking" (Billman 242). Baum once admitted to concealing "a wholesome lesson" behind each episode, and Nye believes one of the pleasures of reading Baum lies in its discovery: a spiritual theme evident in Baum's depiction of Scarecrow, Tin Man, and Lion, for example, is that all people have within them, in embryonic form, the positive attributes they seek (Nye 5).

Baum apparently hoped that *The Wonderful Wizard of Oz* would affect his young readers in much the same way *The Pilgrim's Progress* affected him as a child or youth, opening to him a vision of a spiritual journey from fear to reassurance, from discouragement to hope, from selfishness to compassion. We can be certain he knew he was retelling a Biblically based allegory, and it seems logical that his purpose in using Bunyan was a moral and spiritual one. Baum repeatedly stresses faith in supernatural benevolence, hope in the future, and love for others, but the greatest of these, the "first law" of Oz, is love.

Notes

I should like to acknowledge the encouragement and generous assistance of Lester R. Dickey, Elizabeth Keyser, Roberta Trites, my wife, Jeanine, and our children in bringing this study to completion; and to dedicate it to our granddaughter, Kayla J. Franson.

1. *The Wonderful Wizard of Oz*, shortened to *The Wizard of Oz* soon after its first appearance, has outsold all other American children's books. It was the author's tenth published title. Baum's lifetime output was about 85 books, including 13 *Oz* sequels; and after his death in 1919, six other authors produced 27 additional *Oz* books, the latest appearing in 1963. (For bibliographies of the *Oz* canon, see Gardner and Nye 201–08; Hearn, *Annotated* 363–81; Moore 182–94; and Greene and Martin 178–81.) Despite its immense and enduring popularity, *Oz* has received scant critical attention. The first serious study was by Edward Wagenknecht, *Utopia Americana* (1929) (cited as *UA* in text), supplemented by "'Utopia Americana': A Generation Afterwards" (1962). Subsequent essays worthy of note include those by Gardner and Nye in *The Wizard of Oz and Who He Was* (1957) and the useful collection in Michael Patrick Hearn's edition of *Oz* (1963). The only book-length studies of Baum's work are by Moore (1974) and Nathanson (1991).

2. The map of the Land of Oz first appeared in *Tik-Tok of Oz* (1914), presumably drawn to Baum's specifications by John R. Neill, illustrator of all the author's *Oz* books but the first, which was illustrated by William W. Denslow; a reproduction of the map is readily available in Greene and Martin 44–45. This map should not be confused with a recent map appearing in the Del Rey (Ballantine) Books edition of Baum's series (1979–85), on which the Yellow Brick Road is a winding one.

3. Like Baum's book, *The Pilgrim's Progress* (1678) led to a sequel, part 2, published in 1684. Thereafter, both parts were regularly published together. I cite from the standard critical edition by Clarendon Press, ed. Wharey and Sharrock, without reproducing the edition's frequent italic type.

4. The edition of Baum used in this study is an "unabridged and unaltered republication of the first edition" by Dover Press, 1960, which includes Baum's introduction and Denslow's original illustrations. *Oz* was first published in Chicago by George M. Hill.

5. *Progress*, Darton asserts, "is a children's book, however you frame definitions" (65). Among those who point out Bunyan's strong influence on American literature for children is McMaster (103). Bunyan did write books specifically for children, such as *Divine Emblems, A Book for Boys and Girls,* and *Country Rimes for Children.*

6. Moore claims that Baum refers to the *Arabian Nights, Aesop's Fables,* and *Pilgrim's Progress* in sequels to *Oz* (47), but I have been able to verify only his reference to the *Arabian Nights* (*Dorothy and the Wizard in Oz* [1908], chap. 10). Littlefield (passim) proposes the American political scene as Baum's inspiration for *Oz*, claiming the book was intended as an allegory of America's emergence into the twentieth century. Gardner notes many parallels, but also profound differences, between *Oz* and *Alice in Wonderland* (1865), the most frequently cited Baum source ("A Child's Garden" 19; see also his introduction to Baum's *Magical Monarch of Mo* ix–x, as well as Moore 47, Beckwith 76, and Greene and Martin 47). The standard Baum biog-

raphy acknowledges only the influence of Dickens in the creation of Oz characters throughout Baum's series (Baum and MacFall 24). Other suggested sources include the following: for the episode of the frozen heart in *The Scarecrow of Oz* (1915), Hawthorne's "Feather-top: A Moralized Legend" (Bewley 259–60); for Dorothy's journey beneath the earth in *Dorothy and the Wizard in Oz*, Jules Verne's *Journey to the Centre of the Earth* (1864) (Vidal 40); for an episode in *Ozma of Oz* (1907), Stephen Crane's "The Open Boat" (1898) (Bewley 256–59).

7. Wagenknecht is the first to claim that *Oz* is unique, and he focuses on Baum's ability to turn everyday material into folklore (*UA* 24–28). Carpenter and Prichard label Baum "the first writer to create an unforgettable full-length original American fantasy" (51), and Carpenter and Shirley claim Baum invented "a new kind of fairy tale, uniquely modern and American" (11). Hearn believes Baum to be "among the most experimental and purposeful of American writers for children" ("L. Frank Baum" 65).

8. Baum's statement was reported many years after his death by a friend, Rev. E. P. Ryland (Potter 12; Hearn, *Annotated* 73).

9. Notwithstanding Baum's disclaimer, *Oz* is the most brutal of the series, according to Hearn, dramatic tension deriving from the many "terrifying" dangers to be overcome ("L. Frank Baum" 63).

10. Wagenknecht's statement is typical: Baum's story, he writes, is the sort of romance that we get in *Gulliver's Travels*, in *Pilgrim's Progress*, and other satiric or allegorical travel literature (*UA* 11). Others who are vaguely reminded of *Progress* when reading *Oz*, yet do not recognize it as a Baum source, include Littlefield (50), Nathanson (*Rainbow* 208), and McMaster (103).

11. Baum omits such unsettling episodes as Faithful's torture and death by fire (97), Christiana's being threatened with rape (195), and Timorous and Mistrust having hot irons driven through their tongues (218).

12. From Baum's final seven (of twenty-four) chapters, the MGM screenwriters retain only the bout with the Fighting Trees and Dorothy's return home; in contrast, the only major episode from earlier chapters (those heavily influenced by Bunyan) that is excluded from the film is that of mice rescuing Lion from the poppy field. For an excellent discussion of narrative strengths and weaknesses of both book and MGM film, see the essay by Billman.

13. Barasch 56. In 1890 Baum published an attack on organized religion, and subsequent references in his works to churches and ministers are seldom favorable (Hearn, *Annotated* 73; see also 69–72). Downing calls the MGM film version "one of the most devastating exposés of institutional religion ever to reach the screen" (28). Nevertheless, all his life Baum believed strongly in God and the immortality of the soul (Gardner, "Royal Historian" 28–29).

14. In part 2 of *Progress*, Bunyan often focuses on issues important to children and women that would have been of great interest to Baum as a youth and an adult. An example is Graius's speech on behalf of women, whom he says are "highly favoured" of God and "sharers with [men] in the Grace of Life" (261); an example from part 1 is Bunyan's discussion of whether it is unmanly to be spiritually minded (72). Baum developed a lifelong concern for the welfare of children during a childhood troubled by chronic illness and two unhappy years at a military academy. His inclinations were never typically boyish. He married a strong-willed woman whose mother was a nationally known feminist, and he wrote 17 books for girls under a female pseudonym. For further information on his childhood and personality, see Baum and MacFall (chap. 2), Harmetz (310–21), and Carpenter and Shirley (12–16); on his interest in women's rights, see Nye (12), Gardner ("Royal Historian" 23), Shulman (33), and Nathanson (*Rainbow* 69). Gardner detects in Baum, however, a

discomfort with the New Woman and finds "many sly digs at the suffragettes" in the author's works, *The Marvelous Land of Oz* (1904) being a satire on the movement ("Royal Historian" 23).

15. In Baum's second Oz book, *The Marvelous Land of Oz* (1904), the child hero Tip (who is actually a bewitched girl) is also an orphan. Beckwith notes that in no other American children's books do there seem to be as many orphans as in the Oz tales (85). Moore points out, however, that orphan protagonists in juvenile literature are common (10). Orphans are alluded to in *Progress* (281), although none plays a significant role.

16. Crop failures, Baum later explains, prevent Uncle Henry from making payments on the farm, and the mortgage will shortly be foreclosed (*Emerald City*, chap. 3).

17. Baum claims to have envisioned an island in the South Pacific (Hearn, *Annotated* 99). In *Emerald City* Baum isolates the fairyland behind a Barrier of Invisibility.

18. Although Baum does not give Dorothy's age in *Oz*, evidence from his subsequent Oz books, according to Harmetz (39–40), suggests she is about this age at the time of her first Oz visit.

19. In European folklore, witches are always depicted as evil, their power thought to derive from Satan. For discussions of Baum's creation of good witches, see Baum and MacFall (280 ff.), and Carpenter and Shirley (chap. 15).

20. A reinforcement of this silver image appears when Christian passes Hill Lucre with its silver mine to lure pilgrims away from the road to Zion (106).

21. If Baum were unfamiliar with the Isaiah passage, he might readily have looked it up when reading Bunyan, since Biblical references appear in the margins of most pre-twentieth-century editions of *Progress*.

22. During a scene at the Interpreter's House, straw becomes a metaphor for people (202).

23. Baum's lifelong interest in mechanical gadgetry is noted by Hearn ("L. Frank Baum" 59). McClelland observes that his works display a "strange affinity for decapitation" (49), which may owe something to Bunyan's Great-heart, who decapitates giants, or to Carroll's Queen of Hearts, who is obsessed with chopping off heads.

24. Each of the Oz travelers is assigned a room at the Wizard's palace, Dorothy's containing a fountain spraying green perfume (124). The idea of perfume in the City may come from the letter Christiana receives from the King of the Celestial City, which smells of the "best Perfume" (180); it may owe something, as well, to Mr. Stand-fast's assertion that Christ's name has been "as a Civit-Box, yea sweeter then all Perfumes" (311).

25. As Moore points out (127), only four of the fourteen Oz books by Baum have male protagonists, and one of them (Tip in *Marvelous Land*) is really a girl bewitched. Women wield the power in Oz, for good or ill, and true love, according to Beckwith (84), is found only between girls "when one is a little older than the other, innocent, sterile, and uncompetitive." Moore concludes there are no authoritative father figures in all of Baum's work (127). Others have noted that the men and boys are either ineffectual, wicked, or robotic (Nye 12; Nathanson, *Rainbow* 69). Because Baum's automatons are male, Beckwith is led to believe that Baum rejected the natural process of procreation (85; see also Moore 126–32; and Hearn, "L. Frank Baum" 64).

26. He repeats the episode, in slightly different form, in the tenth chapter of *The Patchwork Girl of Oz* (1913).

27. This description comes from an anonymous review of *Oz*, "A New Book for Children" (605).

28. Nye observes, "Oz is beyond all doubt a little girl's dream-home. Its atmosphere is feminine . . . with very little of the rowdy, frenetic energy of boys." He notes that the few boys in Oz are "girls' boys, drawn as little girls assume boys should

be. Baum could not make Oz fit boys, nor was he capable of making boys who could fit easily and naturally into Oz society" (12–13).

29. For instance, the marginal summaries and comments in *A New Wonderland* (1900, revised as *The Surprising Adventures of the Magical Monarch of Mo*, 1903) repeat a similar practice in *Progress*. So does Baum's custom of including poems in the text: e.g., one appears in *Oz* (232), fifteen in *Patchwork Girl*. Baum's penchant for proper nouns describing characters' attributes, such as Jellia Jamb, the "very sweet" housekeeper in *Marvelous Land*, or Squealina Swyne in *The Tin Woodman of Oz* (1918), may have been inspired by Bunyan's allegorical practice of naming characters after their most notable traits. Baum often tinkered with spelling when coining proper nouns: General Jinjur (*Marvelous Land*) and the Nome (Gnome) King in *Ozma* (for names of over 630 characters in the Oz series [not all Baum's] and descriptions of each, see Snow). Other episodes in Baum's Oz sequels that appear to derive from Bunyan might be cited, such as Tip's box of "Wishing Pills" in *Marvelous Land* (chap. 18), a scene probably influenced by the box of "universal Pill[s]" prescribed for one of Christiana's boys (229–30). Another echo is Baum's creation of Billina, the Yellow Hen in *Ozma*, and an earlier hen in the thirteenth tale of *New Wonderland*, both of which may have been inspired by Bunyan's scene at the Interpreter's House of a hen and her chicks (201–02).

30. Glinda's transcendence in Baum's myth climaxes in his final Oz book, *Glinda of Oz* (1920), the final chapter appropriately entitled "Glinda's Triumph." One of Glinda's sources of power, as explained in *Tik-Tok*, is "a wonderful magic Record Book, in which is printed every event that takes place anywhere, just as soon as it happens" (28), an obvious allusion to the Christian Book of Life (Revelation 20:12).

Selected Works Cited

Barasch, Marc. "The Healing Road to Oz." *Yoga Journal* Nov.–Dec. 1991: 54–57.
Baum, Frank Joslyn, and Russell P. MacFall. *To Please a Child: A Biography of L. Frank Baum, Royal Historian of Oz*. Chicago: Reilly, 1961.
Baum, L. Frank. *Tik-Tok of Oz*. Chicago: Reilly, 1914.
———. *The Wonderful Wizard of Oz*. Introduction by Martin Gardner. New York: Dover, 1960.
Beckwith, Osmond. "The Oddness of Oz." *Children's Literature* 5 (1976): 74–91.
Bewley, Marius. "The Land of Oz: America's Great Good Place." *Masks & Mirrors: Essays in Criticism*. New York: Atheneum, 1970. 255–67.
Billman, Carol. "'I've Seen the Movie': Oz Revisited." *Literature and Film Quarterly* 9 (1981): 241–50.
Bunyan, John. *The Pilgrim's Progress from This World to That Which Is to Come*. Ed. James Blanton Wharey. 2d ed., rev., Roger Sharrock. 1960. Oxford: Clarendon, 1967.
Carpenter, Angelica Shirley, and Jean Shirley. *L. Frank Baum: Royal Historian of Oz*. Minneapolis: Lerner, 1992.
Carpenter, Humphrey, and Mari Prichard. *The Oxford Companion to Children's Literature*. Oxford: Oxford U.P., 1984.
Darton, F. J. *Children's Books in England: Five Centuries of Social Life*. Cambridge: Cambridge U.P., 1966.
Downing, David C. "Waiting for Godoz: A Post-Nasal Deconstruction of *The Wizard of Oz*." *Christianity and Literature* 33 (1984): 28–30.
Gardner, Martin. "The Royal Historian of Oz." In *The Wizard of Oz and Who He Was*. By Martin Gardner and Russel B. Nye. East Lansing: Michigan State U.P., 1957. 19–45.

————. "A Child's Garden of Bewilderment." *Saturday Review* 17 July 1965: 18–19.

————. Introduction to *The Magical Monarch of Mo*. By L. Frank Baum. New York: Dover, 1968.

Georgiou, Constantine. *Children and Their Literature*. Englewood Cliffs, NJ: Prentice, 1969.

Greene, David L., and Dick Martin. *The Oz Scrapbook*. New York: Random, 1977.

Harmetz, Aljean. *The Making of the Wizard of Oz*. New York: Knopf, 1977.

Hearn, Michael Patrick. "L. Frank Baum and the 'Modernized Fairy Tale.'" *Children's Literature in Education* 10 (1979): 57–67.

Hearn, Michael Patrick, ed. *The Annotated Wizard of Oz*. By L. Frank Baum. New York: Potter, 1973.

————, ed. *The Wizard of Oz*. By L. Frank Baum. New York: Schocken, 1983.

Littlefield, Henry M. "*The Wizard of Oz:* Parable on Populism." *American Quarterly* 16 (1964): 47–58.

Lowes, John Livingston. *The Road to Xanadu: A Study in the Ways of the Imagination*. Boston: Houghton, 1927.

Mannix, Daniel P. "The Father of the Wizard of Oz." *American Heritage* 16.1 (1964): 36–47.

McClelland, Doug. *Down the Yellow Brick Road: The Making of The Wizard of Oz*. 1976. New York: Bonanza, 1989.

McMaster, Juliet. "The Trinity Archetype in *The Jungle Books* and *The Wizard of Oz*." *Children's Literature* 20 (1992): 90–110.

Moore, Raylyn. *Wonderful Wizard: Marvelous Land*. Bowling Green, Ohio: Bowling Green U. Popular P., 1974.

Nathanson, Paul. "*The Wizard of Oz* as a Secular Myth of America." American Academy of Religion Convention. Kansas City, 25 Nov. 1991, as reported by Peter Steinfels, "Following the Yellow Brick Road, and Finding a Spiritual Path," *New York Times* 28 Nov. 1991: A16.

————. *Over the Rainbow: The Wizard of Oz as a Secular Myth of America*. Albany: State U. of New York P., 1991.

"A New Book for Children." *New York Times* [*Saturday Review of Books and Literature*] 8 Sept. 1900: 605.

Nye, Russel B. "An Appreciation." In *The Wizard of Oz and Who He Was*. By Martin Gardner and Russel B. Nye. East Lansing: Michigan State U.P., 1957. 1–17.

Potter, Jeanne O. "The Man Who Invented Oz." *Los Angeles Times Sunday Magazine* 13 Aug. 1939: 12.

Shulman, Alix Kates. "Ozomania under the Rainbow." *Village Voice* 3 Mar. 1975: 33, 35.

Snow, Jack. *Who's Who in Oz*. Chicago: Reilly, 1954.

Steinfels, Peter. "Following the Yellow Brick Road, and Finding a Spiritual Path." *New York Times* 28 Nov. 1991: A16.

Vidal, Gore. "On Rereading the Oz Books." *New York Review of Books* 13 Oct. 1977: 38–42.

Wagenknecht, Edward. *Utopia Americana*. 1929. Folcroft, Pa.: Folcroft, 1970.

————. "'Utopia Americana': A Generation Afterwards." *American Book Collector* Dec. 1962: 12–13.

Dwarf, Small World, Shrinking Child: Three Versions of Miniature

Caroline C. Hunt

The tiny hero in a world of big people goes back to the earliest days of children's literature; Tom Thumb comes immediately to mind, as well as later figures like Le Petit Poucet and Andersen's Tommelise. In another kind of story, a child protagonist of normal size consorts for a time with smaller beings; Snow White is the obvious example from fairy tale, while many other tales also present morally significant interludes with very small creatures (often semihuman). Swift in the eighteenth century set the pattern for that kind of exploration beyond fairy tale as did Carroll a century later for yet a third variant, in which a child's body size fluctuates uncontrollably; and no later adapter has ever improved on either Gulliver or Alice.

Whatever the precise situation of the miniature character, the appeal of the underlying idea, the miniature, is great. Perry Nodelman and Susan Stewart, among others, point out the relevance of Claude Lévi-Strauss's dictum that *all* works of art may be viewed as, essentially, miniatures (Nodelman 199, Stewart 48, 54). Stewart, whose highly theoretical *On Longing* includes, in a chapter on miniatures, examinations of doll houses and miniature books as well as more conventional texts, considers the miniature to be "a metaphor for the interior space and time of the bourgeois subject" (xii). Nodelman, more practical in orientation, identifies the main reason for this appeal: "So when these small beings prevail over insurmountable odds, as they always do, they represent a potent version of the wish-fulfillment fantasy: the very small can triumph over the dangerously large, the very powerless over the exceedingly powerful" (199).

Imagine a protagonist of keen intellectual perception—but, at the same time, one who is ignored or underestimated by nearly everyone. Within the limits of text length, syntax, and vocabulary that govern writing for children, the straightforward presentation of such a character might resemble a diluted version of *Notes from*

Children's Literature 23, ed. Francelia Butler, R. H. W. Dillard, and Elizabeth Lennox Keyser (Yale University Press, © 1995 Hollins College).

Underground: unbalanced, almost paranoid. Dostoevsky's antihero touches on this dwarf/child comparison in describing himself as a child whose classmates "began by degrees to grasp that I had already read books none of them could read," even books "of which they had not even heard" (83). As an adult, he says he has "a great deal of *amour propre*"; he then goes on, significantly, "I am as suspicious and prone to take offence as a humpback *or a dwarf*" (30, my italics).[1] The direct portrayal of such a degree of alienation is not a usable option for a "normal" child protagonist—yet many children, in particular children who are keen readers at an early age, experience precisely this combination of a highly developed perceptive faculty with a lack of importance in the eyes of others. The metaphor of miniaturization addresses this dilemma by presenting a protagonist who is independent, resourceful, and intelligent but very, very small.

To be a dwarf is to differ from the norm. The metaphor allows an author to suggest something abnormal, perhaps pitiable, about the small protagonist. The small size of the body presents a tangible symbol for a small degree of importance or status—"stature," in both senses. To be a dwarf is to remain permanently at the disadvantage that children, literally, outgrow. The dwarf, however, more than other humans differing from the physical norm, has played a part in European and Oriental culture for centuries, as outlined by a sympathetic Leslie Fiedler in the opening chapters of *Freaks*. Little people have been not only curiosities but jesters, courtiers, even prime ministers. In fiction, the dwarf or other single miniature character, usually presented as a very small adult, can articulate in adult language the humiliation and powerlessness felt by dwarf and child alike.

Although excellent work has been done on various aspects of this topic, most writers have dealt with "the miniature" as a single idea. In practice, though, most readers experience a story about a solitary tiny hero rather differently from one about an entire tiny society— and very differently from a story about someone whose body size fluctuates. Rather than repeating the obvious and well-documented connections between the small and powerless (in fiction) and the marginalized (in life), I will emphasize the rich variety of metaphors of the miniature and suggest a hierarchy among them. Of the three, the solitary dwarf presents the clearest kind of simple wish fulfillment (as indicated by Nodelman's comment). The miniature society, less obvious in its appeal, offers a dual perspective; the child reader may identify either with the little people or with a normal-sized character (who is almost always present in the story). The tale of a character who shrinks and grows, unlike the other two, addresses fundamental questions of body image and perception, of origins and annihilation.

The three works to be examined here—*Stuart Little, The Borrowers*, and *The Shrinking of Treehorn*—were written in, respectively, the 1940s, 1950s, and 1970s. Each of these books exemplifies a different variant of the miniature: the solitary little hero, the miniature society, and the protagonist who shrinks. Within each type, I have chosen the text which best exploits the possibilities of the type without trivializing the metaphor. The great forerunners, *Gulliver's Travels* and *Alice in Wonderland* (for Alice shrinks only in the first Alice book), are major literary feats by any standard, and it is appropriate that the texts from the twentieth century be of high quality also (*Stuart Little* rather than the Digit Dick books). And because books for young readers comment on their times just as much as books for adults, I have chosen works which reflect their society through the metaphor of size (*The Borrowers*, a commentary on postwar England, rather than *Sleepy People*, a bland picture book; *The Shrinking of Treehorn*, a wicked takeoff on childraising theory, not the one-joke film *Honey, I Shrunk the Kids*).

The Solitary Hero

E. B. White's *Stuart Little*, first published in 1945, represents to war babies what the later *Charlotte's Web* does to their younger siblings, the postwar baby boomers. In some ways, this is the ultimate New York book—and where, indeed, can one feel smaller than in New York City? From the beginning, White emphasizes the differentness of Stuart from his family: "unlike most babies, Stuart could walk as soon as he was born," explains the narrator (2); the family physician "was delighted with Stuart and said that it was very unusual for an American family to have a mouse" (3). His parents delete the rhyme about three blind mice from the nursery songbook. "It is such things that make children dream bad dreams," observes Mr. Little (9). Stuart's rapid maturation enables White to skip over any sort of "childhood" and to present him at once as a more or less grown character.

Like the child/reader, Stuart is in many ways helpless. When accidentally rolled up in a window shade, he fails to escape or even to attract attention until his brother pulls the shade down; indeed, he cannot even make himself heard. He appears, externally, to be of slight importance because of his size. While he is rolled up in the shade, his father calls the Bureau of Missing Persons, "but when the man asked for a description of Stuart and was told that he was only two inches high, he hung up in disgust" (23). Critics sometimes echo this disgust: Margery Fisher refers to *Stuart Little* as an "odd (and, to me, rather frightening) fantasy," in which Stuart's ingenious arrangements "all emphasize the fact that he is trying, agonizedly, to act as a human being" (63).

So much for the obvious disadvantages of being two inches tall. On the inside, though, Stuart is a giant. He is resourceful, as when he makes a trip down the drain to retrieve his mother's ring or when he figures out how to patch a birchbark canoe with pine gum. He has unexpected skills, such as competitive sailing and fast driving. (Perhaps these represent some sort of compensation for his small size. White makes comparisons unavoidable by juxtaposing, against Stuart's nautical skills, his brother George's half-hearted efforts with a rowing machine, and, against Stuart's constant voyaging, Mr. Little's unwillingness to leave home.) He is outgoing and can use his size and unusual appearance to make friends, as in his carefully cultivated relationship with a dentist whose boat he sails and whose miniature car he borrows. Most important, Stuart has an eye for what matters: during his single day of substitute teaching, Stuart's pupils probably learn more than in the rest of the school year. The appealing aspects of Stuart's personality cause many readers to echo Marcus Crouch's response, "*Stuart Little* is a book which inspires affection" (104).

White's skill lies partly in making these things seem so natural— and, on the surface at least, nonthreatening. In the hands of authors with other talents and purposes, the same *topoi* take on a very different tone. Stuart down the drain? Think of that nightmare scene in Rumer Godden's *In This House of Brede*, when Philippa's young son is trapped underground after falling down a mine shaft. The smallest available adults volunteer to go down after him; they fail because they are simply not small enough and using an actual child is out of the question. The boy dies. No wonder that this scene, related only as a flashback, lingers in the memory. Stuart's exploitation of his size when he meets the dentist, several policemen, and a friendly shopkeeper? Look at the manipulative little people in M. E. Kerr's *Little Little*—Knox Lionel, for instance, known as "Opportunity Knox," described by his best friend as "a combination preacher and con man" (3), who uses his stature to become a successful evangelist. Or consider the compelling dwarf figures in Dickens: Miss Mowcher in *David Copperfield,* who relentlessly pursues Littimer and brings him to justice for his part in the seduction of Emily, and Quilp, the bizarre yet sexually powerful villain who causes the death of Little Nell. It is no accident that both of these dwarf figures are connected closely to characters who are childlike and specifically described as small: the benevolent Mowcher acts on behalf of the small, childlike Emily ("*Little* Em'ly") while Quilp, quite the opposite, persecutes a helpless child, *Little* Nell. Indeed, Quilp's actions ensure among other things that Emily will never be full size, never live to grow larger than he. Stuart's ability to see beyond the façade? Look at *The Tin Drum,* in which the protagonist is not only (physically and symbolically) stunted in body but also (physically and symbolically) inarticulate.

The solitary little person in a big world is perhaps the ultimate Invisible Man. Stuart's borrowed automobile can actually become invisible; of Stuart himself, White observes early in the book, "Nobody noticed him, because he wasn't tall enough to be noticed" (29). Though apparently a sexist term, invisible man is accurate; the solitary dwarf, as a main character, usually is male. (Thus "hero," in this variant of the metaphor, happens to coincide with the traditional meaning of a male protagonist; however, it should be considered a genderless term and is so used in discussing the other two variants.) He is usually of an indeterminate, more or less adult age, with the exception of the unfortunately named Digit Dick, a young Australian boy who is the size of his mother's big toe and can speak with animals.

But Stuart is not just small; he is, at least in appearance, a mouse. White himself was ambivalent about this, but the printed text and Garth Williams's illustrations present a character more mouselike than human in appearance. This would seem to put him in a class with traditional animal miniatures, from Beatrix Potter's Peter Rabbit to Beverly Cleary's Ralph with his motorcycle. White's use of a mouselike hero born into a human family, however, raises questions which would not occur in either the animal miniature type as

1. From *Stuart Little* by E. B. White, illustrations by Garth Williams. Illustrations copyright renewed © 1973 by Garth Williams. Reproduced by permission of Harper-Collins Publishers.

used by Potter and Cleary (in which humans are a clearly "other" species) or in Tom Thumb–type stories with clearly human miniatures (where the hero is smaller than others but not different from them). Stuart wears clothes, including a hat and cane, and, in his "long bathrobe trailing around his ankles," he resembles "a little old friar pulling the bellrope in an abbey" as he pulls the chain to turn on the bathroom light (13) (fig. 1). Note the word "ankles" and others normally used to describe *human* bodies: Stuart's firm stomach muscles (17), "the sweat rolling down his cheeks" (6), his touching "his toes every morning to keep himself in good condition" (11) (fig. 2). Stuart can grasp a window shade (17) or hang onto a bird in flight (59) with his hands, which are never referred to as paws. Cleary's Ralph, in contrast, has *paws* throughout *The Mouse and the Motorcycle*. There can be no doubt as to Ralph's nature: "He took hold of the handgrips. They felt good and solid beneath his paws. . . . The seat was curved just right to fit a mouse" (23). People who meet Stuart respond to his size, not his mouselike appearance. To a bus conductor who remarks, "You're no bigger than a dime yourself" (28), Stuart responds, "I didn't come on this bus to be insulted." The conductor apologizes:

2. From *Stuart Little* by E. B. White, illustrations by Garth Williams. Illustrations copyright renewed © 1973 by Garth Williams. Reproduced by permission of Harper-Collins Publishers.

"I beg pardon," said the conductor. "You'll have to forgive me, for I had no idea that in all the world there was such a small sailor."

"Live and learn," muttered Stuart, tartly, putting his change purse back in his pocket. (29)

This intersection of animal miniature and tiny human may well be what caused revulsion in some critics; Anne Carroll Moore tried to persuade White not to publish *Stuart Little,* and the same reaction appears in Margery Fisher's remark, quoted earlier.

White suggests, with his usual delicate touch, that Stuart is not like the others in his society—hence, not "normal." Thus, although most adult humans respond to him simply as a tiny person, Mr.

Little, and sometimes Stuart himself, fear that he may really be a mouse. Stuart's letter to Harriet Ames reveals this fear all too clearly, for it is the one time that his usual fine command of language deserts him. The letter is full of contradictions, circumlocutions, and awkward phrasing, highlighted by the worry that "your parents may object to the suddenness . . . as well as to my somewhat mouselike appearance"; Stuart suggests that "it might be a good idea if you just didn't mention" the letter, as "what they don't know can't hurt them." He veers off into flowery language: "These tranquil spring evenings are designed by special architects for the enjoyment of boatmen," and assures her that his "canoe is like an old and trusted friend" (Stuart does not yet have a canoe) and that he will wait for her "with all the eagerness I can muster" (102). In this rather sad chapter, Stuart is both reluctant to face no longer being unique—Harriet is almost exactly his size—and unwilling to consider honestly just how mouselike he may really be. "Mouselike" seems to mean "nonhuman"; Stuart never worries about appearing mouselike in his warm and satisfying relationship with the bird Margalo even though she is also another species. And Mr. Little's obsession with the mousehole, down which he fears Stuart may one day vanish, seems odd compared to his enthusiasm for Stuart's ability to descend the drain—but fishing in drains for valuables is a "human" activity, and exploring mouseholes is not.

The dehumanizing aspect of small stature figures heavily in Dickens, whose dwarf figures are physically misshapen, and in M. E. Kerr's *Little Little,* where a running joke is the difference between the LaBelle family's insistence on associating only with PFs (perfectly formed little people) and Sidney Cinnamon's equally strong emphasis on the grotesque (for instance, by wearing his roach costume from an exterminator's commercial). Thus, if Stuart is not just a smaller version of his parents but is a different *kind* of being, perhaps he does not possess the ordinary rights of humans. The possibility, with its terrifying implications, lies behind many miniature hero stories and represents one of childhood's deepest fears. To be a child is, potentially, to be a nonperson. Custody battles and child abuse cases attest to this problem every day. White's book also shows traces of other approaches to the question, "Who is human?"—approaches which threaten adults, too, even those of "normal" size. The dehumanization of thousands during the Depression was a very recent memory; more recent was the war, which was still in progress while White was composing *Stuart Little*. "Who is human?" hints at some possible answers based (as in Mr. Little's obsession with the mousehole) ultimately on origins: "Not the Japanese" in the United States; and, obviously, "not the Jews" in Germany. The full potential of the latter association remained to be explored more than 40 years later by Art Spiegelman in his brilliant *Maus* and *Maus II*.

Small World

In his many adventures and the open-ended quest at the conclusion of his story, Stuart consistently affirms the worth of the small hero/ child while acknowledging that fears of being regarded as non-human are legitimate. Stuart is a solitary tiny figure in a landscape peopled by giants, and his relationship to others depends on his uniqueness. But what if he were not one of a kind? Turning from the figure of the solitary little person, consider the possibilities of a miniature society, where the world of the little person becomes the norm—or at least *a* norm that challenges the values of the larger world. Mary Norton, for instance, uses the metaphor of size very differently from White. Her Borrowers are a separate society, parallel to that of the full-size humans in the story. It is the Borrower society that is real, the Borrowers with whom the reader, at least most of the time, is to identify. Thus, although the Borrowers are understandably viewed by full-sized adults in the books as vermin to be exterminated, readers empathize with their fear of being seen and with the constant threat that hangs over them. Some see the plight of the Borrowers, always in hiding, as analogous to that of hidden Jews (especially children) during World War II—another instance in which being seen could, and did, often mean destruction for beings who were officially considered less than human by those in power. Meanwhile, the reader has another option: to dissociate from the Borrowers and feel superior to them (like the Boy in the first Borrowers book).

The world of the Borrowers exudes coziness. They are self-contained—not just as a society, but as a family unit. The group is homogeneous and roles within it well defined; indeed, Arrietty becomes a "borrower" outside her home only because Pod has no son to learn the trade. The charms of a cigar-box ceiling, pictures made of postage stamps, and rugs of blotting paper are exploited

3. From *The Borrowers,* copyright 1953, 1952 by Mary Norton and renewed 1981, 1980 by Mary Norton, Beth Krush, and Joe Krush. Reproduced by permission of Harcourt Brace & Company.

to the full (fig. 3). A possible role for the child/reader here is that of collector—like playing with a doll house. As Lois Kuznets points out, the "lure of the dollhouse," seen from a Freudian perspective, "may betray a longing to be small enough to return to the womb" (119). Alternatively, Nigel Hand has applied some principles earlier articulated by Fred Inglis and Peter Laslett to Mary Norton's series, distinguishing escapism of the (political) left from that of the right according to "the kind of consolation which each writer constructs for the loss of a fully satisfying social world in the here and now" (Butts 87). If the escape to the left results in the sort of fantasy exemplified by certain works of Helen Cresswell, Hand suggests, "then hankering after the past (seen as a world of ordered and stable values) takes us off to the right." This idea makes sense in connection with the Lilliputian descendants of *Mistress Masham's Repose*, the escapist fantasy by that master of escapism, T. H. White— a book which antedates Norton's by five years. An important difference between Norton's brand of nostalgia and White's is that his hero is not miniature but a normal-sized girl who is the victim of unkind and grasping caretakers. Her power over the little people is an ironic reflection of theirs over her—except that she is benevolent and they are not.

Although adult readers of *The Borrowers* have generally been conscious of its conservatism, they have seen that conservatism in quite different ways. Following Lois Kuznets, Patricia Pace thinks that the book "combines a progressive story of a girl's struggle to leave her home with a regressive yearning for a domestic ideal, a childhood innocence imagined in the figure of the miniature itself" (283). The golden age thus lies not in the past of a culture, but in the past of the human life cycle: a time "when the body-self feels whole—before the intrusions of adult sexuality and its felt contradictions." The idea that miniatures present the possibility of an ideal body "erased of sexuality" has been explored by various critics, usually with references to Bakhtin, Freud, Lacan, and so on. Though fascinating, it has two weaknesses when applied to actual texts: it treats all miniatures as essentially the same, and it addresses exclusively female heroes, female writers, and (presumably) female readers. Thus the idea that miniaturization and asexuality connect naturally with conditions like anorexia nervosa may fit the world of *The Borrowers* (female writer, female hero) but ignores parallel texts like Swift's (male writer, male hero) and T. H. White's (male writer, female hero). Though both Swift and White had sexual attitudes which might have contributed to their creation of miniature societies, they also had highly developed conservative tendencies of more obvious kinds. Their resistance to political and linguistic change and their tendency to view England (from their respective exiles in Ireland) as frozen in time, as well as their suspicion of government in real life, suggest that their miniature societies reflect societal, not merely sexual, wish fulfillment.

The cozy little world of the Borrowers, whether or not one sees in it an expression of conservatism, offers the reader an unexpected gift: the recovery of wonder at objects long overlooked. Who pays any attention to blotting paper, or stamps as such—or even cigar boxes? Every reader does, after finishing *The Borrowers*. Another advantage of the Borrowers' smallness is their ability to coexist with full-size humans and observe them without being observed themselves; the venal housekeeper and sottish owner of the house have no secrets from their invisible little critics, the Borrowers. Anyone who thinks this idea so obvious as not to need mentioning should take another look at a text by a very different (though still conservative) writer: Henry James's *What Maisie Knew*.

On the minus side, the Borrowers' size makes them sometimes less than sympathetic characters. To begin with, they are essentially parasites. "I'd call it stealing," the Boy tells Arrietty (84). She laughs and explains, "Human beans are *for* Borrowers—like bread's for butter!" Unlike Stuart, the Borrowers do not differ from larger humans in any important way except their size. Homily's vanity, shown by her refusal to be seen in curlers, is just like that of a "human bean." Some Borrowers are snobbish, some silly, some mean. When her Borrowers are so like the larger people, Norton risks making them merely charming; they see the weaknesses of "human beans" but not their own parallel faults. Curiously, in their behavior the Borrowers resemble mice far more than Stuart does: he looks mouselike but acts human, whereas they look human and act, in many respects, like mice. The various references to them as vermin, and attempts to get rid of them with smoke, ferrets, and so on underscore this parallel.

Because the appeal of *The Borrowers* lies in the completeness of their tiny world, a series of sequels was possible, and the volumes that followed were also of high quality. This suggests, though, that no major issues are either brought up or solved in the original book.

The sequels have their own charm: life in a boot in *The Borrowers Afield,* a voyage downstream in a kettle in *The Borrowers Afloat,* a balloon trip in *The Borrowers Aloft,* life in a church in *The Borrowers Avenged.* Yet each plot holds to the charming and rejects real development: after a long trip down a drain, climaxed by a flood of soapy bath water which almost drowns them, the Borrowers are merely relieved at not having to do any laundry: "Arrietty, too, felt somehow purged, as though all traces of the old dark, dusty life had been washed away—even from their clothes. Homily had a similar thought.

'Nothing like a good, strong stream of soapy water running through the fabric . . . no rubbing or squeezing' " (*Borrowers Afloat* 113).

The subgenre of the miniature society flourished during the 1940s and 1950s, especially in Great Britain—mirroring, perhaps, the perceived decline of the country. *The Little Grey Men,* a nostalgic tale of the Warwickshire countryside, won the Carnegie medal for its portrayal of a small society of gnomes. Lorna Wood's *The People in the Garden* and various other little-people stories carried out the Mistress Masham theme in a lighter key.[2] The pervasive shabbiness of the Borrowers, the unfairly imposed poverty in *Mistress Masham's Repose,* and the determinedly cheerful survivor mentality of most of these books suggests the reality of economic hardship in postwar Britain. The theme of giving up power sometimes appears explicitly. Lois Kuznets suggests that *The Return of the Twelves,* by Pauline Clarke, "emphasizes the individual toy soldiers' vulnerability and thus suggests relinquishing the use of power that comes with greater size and strength" (89). To readers whose world was conspicuously changing in the postwar years, books about miniature societies offered a sense of something wholly manageable.

Shrinking Child

The Shrinking of Treehorn, unlike the Borrower books and *Stuart Little,* is literally a small book, wider (7¼") than it is tall (6¼"). Thirty unnumbered pages of text (many closer to half a page in length) face thirty black-and-white Edward Gorey drawings, each in a neat black 4" × 5" frame. Florence Parry Heide's story concerns a boy who shrinks and who is ignored by adults, especially his parents; both phenomena are equally important (fig. 4). When

4. Illustration copyright © 1971 by Edward Gorey. Reproduced from *The Shrinking of Treehorn* by Florence Parry Heide by permission of Holiday House, Inc.

Treehorn first remarks to his mother that his clothes seem suddenly too big, she—as usual, apparently—pays no attention. "'That's too bad, dear,' said his mother, looking into the oven. 'I do hope this cake isn't going to fall,' she said." When his parents finally look at him more closely, they have a discussion:

> "He really is getting smaller," said Treehorn's mother. "What will we do? What will people say?"
> "Why, they'll say he's getting smaller," said Treehorn's father. He thought for a moment. "I wonder if he's doing it on purpose. Just to be different."

The school bus driver, Treehorn's friend Moshie, and his teacher react similarly. Sent to the principal's office (fig. 5), Treehorn fills out a form with the word "shrinking," which the principal misreads as "shirking." "We can't have any shirkers here, you know," the prin-

5. Illustration copyright © 1971 by Edward Gorey. Reproduced from *The Shrinking of Treehorn* by Florence Parry Heide by permission of Holiday House, Inc.

cipal tells him. "We're a team, and we all have to do our very best." Treehorn tries to correct him, but the principal, in a wonderful burst of jargon, goes right on: "Shrinking, eh? . . . Well now, I'm very sorry to hear that, Treehorn. You were right to come to me. That's what I'm here for. To guide. Not to punish, but to guide. To guide all the members of my team. To solve all their problems." The conversation goes on like this; in one illustration the principal emerges from behind his desk to loom over Treehorn. No wonder Treehorn, finally cured of shrinking and restored to normal size but afflicted with green skin, decides not to tell anyone; he knows no one will notice. That, indeed, is a frequent problem of the child in the (adult) world: not to be noticed, not to be taken seriously. Alternatively, some readers have found in Treehorn a kind of wish fulfillment: not to be bothered, not to be constantly supervised. In consequence the adults have just as little individuality from Treehorn's point of view as he has from theirs: all three of the adult men in the book look alike, with shaggy hair, mustache (plus beard, for the principal), and highly textured, fashionable suits.

The sequels explore the same idea of marginalization through different central metaphors. In *Treehorn's Treasure,* the hero is unable to attract anyone's attention to the money tree in the backyard, or indeed to anything about his existence or needs; a trip to an elegant restaurant begins with Treehorn's mother and aunt sitting behind immense black menus ("There wasn't anywhere for Treehorn to sit, so he stood up") and culminates in his missing the entire meal while running errands for the aunt. "'Wasn't this a delicious dinner, Treehorn?' asked his mother. Treehorn unwrapped another piece of bubble gum. He wished he'd brought one of his candy bars." *Treehorn's Wish* takes place on his (inevitably forgotten) birthday: "'It's my birthday,' said Treehorn. 'So it is, dear,' said his mother. 'I wonder if we should have a cake or something. Maybe your father will see about it. Your prunes are on the table, Treehorn.'" In both of these sequels, money, food, and clothing symbolize the plight of Treehorn. Money is capriciously withheld or impermanent; the bills that grow in the backyard fade to plain paper. Food is also withheld whenever it is symbolically important and provided only when it ceases to matter ("Your prunes are on the table"). Throughout the three books, Treehorn's simple outline contrasts to the tweeds, zigzag patterns, and "busy" interiors of his hostile world. Notably, the alternative metaphors have less immediate appeal than that of size alone.

The story of Treehorn differs in one important way from the stories of Stuart Little and of the Borrowers: Treehorn is small only temporarily. This puts him into a class with Alice, with Gulliver in Brobdingnag, and with a host of comic adaptations.[3] In its implications, however, the idea of shrinking is more threatening than humorous. Numerous commentators, both literary critics and psychiatrists, have discussed the metaphorical connection between shrinking child-figure and phallus; significantly, the classic approach to this is that enumerated by Martin Grotjahn half a century ago, girl = phallus. "It is very important to recognize . . . that the phallus must be represented only by a girl, not by a boy," he observes. "The sexually undifferentiated boy is better suited for a highly sublimated symbolization: the angel. There are no female angels" (36). Whatever may have been the case in the 1940s, more recent children's books use both male and female children in the shrinking metaphor. Perry Nodelman comments on the phallic symbolism in William Joyce's picture book *George Shrinks,* and reprints a picture of George shooting off a toy cannon "strategically placed in front of his lower torso" (143). Joyce's book makes the Freudian connections explicit. George becomes small in a dream and wakes to find it true; his own size is restored when he dives under the covers to escape a cat. Over half the illustrations show long hollow objects—a garden hose, a toothpaste tube, a soda straw—prominently displayed with, usually, a stream or drop of fluid emerging. An image of flight dominates the central part of the book. George's rescue from the land of forbidden fantasies is shown by the reappearance of his parents as he comes out of the bedclothes, while at the same time the back half of the predatory cat is seen receding.

Jacqueline Rose shows how J. M. Barrie's David, in *The Little White Bird,* fears the story of his own birth because it goes back to a time when he did not exist: "'It doesn't make me littler does it?'" she quotes from a crucial scene, "by which he hoped that it would not do for him altogether"; the question of size is connected, in Rose's interpretation, with "the question of origins, of sexuality, and of death" (24). John Gould's poignant *The Withering Child* describes a five-year-old boy's near death from anorexia when his family goes to England on sabbatical: "he keeps growing smaller, shrinking into himself like a dying flower," observes the boy's distraught father (177). There is indeed something terrifying about the idea of shrinking—and not only to children. In China and on the West Coast of the United States, outbreaks of a psychiatric disorder called koro illustrate this fear; patients believe that their genitalia are shrinking to the point of disappearing within the body.[4]

Books about shrinking, therefore, allow the child/reader to confront otherwise impermissible (and specifically sexual) themes, while addressing at the same time the feeling of vulnerability in tracing one's origins to a time of nonexistence, of total oblivion.

Were you ever a little *kid?*

But what about those child readers mentioned at the beginning, the ones who identify so wholeheartedly with Stuart and the Borrowers? This investigation began with a chance conversation with an acquaintance who is now an academic. He had been an early and voracious reader, he said (nothing odd here); and, he went on, one of his favorite books had been *Stuart Little*. When questioning revealed that he had been unusually small for his age, speculation set in. Since then, I have conducted an intermittent survey. First question: Were you undersized as a child? (If not, the interview ends.) Second question: What were your favorite books? This highly unscientific poll, conducted over many years, suggests a high correlation between a sense of oneself as abnormally small and a fondness for books in which the hero or the whole society is diminutive; in fact, the word "little" appears in the title of most of the books mentioned, even if there is no miniaturization in the book. Among animal and inanimate heroes were Little Bear, the Little Engine that Could, even the Little House. Royalty was represented by the Little Prince and the comic strip figure of the Little King. Gregory Maguire recalls hoping that all the books about "small creatures who lived on the underside of our world" could be "true, simultaneously," so that "the world [would be] crawling with intelligent, articulate vermin and their many small friends and relations" (103). He envisioned the Milne characters, Margery Sharp's Rescuers, and the rats of NIMH, along with, perhaps, "the Borrowers stumbling across the mammoth meadows of Malpalquet, and falling upon the necks and breastbones of their literary kind, the Lilliputians from *Mistress Masham's Repose*." For the twelve-year-old that he then was, "adult life on a miniature scale seemed perfect—both a toy to be manipulated and a small-scale wonder of complexity to be examined and over which to brood, god-like" (103). To very small twelve-year-olds, this happened even more strongly.

This group of readers probably represents an acute form of a general childhood condition. The survey respondents were very much aware of their feeling of powerlessness; they would have to be, as not only adults but other children towered over and seemed to threaten them. Even as normal-sized adults, many of them visibly flinched at these memories. They were also exceptionally aware of the comfort brought to them by the kind of books discussed here. But these people were not fundamentally different from their larger peers; and what Stuart, Pod, and Treehorn offered to them is a metaphorical escape that works for other children—and for adult readers, too.

What should by now be apparent is that different miniature hero metaphors work in different ways. The solitary hero metaphor emphasizes a one-against-the-world mentality. A central question in these books is usually the discrepancy between the real importance of the hero—of which he is fully aware—and society's failure to recognize it. (Of all the stories with miniature characters, those with solitary heroes were best liked by the once-undersized readers in my unscientific survey.) Miniature society books, by contrast, tend to emphasize an unchanging cuteness which excludes the unpleasant, the sordid, and, often, the sexual aspects of life; their main appeal seems to lie in their assurance of a world which can be controlled so that change does not enter. (Critics have observed that Norton's small characters are basically pre-industrial artisans in a post-industrial world. White's Lilliputians have not developed much from their eighteenth-century forebears.) Finally, the most powerful of the three variants, the shrinking metaphor, plays to universal uncertainties about the human body. Stuart, like all solitary miniature heroes, knows that he is real and important; both the Borrowers and T. H. White's normal-sized girl hero understand the relationships between the large world and the small; but the shrinking hero, unlike the other two sorts of miniature characters, must constantly confront the questions of what is real and whether his or her perceptions are actually valid. (That is one of the ways in which *Alice in Wonderland,* with its relentless examination not only of "real" logic but of the logic of fantasy and even of language itself, addresses issues that are not even hinted at in the other variants.)

A kind of hierarchy appears among miniature hero metaphors. Most adults, however much they may have enjoyed solitary hero books earlier in life, move eventually beyond them. I must confess that, though the enjoyment was still there in rereading *Stuart Little,* the magic was gone; the book was no longer *special* as it had once been. Miniature society books, however, appeal to a particular need to step outside of the world of change, even if only temporarily; their adult analog is perhaps the mystery novel. Solitary hero books vindicate the underprivileged and usually misunderstood character (and hence the reader), whereas miniature society books offer a safe and stable world of escape. Books about shrinking, however, retain their fascination; they pose questions which matter to child and adult alike. The matter of one's origin and eventual dissolution underlie questions of control over one's body, societal response, and changing perceptions. These books deal with the inescapability of change, the unreliability of perception (both the hero's perception of others and theirs of him or her), and the unpalatable fact that life has a beginning and, thus, an ending. Like the other varieties of the miniature hero metaphor, this one satisfies a widely felt need among young readers; unlike the other two, its fascination does not recede in adulthood.

Notes

1. Dostoevsky's use of the dwarf image reflects his familiarity with Dickens, in particular *The Old Curiosity Shop* and *David Copperfield*, two of his favorites, both of which contain dwarf characters. Dostoevsky's antihero combines in his remark the sentiments of Dickens's Miss Mowcher, who sometimes has to remind larger people that her tiny frame houses feelings just as valid as theirs, with the contorted thinking of Quilp, whose villainy is fueled by his need to triumph over full-sized people.

2. Swift's nostalgia for a manageable, unchanging version of English society contributes to his portrayal of the Lilliputians (though this was not, of course, his only point in that richly satiric work); T. H. White's wartime excursions into the Arthurian past gave way to the postwar miniatures of *Mistress Masham's Repose.* The atmosphere of the late 1940s and early 1950s has been largely eclipsed by the more turbulent 1960s; nevertheless, these were years of change. In the United States, suburbs began with the first Levittown; the automobile entered its ascendancy; and social changes led to *Brown v. Board of Education,* which was still making its way through the courts in the year of *The Borrowers's* publication. In Britain, even more clearly, there was a sharp break with the rise of the Labour party and the creation of the welfare state. The attitude of many conservative authors is exemplified in Angela Thirkell's Barsetshire novels, a continuation of Trollope; in the postwar novels, the government is always referred to, scornfully, as They.

The results of miniaturization for its own sake, on the other hand, may be seen in two American picture books of the 1960s. M. B. Goffstein's *Sleepy People* depicts a race of tiny characters. "There may be a family of sleepy people living in one of your old bedroom slippers," the only picture which portrays anything in addition to the little people themselves, shows four of them snoozing in a furry slipper. John Peterson's *The Littles* involves a family of tiny people with mouselike tails who confront the problem of a visiting cat when their host family (inevitably called the Biggs) goes on vacation. Twenty years later, Zilpha Keatley Snyder writes of little people in Tiddletown, the Tooleys. Gone are the ironies, the exposés of social pretensions, and the elegiac sense of a dying society that made *The Borrowers* more than just a gimmick. Gone, even, are the elaborate details, verbal and pictorial, that had adorned the much earlier American little worlds of Palmer Cox's Brownies and William Donahey's Teenie Weenies.

3. Well-known examples are Raquel Welch and friends slithering through a hapless patient's veins in *Fantastic Voyage,* and the children in the movie *Honey, I Shrunk the Kids* and in books like Elvira Woodruff's *Awfully Short for the Fourth Grade* and *The Magic School Bus: Inside the Human Body.* Clearly this idea can be applied equally to the exciting, the disturbing, the comic, or even the trivial (as in Lorna Wood's overly cute *The People in the Garden,* in which the humans shrink or grow at will by swallowing pills and powders supplied by the Hag Dowsabel). Elvira Woodruff's *The Summer I Shrank My Grandmother* touches superficially on a darker side of the metaphor: the grandmother, thanks to an out-of-control chemistry experiment, gets younger and younger until she is on the verge of disappearing.

4. Epidemics of this panic disorder occurred in Guangdong during the 1980s. Reports of koro in the United States were said to be largely anecdotal at first, but enough cases have been seen to warrant proposals for the disease's inclusion in the fourth edition of the *Diagnostic and Statistical Manual of Mental Disorders* (DSM-IV), according to Bernstein and Gaw's 1990 article in the *American Journal of Psychiatry*.

Even in a comic mode, the idea of shrinkage has powerful overtones. Alf Prøysen's Mrs. Pepperpot stories concern an old woman who periodically becomes as small as a pepperpot, usually for less than a day. His first collection, *Little Old Mrs. Pepperpot* (1959), appeared in an English translation in 1960; the tiny woman was so popular that three further collections appeared in translation, both in Britain and in the United States, through the 1960s.

Works Cited

Bernstein, Ruth L., and Albert C. Gaw. "Koro: Proposed Classification for DSM-IV." *American Journal of Psychiatry* 147.12 (1990): 1670.

Butts, Dennis, ed. *Good Writers for Young Readers*. St. Albans: Hart-Davis Educational, 1977.

Cahn, Joseph M. *The Teenie Weenies Book: The Life and Art of William Donahey*. La Jolla, Calif.: Green Tiger Press, 1986.

Carroll, Lewis. *The Complete Works of Lewis Carroll*. London: Nonesuch Press, 1959.

Cleary, Beverley. *The Mouse and the Motorcycle*. Illus. Louis Darling. New York: William Morrow, 1965.

Cole, Joanna. *The Magic School Bus: Inside the Human Body*. Illus. Bruce Degen. New York: Scholastic, 1989.

Cox, Palmer. *The Brownies: Their Book*. New York: Century, 1887. Rpr. Dover, 1964.

Crouch, Marcus. *Treasure Seekers and Borrowers: Children's Books in Britain 1900–1960*. London: The Literary Association, 1962.

Dickens, Charles. *David Copperfield*. Ed. Nina Burgis. Oxford: Clarendon Press, 1981.

———. *The Old Curiosity Shop*. London and New York: Oxford University Press, 1951.

Dostoevsky, Fyodor. *Notes from Underground*. New York: Dell, 1960.

The Fantastic Voyage. Dir. Richard Fleisher. Twentieth-Century Fox, 1966.

Fiedler, Leslie. *Freaks: Myths and Images of the Secret Self*. New York: Simon and Schuster, 1978.

Fisher, Margery. *Intent Upon Reading: A Critical Appraisal of Modern Fiction for Children*. 2d ed. Leicester: Brockhampton Press, 1969.

Godden, Rumer. *In This House of Brede*. New York: Viking, 1969.

Goffstein, M. G. *Sleepy People*. New York: Farrar, Straus & Giroux, 1966.

Gould, John A. *The Withering Child*. Athens and London: University of Georgia Press, 1994.

Grass, Günter. *The Tin Drum*. New York: Pantheon, 1962.

Grotjahn, Martin. "The Symbolization of Alice in Wonderland." *American Imago* 4.4 (1942–46): 32–41.

Heide, Florence Parry. *The Shrinking of Treehorn*. Illus. Edward Gorey. New York: Holiday House, 1971.

———. *Treehorn's Treasure*. Illus. Edward Gorey. New York: Holiday House, 1981.

———. *Treehorn's Wish*. Illus. Edward Gorey. New York: Holiday House, 1984.

Honey, I Shrunk the Kids. Dir. Joe Johnston. Buena Vista Pictures, 1991.

James, Henry. *What Maisie Knew*. Oxford: Oxford University Press, 1980.

Joyce, William. *George Shrinks*. New York: Harper and Row, 1985.

Kerr, M. E. *Little Little*. New York: Harper and Row, 1982. Rpr. Bantam, 1983.

Kuznets, Lois Rostow. *When Toys Come Alive: Narratives of Animation, Metamorphosis, and Development*. New Haven and London: Yale University Press, 1994.

Maguire, Gregory. "Belling the Cat: Heroism and the Little Hero." *Lion and the Unicorn* 13.1 (1989): 102–119.

Nodelman, Perry. *The Pleasures of Children's Literature*. White Plains, NY: Longman, 1992.

Norton, Mary. *The Borrowers*. Illus. Beth and Joe Krush. Orlando: Harcourt, Brace, Jovanovich, 1953.

———. *The Borrowers Afield*. Illus. Beth and Joe Krush. New York: Harcourt, Brace, Jovanovich, 1955.

———. *The Borrowers Afloat*. Illus. Beth and Joe Krush. New York: Harcourt, Brace, Jovanovich, 1959.

———. *The Borrowers Aloft*. Illus. Beth and Joe Krush. New York: Harcourt, Brace, Jovanovich, 1961.

———. *The Borrowers Avenged*. Illus. Beth and Joe Krush. New York: Harcourt, Brace, Jovanovich, 1982.

Pace, Patricia. "The Body-in-Writing: Miniatures in Mary Norton's *Borrowers*." *Text and Performance Quarterly* 11.4 (1991): 279–290.

Peterson, John. *The Littles*. Illus. Roberta Carter Clark. New York: Scholastic, 1967.

Prøysen, Alf. *Little Old Mrs. Pepperpot*. Trans. Marianne Helway. Illus. Björn Berg. New York: McDowell, Obolensky, 1960. (Original publication 1959.)

Rees, Leslie. *Digit Dick and the Tasmanian Devil*. Illus. Walter Cunningham. Sydney and Melbourne: John Sands Pty. Ltd., n. d. [1946]

———. *Digit Dick in Black Swan Land*. Illus. Walter Cunningham. Sydney and Melbourne: John Sands Pty. Ltd., n. d.

Rose, Jacqueline. *The Case of Peter Pan, or The Impossibility of Children's Fiction*. London: Macmillan, 1984.

Snyder, Zilpha Keatley. *Squeak Saves the Day and Other Tooley Tales*. Illus. Leslie Morrill. New York: Delacorte, 1988.

Spiegelman, Art. *Maus*. New York: Pantheon, 1986.

———. *Maus II: And Here My Troubles Began*. New York: Pantheon, 1991.

Stewart, Susan. *On Longing: Narratives of the Miniature, the Gigantic, the Souvenir, the Collection*. Baltimore: Johns Hopkins University Press, 1984.

Swift, Jonathan. *Gulliver's Travels. The Prose Works of Jonathan Swift*, ed. Herbert Davis. Oxford: Basil Blackwell, 1939–68. Volume 11.

Watkins-Pitchford, Denis. *The Little Grey Men*. New York: Charles Scribner's Sons, 1951. (Original British publication 1942).

White, E. B. *Stuart Little*. Illus. Garth Williams. New York: Harper and Row, 1945.

———. *Charlotte's Web*. New York: Harper, 1952.

White, T. H. *Mistress Masham's Repose*. Illus. Fritz Eichenberg. New York: G. P. Putnam's Sons, 1946.

Wood, Lorna. *The People in the Garden*. London: J. M. Dent, 1954.

Woodruff, Elvira. *Awfully Short for the Fourth Grade*. New York: Holiday House, 1989.

———. *The Summer I Shrank My Grandmother*. New York: Holiday House, 1990.

Imagination, Rejection, and Rescue: Recurrent Themes in Dr. Seuss

Tim Wolf

Dr. Seuss's first children's book, *And To Think That I Saw It on Mulberry Street* (1937), features three elements—a rejected child, the exercise of childlike imagination, and a rejecting parent whose anger seems focused against the exercise of childlike imagination. The clever whimsical verse and exuberant illustration form a powerful tension with the potentially painful portrait of a child who wants to win the approval of a rejecting parent, and fails. In the end, Seuss attempts to solve the problem of rejection by having the child reject the parent in return. Apparently, this problem mattered deeply to Seuss, and the solution in *Mulberry Street* did not satisfy him, for his next work, *The 500 Hats of Bartholomew Cubbins* (1938), reexplores the problem with a slightly different resolution; the child succeeds in appeasing the angry parent figure and is allowed to depart in peace. This may have seemed a somewhat better answer to Seuss than the counter-rejection he proposed in *Mulberry Street,* but in his next book, *The King's Stilts* (1939), he again picks up the theme and this time seems to arrive at a perfect resolution. The parent does not *really* dislike the child, but rather the parent is suffering from a deep personal unhappiness that makes the parent act angry. Because the child loves the parent, the child assumes the responsibility of healing that unhappiness by reconnecting the parent to the joys of the childlike imagination, and this rescue simultaneously frees the parent to express a previously hidden love for the child.

We might note two powerful aspects of this solution. First, I think that an internalization of responsibility for their parents' behavior, and the assumption of responsibility for rescuing their parents, is a potent psychological force in many children. Second, it makes sense that the very facet of children that seems to provoke parents' wrath—the childlike imagination—is the facet that parents themselves need to reexperience in order to regain happiness; in fact, it

Children's Literature 23, ed. Francelia Butler, R. H. W. Dillard, and Elizabeth Lennox Keyser (Yale University Press, © 1995 Hollins College).

is because parents are cut off from, and longing for, a connection with their own imaginations that they resent children's access to the imagination.

Seuss manages to work out all of these possibilities in the relationships among Eric, Lord Droon, and King Birtram in *The King's Stilts,* and perhaps because he feels he has now truly expressed the complexity of the dilemma and discovered a satisfying resolution, he moves on to other themes. However, I suggest that Seuss returns to the motif 21 years later to write one of his best-selling books, *Green Eggs and Ham* (1960). *Green Eggs and Ham* repeats the perfect resolution to rejection that Seuss discovered in *The King's Stilts,* but does so within the limits of a 51-word vocabulary. This combination of potent theme and highly accessible format may account in part for the book's phenomenal appeal.

I say in part because it would be reductive to limit our understanding of the appeal of these texts to any one factor—even if the factor seems puissant, such as the theme of a rejected child internalizing responsibility for a parent's rescue. Furthermore, we need to guard against a reductive interpretation of this theme itself. For example, if such a theme does manifest itself in the texts, can we also find instances where the texts simultaneously suggest opposite currents? If so, could the tensions and ambiguities of these simultaneous opposites add to, rather than detract from, the texts' appeal? In addition, how do we define such terms as *child* and *parent?* We might take a traditional psychoanalytic approach in which certain symbols represent classic familial conflicts—either androgynous or gender-specific. However, on another level we might attempt a gestalt approach, and because the basic premise of any gestalt analysis is that all aspects of a text (or dream) represent but different aspects of one whole person, we could then view the child and parent in each story as conflicting facets of one person; that is, we could see an "inner child" and an "inner parent" as two members of a constellation of personas within one psyche. But then, whose psyche would we be considering—a child with an inner parent, an adult with an inner child, the psyche of the author himself? Each answer would further multiply perspectives within an already crowded field of possibilities. Yet we can advance even further. For example, could we broaden the meaning of *parent* to see the verbal text as parent to the illustrated text? Could illustration thus carry associations of childlike imaginative freedom, and verbal textuality carry associations of adultlike authoritative delimitation?

Keeping in mind that the ideas in this paper illuminate the complexity of Seuss's appeal only in part, and could suggest wide-ranging, perhaps even contradictory, associations, let us take a closer look at Seuss's first three books, and then *Green Eggs and Ham.*

And To Think That I Saw It on Mulberry Street

We need not look far to discover in *Mulberry Street* the three elements that form the nucleus of a recurrent theme in all four of these stories. The first page of *Mulberry Street* introduces a parent rejecting his child's imagination:

> When I leave home to walk to school,
> Dad always says to me,
> "Marco, keep your eyelids up
> And see what you can see."

> But when I tell him where I've been
> And what I think I've seen,
> He looks at me and sternly says,
> "Your eyesight's much too keen.

> Stop telling such outlandish tales.
> Stop turning minnows into whales."
> Now, what can I say
> When I get home today?

Visually, this large passage of verse looms over a small boy in the lower right corner, almost pushing him off the page. The unbalanced composition correlates to the displacement a child feels under the weight of a parent's rejection. We might say that the parent wants to push the imagination out of Marco's head, just as the large block of text seems to want to push Marco off the paper. Thus, the reader might equate reading and adult oppression.

Several factors could reinforce this equation. First, Marco carries an uncomfortably large book under his arm, for he is going to school. Because few children enjoy going to school, and even fewer enjoy carrying heavy books, the combination further associates verbal text and adult oppression. Furthermore, while Marco tries to obey the adult-prescribed "keeping-up-of-eyelids," and while he dutifully walks the adult-prescribed path to the adult-prescribed destination—in other words, while he marches to the rigid beat of adult dominance—he walks from left to right, the same direction in which the child reads the verbal text. Perhaps in a Hebrew translation, the tyrannized Marco should walk from right to left, for his walk may symbolize our sense of loss and oppression when we first realize that in order to read we must forgo the freedom of letting our eyes wander around the page, and must instead accept the discipline of forcing our eyes into an orderly march along straight lines.

Yet, at the same time, this page also equates reading with pleasure, power, and rebellion. For example, the verbal text reports, in delightfully witty anapestic tetrameter, that the parent wants Marco to "keep his eyelids up," but that the parent also tells Marco that his eyesight is "much too keen." This self-contradiction lets the child reader view the parent as both unfair and stupid, but the child gains this sense of power over the parent through reading—an activity that the page composition may associate with the parent's tyranny; that is, the child gains a sense of pleasure and power through reading, because it allows him or her to participate in a rebellion against reading. Possibly, learning to read, or the act of reading itself, promotes dozens of contradictory internal responses in each of us— power/helplessness, freedom/imprisonment, oral gratification/oral repression—and perhaps Seuss's ability to evoke these oppositions generates some of the dynamic tensions that make his works so potent.[1]

The ambiguous attitude toward the verbal text continues on the subsequent pages of *Mulberry Street,* in a pattern first noted by Perry Nodelman:

> As the boy, Marco, adds details to his complex story of what he saw on Mulberry Street, the pictures become more and more complex, more and more filled with detail—but always in terms of the same basic compositional patterns: the elephant is always in the same place on each spread, and so on. So the pictures build in intensity and maintain their narrative connection with each other, *as the words in a story usually do;* in each picture we look for new information to add to old, rather than having

6. From *And To Think I Saw It on Mulberry Street* by Dr. Seuss. TM and copyright © 1937 by Dr. Seuss Enterprises, L.P. Reproduced by permission of Random House, Inc.

> to start from scratch about what we are seeing each time, as usually happens in picture books. . . . The result is a curious reversal, in which . . . [the] pictures *strain toward the narrative qualities of text*. (255, emphasis added)

Indeed, on the last spread of the parade, Seuss has reversed the situation of the first page; now the illustration overwhelms two pages, almost pushing the four short verbal phrases off the bottom. This could represent the triumph of a free and joyful imagination over the rigid tyranny of verbal textuality—and over the parent's despotic authority. Yet, if we understand Nodelman right, Seuss achieves this coup in part by making the logic of pictorial development resemble the logic of verbal textuality; thus, Seuss may channel the joyful rebelliousness that the illustration inspires toward an acceptance of the logic of verbal textuality.[2]

When we turn the page, we find an illustration of Marco rushing up a flight of stairs to tell his parent about the wonderful parade (fig. 6), and these stairs may suggest other levels of interpretation. For example, could going "up the stairs" symbolize a return to the superego level—or the conscious level? If so, we could read this story as if it were about an adult, whose tyrannical superego, or his inner adult, attempts to control and reject the workings and imaginings of his id, or his inner child. Or, if we remember that Seuss faced much unkind rejection when he first wrote for children, we could interpret Marco as a symbol for Seuss himself—the hero who journeys into the "downstairs" of his unconscious for imaginative inspiration, and then tries to share his treasures with an unreceptive, even hostile, society. Seuss creates a text that allows these readings, and others, simultaneously, so that the next page reverberates with potential meanings. For as soon as Marco reaches his seated (enthroned?) parent, Marco decides not to share his imagination and joy with him:

> There was so much to tell, I JUST COULDN'T BEGIN!
> Dad looked at me sharply and pulled at his chin.
> He frowned at me sternly from there in his seat,
> "Was there nothing to look at . . . no people to greet?
> Did nothing excite you or make your heart beat?"
>
> "Nothing," I said, growing red as a beet,
> "But a plain horse and wagon on Mulberry Street."

Even at its most ostensible level, this passage represents a profoundly disturbing moment. At the beginning of the story we met Marco as a child who wanted very much to win the acceptance of an unhappy parent. In the middle of the story, we discovered along with Marco that the secret of happiness resides in the free exercise of the childlike imagination, for Seuss writes that "Mulberry Street runs into Bliss." Now at the end of the story, we see Marco racing up the stairs with a huge smile on his face. The smile is both an expression of Marco's love for his parent, since he envisions that his story will give the unhappy parent the gift of bliss, and a reflection of Marco's need for his parent's love, since he anticipates that his story will win his parent's acceptance. Yet when we turn the page, we find that both these expectations come to "nothing."

Within Marco's fantasy, we find clues that Marco wishes both to share this happiness with his parent and to have his imagination accepted. For example, after the parade runs into Bliss Street, Marco introduces a number of authority figures who put seals of approval on the celebration—policemen, who escort it on motorcycles, and the mayor and his alderman, who wave flags from their review stand. However, Seuss introduces a more poignant symbol even earlier in the text. Just prior to having his parade "run into Bliss," Marco hitches a little trailer to the end of the procession:

> A band that's so good should have someone to hear it,
> But it's going so fast that it's hard to keep near it.
> I'll put on a trailer! I know they won't mind
> If a man sits and listens while hitched on behind.

The illustration for this text depicts a smiling man with a white fringed bald pate and long white beard sitting on a stool. If we remember that Marco's parade is a story that he intends to tell his father, we might see this smiling man who "sits and listens" as a wishful representation of the father that Marco hopes will listen to and approve of his story about the parade. Several elements support this association. For example, the illustration of the man resembles a prominent western archetype of the patriarch. Furthermore, when Marco later rushes to tell his real father the story about the parade, he finds him also sitting—but, unlike Marco's fantasy father, his real father is frowning.

The presence of a patriarchal archetype in the illustration compels us to consider what parts of the theme could be read as androgynous, and what parts should be read as gender specific. For example, although the text specifies a son and father, I believe that both Marco and his father could be read as either male or female. On the other hand, we would not want to overlook some of the meanings we might glean from a more gender-specific approach. For example, we might associate the son-and-father conflict with classic psychosexual complexes, or with societal gender teachings that may make a father frown on the imaginative daydreaming tendencies of a son, while he smiles on the same tendencies in a daughter.[3] Or we might see the rejecting patriarch as a symbol of our phallocratic society itself and the low status it affords to the imagination.

Whether we interpret the smiling patriarch who follows the parade as an androgynous or a gender-specific fantasy of parental acceptance, the real parent whom Marco encounters at the end of the story "frowns at [him] sternly from there in his seat" and will not follow Marco's stories, either to approve of them, or to share in their joy. Marco's only recourse is to protect himself by hiding his imaginative world. His decision not to tell his parent about the wonders of Mulberry Street constitutes a form of counter-rejection, and thus Seuss seems to end *Mulberry Street* with the problem of the rejecting parent unresolved.

The 500 Hats of Bartholomew Cubbins

Seuss continues to explore the same theme—a rejecting parent whose anger seems focused against the exercise of childlike imagination—in his next book, *The 500 Hats of Bartholomew Cubbins.* Here, King Derwin assumes the role of the parent figure, and his rejection of the child figure, Bartholomew Cubbins, arises from the child's inability to remove his hat in the king's presence. I believe that this hat, and specifically the feather in this hat, might symbolize the imagination—for although the hat itself contains enough magic to constantly reappear on Bartholomew's head, the feather has enough magic not only to reappear, but to sprout, multiply, and grow ever more fanciful and splendid. Furthermore, if we think of the hat as thought, always present about the head, then the feather easily figures as the imagination, the aspect of thought that makes it beautiful and precious. Seuss writes that although the hat was plain, "Bartholomew liked it—especially because of the feather that always pointed straight up in the air."[4] As in *Mulberry Street,* where the parent specifically targets Marco's imaginative stories for rejection, King Derwin specifically targets the feathered hat as his reason for rejecting Bartholomew.

In fact, the text could assume an autobiographical flavor if we remember that a feather quill is a writing implement, and that Seuss strives to express his imagination through writing. We could read Bartholomew as Seuss himself, a boylike man who cannot stop his mind from sprouting wonderful fantasies, no matter how much the ruling forces of society threaten and disapprove. Certainly, Bartholomew's self-reliant pride in his feather could assume a jaunty new light, but another aspect of the story simultaneously assumes a darker shade—Bartholomew's inferior position to the king. The story tells us that King Derwin lives at the top of a mountain, and that Bartholomew feels "mighty small" when he gazes up that hill from his house in the valley. This might translate into Seuss's sense of social inferiority to the "folks on the hill"—the ruling powers of society. If so, then the hundreds of hats that Bartholomew grows could represent Seuss's efforts to make it up the hill, or to impress

the folks on the hill, by penning (feathering) imaginative children's stories, while the king's repeated rejections of the hats could represent the many hostile rejections Seuss endured. In this interpretation, it would hardly be coincidental that, immediately after he had finally sold *Mulberry Street,* Seuss should write a story about a boy who finally grows a hat good enough to sell to a king.

Several aspects of Seuss's youth may be relevant to such an autobiographical interpretation. For example, Ruth K. MacDonald reports that Seuss felt "shame at his German heritage during World War I," that he was nicknamed "the Kaiser" and ostracized (1). Such treatment might lead a person to view himself at the bottom of the hill in society. I think it may be more relevant to note that in Seuss's youth his family suffered a reversal of fortune: during Prohibition his father lost the brewery of which he had just become president. Although the father found another job as superintendent of city parks, the family may have sustained a decline in status, suffering from what Lawrence Stone terms "relative deprivation" (18). In other words, the family may have felt further down the hill, because they had once been further up the hill. Occasionally, children in these types of families will assume an inner burden to rescue the family and restore its lost status, and such a burden would fall especially hard upon an only child, as Seuss was. Certainly the family, or at least the father, was status conscious, for when Seuss told his father that he had applied for a fellowship to Oxford, the father reported to the local newspaper that Seuss had already won a fellowship to Oxford, and when Seuss did not in fact win the fellowship "the father felt forced to send him to Oxford anyway, in order to save face" (MacDonald 3). Seuss himself admired his father, and viewed him as a major influence in his life. He recalls that his father gave him the memento of a plaster cast of a dinosaur track and Seuss interprets it thus: "He was trying to tell me, in joke form, [that] a species can disappear and still leave a track in the sand" (MacDonald 2). Could the young Seuss have unconsciously perceived that it was up to him to leave a mark for the family? If Seuss sensed that his family felt "mighty small" when they looked up the hill, he might have sworn to find a way to plant the family flag on the top, and after failing at his academic ambitions, decided that his best hope in this contest was his genius for imagination, just as Bartholomew's best hope is the magical hat that grows out of his head. The last illustration in *The 500 Hats* depicts Bartholomew returning to his home in the valley with a sack of gold on his back—proof of his conquest of the folks on the hill, and a possible correlative to Seuss's earnings from *Mulberry Street*. The picture gets much of its power from the two tiny figures waving at him from the distant humble cottage—his father and his mother.

Nevertheless, Bartholomew's successful sale does not quite dispel some dark suggestions in this final illustration. For example, we might wonder if Seuss felt that the power structure of his society wanted to slay his imagination, and that he could survive only by imagining something so enticing that the power structure would commodify it. I find it disturbing that, whether he fails or succeeds, Bartholomew's relationship to the power structure dictates that he must eventually lose his beloved hat and feather (if he were to fail, he would wind up with no hat because he would have no head). Because the hatless Bartholomew carries the ungainly, almost burdensome, sack of money, we might wonder whether Seuss felt that he had somehow sold out when he sold *Mulberry Street*. Furthermore, we might conjecture that Seuss feared that he had lost some of his imaginative powers, or that he had forfeited ownership of them. Finally, since Bartholomew returns to his home in the valley, we might suspect that, even though he had been rewarded with money after selling *Mulberry Street*, Seuss in some ways still felt like a "mighty small" person who had not really made it up the hill. These autobiographical speculations present a disturbing picture, a picture of an artist who perceives of his imagination as something that can be killed, or bought, or sold at the whim of the rich and powerful.[5]

Returning from the possible autobiographical interpretation to more ostensible levels, we see that *The 500 Hats* goes a step further than *Mulberry Street* in solving the problem of the rejected child. In *Mulberry Street* the parent and child reach an impasse, but in *The 500 Hats* we see the parent and child walking arm in arm, looking upon one another with happy smiles. I think that most readers would agree that, although this illustration is somewhat gratifying, it fails to carry the emotional charge that a similar illustration would have carried in *Mulberry Street*. In *Mulberry Street*, because we have seen Marco laboring to think of ways to please his parent, and then have seen him happily running up the stairs brimming with stories to share, we deeply regret that the parent and child do not connect. But the relationship between Bartholomew and King Derwin seems more distant and accidental. We are glad that King Derwin smiles upon Bartholomew in the end primarily because we are relieved at Bartholomew's safety. We might have been as glad if the king merely had decided to leave the poor boy alone.

Nevertheless, we should neither overlook that both these stories project the pattern of an unhappy, grouchy parent figure rejecting the imaginative world of a child figure nor ignore the implications of the added reconciliation at the end of *The 500 Hats*. When King Derwin accepts the child's imaginative world, he gains joy, just as Marco had hoped his parent would. If we do not much care about King Derwin's joy, perhaps it is because Seuss is only just beginning to solve the problem of the rejected child, and thus has done so rather imperfectly. The rescue of the parent from unhappiness nevertheless represents a step forward in Seuss's exploration, a step he explores with more success the following year in *The King's Stilts*.

The King's Stilts

To make the rescue of the parent from unhappiness more meaningful in *The King's Stilts*, Seuss not only increases our sympathy for him but also connects his rescue to the survival of the kingdom. Seuss accomplishes the simpler of the two tasks by developing a plot line in which, because of his sadness, the king can no longer protect his kingdom from a salty flood. But how can Seuss increase our sympathy for a parent who angrily rejects his own child? He does so by splitting the parent into two figures—the bad Lord Droon and the good King Birtram—each representing a different side of the parent. We cannot fail to notice the similarity between this device and the stock figure of the wicked stepmother in fairy tales, for the daughter who suffers under the wicked stepmother in fairy tales can usually remember a second mother, her real mother, an ideal loving mother—but unfortunately a mother who is dead, and thus powerless. Freudian and Jungian folklorists have long suggested that this dichotomy not only permits the child reader to vent hostility against her mother with impunity but also offers the child reader a way of explaining the mother's unacceptable behavior, that the person is not really the child's mother (Bettleheim 66–73, Von Franz 207–214).

In *The King's Stilts* the good parent is not dead, but he loses his power to the bad parent, and thus the child must rescue the good parent from the bad parent. This scheme reveals a profound possibility about the psychology of coping with rejection. Perhaps rejected children want to reject their parents in return, as *Mulberry Street* encourages, and maybe they also want to appease the parents, as *The 500 Hats* suggests. However, perhaps they could also interpret parental rejection as a symptom of their beloved parents' unhappiness, and thus want to rescue their poor parents. Of course, children might employ wishful thinking in order to falsely believe that a loving parent is hidden and trapped within an angry rejecting parent, but children sometimes perspicuously apprehend a truth; that is, many parents do suffer daily depressions, discouragements, frustrations, tensions, or wearinesses that lead them to snap at their children, even though they love their children.[6] In either case, Seuss's split parent in *The King's Stilts* allows us to see that rejected children not only must bear their parents' rejection, but might also assume a heartrending burden of responsibility for their parents' rejecting behavior.

In addition, the split parent in *The King's Stilts* yields well to a gestalt reading in which we see all the seemingly separate characters and events of the story as different facets of one psyche—the child becomes an inner child, the saltwater flood an inner flood, and so forth. In the beginning of the story, Seuss presents to the reader the ideal adult in King Birtram—an adult who has achieved a perfect balance between his adult and child natures: "When he worked, he really worked . . . but when he played, he really PLAYED!" Significantly, the first view we have of the king may provide two hints of this ideal balance and unification. First, we see the king doing very adult-looking work—signing royal documents—but we see him doing so in the bathtub with a delicious pink ring (foreshadows of the mischievous Cat in the Hat!), while a wonderful fish spurts huge drops of water. Although the king signs official documents, everything around him looks playfully jolly. Second, we see the king in the presence of both a smiling child—Eric—and a frowning adult—Lord Droon—the figures who, on the gestalt level, could represent the two sides that the king balances.

At the same time, this illustration represents a near-ideal family dynamic, for the child figure is in close, loving, and happy contact with the good side of his parent, whereas the frowning side of the parent stands aside tamed and innocuous (yet somehow still a disturbingly threatening potential).

When we turn the page, we learn how much depends upon the well-being that the king maintains by balancing his child and adult natures, for we see that his land lies in a valley below the level of the seas that surround it, and that only the heavily intertwined roots of the Dike Trees growing all along the edge of the island forestall a devastating flood. Perhaps the salty sea symbolizes the tears and cares of the adult world, a world that threatens to flood and obliterate the happy kingdom (the kingdom of the self in a gestalt reading). The roots that hold back the flood, then, could represent the childlike imagination, for they weave a mysterious living web that reaches down into the fertile earth below the kingdom—a possible metaphor for a healthy connection with the unconscious. It is the joys of this connection, the bliss of the active imagination, that forestalls the woeful flood of adult cares and tears.

The king's most important task by far, we learn, is to protect these roots from the evil black Nizzard birds, who like to peck at the roots. The text associates these Nizzards with adult worries: "'A hard day' [the king would] say, 'full of nizzardly worries.'" In other words, the myriad worries of adulthood constantly threaten to cut us off from the roots of our childlike joy and pleasure, thus allowing the salt flood of tears. King Birtram, however, creates a unique response—an army of "Patrol Cats." How fitting that cats—those most independent-minded, unmastered creatures—should guard the roots of childlike imagination! How inappropriate would have been dogs, with all their worry and obsequiousness to serve their masters. To defend our childlike imagination and joy, Seuss seems to say, we must be like cats toward society, not like dogs. (This may also look forward to the anarchistic Cat in the Hat saving two children from a dull adult-ruled afternoon.)

Finally, the stilts give the king the ability to defend the roots, for they give him his very will to live: "This was the moment King Birtram lived for. . . . 'Quick, Eric!' he'd shout. 'Quick, Eric! The stilts!'" The roots and the stilts may be a double symbol for the same thing—the childlike imagination. The stilts, which we note that the *child* must fetch for the king, lift the king high above the mundane surface of the earth in flights of fancy, just as the roots burrow far below the mundane surface into the rich soils of the unconscious. Furthermore, when the stilts disappear, so do the tree roots, and just as the disappearance of the stilts leads to the king's tears, the disappearance of the tree roots leads to the kingdom's immersion under saltwater. Perhaps the only distinction we can make between these two symbols is that where the roots could represent the healthy state of the imagination, the stilts could represent the prescription for preserving that state—play, or the daily energetic use of the childlike imagination.

Thus, unlike *Mulberry Street* or *The 500 Hats,* which both begin with a parent's rejection of a child, and of a child's imagination, *The King's Stilts* begins with a parent-figure enjoying a friendly relationship with the child-figure and embracing the imagination. After we pass the beginning, however, we find *The King's Stilts* moving into parallel with Seuss's first two books, for we meet the rejecting side of the parent in Lord Droon. Seuss writes: "There was a man in Binn who didn't like fun. He didn't like games. He didn't like laughing. This man was a scowler. This man was Lord Droon." The illustration that accompanies this verbal text depicts Lord Droon scowling at the king's stilts, and so Seuss makes Droon fulfill half of his function—the rejection of the childlike imagination—but this bad side of the parent must reject the child as well. Thus, Seuss has Droon steal the stilts and give them to Eric with the command to bury them.

This plot device accomplishes several objectives. First, it identifies the child in the story as the keeper of the childlike imagination. After all, neither Birtram nor Droon know the location of the stilts. Second, Eric's knowledge of the stilts' location, a knowledge which is dangerous to Droon, gives Droon a reason to attack Eric himself, thus making Droon fulfill the second half of his function as the rejecting side of the parent. Third, Droon's theft of the stilts seems to fix an overserious adult facet of the persona as the culprit in grownups' lack of joy. Fourth, Eric's burial of the stilts could represent the psychological process of repression, in this case the repression of childlike qualities.

Most important, the device forces Eric to assume the burden of rescuing the good side of the parent. Because only Eric knows where the stilts are buried, only Eric can save the king from depression and thus the kingdom from the salt flood. The child reader here may find a strong correlative to his or her own burden to rescue a parent, as well as a powerful portrayal of the bad angry (side of the) parent that keeps the child from reaching the good loving (side of the) parent. Seuss presents this dilemma in a remarkable illustration. Eric runs up a flight of stairs to rescue the king, only to be intercepted at the top by a scowling Lord Droon. In *Mulberry Street* Marco also rushes up a flight of steps to reach a good parent, only to find a disapproving parent instead. However, in *The King's Stilts* we have a second, hidden, good parent—a possibility that this illustration exploits to great effect, for a sad, helpless-looking King Birtram seems to grow like a ghost out of the back of the very solid-looking Lord Droon, almost making the figure resemble a Janus (fig. 7). The king's back is turned to Eric, so although Eric can see the unhappy king, and can long to give that king the gift that will save him from unhappiness, the king cannot see Eric, and Lord Droon stands guard to insure that Eric will not reach the king. In the same way, when children face an angry, rejecting parent, they may see (or think they see) behind that anger a helpless, depressed parent whom they long to rescue by sharing the secret knowledge of childhood joy, but the child may also feel that the approach to the "true" parent is always blocked by the side of the parent that is forever angrily rejecting the child.

The next illustration, though not as remarkable, develops the theme further, for we see that Droon has locked Eric into a prison house under the false pretext that Eric is being quarantined for measles. This may represent the child reader's feeling that she has been locked up by her parent's mistaken opinion of her, an opinion, propagated by the bad side of the parent, that the child is somehow sick. Or, on the gestalt level, the imprisoned child could represent locked up or repressed childlike qualities within a person, qualities that the overserious inner parent mistakenly condemns as sick. Measles' association as a specifically childhood disease supports either interpretation.

The poor child, then, has been condemned as sick, locked into a prison, and separated from the good parent by a bad parent that stands eternal guard. How will the child rescue the parent? The answer is richly suggestive: Eric fools Lord Droon by disguising himself in adult clothes! On the familial level, a child feels that he must maintain a token facade of acceptable grown-up behavior if he wishes to get past, or appease, his parent's anger, and thus have an opportunity both to receive the parent's approval and to share the hidden secrets of childhood joy—the blissful imagination. Or, on the gestalt level, we could see an individual who feels that she can express her childlike qualities and drives only if she somehow disguises them as acceptable adult behaviors (we certainly see

7. From *The King's Stilts* by Dr. Seuss. TM and copyright © 1939 by Dr. Seuss Enterprises, L.P. Reproduced by permission of Random House, Inc.

enough of this type of sublimation around us). Or, on an autobio-graphical level, could we not see here a symbol for Seuss himself—the hero who masquerades as a respectable adult, when within he is actually a child smuggling childhood imagination and joy to an over-Nizzarded world?

In any case, when Eric sneaks past Droon to return the stilts to the king, the king regains his will to live, rallies his patrol cats, and drives off the Nizzards from the Dike Tree roots, thus saving the kingdom from a flood. At the end of the story, the despotic adult-figure is locked up, and we see the king and Eric happily playing together on their stilts. The child has vanquished the bad (side of the) parent by returning the joys of the childlike imagination to the good (side of the) parent, and this rescue has freed the parent to once again express his or her blocked and hidden love for the child. The elements of love and rescue make this a more compelling solution to the dilemma of the rejected child than Seuss found in either *Mulberry Street* or *The 500 Hats,* and perhaps because he has discovered this satisfying resolution, Seuss abandons for a time the theme that he has pursued so single-mindedly; however, he returns to it again 21 years later to write one of his best-sellers—*Green Eggs and Ham.*

Green Eggs and Ham

Within the 51-word vocabulary of *Green Eggs and Ham,* Seuss re-introduces the most important aspects of his first three books—the grouchy rejecting parent and the happy accepting parent, the re-jected child and the child's mission to rescue the parent, the healing power of the childlike imagination and the association of the imagi-nation with childhood libidinal drives—perhaps even a subversion and simultaneous reinforcement of the reading process. As with the other three books, we will treat the text's illustrations as "illumi-nations"—to borrow a term from Maurice Sendak—to notice how they tell *more* than the verbal text and relate stories of their own.[7]

One aspect of *Green Eggs and Ham* that sets it apart from the other three stories is the androgyny of the child protagonist, Sam. Sam has no physical characteristics that mark him or her as either male or female, and Seuss never uses a gender-specific pronoun when re-ferring to Sam. Thus, although I believe females could read beyond the specifically male characters in Seuss's first three books to make

an androgynous identification with the overall parent-child relationship, the readers of *Green Eggs and Ham* are even more free to
view Sam as male or female or both. I have not had to look far to be
convinced that females often do view Sam as female. For example,
one of novelist Pat Cadigan's female protagonists, Samantha, goes
by the nickname of Sam-I-Am. Even closer to home, a Samantha in
one of my children's literature classes went by the nickname Sam,
and has a picture of Sam and the motto "Sam-I-Am" tattooed on
her ankle (I use this example with kind permission). These examples not only bespeak Sam's androgynous nature but also suggest the almost cultlike devotion the book has inspired in several
generations of readers.

I have more difficulty viewing the grouch as androgynous, even
though Seuss never associates the grouch with a gender-specific
pronoun. First, the grouch wears a tall top hat, which in our society
usually carries masculine association. Second, the grouch sits in an
easy chair reading a newspaper, which has almost become a stereotype in our society for the tired father who comes home from work
and doesn't want to be disturbed—the famous "missing American
father." (Unfortunately, part of this stereotype probably developed
because the tired mother came home from work and then went
into the kitchen to cook supper for everyone else!) Nevertheless, I
will attempt grammatically to portray both the grouch's and Sam's
androgyny by referring to them alternately as male and female.

Green Eggs and Ham begins with an illustration of a small smiling
creature dashing around a corner while standing on the back of
a smiling beast. (This illustration on page 3 and the last illustration, on page 62, are the only single-page illustrations. Every other
illustration comprises a two-page spread.) In her right hand the
small creature holds a hat, and in the left a sign proclaiming, "I am
Sam." Beginning readers are at this moment teaching their eyes to
move from left to right along the verbal text so that they can read
these words, and Seuss reinforces the reading process by making
the words themselves part of the sign dashing across the page from
left to right. Furthermore, the child reading the words identifies
with the small creature riding the beast, and because Sam's riding
seems effortless and joyful, the reading seems effortless and joyful
as well. Reading, just like the smiling friendly beast, will take the
reader for a pleasure ride. However, the beast resembles a dog, a
subservient creature that obeys authority with good cheer, and this

begins to hint that the reinforcement of reading may not go entirely unchallenged by other opposing elements of the text.

For example, when we turn the page (4–5), we meet a bigger creature—the parent figure—sitting in an easy chair reading a newspaper. He looks tired and unhappy, and I suggest that children see adults this way more often than adults might like to think. Seuss makes the unhappy parent's newspaper seem dry and lifeless, and by thus associating reading with dull joyless activities and grouchy people (shades of *Mulberry Street*), Seuss may encourage rebellion against the same reading process that he seemed to privilege on the previous page. In fact, if we look carefully, we can see that the grouch's dull, depressing newspaper is actually a beginning reader, an alphabet book with "A, B, C, D, E, F, G" written across the top. In addition, this illustration already hints of parental rejection, for the introduction of the unhappy parent seems to push Sam halfway off the page—an unusual but effective compositional decision. In some ways, this illustration could represent the temporary defeat of happiness, because the grouch frowns and we can no longer see the smiles of either Sam or the beast.

But the tide of battle changes with the turn of the page (6–7). Here Sam comes dashing back into the picture, but with several important transformations (fig. 8). First, he no longer rides a dog, but rather a large cat, an animal that Seuss always associates with anarchy and the imagination. Second, Sam no longer rides from left to right, but rather from right to left, thus introducing a note of rebellion against the reading process. Third, Sam's sign no longer reads, "I am Sam," but rather inverts the syntax to "Sam I am," reinforcing the subversion. Although these elements combine to challenge the gloomy mood of the previous illustration, we should also note that the friendly smile that Sam offers the startled parent injects an element of invitation into the challenge—"I am here to disrupt, and I invite you to join in the fun." The grouch seems temporarily unnerved, and the dull alphabet letters on his newspaper seem to have transformed themselves into the name *Marco*. Could the assertive Sam-I-Am represent the triumphant return of the previously timid and defeated Marco?

When we turn the page (8–9), we find that Sam has partially effected his subversion against reading, for as the result of his right-to-left passage across the page, the newspaper now lies scattered on the floor. Nevertheless, the parent here reclaims some of her

8. From *Green Eggs and Ham* by Dr. Seuss. TM and copyright © 1960 by Dr. Seuss Enterprises, L.P. Reproduced by permission of Random House, Inc.

lost authority. Her countenance glares, and her fist slams the easy chair, as she cries, "That Sam-I-Am! / That Sam-I-Am! / I do not like / that Sam-I-am!" At long last, Seuss no longer equivocates about the rejecting parent; we could not ask for a simpler, more direct statement of rejection. I suggest that many children have experienced almost identical situations. For example we can picture a young child named Sam jockeying for attention by running back and forth in front of a parent who is reading the newspaper, only to have the parent yell at her to go away. Even if the parent says something nonpersonal—"I've been working all day! Can't I have a moment's peace?"—I submit that Sam may hear "That Sam! That Sam! I do not like that Sam!"

At this point, then, I believe that children hold their breaths as they turn the page (10–11). The parent has come right out and said it—"I do not like Sam!" The statement hangs like a cloud. What will happen next? How will Sam cope with the rejection? What will he do? What will he say?

He says, "Do you like green eggs and ham?"

The key to my reading of this story lies in the gap created by this non sequitur response, for the gap forces the child reader to transfer the anxiety about whether the parent will learn to like Sam, to whether the parent will learn to like green eggs and ham. In other words, throughout the rest of the text, every time that Sam asks, "Would you eat them in a house, with a mouse, in a box, with a fox," and so forth, the child hears herself ask, "Please like me, parent," and every time that the grouch responds, "I do not like them, Sam-I-Am," the child hears her parent respond, "I do not like you."

Because Seuss transfers the parent's rejection to the green eggs and ham, we should consider this strange dish carefully. For example, why are the eggs green? Perhaps their unrealistic color highlights their function as an imaginary food, and thus encourages us to see them as a representation of Sam's imaginative world. Furthermore, in order to persuade the parent to like the green eggs and ham, Sam takes him on an increasingly imaginative ride, and thus we come to associate the green eggs and ham with a celebration of the imagination.

In addition, we might also acknowledge the orality of eggs and ham. They promise a tangible pleasure to the mouth, a pleasure that Seuss on one level ties to the oral pleasure of reading the text, especially since the eggs and ham move from left to right. On the other hand, the entrance of the eggs and ham causes the parent's newspaper to blow away, thus intimating that Sam wishes the more tangible oral gratification of eating to replace the dry orality of reading.[8] We have seen this tense ambiguity toward reading before in Seuss's texts, and it increases as *Green Eggs and Ham* progresses.[9]

However, the defeat of the parent's newspaper on page 9 may represent other things in addition to the oral gratification of eating; that is, it could represent the beginning of the child's rescue of the parent, especially through restoring to the parent the joys of the imagination. I have suggested already that children may be highly empathetic to the sadness that they sense (or think they sense) behind the irritable moods of their parents, and we have seen Seuss symbolize this in an angry Lord Droon facing Eric, while a sad King who needs Eric's help is hidden behind Droon. Similarly, in the four illustrations of the parent up to this point in *Green Eggs and Ham*, Seuss makes him look angry only in one, and depressed in the others. As the newspaper, and the dry unimaginative factual world that it symbolizes, seemed to make the parent unhappy, part of Sam's rescue is to get rid of the newspaper and to offer the parent a better alternative. Sam offers this alternative on a long hand

that he reels out of a fishing rod. Not only is the child fishing for
the parent's attention, she is reaching out to him, and the alternative that she offers mixes into a potent brew ingredients such as
the gratification of libidinal drives, a rebellion against reading and
other authoritarian processes, a celebration of the imagination, and
an acceptance of the child.

I think we can see this complex of associations operating in several other parts of the text, such as the train. For example, as the
child reader sees the train rushing powerfully along its track from
left to right, he can associate the train with the reading process,
linking elements as a sentence does. At first, this association seems
to equate reading with the pleasures of the imagination—libidinal
and otherwise. Yet, as the joy and anarchy of the ride increase, the
left-to-right track becomes less straight and stable, finally ending
in a midair terminus that tosses the train and its inhabitants into
chaotic positions (44–50). Significantly, the parent will not eat the
green eggs and ham until the train is off the track, and everyone is
floating haphazardly in the water. This may link oral gratification
and the celebration of the imagination to a chaotic state that rebels
against the fixed track of verbal text, especially as Seuss puts the
illustration in which the parent finally samples the green eggs and
ham onto the only page in the book without verbal text.

However, the most significant aspect of Sam's journey with the
parent involves the celebratory happiness of Sam's imaginative
world, for we must remember that in Seuss the child seeks the parent's acceptance not only in order to fulfill the child's own need
for love, but in order to rescue the parent from unhappiness, and
that this rescue can only be effected by returning the parent to the
joys of the childlike imagination. In *Green Eggs and Ham* the child's
ride of the imagination leads to bliss, just as in *Mulberry Street* the
child's parade of the imagination runs into Bliss Street—but this
time the child does not fail to share that bliss with the parent. We
can easily sense the blissful quality of Sam's imaginative world, for
every denizen of that world wears an expression that Jonathan Cott
calls "blissed out," or that Karla Kuskin describes as "a smile you
might find on the Mona Lisa after her first martini" (Cott 9). The
mouse smiles in a house. The fox smiles in a box. The goat smiles in
a car. The people in the train smile even while the train is flipping
upside down into the smokestack of a boat. In fact, the captain of
the ruined boat bestows a friendly smile on the fox, even as he is

thrown off his boat by the crash (47). In the illustration on pages 48 and 49, everyone is flying everywhere into the water, some upside down, but the only person not smiling serenely is the parent—who has still not eaten the green eggs and ham, and thus has not yet gained the secret bliss of Sam's anarchic childlike imagination.

Much is at stake, then, when the child reader turns to pages 54 and 55 to see the sad-looking parent reaching toward Sam and saying, "Sam! / If you will let me be, / I will try them. / You will see." I think many a child has heard similar weary responses when he has tried to get his parent to play with him: "All right, Sam. I will play with you if you will leave me alone afterwards." For the child who has been fishing for attention, this is the moment when the parent "bites." But will the parent in *Green Eggs and Ham* bite? The child reader turns the page (56–57) to see the characters all holding their breaths as the sad parent eyes a green egg on his fork. The pages contain no verbal text, but the child reader holds her breath along with Sam's friends, for she pictures her own parent putting aside his newspaper grudgingly to give her a few minutes of attention. If only her parent realized that she is trying to give something precious to him—a return to his lost bliss.

When we turn the page (58–59), we see that the parent has eaten the whole egg and is now smiling for the first time. In subsequent pictures, Seuss reduces the number of lines around the parent's mouth and eyes so that he looks increasingly younger and less weary. I suggest that every time the grump in *Green Eggs and Ham* eats the egg, somewhere a tired, grumpy parent puts down his or her newspaper to grudgingly give his or her son or daughter a few minutes of play time, and starts feeling genuine happiness and contentment for the first time that day. Every time the grump eats the egg, somewhere a child's heart feels gladness as she sees sadness, worry, weariness, and years fall away from the face of the parent she loves. Somewhere, if only in the child reader's imagination, a parent stops being angry with his child, and starts to like her instead. For as the child reads *Green Eggs and Ham,* she takes a blissful imaginative journey into a realm where her parents embrace her imagination, thus sharing her joy, and loving her in the realm where she truly thinks, feels, and lives.

We see, then, that every act of reading *Green Eggs and Ham* might relate to two or three levels of a celebration of the childlike imagination. First, the theme of the text itself celebrates the childlike imagination, not only by privileging it as the dominant dynamic within the text, but by positing it as the only force that could restore a parent's happiness and heal the depression that makes the parent seem to reject the child. Second, while children read this text about the imagination, they go on blissful imaginative journeys of their own in which they see themselves sharing the bliss of imagination with their parents, thus making their grouchy, depressed parents happy and receiving the love the depression was blocking. The bliss of imagination can make a parent love a child, even if only in the child reader's blissful imagination. This, of course, suggests the third possible level of blissful imagination that the text may encourage. Although it may be true that a parent's love is hidden or blocked by weariness or depression, it also may be true that the parent simply does not love his or her child; thus, the third level of blissful imagination that the text might encourage is not simply the imaginative act of releasing a parent's hidden or blocked love, but the wish-projection of hidden or blocked love where there is none. Either of the last two possibilities might explain the almost cultlike devotion *Green Eggs and Ham* has inspired.

As the book ends, Seuss has the parent repeat every particular of Sam's ride, and affirm that she would eat green eggs in all of the places Sam has taken her:

> And I would eat them in a boat.
> And I would eat them with a goat . . .
> And I will eat them in the rain.
> And in the dark. And on a train.
> And in a car. And in a tree.
> They are so good, so good, you see!
> So I will eat them in a box.
> And I will eat them with a fox.
> And I will eat them in a house.
> And I will eat them with a mouse.
> And I will eat them here and there.
> Say! I will eat them ANYWHERE!   (59–61)

In this way, Seuss makes sure that we understand that the parent has not only eaten the egg, but that she has joyfully accepted Sam's entire imaginative world.

Finally, on the last page, the platter is empty, the parent is serenely happy, and the child receives the gratitude of the rescued parent

9. From *Green Eggs and Ham* by Dr. Seuss. TM and copyright © 1960 by Dr. Seuss Enterprises, L.P. Reproduced by permission of Random House, Inc.

(fig. 9): "I do so like / green eggs and ham! / Thank you! / Thank you, / Sam-I-am!" (62). Seuss illustrates both characters with their eyes closed, to show not only serenity, but to make their happiness seem dreamlike, and parallel to the happiness that the child reader is experiencing as he daydreams about a resolution with his own parent through the vehicle of the text.

And, most important, although the verbal text of this last page states that the parent has learned to like green eggs and ham, the child reader knows that the parent has actually learned to like something far more wonderful. In the illustration, the parent's arm is now around Sam.

Notes

1. Peter Neumeyer ascribes Seuss's potency to a "sense of anarchy" (Lamb A18), whereas Loreene Lovette Ort suggests that Seuss moves from order to anarchy and then back to order for the purpose of giving the child the pleasure of "secure suspense"; that is, the child may experience the thrilling anxieties of anarchy, while

feeling secure that order will prevail in the end (135–37). I would add that the texts not only move sequentially from order to anarchy and back to order, but also that many parts of the texts incubate order and chaos, and other hierarchical oppositions, simultaneously.

2. These simultaneous oppositions may be more prevalent in Seuss's work than has been generally realized. For example, Michael Steig takes exception to *I Wish That I Had Duck Feet*, a book illustrated by Barney Toby, and written by Seuss under the name Theo. LeSieg, a play upon Seuss's real name—Theodore Seuss Geisel. Steig claims that the ending, in which the boy throws the items of his wild daydreams into a garbage can, makes the book function as a cautionary tale against nonconformity, and even against the use of the imagination (140). Although Steig has done well to notice in a Seuss text something that many would never attribute to Seuss—a rejection of the imagination—we might also notice elements of the text that hold both subversion and privileging of the imagination in unresolved tension. For example, to name but one simple element, a garbage can carries negative connotations on only one side of its hierarchical ordering. On another, it could represent a place of treasures and fascinations, especially to children.

3. For a time Seuss attempted to pursue the life of an academic at Oxford, an occupation that, in Seuss's own words, was filled with "astonishing irrelevance" and ran counter to the grain of his imaginative impulses, as is witnessed by the fact that his notebooks from this attempt are filled with doodles rather than notes. Relevant to a consideration of gender-specific attitudes toward the imagination is the fact that Seuss's father provided the impetus for this venture, whereas Seuss's mother expressed relief and encouragement when Seuss finally abandoned this attempt and dropped out to pursue his creative instincts. In Seuss's own words, she "said she was so happy that I would never be a stuffed shirt." It was partially the urgings of another female, Seuss's future wife, Helen Palmer, that gave Seuss the courage to "follow his natural inclinations away from academia" (MacDonald 9–10).

4. Some readers may wish to consider the theoretical psychosexual implications of a father-figure who is threatened by something on the son-figure that "always *pointed straight up* in the air." The bigger Bartholomew's hats get, the more abundantly the feathers seem to spurt out of the top, while King Derwin's angry response is to shoot "huge arrows" at the hat, a solution that, although realistically improbable, could be symbolically consistent with a phallic duel. Also consistent within such a theoretical framework is the father-figure's decision to solve the problem by cutting off Bartholomew's head, a suggestion of castration and Oedipal revenge. In fact, the very first picture of King Derwin not only shows him high up on a hill—the parent, or even the superego, position we remember from the stairs before the parent in *Mulberry Street*—but also depicts him standing below a huge ax, thus from the beginning associating him with either the threat of Oedipal revenge, or with the censoring power of the superego.

Those who subscribe to such a theoretical framework could thus read a classic Oedipal challenge into Bartholomew's unruly hat, or in a different interpretation might even consider the possibility of a homosexual presentation toward the father, with a longing for the father's acceptance and the fear of the father's angry rejection of the phallus.

On the other hand, a slight rereading of classic psychoanalytic theory could allow us to acknowledge the possibility of psychosexual imagery in the upright feather without forcing any of the above conclusions. For example, the feather could conceivably be seen as a symbol of the libido in a wider sense than sexuality, as a symbol of a person's life forces, the deepest sense of a person's identity. If we can justify associating the upright feather with both the beauty of the imagination and with the libido, we might see within this story a suggestion that the act of imagining is a part of our libido, that it is one of the several primal urges that fuel our will to live and constitute the deepest roots of our sense of self. Within this framework, we might reinterpret the possible suggestions of castration in the story as a correlative to the psychic mutilation that our phallocratic society effects upon its males when its narrow conception of masculinity drives them to cut off the imaginative impulses of their being.

5. For a more optimistic reading of this last illustration see Mavis Reimer's interpretation of Bartholomew's trials as a journey of growth, and therefore the gold as a symbol of spiritual wealth: "The roads the child Bartholomew travels are paths of exploration rather than streets of possession. . . . And it seems to me that, in front of the silhouetted figures of his parents, there is the faint suggestion of a path meandering past the house and on into the fields beyond" (141). This reading reveals Seuss's extraordinary ability to suggest powerful oppositions within a seemingly simple framework.

6. For any who doubt a child's ability to arrive at such a perspicuous apprehension, I recommend Gareth B. Matthews's *Philosophy and the Young Child*, especially the section on children's reasoning ability (23–36).

7. Maurice Sendak is quoted as having said: "There are basically two types of illustration. First, there is the direct no-nonsense approach that puts the facts of the case into simple, down-to-earth images: Miss Muffet, her tuffet, curds, whey, spider and all. Then there is, for want of a better term, illumination. As with a poem set to song, in which every shade and nuance is given greater meaning by music, so pictures can interpret texts" (Lanes 109).

8. Of course, the green eggs and ham are not the only edible-looking elements of the text. Part of Seuss's genius is that he appeals to children's orality throughout his books by giving many of his objects soft, rounded "gummable" textures. In addition, he may appeal to children's anality (witness the squishy tree tops) or even their sexuality (witness the trains and tunnels and smokestacks). In all of these cases, the appeal sets up a tension between a physical gratification that is preferable to reading, and the attainment of these pleasures on an imaginative level as part of the pleasures of reading.

9. Readers who wish to pursue the possible gender-specific psychosexual implications suggested in note 4 on Bartholomew's feather might see the piece of ham with an egg on either side as a phallic symbol. Within such a theoretical framework, the hats of the son and father figure might be analyzed for suggestions of a phallic duel. For example, does the father's hat seem to wilt on page 6 when Sam presents his challenge? Does it tend to regain height when the father-figure regains authority on page 9? Could the odd compositional arrangement of page 5 that removes Sam's head from the page suggest castration? Conversely, could Sam's presentation of the green eggs and ham be interpreted as a homosexual invitation? If so, how might the father's posture on page 27 be interpreted? However, as I mentioned in note 4, it may be possible to view the eggs and ham as a sexual symbol (perhaps even as a suggestion of the uterus and ovaries) without having to accede to the possibilities of classic psychosexual complexes. A sexual symbol here might be seen as Seuss's way of associating the imagination with the child's libidinal drives, not only making us want the imagination to triumph, but causing us to associate the imagination with the will to live and with the deepest roots of personal identity. Perhaps in Seuss, the parent's acceptance of the child, of the child's sexuality, and of the child's imagination become indistinguishable.

Works Cited

Bettleheim, Bruno. *The Uses of Enchantment: The Meaning and Importance of Fairy Tales.* New York: Random House, 1977.

Cott, Jonathan. *Pipers at the Gates of Dawn: The Wisdom of Children's Literature.* New York: McGraw-Hill, 1981.

Lamb, J. R. "Dr. Seuss Dies." *San Diego Tribune* Sept. 25, 1991: A18.

Lanes, Selma G. *The Art of Maurice Sendak.* New York: Harry N. Abrams, 1980.

LeSieg, Theodore [Theodor Seuss Geisel]. *I Wish That I Had Duck Feet.* Illustrated by Barney Toby. New York: Random House, 1965.

MacDonald, Ruth K. *Dr. Seuss.* Boston: Twayne, 1988.

Matthews, Gareth B. *Philosophy and the Young Child.* Cambridge, Mass.: Harvard U.P., 1980.

Nodelman, Perry. *Words About Pictures: The Narrative Art of Children's Picture Books.* Athens: U. Georgia P., 1988.

Ort, Lorrene Love. "Theodor Seuss Geisel: The Children's Dr. Seuss." *Elementary English* 32 (1955): 135–42.

Reimer, Mavis. "Dr. Seuss' *The 500 Hats of Bartholomew Cubbins:* Of Hats and Kings." *Touchstones: Reflections on the Best in Children's Literature.* Vol. 3, *Picture Books.* Ed. Perry Nodelman. West Lafayette, Ind.: Children's Literature Association, 1989. 132–41.

Dr. Seuss [Theodor Seuss Geisel]. *The 500 Hats of Bartholomew Cubbins.* Eau Claire, Wisc.: E. M. Hale for Vanguard Press, 1938.

——. *And To Think That I Saw It on Mulberry Street.* New York: Random House, 1937.

——. *Green Eggs and Ham.* New York: Random House, 1960.

——. *Horton Hatches the Egg.* New York: Random House, 1940.

——. *The King's Stilts.* New York: Random House, 1939.

——. *McElligott's Pool.* New York: Random House, 1947.

Steig, Michael. "Dr. Seuss's Attack on the Imagination: *I Wish That I Had Duck Feet* and the Cautionary Tale." *Proceedings of the Ninth Annual Conference of the Children's Literature Association: University of Florida, March 1982.* Children's Literature Association (U.S.). New Rochelle, NY: Iona College, 1983.

Stone, Lawrence. *The Causes of the English Revolution: 1529–1642.* New York: Harper, 1972.

Von Franz, Marie-Louise. "The Beautiful Wassilissa." *Problems of the Feminine in Fairy Tales.* New York: Spring Publications, 1972. 143–157. Rpt. in *Cinderella Casebook.* Ed. Alan Dundes. Madison: U. Wisconsin P., 1988. 200–218.

Leap of Faith in Astrid Lindgren's
Brothers Lionheart
Eva-Maria Metcalf

I believe in children's need for consolation. When I was a child, people believed that when you die you go to heaven; that was not one of the most amusing things one could imagine, to be sure, but if everyone went there. . . . That would at least be better than lying in the ground and not existing any more. Today's children no longer have this consolation. They no longer have this tale. So then I thought: one could perhaps give them another tale that can provide them with a little warmth while they wait for the unavoidable end.

Astrid Lindgren to Egil Törnqvist, 1973

If we believe Astrid Lindgren, a major driving force behind *The Brothers Lionheart,* to which she refers above, was her desire to console. Despite the prevalence of violence and death and despite the novel's controversial conclusion in death and suicide, it is both a consoling and a hope-inspiring book. Not everybody has interpreted the novel in this fashion, however. Like Lindgren's early success, *Pippi Longstocking,* it was greeted with sharp criticism as well as with praise when it first appeared in 1973, and the debate has not quite subsided yet. The reason for the different readings can be sought in the novel's complexity and ambiguity, the main focus of my reading.

The Brothers Lionheart follows the tradition of the fantasy tale, in which primary and secondary worlds are closely linked in a tension-filled coexistence. Lindgren carefully crafted the fantasy paradigm to allow readers a choice. In fact, the novel is designed to work on two levels: for the child to enjoy and escape and for the adult to understand and empathize. Thus, it can be read as a heroic quest, providing the reader with plenty of adventure and a story about love that conquers death; but it can also be read as a psychological portrayal of a sick boy coming to terms with approaching death and a developmental novel that traces the main character's growing self-confidence. In my discussion of *The Brothers Lionheart* I found

Children's Literature 23, ed. Francelia Butler, R. H. W. Dillard, and Elizabeth Lennox Keyser (Yale University Press, © 1995 Hollins College).

Zohar Shavit's concept of the ambivalent text quite helpful, because this novel, which speaks to children and adults alike (but does so in very different ways) constantly crosses borders and hovers between two distinct discursive practices (Shavit 63–69).

The story is told in retrospect and in the voice of Karl Lion, called Rusky, who is confined to his sofa-bed in the kitchen and is slowly dying of a lung disease. His beloved brother Jonathan died in his attempt to save Rusky by jumping from the window of the burning house with Rusky on his back. Rusky survives but is shortly thereafter carried off to Nangiyala, a land of dreams and magic, already familiar to him from his brother's stories. There, the brothers are reunited and experience a brief moment of peaceful bliss, but all too soon they are separated again as they struggle against the forces of evil embodied by Lord Tengil. Tengil, who reigns over the neighboring Wild Rose Valley with the help of a cruel dragon named Katla and scores of mindless and ruthless soldiers, threatens to bring Cherry Valley where the two brothers live under his control too. A long and dangerous struggle for freedom ensues in which both brothers play key parts. In the final battle between the forces of liberty and the forces of oppression, Tengil is killed by Katla, who remains a threat. Jonathan volunteers to rid Wild Rose Valley of the fire-spewing dragon but is paralyzed by Katla's flames in the process. Now, roles are reversed, and it is up to Rusky to rescue Jonathan from terrible suffering by leaping into the looming abyss with Jonathan on his back in order to reach the paradisiacal Nangilima, where they will be restored to health and happiness and stay together forever.

Rusky's leap into death and darkness is cushioned by his faith in Jonathan's story that his step into the abyss will take him to lush and peaceful Apple Valley, where he will enjoy eternal happiness together with his brother. The novel operates similarly to assuage child readers' fears of loneliness and the horrible unknown of death. Lindgren's role as a storyteller is mirrored in the novel by Jonathan, who invents stories so powerful that they take hold of Rusky's imagination and literally carry him to Nangiyala and later to Nangilima. Both are lands of "campfires and stories," which resemble the earthly paradise of many adventure stories. Although the novel is set in a period when most children still believed in heaven, Rusky resembles the growing number of today's children for whom this novel is written—in Sweden and elsewhere—children who face a terrifying abyss of nothingness at the end of life. Rusky, too, needs Jonathan's stories to help him confront the fear of the threatening unknown. A common topos in children's literature underlies the story about the Brothers Lionheart, namely, that imagination and stories can change one's outlook on life and, ultimately, change one's life by providing both the inspiration to fight and to persevere as well as the means to escape an unbearable reality.

Healing and Empowerment

In the early 1970s, when fantasy and fairy tales had fallen out of favor in Sweden and the United States and when many Western countries were riding high on a wave of social realism, Lindgren sensed a spiritual void in children's books that she sought to fill with her fantasy novel with fairy-tale elements about the Brothers Lionheart. Most likely, she also wanted to soothe and console the child within, the inspiration and ultimate critic of her work. Lindgren has said that she never loved anyone more than her father, who died in 1969 and left a void in her that needed to be filled, a loss that needed to be explained.

At the same time, Max Lüthi defended children's need for fairy tales in *Once Upon a Time,* and Bruno Bettelheim adopted and popularized the idea of the fairy tale's therapeutic value in *The Uses of Enchantment.* Both argued that the fairy tale's poetic visions about existential questions build children's confidence by providing models for satisfying conflict resolutions. In Bettelheim's Freudian parlance the fairy tale presents models for sublimation that allow children to distance themselves from overwhelming and potentially harmful subconscious pressures. Fairy tales, Bettelheim argues, match the mindset of children better than realistic children's books written in the relativistic discourse of the scientific age (53). For children an escape into fantasy and illusion can be a constructive and empowering experience.

Lindgren's choice of the fantasy paradigm to help children combat fear and trauma goes along the same lines. Readers who need reassurance can sublimate their fears and anxieties by identifying with Rusky and enter the secondary world of heroic adventure. The critical, psychoanalytically versed reader, however, will recognize that this very process takes place in Rusky's mind. In the opening lines of the novel Lindgren has Rusky tell her readers what lies ahead: "Now I am going to tell you about my brother. My brother Jonathan Lionheart is the person I want to tell you about. I think it's almost like a saga and just a little like a ghost story, and yet every word is true, though Jonathan and I are probably the only people who know that" (7).

With decades of experience as children's book editor, Lindgren recognizes how important it is to capture the young readers' imagination in the opening paragraphs. A mythical and thrilling read, the novel is tightly composed and filled with dramatic action. Lindgren fulfills her initial promise by giving her readers suspenseful action, catharsis, and the happy ending that children are accustomed to from fairy tales. In fact, she appropriates the fairy-tale paradigm of "overcoming of dangers and entry into the realm of glory" for the ultimate trip into the unknown (that is death), as Kingsley, MacDonald, and C. S. Lewis had done before her (Lüthi 140).[1]

Through the first person narrative Lindgren establishes a close bond with the reader, which is reinforced by familiar rhetorical devices from folktales and fairy tales, such as the repetition of phrases and motifs, magic numbers and agents, and the rhythm and formulaic style characteristic of the oral tradition. True to the fairy-tale tradition, Lindgren does not spare her readers strong emotions like love, hate, elation, despair, and existential fear. She gives them clear objects of identification in the black-and-white protrayal of Tengil, the villain, and Jonathan, the hero. Other protagonists are more fully delineated novelistic characters that lend the story both body and complexity.

While recreating the emotional level and quality of the child perspective, Lindgren's rendition of events in the primary world before they gain a heroic dimension in the secondary world at times borders on the sentimental or skirts the melodramatic. Death itself is not sentimentalized, however. Lindgren avoids this danger by sublimating it, that is, by transmuting events into the secondary world of campfires and stories. In her description of this world Lindgren relies heavily on traditional imagery, but she does not always endow these images with traditional values. Until fairly recently death in children's literature was almost without exception embedded in the punishment-reward discourse of Christian conceptions and representations of death. The paradise of Nangiyala, however, has nothing to do with reward for good behavior in life. Lindgren's narrative is equally far removed from the cautionary tale, an inheritance from the Enlightenment. As Maria Tatar has convincingly shown in *Off With Their Heads!* nineteenth-century cautionary tales used the death of the protagonist as a common scare tactic against even minor sins like disobedience or obstinacy. The romantics scorned such drastic crudeness and aestheticized death instead. Yet even the romantic discourse about death retained traces of punishment and reward in the message that the gods love those who die young, a message that rewards purity and innocence.

Lindgren breaks with the nineteenth- and early twentieth-century literary tradition that Susan Sontag describes in her essay "Illness as Metaphor" as the "inveterate spiritualizing of TB and the sentimentalizing of its horrors" so that "the virtuous only become more so as they slide toward death" (41). Lindgren has little patience for this attitude that permeates children's literature of the nineteenth and early twentieth centuries and reverberates still in some of today's children's books. (MacDonald's *At the Back of the North Wind* is a prime example among earlier books, and Elisabeth Kübler-Ross's *Remember the Secret* shows the continued vitality of this attitude toward death in recent children's literature.)[2] Crippled and coughing, Rusky is dying a slow death from tuberculosis at home in the kitchen sofa-bed. Nothing about this image is the slightest bit beautiful. Nor is Rusky defined as one of God's chosen children displaying spiritual refinement like Diamond in *At the Back of the North Wind*. Death hits Rusky with all its grim cruelty, because he believes himself to be the cause of his idolized brother's death and he is dying himself. Rusky therefore refutes Jonathan's schoolteacher's utterance that "the gods love those who die young" as "pretty silly" (16).

Initially, Rusky picks up the threads of Jonathan's stories about Nangiyala with slight trepidation. What if this is just one of the many stories without any claim to truthfulness that Jonathan told him? But when he sees the white dove on the windowsill, the messenger from Nangiyala that Jonathan had promised would come, all his doubts vanish. From now on, Nangiyala is his real world, and he can only remember his wretched, lonely existence on earth as a thing of the past. And so do the readers who join him in his adventures in Nangiyala. Or is it possible—or even desirable—to linger imaginatively in the kitchen where Rusky is close to dying? Lindgren herself has this to say about reading the novel:

> For me—as an adult—it is clear that Rusky is so devastated when his brother dies that he must continue fabricating the story about Nangiyala that Jonathan tried to console him with. What happens in the book happens in Rusky's imagination, and when he dies on the last page, he dies at home in his kitchen sofa-bed. My adult self understands that, but the child in me will never accept such an interpretation; I *know* that everything happens just as it does in the book. Then everybody may interpret the book after his or her own fashion. (Holmberg 79)[3]

Imbricated Texts

Few authors have reflected so openly on the ambiguous nature of their creative impulse or have as consciously admitted to appeasing the doubting adult self by wholeheartedly entering into the realm of fantasy and magic. Lindgren speaks simultaneously to two distinct audiences, addressing them with one text in two voices. The story's complexity lies in, among other things, the fact that both child and adult perspectives are executed with the same painstaking care.[4] Each voice originates in a different narrative mode and genre which are seamlessly interwoven, at times obscuring the difference between primary and secondary worlds: the novel on the one hand and the fairy-tale quest on the other. Lindgren's ardent desire to console children tips the balance in favor of the child's perspective, which she takes great pains to reinforce. The child, not the adult, is Lindgren's primary and preferred audience. Whereas Lewis Carroll in his equally double-tiered, ambivalent *Alice in Wonderland,* often uses the child as a pseudo-addressee, while talking over the child's head to adults, Lindgren always prioritizes the child audience.[5] One could say that Lindgren stands Carroll's textual ambivalence and complexity on its head. The voice of the omniscient storyteller who firmly controls the fictional worlds predominates and hides the fact that Rusky, lying in the kitchen, has no control over his life or knowledge of death.

In the opening sentences of the novel, Lindgren assures her

readers that the story they are about to read is true. The claim to truthfulness is, however, qualified by the statement that Jonathan and Rusky are probably the only people who know that it is true. The narrative thus represents subjective rather than objective truth, a claim that is sustained in both perspectives. Lindgren promotes the reader's desire to believe in the truthfulness of Rusky's adventures in Nangiyala throughout the novel. Through the first person narrative she augments the readers' proclivity to identify closely with the thoughts and feelings of the main protagonist. To dispel any remaining doubts in the readers' minds, Rusky informs them about Nangiyala, "And it really was exactly as he'd [Jonathan] told me, while he'd sat there with me in the kitchen at home. Though now I was able to see that it was true, too, and I was pleased about that" (25). On numerous occasions Lindgren buttresses the reality of the land of campfires and stories by making Rusky recall his former self and his former environment from his new vantage point of Nangiyala: "I remembered suddenly how things had been that time when Jonathan was dead and away from me, and I was lying in my sofa-bed, not knowing whether I'd ever see him again; oh, it was like looking down into a black hole, just thinking about it" (47). And "Jonathan liked dressing up. He used to playact for me in the kitchen in the evenings, when we lived on earth, I mean" (105). Lindgren even plays with the concept of imagination by introducing yet another dreamworld into the imaginary reality of Nangiyala. When Rusky arrived, "he couldn't even imagine anywhere better to live" (24), and on his way to Katla Cavern he says to Jonathan, "this can't be real. It's like something out of an ancient dream" (128).

The dual structure of *The Brothers Lionheart* allows Lindgren to commit herself openly to bibliotherapy, yet to write a demanding and uncompromising novel. In recent decades, a shift in the social construct of childhood has led many juvenile authors to adopt new attitudes toward their readers. Many children's writers have moved from a controlling, protective, and sometimes patronizing narrative position to the decentered, integrative, and dialogic narrator of the modern novel tradition. Following Shavit's argument about the peripheral status of children's literature within the total system of literature, we can view children's literature's appropriation of novelistic discourse as a shift of the system's center away from the novel— or children's literature's move toward the former center—putting the novel within reach of children's literature. (Accepting this premise, this shift becomes another indicator of the death of the novel in "high" literature.) In *Bridge to Terabithia,* for example, Katherine Paterson appropriates the novelistic discourse to children's literature. Her book about death does not give children ready-made answers.[6] Paterson does not take her readers by the hand to enter a ready-made fantasy world; instead, she leads her readers right up to the threshold and then invites them to find their own way, for "Terabithia should not be used as a cure or a fast solution to the problems children face" (Chaston 239). In Paterson's book there is only one text that addresses both children and adults.

Born in 1907, Lindgren belongs to an older generation of writers for whom the worlds of childhood and adulthood are more separate in kind than for younger writers. I see *The Brothers Lionheart,* however, as a step in the development toward a unified text for a nonstratified audience that Lindgren perfected in her last novel, *Ronia, the Robber's Daughter.* Through the dual structure of the text, which is carefully calculated to work on two levels, Lindgren has devised a way to address both children and adults on equal terms.

Read from the adult psychoanalytic perspective, Rusky's emphatic assurances that Nangiyala resembles Jonathan's story world in everything and Rusky's repeated references to life "on earth" anchor his vision in his real-life experiences and reveal them as projections of his inner conflicts. Structural similarities unite his real and his imaginary world. The brothers' old farmhouse in Nangiyala has the same layout as does their home on earth. It, too, has only a kitchen which they inhabit and a room in which their mother will be able to do her sewing when she arrives. Rusky's imagination transports him to remote, beautiful, and terrifying places that he has never seen before, but it also transports him from kitchen to kitchen, each time providing him with a safe point of departure. The mother's singing of the popular song "La Paloma" (Spanish for dove) is also integrated into Rusky's fantasies. Lindgren skillfully uses the double symbolism of the white dove as messenger of both death and peace. A white dove leads him to Nangiyala, where white doves are Sofia's messengers in the struggle against Tengil and his terror regime.

The attacks of fear, distress, loneliness, and insecurity Rusky experiences while lying in his sofa-bed resurface in the otherworld in connection with his solitary adventures which follow one upon the other in renewed patterns of suspense and resolution. Rusky's struggle against the forces of evil is the concretization of his internal struggles and ambivalent feelings toward death. He longs to join his brother, Jonathan—the only person who had shown him love, kindness, and devotion in life—in the other world, but his horror of death turns this final step into a fierce battle. Gazing into the abyss of death becomes too horrifying to bear for Rusky, as is the sight of Katla, the dragon, symbolizing evil incarnate. But once he has replaced these monstrous apparitions with a vision of paradise, he can take the final step to join his brother.

Even though adult readers may suspend disbelief in the process of reading and let the current of the narrative carry them along, rational and analytical minds are likely to dismiss Rusky's adventures as compensatory dreams in the end. For the critical reader it is not death but imagination that provides the passage to Nangiyala, and Rusky's leap to Nangilima is but a leap of faith. The different ways Nangiyala and Nangilima are reached support an underlying agnostic attitude. Rusky flies to Nangiyala without being able to answer the question of how he got there (20), but the way to reach Nangilima is incomparably more difficult, for Rusky himself has to take the step which will precipitate him into the dark abyss below.

When the book first appeared, many adult readers and critics were shocked and dismayed at its ending. Reactions to the novel divided sharply along lines of age, attitudes, and aptitudes. Although quite a few adults found the ending depressing and demoralizing, letters came pouring in from young readers thanking Lindgren for giving the book such a happy ending. What accounts for this discrepancy in reader reception? The fact that an adult perspective is interwoven skillfully and hidden deep within the narrative of *The Brothers Lionheart* may have misled some adult readers, but it still does not adequately explain the fact that 23 of the 24 critics who reviewed *The Brothers Lionheart* when the novel first appeared in Sweden "misread" the ending as suicide and were highly critical of it (Törnqvist 30).

The debate concerning the ending of *The Brothers Lionheart* raises questions about how children's book critics ought or ought not to read literature written for children, which should be and have been discussed in a different setting and on a wider scale. Within its context I would like to raise a few questions and venture some answers. How can we as adults recreate a child's way of reading? Should we even try? And what happens if we do? Because adult and child per-

spectives are at great variance with one another in this case, the
perspective adopted by the critic becomes an issue. As it happened,
the great majority of—most likely well-intentioned—critics failed
to adopt or see either perspective, which may be as much an indictment of that kind of children's literature criticism as it is a comment
on the difficulty of combining a naive, childlike reading with the
analytical approach demanded of a critic. The blindness to the adult
perspective may be explained by a critic's penchant for approaching
a story written for children differently from an adult novel. Disparate evaluative methods come into play. The critics' interpretations
and verdicts were in all likelihood based on somewhat schizophrenic
attempts at assuming the child's point of view while retaining the
grown-up's concern for the well-being of the child. A positive portrayal of suicide, be it real or imagined, is still taboo in children's
and young adult novels. In most books from the 1970s and 1980s
that deal with suicide, the actual suicide is either averted or condemned as an undesirable, unethical solution. By openly condoning
an escape into death in the realm of fantasy and imagination, Lindgren puts herself at odds with accepted societal norms for holding
on to life at any cost. But her deepest concern is with the quality
not the length of life, and her concern for a good, satisfying, and
truly humane life for everyone is at issue in this tale about death
and dying. Moreover, the tale itself contributes to making life more
bearable and more valuable, as many child readers have declared
in letters to the author.

Ethical Directive

Lindgren may present existential and ethical questions in the traditional framework of a fantasy and adventure story, but the questions she raises and the answers she provides are anything but conventional. Death in this novel appears in many forms: accidental,
natural, and violent. For a children's book the death toll is impressive: the villains, the two brothers, Mathias (Rusky's adopted
grandfather), two messenger pigeons, the horses Fyalar and Grim,
Tengil soldiers, and many innocent people from the Wild Rose Valley. Despite the persistent threat and presence of death, the tone
of the book is positive and hopeful. The freedom fighters win, and
Rusky's final leap of faith, which exactly mirrors Jonathan's jump
from the burning house, promises and achieves Rusky's ultimate

redemption. The novel's closing words assure us that both will come to Nangilima: "Oh, Nangilima! Yes, Jonathan, yes, I can see the light! I can see the light!" (183). An otherwise uncontrollable and unbearable situation has been and, by implication, can be set right by means of willpower. Imagination can provide the means to pull yourself up by your own bootstraps. The defeatist attitude lodged in the idea of suicide is turned into constructive self-help, and then counterbalanced by the moral imperative of courage, which runs through the novel like a red thread: "But there are things you have to do, otherwise you're not a human being, but just a bit of filth" (48, 52, 130, 183).

Much courage is needed to overcome great fear, and seldom before has the fear of death been treated with such candor in a children's book. Rusky's ever-present feeling of fear, which he is forced to overcome again and again, reveals the dialectic notion that one cannot be courageous without knowing fear. Despite the fact that Rusky is presented as a bundle of fear until the very end, there is much fighting spirit in him. In Nangiyala he manages to help the freedom fighters in various ways when he is separated from Jonathan and left to his own resources. And it is he who takes the decisive step at the end. "Afraid" is the last word Rusky utters before he jumps off the cliff in the firm conviction that he will never again have to be afraid.

The courage Lindgren fosters in *The Brothers Lionheart* is the courage of the heart, which is spelled out in the brothers' surname. But the obvious reference to King Richard the Lion-Heart is misleading, for Jonathan differs from his namesake in at least one important aspect: he is a champion of nonviolence. Jonathan, who dares to confront the dragon Katla, is not the valiant dragonslayer familiar from fairy tales and sagas. He is a warm, tender, and loving person who would neither hurt nor kill anybody—not because he does not dare, but out of conviction. Jonathan is a pacifist, fighting for a world where peaceful cooperation replaces oppression and aggression.

By raising the question of pacifism, Lindgren lends considerable complexity to the struggle of good versus evil, for in this novel there are heroic figures who do not shrink from using violence to combat oppression and abusive cruelty. Among them is Antonia, who prepared to avenge the murder of her husband ordered by Tengil. Antonia has cut off her long beautiful hair and transformed it into bowstrings. (To the reader familiar with Icelandic sagas this action evokes a famous episode in Njal's saga, where Gunnar's wife Hellegerd refuses to save her husband by cutting off her hair for his bowstring.) The intrepid rebel and freedom fighter Orvar also sees violence as the only recourse to liberate his country from the forces of evil. His argument, that if everyone were like Jonathan, evil would forever reign in the world, is contradicted by Rusky, who gets the last word: "If everyone were like Jonathan, there wouldn't be any evil" (165). It is also contradicted by the course of events, for Wild Rose Valley is ultimately freed from evil due to Jonathan's nonviolent courage.

Courage in *The Brothers Lionheart* is not synonymous with bravery and definitely not with ostentatious fearlessness. This becomes evident in an episode when a Tengil soldier named Park, bragging about his strength yet neglecting his and his horse's life, foolhardily leads his horse into the swift rapids of the River of the Ancient Rivers to prove his courage. The narrator calls him a fool and a coward because he frivolously gambles his own life and that of his horse on a bet and because he does not have the human decency and courage to thank his savior, Jonathan. Park's blatant disregard for life and personal integrity, incidentally, is indicative of the oppressive Tengil regime in Wild Rose Valley he represents (156). Both the pervasive message of nonviolence and the condemnation of meaningless tests of manliness in Park's near-suicidal mission make up this "suicide" book's subtext, namely a deep respect for life.

There is as much tenderness and love in this fantasy novel as there is cruelty and violence; and in the end love wins out over hatred, indifference, and death, for Rusky's love for Jonathan transcends and conquers death. The love story of the two brothers forms the metatext which unifies the dual structure of the novel. After all, the whole story concerns Jonathan, as Rusky, the narrator, tells us in the first lines of the novel: "Now I'm going to tell you about my brother. My brother, Jonathan Lionheart, is the person I want to tell you about" (7). By the same token, this novel is Lindgren's declaration of love to the courage of the heart in an imperfect world. In this ambivalent text the message is uniform. It tells us about the courage of those generally deemed weak, about human brotherhood that does not differ from sisterhood, of the power of love, and, above all, about the power of words to provide fortitude and consolation.

Notes

Note to Epigraph: Egil Törnqvist, "Astrid Lindgrens halvsaga: Berättartekniken i Bröderna Lejonhjärta." *Svensk Litteraturtidskrift* 2 (1975): 30.

1. One could even find traces—in plot development of motifs—of specific myths, sagas, and fairy tales in *The Brothers Lionheart*. There are certain—if tenuous—similarities between the Grimms' tale "The Two Brothers" and *The Brothers Lionheart*. The separation of the brothers at decisive moments, their reunification, the confrontation with the dragon, and the use of wit to overcome a superior enemy are elements both tales share. The paradigm of adventure and exploration in an otherworld beyond death is also used in *The Water Babies* and in *The Last Battle*. Tom in *The Water Babies* drowns before he experiences the lovely underwater realm, and Aslan explains to the children in *The Last Battle* that they have been killed in a railway accident.

2. Elisabeth Kübler-Ross, known for her research on dying and efforts to console children in the face of death, displays the same desire in her fiction. In her picture book, *Remember the Secret*, she employs the traditional TB metaphor as well as traditional Christian conceptions of paradise. Unfortunately, Kübler-Ross's didacticism far outweighs her artistic talent, and text and pictures in *Remember the Secret* are artificially sweet and sentimental.

3. Lindgren has made similar statements about *Mio, My Son* and "South Wind Meadow." Here, too, the adult reader knows that Mio remains all alone on his park bench and that Mattias and Anna die in the winter cold, but all children, including the child in the author, know that both Mio and Mattias and Anna live on surrounded by warmth, love, and happiness. In interviews Lindgren has repeatedly defended the final scene of *The Brothers Lionheart* by pointing to the overwhelmingly positive reception by children, and she also cites specific cases in which her tale about the brothers Lionheart has comforted and helped dying children. She has even gone a step beyond her book in order to appease any doubts and to assuage the remaining fears of her readers. In a letter to the newspaper *Expressen*, dated February 26, 1974, Lindgren has assured her readers that Tengil and his men and the horrifying monsters Karm and Katla will never come to Nangilima.

4. For simplicity's sake, and cognizant of the oversimplification this implies, I will use Lindgren's own terms of child and adult perspective. If one considers that, according to a recent poll, two thirds of all Americans believe in a life after death, more accurate terms may be gnostic and agnostic perspective or naive and critical perspective.

5. For a detailed analysis of the status of children's literature within the field of literature, see Zohar Shavit in *Poetics of Children's Literature*, especially chapter 3, "The Ambivalent Status of Texts," 63–92.

6. See Joel D. Chaston's analysis, especially 239.

Works Cited

Bettelheim, Bruno. *The Uses of Enchantment*. New York: Vintage Books, 1977.

Chaston, Joel D. "The Other Deaths in *Bridge to Terabithia*." *Children's Literature Association Quarterly* 16, 4 (1991/92): 238–241.

Holmberg, Hans. "Astrid Lindgren—en litterär imagiker." *Artes* 13 (1987): 73–79.

Kübler-Ross, Elisabeth. *Remember the Secret*. Berkeley: Celestial Arts, 1982.

Lindgren, Astrid. *Bröderna Lejonhjärta*. Translated by Joan Tate. Stockholm: Rabén & Sjögren, 1973.

———. *The Brothers Lionheart*. New York: Puffin Books, 1987.

Lüthi, Max. *Once Upon a Time: On the Nature of Fairy Tales.* Bloomington: Indiana University Press, 1976.

MacDonald, George. *At the Back of the North Wind.* New York: Macmillan, 1964.

Ritte, Hans. "Die Unzugänglichkeit von Kinderliteratur für Erwachsene: Astrid Lindgrens Äußerungen zur Rezeption ihrer Werke." *Fundvogel* 41/42 (1987): 13–16.

Shavit, Zohar. *Poetics of Children's Literature.* Athens and London: University of Georgia Press, 1986.

Sontag, Susan. *Illness as Metaphor and AIDS and Its Metaphors.* New York: Doubleday, 1989.

Tatar, Maria. *Off With Their Heads! Fairy Tales and the Culture of Childhood.* Princeton: Princeton University Press, 1992.

Törnqvist, Egil. "Astrid Lindgren's halvsaga: Berättartekniken i Bröderna Lejonhjärta." *Svensk Litteraturtidskrift* 2 (1955): 17–34.

Reinventing the Past: Gender in Ursula K. Le Guin's Tehanu and the Earthsea "Trilogy"

Perry Nodelman

The publication of an unexpected sequel to a novel or series of novels, always disconcerting, is especially so when it occurs some years after the appearance of the original. What seemed complete for so long turns out not to be, and, inevitably, the events of the new story change the meaning of what went before.[1]

So it is with Ursula K. Le Guin's novels about Earthsea. For almost two decades after *The Farthest Shore* appeared in 1972, they were widely known as the Earthsea Trilogy. Then, in 1990, Le Guin published *Tehanu*—a fourth member for the former trilogy, teasingly subtitled "The Last Book of Earthsea." In continuing her story past the now only apparently concluding events of *The Farthest Shore*, Le Guin clearly signaled that she had new thoughts about her old conclusions, and that she wanted readers to reconsider their understanding of what they had read earlier.

In "From Master to Brother," Len Hatfield describes how a perceptive reader can read the former trilogy in terms of its new addition. He argues that the difference between *The Farthest Shore* and *Tehanu* mirrors Le Guin's espousal, in articles and speeches, of the feminist analysis of patriarchal assumptions that emerged in the years between the appearance of the two novels, and "marks a similar movement from a representation of patriarchal structures of authority to a critique and displacement of them by means of a 'mother tongue,' a phrase Le Guin has usefully borrowed and developed from feminist theory" (43).

Hatfield does not see this movement as representing the abandonment or even the revision of old ideas; for him, *Tehanu* merely acknowledges openly what was hidden in the earlier books: "Implicit subversions of patriarchy become explicit" (61). Hatfield appears to have done exactly what I assume Le Guin wished: he has

Children's Literature 23, ed. Francelia Butler, R. H. W. Dillard, and Elizabeth Lennox Keyser (Yale University Press, © 1995 Hollins College).

reinterpreted the old story in the light of its new ending—and done it persuasively.

Nevertheless, my first response, both to the existence of *Tehanu* and to Hatfield's reading of it, was deep suspicion. I found myself unable to forget the almost 20 years in which there was *no* explicit subversion of patriarchy in the Earthsea books. I found myself wondering if, before *Tehanu*, it would have been possible to notice—or, having noticed, to see as important enough to concentrate on—the implicit subversion the later explicit statement now makes so obvious. Is Le Guin engaged in reinventing the history of her own attitudes? Is Hatfield helping her to blot out the past?

But then I remembered the unsettling transformations that had occurred in my understanding of the Earthsea books long before *Tehanu* existed, as I first read them some years ago. Just as *Tehanu* influenced Hatfield's understanding of the former trilogy, my own reading of the second book, *The Tombs of Atuan*, had significantly changed my original understanding of the first book, *The Wizard of Earthsea*. It had been clear to me then that Le Guin had wanted me to experience this transformation, to understand *Wizard* first one way and then the other: she had taken advantage of the fact that new events change the meanings of old ones in a particularly pointed and clever way. Furthermore, the way *Tombs of Atuan* changed my reading of *Wizard of Earthsea* related specifically to questions of gender—just as Hatfield suggests the move from *Farthest Shore* to *Tehanu* does.

Apparently, then, *Tehanu* is not so much an attack on history as a continuation of it. It merely repeats what was always true of the Earthsea books: although each book always could—indeed must, for new readers—be read and understood without knowledge of its sequels, the new information provided by the sequels always forced readers into a revised understanding of what went before.

Nevertheless, I still feel a little unease about what Le Guin tries to do in *Tehanu,* and the way in which Hatfield has responded to it. Eighteen years is a long time between books; and in the history of North American ideas about gender, they were busy years. If we allow the revised version of something that seemed complete for so long to blot out our memory of what we earlier thought to be true, we misrepresent both our earlier experience of these books and the two decades of cultural history during which they meant something different.

What follows, then, is an attempt at Earthsea archaeology. I try to remember what Le Guin appears to want me to forget, and what Hatfield seems to have forgotten: what the trilogy meant before it had a fourth book. Nevertheless, my method is akin to Hatfield's, exploring how reading *Tombs* evokes meanings not otherwise perceivable in *Wizard*.

Although I am returning to a long-standing perception that *Tombs* forced me to revise my reading of *Wizard*, I can no longer understand that difference as I once did. New events have changed the meanings of old ones; if I want to make sense of my old perceptions now, I have no choice but to do so in terms of interpretive strategies I have since learned, from a variety of critical theorists—many of them, like Annis Pratt and Eve Kosofsky Sedgwick, feminists. I offer these readings and rereadings as a prelude to the rereading of all three books implied by *Tehanu* and presented by Hatfield, in the faith that tracing the archaeology of the older ideas submerged under the latest transformation might offer insight, not just into Le Guin's fiction, but also into the shifting history of cultural conceptions of gender, and of feminist responses to them, between 1972 and 1990.

To begin at the beginning: how did I, and other readers, once understand *Wizard of Earthsea*? What might it mean on its own, without consideration of what follows it?

In a talk given in 1975, Le Guin said that "the great fantasies, myths and tales . . . speak *from* the unconscious *to* the unconscious, in the *language* of the unconscious—symbol and archetype" (*Language* 62); in other words, they represent allegories of psychological processes. In a 1973 essay in which Le Guin made it clear that she saw *Wizard* as such a fantasy, she named its specific subject as "coming of age" (*Language* 55). Since then, many readers have echoed her assertion that *Wizard* is an allegory of individuation, some even insisting that the experience of reading it itself offers psychological benefits. According to Jean Murray Walker in 1980, "What is from Ged's point of view the experience of socialization is for the reader an experience of isolation from society which passes him through an artificial, highly patterned action, limited in space and time—a rite of passage" (183). According to Margaret M. Dunn in 1983, "a young reader cannot escape the implications which the story holds for him" (56).

What I find most instructive about these comments, from the perspective of a different decade, is that both Dunn and Walker refer to readers as "him." The pre-*Tehanu* Le Guin would not have been upset by this: explaining why she called the genderless characters in her adult science-fiction novel *The Left Hand of Darkness* "he," Le Guin once said, "I utterly refuse to mangle English by inventing a pronoun for 'he/she.' 'He' is the generic pronoun, damn it, in English" (*Language* 168). It seems that Dunn's and Walker's readers are similarly generic: obviously, not all of Le Guin's actual readers are male, and I doubt that Dunn or Walker would wish to exclude female readers from the benefits they ascribe to the book.

But a male hero like Ged in *Wizard of Earthsea* can represent the psychological situations of female readers only to the degree that his maleness is *not* a focus of attention—only if the specifically male features of the story are ignored as insignificant or seen as symbolic of the generic human condition, beyond consideration of gender. That is how I first read the book.

Indeed, nothing in *Wizard of Earthsea* suggests that Ged's problems or his way of solving them relate significantly to his masculinity. For readers who understand his story as a model for psychic integration, it is merely accidental that he happens to be a male. Few of the critical analyses of *Wizard* that appeared prior to the publication of *Tehanu* attach much significance to Ged's gender.[2]

But for me, Ged's status as representative of generic adolescence was thrown into question as soon as I read the second book of the series. *The Tombs of Atuan* describes how a second person, Tenar, follows a second, different path toward maturity—a symbolic journey of psychic significance, but one different enough from Ged's to throw its "generic" status into doubt.

What could account for this variation from an apparently universal psychic pattern? The most obvious difference between Tenar and Ged is that she is female.[3] If a story like Tenar's must be told, then could Ged *not* have been female? Is his story in fact a specifically male one after all? It seems so. I found myself rethinking *Wizard* in terms of the new focus on gender implied by the new information from *Tombs*.

I quickly realized that the most obvious explanation for the differing stories of psychic integration experienced by the male Ged and female Tenar could be found in Jungian psychoanalytic theory. Le Guin reveals her knowledge of Jung when she speaks of "the timeless archetypes of the collective unconscious" (*Language* 69) and names Ged's adversary in *Wizard* a "shadow." Jung asserts significant differences in the psychological makeup of males and females when he posits the existence of a female principle in males, the anima, and an equivalent male principle in females, the animus. Although the goal of psychic integration for both males and females is an androgynous state achieved by accepting this "other" as part of one's self, what men and women see as other and must integrate are two opposite qualities. That means that female integration operates differently from male integration, and requires its own story with its own cast of characters—a story like *Tombs*.

Just as Jung saw the components of the psyche as an inner cast of characters that need to come into balance with each other, Le Guin describes the characters in her novels as "psychic factors, elements of the complex soul" (*Language* 66). We could certainly understand Tenar's meeting with Ged as the awakening of her animus, and read *Tombs* as an allegory of female coming of age parallel to Ged's story, now clearly revealed as a specifically male one.[4]

At that point, I thought I had figured out why Tenar needed her own story and was quite content not to think of the implications of Ged's story then being exclusively a male one. I suppose I assumed what Le Guin's comments on the use of "he" implied: that the universal human condition was in fact male, and that being female was therefore a variation from the human norm.

In accepting that notion, I neglected to notice other problems— the most obvious being the fact that the next novel, *The Farthest Shore,* is yet another story of an adolescent apparently accomplishing psychic integration, even though Le Guin had already used up the two genders in the two earlier books. In light of the universalist claims of Jungian theory, why would a different male require a different story?

Another sort of Jungian reading might avoid that problem by seeing all three books of the trilogy as a sequential story of one psyche's integration, as represented by Ged. In *Wizard,* he confronts his shadow, those aspects of himself his conscious mind has rejected and must acknowledge; then in *Tombs* he moves down into his unconscious, as represented by the underground tombs of Atuan, and there confronts his anima, Tenar, and integrates it into himself as he places the ring of Erreth Akbe on Tenar's wrist; in *The Farthest Shore,* finally, the anima Arha is replaced by Arren (note the similarity in their names). Arren is a "girlish lad" who seems androgynous and whose destiny as high king over all might well represent psychic individuation and wholeness.

In retrospect, of course, the mere existence of *Tehanu* denies the possibility of such an interpretation: past wholeness, what further psychic activity could a narrative possibly represent? But even before the existence of *Tehanu* such a reading is problematic. If Tenar most significantly represents Ged's anima, then why do we see the events of *Tombs* from her point of view?

John H. Crow and Richard D. Erlich assert that "narrating the story from the Anima-figure's point of view . . . allows Le Guin to treat the woman as a person with an individuality of her own, rather than making her nothing more than an adjunct of the male, as often happens in myths and stories of this type" (203). But the idea that this could even be possible suggests a confusion inherent in Jung's own writing: according to Demaris Wehr, "He often states specifically that he is going to discuss the anima—an aspect of male psychology—and then launches into a discussion of the psychology of women" (104). Indeed, the rhetoric of *Tombs*, which focuses on Tenar being freed from the false idea of femininity represented by Arha and becoming herself, gives us no choice but to see her as an individual rather than just the nameless expression of the anima she was—as a character, that is, rather than a psychic component. Instead of disguising the pattern, the fact that she is "a person with an individuality of her own" actively conflicts with the possibility that she is merely part of Ged's psyche.

In the light of that, I now understand that the way Le Guin's characters waver between representing psychic entities and representing people prevents any consistent Jungian interpretation of the trilogy; Le Guin's Jungian ideas are more suggestive than exact.

Nevertheless, they are suggestive. For instance, the dark powers worshipped by women in the tombs of Atuan clearly relate to Jungian archetypes of the feminine—they are irrational, passive, silent, and below consciousness, and their place is dark, labyrinthine, womblike. Their worshipper Arha is then the anima as a distorted representation of femininity that must be discredited, to be replaced by the individual person Tenar. Seen in this way, which is hard to avoid in the context of strategies of reading texts for unconscious assumptions about gender that feminist criticism has taught us in the past decade or so, *Tombs* seems to be the story of how Tenar learns to be whole by rejecting femininity as conventionally defined. It is easy to see why Le Guin, at a point in the history of feminist thought when a once-powerful ideal of genderless equality for all seems to have lost ground to a celebration of once-marginalized feminine values (such as a "mother tongue"), might wish to reconsider the significance of Tenar's story through the addition of *Tehanu*, which, in finally telling something of Tenar's later life, specifically engages and revises the apparent assumptions of *Tombs*.

Because those assumptions seem to be versions of Jung's archetypes, it would be useful to take a closer look at feminist responses to Jung in the years since the Earthsea trilogy first appeared. Annis Pratt asserts that "although he sees androgyny, involving the transcendence of gender, as a necessary element in human development, his definitions of these gender qualities tend to be rigid to the point of stereotyping" (7). The archetypes are stereotypes; as a result, as Demaris Wehr suggests, women not only "challenge certain dimensions of Jung's view of the unconscious—dimensions stemming from his androcentrism"; they are actually "claiming that in some ways they stand outside of the psyche that Jung proclaimed as universal" (97). The conclusion is obvious: despite Jung's claims otherwise, the "generic" psyche he describes is specifically masculine—and can be read as such.

Because commentators now explore Jung's thought for what its claims about femininity might reveal of his assumptions about the masculinity he disguises under the name of universality, I can now read Le Guin's Jung-influenced novels in terms of what their claims about femininity, as expressed in Tenar, might reveal about masculinity, as expressed in the earlier and theoretically gender-neutral story of Ged. If Tenar's story is different from Ged's *because* she is female, then it invites a rereading of Ged's story, in particular its differences from Tenar's, as a description of specifically male experience. In other words: the same climate of change in our ideas about gender that seems to have led Le Guin to produce *Tehanu* as an encouragement to one particular way of rereading the earlier books might also lead to another, quite different rereading, one that focuses on the books' hidden assumptions about maleness.

That project seems particularly relevant to me when I view *Tombs of Atuan* through the lens of Annis Pratt's description of how novels about girls by women contain different views of archetypal patterns than novels about boys by men. Pratt believes that "women's fiction reflects an experience radically different from men's because our drive towards growth as persons is thwarted by our society's prescriptions concerning gender" (6). Traditionally, male maturity represents the freedom to wield power, female maturity a regressive acceptance of dependency and lack of power. Consequently, women's books about girls tend to take a positive view of their heroine's attempted escape from societal demands into a solitary and blissfully uncivilized place, often a "green" world of nature: "About to be conquered by 'human' society, she turns to something 'inhuman'; about to be dwarfed at the moment of the first development of her energies, she feels that the natural universe as a whole is her kingdom" (17). Frequently, this blissful solitude is destroyed by a male intruder, who rapes the girl and forces her back into the more repressive conventional world.

Tombs follows this pattern, but in a strangely distorted way. The solitary place Arha escapes into is a bleak cavern that imprisons her, and the hostile rapist is replaced by an admirable rescuer who makes her aware of her individuality rather than restricting it. Despite the fact that Le Guin is female, this sounds like a male version of a female story, a rejection of the freedom Tenar experiences in the solitary femininity of her Jungian caverns as imprisonment, and a celebration of entrapment by a male into a male-dominated society as freedom.

We can accept such views only if we see the society Ged represents as universally egalitarian rather than male-dominated, only if we see the Nameless Ones as universal evil rather than rejected femininity; even then, it is hard to neglect the opposite possibility, to wonder, as Cordelia Sherman does, if "the subliminal message" is "that women living without men become twisted and purposeless" (26), or to note, as Lois Kuznets does, that the novel "actually depicts the suppression of a female cult" (32). If *Tombs* reveals this much acceptance of a masculinist point of view, then it becomes important to explore the assumptions about masculinity implied by the apparently generic story of *Wizard*. Only after doing that can we see how cleverly Le Guin reinvents the past in making the explicit antipatriarchalism of *Tehanu* seem implicit in the earlier books.

Reading *Wizard* in the light of how *Tombs* varies from it reveals many aspects of *Tombs* that counterpoint *Wizard* in ways suggestive of traditional differences between femininity and masculinity: what happens to Ged is often directly opposite to what happens to Tenar. Whereas Tenar is passively thrust into darkness against her will, Ged himself aggressively invites the darkness. Tenar remains in her caves and has her fate come to her, yet Ged travels the world and goes to meet his fate. As priestess, furthermore, Tenar has a role to fill that blots out and replaces her self; as wizard, Ged has a job to do that expresses and fulfills himself. Tenar's role separates her from others, and she begins to triumph when she learns to care more about them and their attitudes toward her; Ged's job puts him in competition with others, and he begins to triumph when he learns to care less about them and their attitudes toward him.

Tenar must learn to define herself more in terms of others, Ged less; but in both cases, the others are men, which suggests that self-definition is a matter of seeing oneself connected to men if one is female, and separate from other men if one is male. After meeting Ged, Tenar rejects her entire sex: "All these women among whom she had always lived and who made up the human world to her, now appeared to her as both pitiable and boring" (83). After meeting women, Ged rejects them rather than himself. Just as Tenar's story centrally involves Ged, Ged's story centrally involves himself; a woman, Serret, has only a peripheral role in it. Nevertheless, the climax of Ged's story comes when he rejects what the woman Serret offers; the climax of Tenar's story comes when she accepts the truth of what the man Ged offers. And finally, Tenar is saved by Ged, whereas Ged saves himself.

As "the Eaten One," Tenar is absorbed into a darkness exterior to herself, and must be disgorged from it in order to be free; but Ged's darkness comes from within and he must seek and reabsorb it in order to become free. She first accepts and glories in her darkness as she learns the mazes of the Tombs, and must be taught to run from it; he first runs from his darkness and must learn to pursue it. Her goal is separation; his, wholeness. Her absorption into darkness gives her a power which is shown to be illusory, and his disgorging of darkness is a use of his power which signals his lack of power over himself. But both darknesses represent what each must conquer in order to be free, so that she must conquer what strengthens her while he must conquer what weakens him. In other words, she triumphs by giving up power, he by regaining it. Furthermore, her absorption into the darkness diminishes her, and she becomes more at the end by separating from it and becoming less; his unleashing of his darkness into the world diminishes him; and he becomes more at the end by uniting with it.

Not surprisingly, Tenar's loss of the power of darkness earns her the right to be ordinary, but Ged's integration of that power earns him the right to hold power and wield it. There is a deep irony here: the endings of both *Wizard* and *Tombs* seem to contradict what they most obviously try to persuade us of. *Tombs* contains many statements about the dangers of solitude and separation; but Tenar is saved from solitude and finds herself separate. Saved from the darkness of the caves, she finds the larger and scarier darkness of the sea, and saved from silence, she goes to live with Ogion, "the Silent." Meanwhile, *Wizard* is clearly meant to be about the dangers of pride and wilfulness, but Ged is saved from using his power in order to assert himself and ends up wielding his power in a way that allows him to assert himself in an even more intense way. He has become "a man who, knowing his whole true self, cannot be used or possessed by any power other than himself" (199).

These different fates clearly relate to traditional conceptions of femininity and masculinity. Tenar's enclosed life in the caves is an extreme form of the role she must eventually play as wife and housekeeper, and Ged's releasing of his shadow is an extreme form of the machismo he must express as a male and a hero. In a sense, both first experience and reject extreme and therefore less useful versions of the roles that rightly await them because of their genders; and the roles both Tenar and Ged fill after theoretically learning to balance the extreme are less androgynous than surprisingly traditional feminine and masculine ones.

Throughout *Tombs*, Le Guin makes traditional connections between femininity and receptivity, silence, darkness, touch, and emotion, on the one hand, and between masculinity and authority, speech, light, sight, and reason, on the other. The sign of Tenar's power is a dark uterine cave, of Ged's a phallic staff and a light, and Le Guin's description of his entry into her cave is fraught with sexual overtones: "He had come here into the hollow place that was the heart of the tombs. He had entered in" (59). Later, when she holds him captive, his knife is "useless": "the blade of it was broken short" (71). Eventually, however, he replaces the eunuch Manan as the man in her life, calling her "little one" as Manan did (117), and raising the staff she had brought him and his light to free her from darkness. When Ged identifies the emasculated Manan as a servant of darkness (120), disregarding his obvious love for Tenar, the implication is that the evil that enmeshes Tenar is a rejection of male power; and Le Guin's language clearly implies that her salvation through her contact with him is an awakening of heterosexual desire.

Men held captive in the caves earlier had suffered a different form of mutilation from Manan's: they had their tongues cut out. Traditionally, the ability to speak, to name and have the name you give accepted, is a pure form of mastery, the strongest evidence of authority—like God's originary speech that simultaneously gives a name to light and produces it, or like Adam's naming of the beasts. Such authority is also, traditionally, male. It is then not unrelated to conceptions of gender that the female order of Atuan considers the reading of words as "one of the black arts" (112), or that Tenar's world is dark and silent except for Ged's words, or that Ged carries light and has the power of naming.

A female priestess takes away Tenar's original name as she begins her apprenticeship, and the male Ged later gives it back to her. Without a name she chants meaningless words, empty signifiers—and is herself an empty signifier, a nameless container, until Ged's voice speaks her name. Similarly, a wizard takes away Ged's original true name and gives him a new one as he begins his apprenticeship; but that new name remains his true name, so that while Tenar's truest self is defined by what she always was, the person under the role, Ged is defined by what he is chosen to become, the job imposed on the person. Not surprisingly, Tenar learns after her escape from namelessness that she cannot call a rabbit to her by naming it, as Ged can; wizardry, Le Guin tells us a number of times, is essentially the art of controlling something by naming it—in Earthsea, an exclusively male profession.

He who names, names what he sees; his gaze defines what is. Tenar first fears Ged's "dark gaze" (80), ordering him not to look at her, and she defends herself from the temptation to look at the visual wonders of the dark cave she has previously known only by touch, and has now seen as revealed by his light, by denying the truth of what the eyes see: "All I know is the dark, the night underground. And that's all there really is. That's all there is to know, in the end" (86). But Tenar gives in to the temptation to trust her eyes when Ged shows her something he considers "worth seeing": herself in a beautiful gown, dressed as he imagines her and in a way meant to be conventionally attractive to the male gaze.[5]

Tenar's salvation occurs when she acknowledges the truth of the name Ged gives her and accepts his vision of her, the male-oriented image he imposes over her. Acknowledging his power to name her, she goes to him bearing a light and names him with the name he has told her (104). Her ability to speak his name signifies her moment of salvation; in *Wizard,* his salvation is also signaled by the ability to speak the name of the same person: himself. Both salvations signify acceptance of Ged's values—his words instead of her silence, his light instead of her darkness. Tenar claimed earlier that there is darkness buried under all the light; now she accepts his reverse definition of her as a light buried in darkness, "a lantern swathed and covered, hidden in a dark place" (108). Vision has triumphed over touch, light over darkness, naming over namelessness—male over female. And in the process, both masculinity and femininity have been defined.

A closer investigation of *Wizard,* in the light of this new information from *Tombs,* reveals that the same thing has already happened there. Although the bulk of *Wizard* has nothing to do with Ged's involvements with women, they play a surprisingly important part.

As soon as Ged first discovers his power as a wizard, his aunt (a witch) tries "not only to gain control of his speech and silence, but to bind him at the same time to her service in the craft of sorcery" (15). The aunt's action clearly parallels Tenar's first response to Ged when she finds him in her caves, and is equally doomed, for Ged's male power of speech is stronger than the female power of binding. Le Guin reports two Gontish sayings which make clear that this is a specifically female attempt to control male power: "weak as woman's magic" and "wicked as woman's magic" (15).

This is merely the first of a number of key points in Ged's maturation which involve his dealings with women, and his growing understanding of the dangers both of the female power that might bind him, and of the danger of being bound by his own desire for women and what that desire represents. He first evokes the shadow that later haunts him in response to a young woman, the daughter of the Lord of Re Albi, because he had "a desire to please her, to win her admiration" (31); this desire causes him to forget what his master Ogion reminds him, that the young woman is "half a witch already," and that "the powers she serves are not the powers I serve" (35). Ged's wish to please the young woman by showing off his strength is a recognizable expression of machismo that binds him to the dark powers. Ged apparently needs to learn that the desire women awaken in men makes men dangerously vulnerable, and that like women's magic it wickedly encourages weakness.

The weakness is a misuse of strength in the name of vanity, to win admiration. Ged exhibits the same weakness in the central episode of the book as he looses the shadow he then must flee. This time it seems to have nothing to do with female power, for it is a male he is trying to impress, the apprentice wizard Jasper. Even so, the act centrally involves Ged's machismo, his need to prove himself more powerful and more manly than Jasper, and so, it also centrally involves a woman. The spirit Ged chooses to awake from the dead is that of the ancient queen Elferran.

Eve Kosofsky Sedgwick's analysis of "male homosocial desire" suggests a possible interpretation of Elferran's part in Ged's action here. Sedgwick claims that the major force driving heterosexual men has traditionally been their desire for approbation from or mastery over other males, and that men's dealings with women have most significance as the medium by which men develop their bonds and establish their hierarchies of power with each other. Lévi-Strauss calls this "the male traffic in women"—in Sedgwick's words, "the use of women by men as exchangeable objects, as counters of value, for the primary purpose of cementing relationships with other men" (123). Seen in these terms, Ged's desire to prove himself more powerful than Jasper is a readily understandable expression of homosocial desire, and it makes good sense that he should choose to express it by showing his power over a woman.

As Sedgwick suggests, many novels depict the transfer of power between men "over the dead, discredited, or disempowered body of a woman" (137). Elferran's body is all three; in an aside some pages later we learn that it was the great king Morred's love for Elferran that led to his country's ruin.[6]

But Sedgwick sees this sort of transfer of power as a culturally approved action, and Le Guin shows us that Ged is clearly wrong to try to wield his power in this way. His attempt to prove his mastery over another man by mastering a woman's spirit looses the shadow that then haunts him. If the male homosocial desire to better other men defines masculinity, then Le Guin seems to be demanding that Ged achieve his power (and the ability to better other men) only by denying that form of masculinity.

That possibility becomes more certain in his next encounter with a woman. Serret, the woman who first aroused his desire to be admired, now tries to involve him in a traditional triangle of the sort Sedgwick describes as a representation of homosocial desire: she offers him herself as a way of proving himself more powerful than her own husband and all other men: "You will be mightier than all men, a king among men. You will rule, and I will rule with you" (134). Ged rejects this possibility, apparently because he feels no desire for Serret; he has already learned in his dealings with Jasper to separate his power from the machismo that involves valuing females as goods traded to establish male authority.

Nevertheless, Ged's power is still clearly identified with maleness; he rejects Serret's offer because it would require him to give himself over to the Stone of Terrenon, an object connected to the same "Old Powers" that rule in the Tombs of Atuan and therefore, a female force, dark, ancient, before and below light and speech. In opposing this female force with his own ability to name and to give light both here and in *Tombs*, Ged defines his power as male. In this way, Le Guin preserves and passes on conventional ideas about how both females and femaleness weaken male power.

According to Sedgwick, male homosociality operates by expressing its desire for power over other males through heterosexual lust, and therefore has developed over the past few centuries in our culture a vested interest in marginalizing and anathematizing homosexual lust as a defiance of the established hierarchy. Homophobia is then a necessary corollary of homosociality, as is the secret fear of successfully homosocial men that in their focus on other men they might themselves be homosexual. Considering the degree to which Le Guin's vision of Ged evokes so many of our cultural assumptions about maleness, it seems worthwhile to consider the possibility that this sort of homophobic panic might also be present.

Once more, the possibility emerges only if we refuse to ignore the implications of the specific vehicles Le Guin uses in her metaphors for psychic components—if we explore the degree to which the specific characters and actions that are meant to stand for abstract qualities might be seeping their own meanings into those abstract qualities. From that point of view, Ged's shadow, a distorted image of himself as other that is evoked in his desire to master another man, can be seen as a representation of homophobic fear. The shadow as Le Guin describes it looks something like him, pursues him, wants to hold him and enter into him (121)—and in two key scenes he most fears its presence behind him, first just prior to his entry into Serret's castle as it tries to "catch hold of him from behind" (122), and later as he pursues it and looks over his shoulder to see it standing behind him (164).

In this latter instance, Ged has pursued what he fears into a "dark cleft . . . dark trap under the roots of the silent mountain, and he was in the trap" (163–64) as the shadow comes up behind him and attempts once more to enter him. The place might well be seen as a representation of his own body and what he fears for it; he is both trapped in it and about to be defiled through his entrapment in it. It counterpoints the Tombs of Atuan, a place that seems to represent parts of the female body and their ability to entrap and, sometimes quite literally, castrate males.

Although the public story of Ged's involvement with women is his learning how his own interest in them can weaken him, the subtext implied by these dealings with the shadow is how his knowledge of the dangers of women evokes a fear of his own homosexuality that then must be resolved. Ged's first fearful attempt to beat off the shadow with the staff which symbolizes his manly power unmans him, as the staff burns up; he then flees from the shadow's literally homosexual attempts to enter him from behind into the protective space of the woman Serret's castle, where he must once more reject the possibility of heterosexual desire. The result is the scene in the cleft, where Ged prevents what sounds like a homosexual rape by inviting it—in essence, dissipating the homosexual implications by acknowledging and defying his homosexual fears.

Freed of those fears, he can take a male companion, his friend Vetch, on his final voyage to confront the shadow. Vetch is the antithesis of Jasper—a male Ged can bond with without the pressure of the machismo of homosociality, which might explain why Ged pursues his relationship with Vetch only *after* the scene in the cleft. Vetch is black, like Ged's shadow; but it is a blackness now divested of danger, an unthreatening version of a threatening image.[7]

If taken literally, Ged's final meeting with his shadow also suggests a concern with homosexuality; he unites with it only after it transforms itself in turn into all of the important men in Ged's life except Vetch—all the males with whom he experienced homosocial desire. It then advances toward him as a phallic "blind unformed snout" that "heaved itself upright" (197), and finally Ged drops his own phallic staff, embraces the shadow, and invites it in.

But as it turns out, this is Ged's union with himself, not with another who looks like him. The combined sameness/otherness of homosexual desire has dissolved; the other is separated out as Vetch, who merely observes the union rather than taking part in it. In other words, Ged achieves integration only after he rids himself of all desire and all fear of desire, heterosexual or homosexual. The male shadow Ged fears turns out to share his name—and therefore to share the name of the male power Tenar feared. But while her acceptance of it ties her to him, his acceptance of it separates him from all ties. Cut off from desire, he becomes totally self-enclosed, and ironically in possession of great social power.

Paradoxically, the power Ged achieves as wizard and namer is a male power that he can achieve only by ridding himself of the sexual desires that would cause him to wield it specifically as a male; a wizard must be a man, but a man who feels no male desire. If male power transcends male desire, then gender is divorced from sexuality; indeed, Ged's story replicates the conditions of grammar Le Guin postulated in her discussion of the generic human as "he." It is only when the fact of Ged's gender ceases to be an acknowledged operative factor that he can most express a power theoretically generic and universal but in fact unavailable to females.

Similarly, despite the sexual implications of Ged's staff and Tenar's cave, their relationship is meant to be purely symbolic— not a sexual union but a desirably sexless integration of the idea of maleness and the idea of femaleness. But Ged and Tenar are real people as well as representations of ideas, and so their gender and their sexuality transcend the symbolic and become real issues that reveal the gender bias in the ideas they represent.

The third book of the trilogy tells a different story about a different kind of male; Arren's destiny is to become king over all of Earthsea. Like Ged and Tenar, Arren is a psychic factor as well as a character, and his story adds to Le Guin's exploration of gender and causes readers to reinvent their previous understanding of both Tenar and Ged.

Arren's story counterpoints Ged's enough to seem almost directly opposite to it. The forces Le Guin represents by shadow and darkness are aspects of the self that have been rejected and buried in the unconscious; but whereas Ged buried and then confronted his aggressive cockiness, Arren appears to have buried and has to confront his unaggressive wish to ignore his responsibility. Whereas

Ged confronts his shadow by wielding the phallic sign of his power, his staff, Arren resists wearing the sword which is the phallic sign of his power, and for a time carries a small knife instead—a rejection of the male power he has been fated to wield. When Ged enters most fully into the thrall of his shadow, he experiences egotistic vanity and replaces concern for others with self-concern, but when Arren is most fully in the thrall of his shadow, he experiences only numbness, and replaces concern for others with a perception of total meaninglessness that justifies the absence of concern: "At the depths of the dream . . . there was nothing—a gap, a void. There were no depths" (109).

I suggested earlier that Ged's and Tenar's experiences of darkness both represent extreme versions of their fated roles, and the same is true of Arren. Paradoxically, his wish to do nothing is a wilful rejection of his fate, which he must will himself to accept even though doing so means giving up his will. In this way, his story reverses Tenar's: as Arha, she had a role she must step away from before she can become a self, but Arren has a wilful self he must shed before he can take on his fated role as king.

Furthermore, that role itself represents a form of lack of wilfulness. The sword which symbolizes it "never had been drawn, nor ever could be drawn, except in the service of life" (3). Throughout the book, Le Guin insists that what Arren must learn is, as Ged says, to "do nothing because it is righteous or praiseworthy or noble to do so; do nothing because it seems good to do so; do only that which you must do and which you cannot do in any other way" (67). If Ged's story represents the aggressiveness of male power and its need to define its proper use, then Arren's story represents the ordering nature of male power and its need to define its proper use.

At a key point, Ged tells Arren, "that is the power, not to take, but to accept" (138). To learn this is a triple-barreled form of acceptance; Arren must, first, accept his fate, second, accept a fate that inherently demands the acceptance of an ideal of control and restraint, and third (perhaps most significant), accept Ged's word. For Arren, to be in darkness is to mistrust Ged; throughout the book, the central question for Arren is whether or not he will accept Ged's word.

Furthermore, Ged's word is still connected with Ged's gaze. In one of the book's key scenes, Arren responds to a look of "great wordless, grieving love" he sees in Ged's eyes as Ged looks at him:

"Arren saw that, and seeing it saw him for the first time whole, as he was" (165). Having seen Ged as Ged sees himself, he then accepts Ged's vision of everything, including himself: "Arren saw the world now with his companion's eyes" (165).

According to Pratt, "In the Bildungsroman proper, with its expectation that the hero is learning to be adult, there is [for girls] the hidden agenda of gender norms, where 'adult' means learning to be dependent, submissive, or 'nonadult' " (16)—just as Arren becomes in relation both to Ged and to his fated role as king. Paradoxically, Arren can become the ultimately powerful and inevitably male king over all only by learning to act as females have traditionally learned to act.

In fact, Arren, the "girlish lad" (80), is in the same situation as the female Tenar, and his emotions at the beginning of *Shore* directly mirror Tenar's at the end of *Tombs*. Upon seeing Ged and experiencing "the gaze of those dark eyes" (6), he immediately "had fallen in love" (7). In fact, all his thoughts are about Ged, and so this book reads like a continuation of the one before it, but with the female point of view disconcertingly become that of a male. Like Tenar, Arren resists what Ged stands for, at moments when he finds himself in darkness, and like Tenar he triumphs when he looks at Ged looking at him and accepts Ged's vision of himself and the world.

Le Guin further reinforces the femininity of the role Arren plays by placing him in situations traditionally occupied in fiction by females. Enslaved by a cruel villain, he is like a typical damsel in distress, helpless to do anything himself about his "bonds" (61) until he is saved by Ged, whose "grip" on his arm replaces the chains (62) and pulls him to safety. As with many heroines of romance, the issue is not his being bound, but who is doing the binding. Furthermore, when Arren tries to use his sword aggressively, he is "silly . . . whereas going into a trance at the wrong moment had been wonderfully clever" (64). Like Snow White, Sleeping Beauty, and many other female protagonists of fairy tales, he triumphs most when he is most passive. In the novel's climactic scene, it is Ged who fights, while Arren mainly watches. This scene parallels the one in which Vetch watched Ged confront his enemy, but now the great hero is in the role of the watcher rather than the doer.

This new definition of male power as "female" passivity in relation to a greater male power might logically raise the issue of male fear of homosexuality. But there is certainly no evidence of any fear in the forthright references to Arren as a "girlish lad," in the scenes in which Le Guin refers to Ged observing Arren's naked "golden and supple" body "with impartial tenderness" (69), in the imagery of romance used to describe Arren's love for Ged. Arren achieves a homosocial bonding with Ged without any question of or fear of sexuality. The main reason probably relates to Jungian concepts of individuation: if Arren represents what the psyche becomes after it integrates the anima, then presumably it has transcended the sexual fears that earlier haunted Ged. It has achieved a higher and more spiritual plane of existence, a plane where the focus is on philosophical discussion rather than on physical urges. In fact, Arren is always what Ged becomes at the end of *Wizard*—not so much the adolescent he is purported to be as a mature and therefore, apparently, sexless being. The "girlish lad" is less androgynous than passionless.

Furthermore, it is probably no accident that Arren's title in the old tongue, "Agni Lebannan" (152), contains something so much like *agnus,* the Latin word for lamb. Like Christ, Arren is lamblike in his lack of sinful thoughts and his innocence. He is the child Ged sends before him into the dark (122), as Christ is the child God sends into the dark world to announce his salvation. If Ged as wielder of light and speaker of words parallels God the father, then Arren, who becomes king of the world through resisting aggressive action and following God's word, is Christ—and presumably like Christ, his kingly power is signaled specifically by the fact that he is inhabitant of a male body but blind to its sexual impulses.

Nevertheless, this story of psychic individuation, like the story of God and Christ, carries its larger truths within the metaphor of a loving relationship between two males. In hiding or ignoring the sexual possibilities of such a relationship, both stories achieve the ultimate goal of homosociality: a deep and deeply significant love between two males without any homosexual overtones. So Le Guin's story once more replicates ideas of masculinity key to our cultural definitions of ourselves: in both Jungianism and Christianity, the most intense and most important relationships for males are with other males and decidedly without homosexual content. In this way, male power declares its universality and its universal sway by denying the specific significance of its gender.

I am not suggesting that Le Guin herself intended to affirm such ideas, or even to present an analysis of maleness in relation to male

sexuality—merely that the supposedly generic archetypes she tries
to describe are inevitably located in assumptions about gender differences that are less universal than cultural and local; in the first
three Earthsea books, she was merely taking for granted what her
culture believed, and expressing it in metaphors her culture commonly used. Because of the ways in which the vehicles for those
metaphors secretly but inevitably obtrude their presence into the
meanings they stand for, she reveals more about herself and her
culture's attitudes toward gender than she might care to.

And that, I believe, is exactly the significance *Tehanu* takes on
when viewed as the sort of addendum which requires reinterpreta-
tion of what precedes it. If, for a moment, I reject Le Guin's invitation to forget what I have already understood about the earlier
books and just described, I see *Tehanu,* not as an explicit statement
of formerly implicit themes, but rather, as a profound criticism and
reversal of what went before.

Tehanu most clearly asserts itself as a revisionist act by the fact
that it is not the kind of story one expects in a novel supposedly for
young adults. Although it does tell how a child grows into knowledge of her power, that is not the central issue. The protagonist is
Tenar as a middle-aged woman, someone more like Le Guin herself than like her intended audience, and the story centers on the
awakening of her consciousness of the evil in the world, specifically
the evil done to women by men.

The shadow Tenar confronts here is clearly exterior to herself:
machismo as sheer brute force directed against women by men
whose self-esteem depends on their ability to mistreat those weaker
than themselves—Tenar herself and the gipsy child she saves from
a horrible death by burning. Tenar comes to understand that this
sort of violence is merely an extreme form of the power her culture
has traditionally invested in males. It turns out to be a good thing
that Ged loses his wizardly power of controlling through naming,
and that he must learn to be happy as a goatherd with no worldly
authority at all.

Ged comes to represent a new kind of maleness divested of its
traditional authority; he happily takes a hand in washing the dishes,
whereas Tenar's son reveals a retrogressive machismo in his refusal
to do so. Not incidentally, Ged must also rediscover his sexuality,
and we hear how he finally in middle age loses his virginity to
Tenar, paradoxically free to express his biological maleness now

that he has been divested of his male power. Earlier, he represented a separation of power from sexuality that allowed male authority by denying the significance of its maleness; now he represents a separation of sexuality from machismo that redefines maleness by separating it from the need for authority.

Furthermore, the power Ged has lost is in the process of being superseded by a new form of power, one that finds expression in the female child Tehanu, who intuitively knows the language of dragons. As Arren presumably unified male and female in an androgyny that transcended sexuality, Tehanu unifies human and dragon in a condition that transcends the need for the reasoned control of male authority—for the dragon parallels all those dark unconscious forces that Le Guin earlier both identified with women and rejected as evil.

Seen in this way, then, *Tehanu* suggests that Le Guin has reversed her earlier position on male and female qualities: just as she had earlier accepted the identification of traditionally female qualities as an evil that must be transcended, she now seems to be doing the same thing with traditionally masculine qualities. By showing how much supposedly universal archetypes can change in a decade and a half, *Tehanu* reveals the transitory nature of all the supposedly eternal assumptions human beings make about gender and sexuality. By creating the conditions that allow readers like Hatfield to read what came before in the light of an addendum, so that the now-current assumptions seem to pre-date their coming into existence so firmly as to seem omnipresent and universal, *Tehanu* reveals the continual process by which all of us constantly reinvent the past.

Notes

1. The existence of new information inevitably changes our understanding of old information: even during our reading of one novel on its own, an apparently insignificant reference to, say, a broken stair in the first chapter comes in retrospect to seem far more meaningful, after the hero trips on it and dies in chapter fifteen. Furthermore, as Frank Kermode suggests in *Sense of an Ending*, it is exactly our knowledge that events conclude in a certain way that allows us to understand their significance: interpreting fiction is a matter of keeping the end in mind as we reconsider what led up to it and defined it as a conclusion.

2. Indeed, gender rarely appears as an issue even in discussions of the trilogy as a whole. Bittner, Slusser, Walker, Dooley, Dunn, and Bailey discuss individuation without reference to gender. Galbreath so far ignores the issue of femininity that he doesn't even mention *Tombs*, and Attebury also focuses his discussion on the first and last books. While Remington mentions sex symbolism, he doesn't explore its

implications, and both Manlove and Patterson see significant differences in Ged's story in *Wizard* and Tenar's in *Tombs* but deny they relate to gender. Esmonde and Sherman do begin to relate the differences to questions of gender but then deny the conclusions their own insights imply, and Crow and Erlich solve the problem by seeing Tenar in Jungian terms, as Ged's anima. For these and most critics, furthermore, it is also incidental that Ged lives in a world where the sailors, fishers, and farmers are all male, where the powerful wizards are all male, where it is never questioned that the king whose rule will eventually bring peace will be male, and where women do the cooking and cleaning and are silly superstitious witches rather than powerful wise wizards. In such a vision of the universal human psyche, the patriarchal male authority we know to exist in a transitory social world is meant to represent universal psychic power, and readers are expected to understand that psychic power has no inherent connection to maleness.

3. It is instructive that *The Left Hand of Darkness,* Le Guin's novel about a planet whose citizens are inherently genderless, appeared in 1969, sandwiched between the male story of *Wizard of Earthsea* (1968) and the female one of *Tombs of Atuan* (1971)— and at just that moment in North American cultural history when the contemporary feminist movement began to gather strength.

4. Indeed, a number of critics suggest that the three books present parallel tales of coming of age.

5. It may not be accidental that in *Wizard,* Ged's shadow emerges as he evokes the image of another woman in a beautiful gown, or that the old woman who gives him half the ring he eventually places on Tenar's wrist defines herself for him by showing him the elaborate child's dress she wore as an infant princess.

6. Sedgwick is talking specifically about transfer of power from the aristocracy to the middle class, and it is interesting that Ged's discomfort with Jasper relates significantly to his perception that Jasper as an aristocrat looks down on him. The dispute between Ged and Jasper over the body of a dead woman is counterpointed in *Tombs* in the dispute between Kossil and Tenar over the body of a discredited, disempowered, and almost dead man, Ged; but in this case, the man wins.

7. Vetch's household is a safe place in every way. In it, Ged finds not only Vetch but also the one sexually unthreatening female of the book, Vetch's young sister, and Vetch's brother, whom he sees as a less threatening version of himself, someone his own age who has none of his power.

Works Cited

Attebury, Brian. "On a Far Shore: The Myth of Earthsea." *Extrapolation* 21, 3 (1980): 269–277.

Bailey, Edgar C., Jr. "Shadows in Earthsea: Le Guin's Use of a Jungian Archetype." *Extrapolation* 21, 3 (1980): 254–261.

Bittner, James W. *Approaches to the Fiction of Ursula K. Le Guin.* Ann Arbor, MI: UMI Research Press, 1984.

Crow, John H., and Richard D. Erlich. "Words of Binding: Patterns of Integration in the Earthsea Trilogy." In *Ursula K. Le Guin.* Ed. Joseph D. Olander and Martin Harry Greenburg. Edinburgh: Paul Harris, 1979. 200–224.

Dooley, Patricia. "Magic and Art in Ursula Le Guin's Earthsea Trilogy." *Children's Literature* 8 (1980): 103–110.

Dunn, Margaret M. "In Defense of Dragons: Imagination as Experience in the Earthsea Trilogy." *Proceedings of the 9th Annual Conference of the Children's Literature Association.* Ed. Priscilla Ord. Boston: Northeastern U. P., 1983. 54–60.

Esmonde, Margaret P. "The Master Pattern: The Psychological Journey in the

Earthsea Trilogy." In *Ursula K. Le Guin.* Ed. Joseph D. Olander and Martin Harry Greenburg. Edinburgh: Paul Harris, 1979. 15–35.

Galbreath, Robert. "Taoist Magic in the Earthsea Trilogy." *Extrapolation* 21, 3 (1980): 262–268.

Hatfield, Len. "From Master to Brother: Shifting the Balance of Authority in Ursula K. Le Guin's *Farthest Shore* and *Tehanu.*" *Children's Literature* 21 (1993): 43–65.

Kermode, Frank. *The Sense of an Ending: Study in the Theory of Fiction.* New York: Oxford U.P., 1967.

Kuznets, Lois R. "'High Fantasy' in America: A Study of Lloyd Alexander, Ursula Le Guin, and Susan Cooper." *Lion and the Unicorn* 9 (1985): 19–35.

Le Guin, Ursula. *The Farthest Shore.* New York: Bantam: 1975.

———. *The Language of the Night: Essays on Fantasy and Science Fiction.* Ed. Susan Wood. New York: Putnam-Perigee, 1979.

———. *The Left Hand of Darkness.* New York: Ace, 1969.

———. *Tehanu: The Last Book of Earthsea.* New York: Atheneum 1990.

———. *The Tombs of Atuan.* New York: Bantam, 1975.

———. *The Wizard of Earthsea.* Harmondsworth, Middlesex: Penguin Puffin, 1971.

Manlove, C. N. "Conservatism in the Fantasy of Le Guin." *Extrapolation* 21, 3 (1980): 287–297.

Patteson, Richard F. "Le Guin's Earthsea Trilogy: The Psychology of Fantasy." In *The Scope of the Fantastic—Culture, Biography, Themes, Children's Literature.* Ed. Robert A. Collins and Howard D. Pearce. Westport, CT: Greenwood Press, 1985. 239–247.

Pratt, Annis, with Barbara White, Andrea Lowenstein, Mary Wyer. *Archetypal Patterns in Women's Fiction.* Bloomington: Indiana U.P., 1981.

Remington, Thomas J. "A Time to Live and a Time to Die: Cyclical Renewal in the Earthsea Trilogy." *Extrapolation* 21, 3 (1980): 278–286.

Sedgwick, Eve Kosofsky. *Between Men: English Literature and Male Homosocial Desire.* New York: Columbia U.P., 1985.

Sherman, Cordelia. "The Princess and the Wizard: The Fantasy Worlds of Ursula K. Le Guin and George MacDonald." *Children's Literature Association Quarterly* 12, 1 (Spring 1987): 24–28.

Slusser, George Edgar. *The Farthest Shores of Ursula K. Le Guin.* San Bernardino, CA: Brogo Press, 1976.

Walker, Jeanne Murray. "Rites of Passage Today: The Cultural Significance of *A Wizard of Earthsea.*" *Mosaic* 13, 3–4 (1980): 179–191.

Wehr, Demaris H. *Jung and Feminism: Liberating Archetypes.* Boston: Beacon Press, 1987.

Is Flying Extraordinary?
Patricia MacLachlan's Use of Aporia

Roberta Seelinger Trites

Three of Patricia MacLachlan's novels have female protagonists between the ages of ten and twelve: *Cassie Binegar, Unclaimed Treasures,* and *The Facts and Fictions of Minna Pratt.* [1] Each of these novels is a narrative about a girl who feels silenced by external forces and who subsequently regains a more developed interior voice than the one she has lost. As a result, in these stories the traditional narrative of female silencing is itself silenced by revisionary narratives of female articulation.

Many feminists have pointed to female voicelessness as a recurring obstacle for women in our culture. Psychological theorists posit cultural silencing as one of the dominant forces that shape female adolescence,[2] and literary theorists have shown how this social phenomenon of silencing manifests itself in literature.[3] Recently, feminists have formulated strategies that promote narrative as a way for women to connect so that they might overcome this socio-literary silencing.[4]

Those of MacLachlan's novels that focus on the development of preadolescent girls are remarkable in the ways that they combine these literary and psychological theories. After each of MacLachlan's girl protagonists interacts with the narratives of other female characters, she resolves a conflict with her mother [5] and gains understandings of both her own sexuality [6] and of some artistic process. Her increased awareness leads to her ability to formulate a "new fiction" that breaks from traditional cultural silencing. And their victories serve as a literary *tour de force* for feminism.

Central to these victories is the value each of these texts places on language. Until MacLachlan's preadolescent girls learn the power that language gives them, they are frustrated into silence because they try to understand abstract concepts in concrete, physical terms.[7] MacLachlan's texts illustrate this frustration by relying on the rhe-

Children's Literature 23, ed. Francelia Butler, R. H. W. Dillard, and Elizabeth Lennox Keyser (Yale University Press, © 1995 Hollins College).

torical device of aporia: each character temporarily loses her ability to speak because she is placed in a dilemma.[8] As long as she looks to the external voices of authority to solve a dichotomy that disturbs her, she is silenced by aporia; but once she learns to rely on her interior voice, she is better able to express herself.[9]

According to classical rhetoric, aporia results from the impossibility of concluding an antilogical argument wherein two contradictory statements seem either simultaneously true or simultaneously false (Kerferd 65). Because no conclusion can be drawn, the rhetorician is silenced. For example, one might feel perplexed—as does the protagonist of MacLachlan's *Unclaimed Treasures*—by the antilogical paradox that flying is both extraordinary and ordinary: for a human, flying is extraordinary; for a bird, it is ordinary (76–77). Given the original terms of the argument, however, no absolute conclusion can be reached as to whether the act of flying is itself purely ordinary or purely extraordinary. Plato resolves the paralyzing effect of this type of antilogical rhetoric with the implementation of a third term to create the conclusion of a dialectical argument: the synthesis. Unlike antilogic, the dialectic allows for the restating of the original question so that it can be answered (Kerferd 66–67). In this way, with the synthesis that intuitive thinking allows, the aporia that stems from binary thinking can be avoided.[10]

The concept of aporia is pertinent to MacLachlan's works in its metaphorical ability to demonstrate the centrality of language to a girl's subject position. While experiencing the voicelessness of aporia, the individual cannot shape her own experience, nor can she interact with other people. She is only an object in other people's dialogues. But as each of MacLachlan's characters recovers from her aporia, she develops a subject position that gives her new power. No longer silenced, no longer the object of someone else's experiences, she can finally engage with other people by expressing herself. Her increased immersion in language processes, then, is instrumental to her growth.

Significantly, MacLachlan's texts also create temporary aporic experiences for the reader. *Cassie Binegar, Unclaimed Treasures,* and *The Facts and Fictions of Minna Pratt* set up an antilogical argument for the reader to work through at the same time that the protagonist is working through a similar antilogical argument. And just as the character discovers internal synthesis as a solution to the powerlessness of silencing, so, too, can the reader. Thus, MacLachlan's use of aporia demonstrates the primacy of language not only in her characters' lives but also in the reader's life.

In *Cassie Binegar, Unclaimed Treasures,* and *The Facts and Fictions of Minna Pratt,* some form of artistic process serves as a metaphor for the character's immersion in language. For Cassie Binegar, the artistic process is barely metaphorical, since her mode of expression—poetry—is comprised entirely of words. Cassie feels out of control because her family life is so chaotic, a feeling exacerbated by the death of her grandfather. On the first page of the text, she writes in the sand: "I AM INFINITELY ANGRY" (3). She is specifically angry at her mother for not keeping the well-ordered type of home in which Cassie's friend Margaret Mary lives. Cassie longs for "a space of my own" away from her disorderly family (7). She expresses her longing in a work-in-progress, a poem she calls "Spaces." The beginning of Cassie's sense of being silenced by the adult world, however, manifests itself as writer's block, and she has trouble finishing the poem. The reader may understand that Cassie is frustrated because she is too literal in her quest for some kind of order to be externally imposed on her life, but the character must work through several aporic moments before she gains that knowledge for herself.

Cassie's first aporia results from a conversation with a voice of male authority, her older brother James. She says she wants her family to be "like everyone else" (16). James answers her by asking a rhetorical question that Cassie cannot answer: "And what is everyone else like, Cass?" (16). Cassie can't even begin to answer him, so she retreats into herself after she tells him that he just doesn't understand (16).

Another aporia results after Cassie develops a crush on Jason, a writer and another male authority figure. Cassie asks, "Why don't I have a space of my own?" (69), quite literally; she wants an actual, concrete place where she can have privacy. But Jason answers her with a rhetorical question that denies the legitimacy of her question: "Each of us has a space of his own. We carry it around as close as skin, as private as our dreams. What makes you think you don't have your own, too?" (73).

Jason and Cassie are enacting the "semiological enigma" that Paul de Man defines (10). Modifying the classical definition of the aporia to demonstrate how ambiguity influences textuality, de Man describes the tension that occurs when the answer to a rhetorical question delegitimizes the existence of the original question (9–13). An aporic silence invariably results from a rhetorical question when "it is impossible to decide by grammatical or other linguistic devices which of the two meanings (that can be entirely incompatible) prevails" (de Man 10). Thus, to the rhetorical question of a male authority—notably couched in patriarchal diction that denies the legitimacy of her original question—Cassie has no answer. She reinforces the silence she feels by turning out the light, "leaving herself and the questions in the dark" (73).

A later rhetorical question in a dialogue with her grandmother silences Cassie again. Cassie asks, "How come you don't see things the way they are?" (84). Gran answers the literal question with a rhetorical question, "Tell me, just how are things? How *are* things?" (84). Again, Cassie is silenced; "No answers anywhere," she thinks (84). And because she feels bereft of language, she bursts into tears. But rather than leaving Cassie alone to work through her aporia, as James and Jason have, Gran comforts her and suggests that Cassie try to learn "how to look through other people's eyeglasses" (85). Gran tells Cassie that her grandfather never did learn how to look through other people's eyes before he died, showing the girl that her grandfather's rigid attempts to control the world around him externally kept him from enjoying his life (85). While reinforcing the matrilineal bond between them, Gran tries to teach Cassie to develop more than one internal perspective for judging things. In other words, Gran uses a narrative to teach Cassie to shift her subject position. Because this process of adapting various subject positions can be accomplished more easily by someone who relies on her interior self to perceive theoretical possibilities than by someone who judges the world only in concrete terms, Cassie grows into a new stage of psychological maturity.

After Cassie learns the interior process of changing her subject position, she gives up her quest to gain complete control over her environment, and she recovers her poetic voice. She finishes her poem "Spaces" by proclaiming that her mind is her favorite space. She describes her mind almost entirely in terms of language, as "Where I sort out my thoughts and sighs / and shouts! / and cries" (116). Having understood that the language of her thought processes is the only tool she has to exist peacefully in the world, Cassie concludes that the best space of all is the subjectivity of her mind:

"That is where I like to be / Because I know that's really me" (116).

After Cassie comes to understand the power of her own mind, she recognizes that she is more in control of her life than she had previously realized. As a result, she is able to forgive her family (and especially her mother) for being disorganized. Moreover, Cassie recognizes that perhaps she is not a suitable partner for Jason, and she rejoices when he falls in love with her cousin. Cassie tells her grandmother, "I suppose . . . this means no more pain and anguish for Cousin Coralinda. They'll probably get married and swim naked in the sea" (111). The girl can empathize with other people's needs, and she has acknowledged what is sexually appropriate for herself at this stage in her life. (Swimming naked in the sea with Jason is *not* one of her dreams!) Cassie's quiet acceptance of her sexuality and her forgiveness of her mother denote an acceptance of her own femininity. With the help of a matriarchal figure, Cassie has learned to embrace the powers of both her mind and her body, recovering both her interior and her exterior voice.[11]

Willa Pinkerton, the protagonist of *Unclaimed Treasures*, undergoes many of the same experiences. Initially, she seeks to understand abstract ideas in concrete terms; she develops a crush on an older man; she is angry at her mother for not understanding her; and she works through these problems by understanding an artistic process. Most important, Willa experiences her frustration as the aporic silencing of her interior voice.

The summer Willa is twelve, she seeks to do something "important and extraordinary." Her definition of an extraordinary woman involves a number of concrete activities:

> She would be tall and sleek-haired, dancing somewhere perhaps. Or playing bouncy music on an organ in a restaurant while people ate mushrooms. She would be wearing lavender eye makeup and a fur coat and diamonds the size of apricots. After each performance she would eat chicken salad or toasted cheese sandwiches (Willa's favorites) by candlelight. There would be waiters in red jackets with brass buttons waiting to light her perfumed cigarette in its sequined holder. There would be ice-cream sundaes with sprinkles for dessert (another of Willa's favorites). And a tall, splendid, solemn-eyed man . . . would be there, looking loving over the appetizer. (30)

At this point in her life, Willa specifically defines "having babies" as something that is not "important and extraordinary" (9). As Willa's mother is pregnant, the girl's rejection of this powerful expression of feminine sexuality is also a rejection of her own mother.

The first adult who hears Willa's plan to do something important and extraordinary interprets her goal rhetorically. Matthew, a man of whom Willa is enamored, asks her if she means "going-skydiving important and extraordinary or saving-a-life important and extraordinary or creating-something-beautiful important and extraordinary? . . . Or just plain everyday important and extraordinary?" (10) In response to these questions, Willa blinks and is silent (10). And just as the men who ask Cassie rhetorical questions leave her to struggle in voicelessness, Matthew does not help Willa. By introducing an abstract level to her questioning, the man has invalidated Willa's original goal, so the rhetoricity of a male voice of adulthood has denied the legitimacy of how the girl has defined "extraordinary."

The rhetorical question stuns Willa into a silence so complete that she no longer possesses the definition of a word that has been essential to her self-perception. Her initial understanding of the term "extraordinary" now seems inadequate, so she temporarily loses her use of language. Willa's silence, by underscoring that language is central to the individual's ability to make meaning, shows in part how language creates the individual. When Willa loses her original definition of the word "extraordinary," she loses the certainty of her plans for the future.

The reader, however, probably sees the resolution of Willa's aporia before she does: her aporia can be resolved with the use of synthesis, as an aporia reconstructed by classical dialectical rhetoric would be. Having the benefit of other characters' perceptions, the reader understands that extraordinariness is not a matter of either/ or but a matter of both/and. For instance, Willa tries to make a list of *"Things Ordinary"* and *"Things Extraordinary."* She lists as ordinary: "Eating," "Sleeping," "Bathroom," and "Chores" (76). But her father points out, "Chores can be extraordinarily important" (76). And when he defines "Flying" as extraordinary, someone who employs classical antilogic points out that, to a parrot, "Flying is not at all extraordinary" (76–77). The reader begins to recognize that flying is both ordinary and extraordinary, so she or he may at this point understand the resolution of aporia as a need for language that synthesizes. But Willa, still stuck in a concrete, binary interpretation of the world, rejects this possibility. She furiously throws her list of *"Things Ordinary"* and *"Things Extraordinary"* away (77). "How will I ever know?" she asks, "stomping off" (77).

But Willa eventually does know; she arrives at her synthesis through her recognition that language shapes the lives of those around her. Matthew is an artist who lives next door to her, and she has gladly posed as his model. When the painting is finished, hoping for the fulfillment of her romantic longing, she sneaks into his studio to see the picture for the first time. She plans to leave him a note that professes her eternal love, but when she arrives at the studio, she finds the artist's estranged wife gazing at the picture.

When the woman leaves, Willa recognizes that she is not the figure in the painting as she has expected to be; the artist has drawn a composite of Willa and his wife. Art serves as a type of language here: the painting is the artist's form of communication. The figure in the painting emblematizes that Willa exists not as a readily identifiable autonomous ego formed separately from all the other autonomous egos in the world; rather, she—and the painter's wife and all people—exist in a state of dialogic interaction with other people.[12]

Willa leaves the note she has brought, but she rips her name off of the paper to make it look as if the artist's wife has left it. Although the girl intended the note to be the signifier of her emotions, in editing out her name, she makes the note the signifier of another person's feelings. This time, she has chosen silence; it has not been imposed upon her. The words that Willa chooses to leave change both the couple's life and the young girl's understanding of life. She begins to think that all people are partly ordinary and partly extraordinary. In other words, it is both commonplace and miraculous that everyone has an interior world that depends on some form of language production for its existence. Moreover, after Willa realizes that Matthew is not her true love, she is able to enter into a satisfying romantic relationship with a boy closer to her own age.

This realization has been reinforced by her recognition of how ludicrous one of her father's students is for having a crush on him. Thus, Willa's reconciliation of her verbal aporia coincides with an acceptance of her own sexuality. The key factor in her reconciliation has been her understanding the narratives of two women,

Matthew's estranged wife and her father's lovelorn student: "Two people, unrelated, who would never come to know one another, never even hear the whisper of each other's name" (79). Nevertheless, their stories have changed Willa's life, placing Willa squarely within the call for women to learn from other women's stories (Heilbrun, "Silence and Women's Voices" 10–11).

After Willa understands the stories of these two women, she forgives her mother. When Mrs. Pinkerton gives birth, Willa considers her new sister to be both ordinary and miraculous: "Willa nearly cried out with happiness, with joy; the baby was that ugly. . . . You are the most wonderful thing I have ever seen, thought Willa. So small, curled fingers, eyelids like rice paper" (112). No longer does Willa believe that having babies is not "important or extraordinary." The frustration of her aporia is gone. She can now think more theoretically, so she can see that abstractions like love and language rather than concrete physical actions are what allow things to be simultaneously ordinary and extraordinary.

The binary tension that confuses Minna Pratt is also linguistic, for she wants to distinguish "fact" from "fiction." Minna's mother is a writer, so running through the text is a metafictional narrative about how fiction is created and how it works. For instance, Mrs. Pratt has posted over her desk signs that read "FACT AND FICTION ARE DIFFERENT TRUTHS," "FICTION IS FACT'S ELDER SISTER —KIPLING," and "FANCY WITH FACT IS JUST ONE FACT THE MORE —BROWNING" (21). Because Minna does not understand how her mother creates fiction out of facts, much of the story deals with the ontology of written language. A dialogue between Minna and her brother, McGrew, illustrates Minna's confusion:

> "Made-up facts are not true," she [Minna] said, exasperated. . . .
> "But Mama makes up facts," said McGrew. "In her books. I can too."
> "That's fiction!" said Minna, her voice rising. "It's not true!"
> "It's about people and feelings and places," said McGrew, "and all those things are true." (65)

Minna, however, interprets facts and fiction as being mutually exclusive.

Mrs. Pratt's readers frequently send her letters asking diverse questions. As one young reader puts it: "I have TWo questions that only you, a WRiter, can ansxxswer because I know that writerxs know the anSwers" (61). But Minna is angry at her mother: "She doesn't listen. She asks me the wrong questions. She answers with wrong answers" (67). Minna rejects her mother as an authority when she concludes that Mrs. Pratt does not have all the answers because her mother is unable to help resolve her confusion (64).

Because Minna is unable to articulate her confusion verbally, she writes letters to a variety of people, including her mother, the ballet dancer Mikhail Baryshnikov, and Mozart. The letters provide the girl with a forum for self-expression. In writing letters to people who either do not know her or who she feels ignore her, she uses language to shift herself from an object position to a subject position. And as a result, she can work through her confusion and her anger at her mother so that she is able to resolve her inner turmoil herself. The letters are yet one more example in MacLachlan's writing of the privileging of language: the character must have some linguistic means of self-expression before she can recognize the power she has in her own life.

The narrative of another woman that helps Minna the most turns out to be her mother's—the very narrative that has been confusing Minna. Because Mrs. Pratt's narrative is largely the story of how she creates fiction, Minna eventually connects with another woman not only by means of language, but by discussing language. Mrs. Pratt tries to understand life by asking questions that have myriad answers. Minna—like Cassie—wants the questions to have specific answers. Early in the text, Minna is annoyed with her mother for thinking out loud, "answering her own questions" about life, not Minna's (22). Later, Minna catches herself asking similar questions about a friend of hers. She is surprised to recognize, "I am thinking just like my mother" (52). The mother and daughter connect again over the source of Minna's aporia when Mrs. Pratt reminds Minna of the time she was five and answered a query of her mother's, "It's *one* of the truths, Mama!" (66) After Mrs. Pratt quotes her daughter, Minna loses her voice. "There was silence then. Minna stared at her mother. What did I know then, thought Minna, that I've forgotten?" (66) Rather than being silenced by a voice of the patriarchy, Minna has been silenced by the voice of her own childhood.[13]

Confronted by the signs over her mother's desk late in the text, Minna thinks, "There is something here I almost know. . . . I am beginning to remember" (124). She reads a letter a child has written her mother asking if all her stories are "lies" (124). Mrs. Pratt says that she has answered the boy's letter: "Some of them are and some of them are not. But they are *all* true" (124). For the first time, Minna does not feel confused by the distinction between fact and fiction. Instead, she nods her head in agreement and understanding.

One of the signs over Mrs. Pratt's desk has provided the reader of *The Facts and Fictions of Minna Pratt* with a clue for the resolution of Minna's aporia. "TRUTH" in writing is the synthesis between fact and fiction, which are not mutually exclusive. Minna's burgeoning maturity emerges at the midpoint of the novel when she decides that *"Surely love is a fact"* (73). This is her first recognition that many truths can only be understood in abstract and intuitive ways.

The text makes clear early in the novel that maturity is one of Minna's primary goals: "Minna Pratt, age eleven, is sitting patiently next to her cello waiting to be a woman" (3). Although she is a cellist, she hasn't yet learned how to play with a vibrato, which, for Minna, is an act of maturity. Just as Cassie Binegar defines security as something she can physically find, Minna mistakenly considers her vibrato (and therefore her maturity) to be something she can find in the material world: "She will practice and practice until she finds her vibrato, wherever it may be" (23). Minna's search for a vibrato parallels her search to understand the difference between fact and fiction, so music serves as a metaphor for her growing understanding of language. Her aporia occurs because she tries to answer rhetorical questions—"Facts were true. Wasn't fiction invented? Untrue?" (21) and *"Where is* [my vibrato]?" (44)—literally. As long as Minna thinks only in concrete terms, she can neither understand "fact" and "fiction" nor play with a vibrato because she does not yet know how to listen to her interior voice.

Minna's friends who can play with a vibrato describe the first time they achieved it as something they have experienced rather than something they have found. (Their stories even seem at times like narratives about the discovery of sexuality.) Her boyfriend tells her, "I got it at music camp" (13). Her music teacher assures her that "life and music are not separate" and tells her: "Your vibrato is not something that is there, I mean that exists, like fingernails, or hair. . . . It is something you can work at, yes, and think about, yes, but it is much more like . . . understanding something for the first time" (45). Willie, a street musician says, "It was like magic. Almost like magic. One day I was playing and it happened" (75). He goes on to equate a vibrato and maturity: "Sometimes it comes as a great surprise after a lot of hard work. . . . Like becoming an adult" (76). Another friend brags that after she has heard a moving story, "I just *know* that my vibrato will come to me if I *practice*. I *practice*. And it *does!*" (99).

These narrations help the reader see that Minna is toiling too ardently. Willie even tells her so: " 'Don't work so hard,' . . . . 'Think about the music, not just the notes. It will creep up on you, like moonlight' " (83). And once Minna gives up looking for her vibrato, she "finds" it. She awakens in the moonlight the night after an important musical competition, and having come to terms with her aporia and her subsequent frustration, she can finally play with a vibrato. She has learned to feel the music. She also seems to have redefined the terms of one of her rhetorical questions. Instead of thinking about where her vibrato is located, she simply experiences the music: she "smiles at the new rich sound" (135). She has discovered that playing with a vibrato is not something that one can rush by searching for it.

For that matter, neither can the physical maturity that she has longed for in the book's opening. The reader, however, may feel reassured about Minna's sexuality, for the text clearly communicates that Minna eventually achieves at least part of the maturity she seeks. Unlike Cassie and Willa, Minna is already past the stage of unrequited puppy love when the novel opens. She admits to having been in love with the man who sells her family eggs and with one of her father's clients (11–12). But those crushes are long over, and for the duration of the novel, she shares a reciprocal relationship with a boy her age, whom she calls to tell about having achieved her vibrato.[14] Her discovery seems particularly sexual, since first she "leans over the edge of the bed to touch her cello, lying by her bed like a sleep-over guest" (135). She then plays in a closet with the light turned on, "softly at first, then a bit louder" (135). After awhile, she stops, sits silently a few moments, reaches up to turn off the light, slips back into bed and stares at the moonlight. Then she calls her boyfriend. With the images of the bed, the moonlight, the lit closet, the vibrating intensity of a musical instrument so evocative of the female body, and Minna's pleasure (which she wants to share with her boyfriend), the passage creates a beautiful metaphor of female *jouissance*. Significantly, she achieves this climax independently of other people, but only because of what she has learned from them. She has moved from relying on authorities to define her experiences to relying on her own sense of intuition.

While Minna searches in the external world for concrete solutions to her problems, she is isolated from the full expression of her metaphoric language, music, but when she finally turns inward and accepts abstractions, she begins to experience the potential of that metaphoric language. She finally recognizes that—like "ordinary and extraordinary"—fact and fiction combine to create something greater: truth. She realizes that truth is what transforms fact into fiction, just as a vibrato transforms music into art. Once she restates the question "what is the difference between fact and fiction" to ask "what is truth," she achieves a synthesis that allows her to resolve her confusion about the nature of written language. She is no longer silenced verbally, physically, or artistically.

MacLachlan's novels all define art as something that transforms life. In *Sarah, Plain and Tall,* Sarah uses visual art to reconcile herself to her loneliness; Anna and Caleb use music. Journey uses photography in the novel that bears his name. Larkin finds poetry comforting in *Baby.* Arthur uses writing to make himself feel better in *Arthur, for the Very First Time.* Cassie Binegar does, too. Moreover, Cassie's mother plays the flute. Willa Pinkerton watches other people use painting, music, and writing; her mother dances. Willa herself is a writer who jots down on small pieces of paper things that disturb her (13), and she and her brother tell each other the story of their twelfth summer in order to make meaning of it. Minna Pratt watches her mother write to make sense out of life, and Minna writes and uses music to come to terms with her life.

The three novels that focus on a young girl's development of her interior voice make specifically metafictional comments on writing and storytelling. For example, the third sentence of *Cassie Binegar* is "What's written becomes truth" (3). The opening of *Unclaimed Treasures* is an italicized framing tale that describes the story to follow: " 'It was like a short story, that summer,' said the woman [Willa], settling in the wing chair by the window. 'A short story with a beginning, a middle, and an end' " (1). The framing tale concludes with Willa's brother promising their sister: "I'll . . . tell you a story about extraordinary things. A story with a beginning and a middle. And an end that begins another story" (118). Minna Pratt, too, is concerned about writing stories with "a beginning, a middle, and an end," mostly because her teacher requires such stories of her (26). Even before her teacher requires linear narratives of her, Minna "had written in a journal, keeping track of herself on paper, reading herself from time to time" (23). Minna also expresses her feelings by writing letters. She, Willa, and Cassie all find writing to be a process of self-creation.

Language, then, provides these girls with the ability to construct the narratives that organize their lives. As Willa marvels in *Unclaimed Treasures,* "You know what? . . . If you put all the letters of the alphabet in a box, there is every story ever written. Every story possible" (18). Carolyn Heilbrun puts it this way: "We live our lives through texts. They may be read, or chanted, or experienced electronically, or come to us, like the murmurings of our mothers, telling us what conventions demand. Whatever their form or medium, these stories are what have formed us all; they are what we [women] must use to make new fictions, new narratives" (*Writing a Woman's Life* 37).[15] Artistic processes, especially narratives, are a means for the subject to feel connected to other people, and they provide a specific way for females to empower themselves. Thus, art generally serves in MacLachlan's fiction as a metaphor for how the subject functions: she is created by language and in turn uses language to recreate the world so that she can understand it. The subject is engaged in a dialogic process of being structured by and restructuring language, and she can use language to ensure that she is not repressed by patriarchal traditions.

These metafictional metaphors about the process of artistic creation allow the reader to enter into the story. *Cassie Binegar, Unclaimed Treasures,* and *Minna Pratt* each make a statement about writing narratives that is paradoxical. On an antilogical level, how can someone "read herself" by *writing,* as Minna does? How can Willa's story be both a beginning and an ending? What does the act of writing something down have to do with the creation of truth, as Cassie's teacher claims? Just as Willa, Cassie, and Minna are silenced into aporia, the reader may also be temporarily silenced by these metafictional paradoxes.

The literal answers to such questions disrupt the text, momentarily forcing the reader into an aporia until she or he performs the same synthesizing process the characters are learning. The text thus shifts the reader's subject position, so language has affected her or his subjectivity. When the reader synthesizes a response, she or he reciprocally affects what the language in the text means and how it achieves that meaning. The metafictional aporia, then, is an exploration of how language determines the reader's experience. If the reader has questioned the metafictional paradoxes, then she or he both determines and has been determined by the language of that text.

Thus, rather than providing authoritarian prescriptions, MacLachlan's metafictional aporias ask the reader to engage in abstract, dialectical thought. Syntheses would be different for each reader, but I worked my way out of the aporia by concluding that a story isn't a goal to be reached; it's a linguistic process that helps us understand ourselves and other people. If we accept the postmodern premise that all people are subjects created by language, then we can interpret stories as a function of subjectivity. When we as readers partake in the narrative process, the language of the narrative shapes our subjectivity so that we emerge from the experience with a changed awareness. We shape the text, and the text shapes us.

Anita Moss describes one use of metafiction as a way for an author to demonstrate child writers in the "process of discovering their identities" (91). MacLachlan's use of metafiction certainly draws attention to the female subject's growing awareness of how language affects her identity: through various artistic explorations, Willa, Cassie, and Minna intuitively accept the primacy of language. Perhaps even more important, when metafictions engage the child reader in constructing meaning, they can empower child readers to explore how language creates them as subjects.

In MacLachlan's novels, art is a bridge between the subject and the forces that shape her or him. When Willa, Cassie, and Minna employ art to better understand the connection between the abstract and the concrete, they are metaphorically creating a way for themselves to understand the interior power that language gives them. On a metafictional level, if all people are subjects created by language, then novels—fashioned entirely as they are by language—become a sort of microcosm for investigating how language serves to construct the individual (Waugh 3). Metafictional aporias, therefore, also provide a process for exploring how art—especially narrativity—enables the subject who is reading the text to construct and be constructed by language.

Patricia Waugh defines metafictional writing as a genre that "self-consciously and systematically draws attention to its status as an artefact in order to pose questions about the relationship between fiction and reality" (2). Waugh provides an explanation for what an author such as MacLachlan gains with metafictional explorations of reality:

> Metafictional novels allow the reader not only to observe the textual and linguistic construction of literary fiction, but also to enjoy and engage with the world within the fiction. For the duration of the reading at least, this world is as "real" as the everyday world. Such novels reveal the duality of literary-fictional texts: all fiction exists as words on the page which are materially "real," and also exists in consciousness as worlds created through these words. . . . The reader is made aware that, in the fiction-reading process, an act of consciousness creates an "object" that did not exist before. (104)

This explanation of metafictionality is especially important to children's literature because children exist in a continual process of exploring the nature of reality and of being. When children begin to wonder about reality (as, for example, Minna does), they are beginning to wonder what it means to *be*. And—they are thinking abstractly and intuitively. Best of all, in MacLachlan's narratives, the *be*-ing of girls is ultimately not silenced by linguistic and/or sexual forms of repression. Instead, language is the liberating force that keeps these girls from reenacting the age-old psychosocial methods of silencing females.

MacLachlan's novels contain a trove of sophisticated abstractions. The characters experience how the transformative power of language establishes their subjectivity and so, in a similar process, can the reader. MacLachlan's use of aporia demonstrates how children—regardless of gender—are shaped by language and how they might experience their subjectivity; her metafictional aporias draw the reader into an experience that parallels her characters' abstract explorations of subjectivity.

In *Unclaimed Treasures, Cassie Binegar,* and *The Facts and Fictions of Minna Pratt,* language—and especially narrativity—is the synthesizing connection between the physical, exterior world and the abstract, interior world. As the resolutions of aporias eventually authorize each character's subject position, so too do the metafictional aporias authorize the reader's subjectivity. Because MacLachlan tells a story so well, the elegance of her narratives initially cloaks the intricate underpinnings of these novels. But the deceptive simplicity of these texts seems to be part of the narrative process. MacLachlan ultimately implies that in the language process, the female subject has a power as ordinary—and as extraordinary—as flying.

Notes

The author would like to acknowledge with gratitude the significant contributions made to this paper by the two anonymous readers for this journal.

1. MacLachlan's 1993 novel, *Baby*, is also about a young girl protagonist who experiences patriarchal silencing. Focusing more on aphasia (voicelessness) than on aporia (undecidability as a rhetorical trope), *Baby* is a treatise on how necessary words are to girls' development.

2. In *Meeting at the Crossroads,* a study that painfully delineates much of what causes psychological problems for women in our culture, Lyn Mikel Brown and Carol Gilligan describe the transformation of adolescent girls from being outspoken and confident at the age of eight or nine to being so concerned with being socially acceptable that they have learned to silence themselves by the age of thirteen or fourteen. All three of MacLachlan's preadolescent girls fall between these ages, and they all experience the type of silencing that Brown and Gilligan demonstrate as central to the female adolescent experience (4–6, 20–21). Yet MacLachlan defines reliance on interior language as a means for these girls to overcome cultural silencing.

3. Elaine Showalter relies on feminists from Virginia Woolf to Adrienne Rich to demonstrate how "women have been denied the full resources of language and have been forced into silence, euphemism, or circumlocution" (193). Studies by Sally L. Kitch, Marianne Hirsch, Janis P. Stout, and Brenda O. Daly and Maureen T. Reddy, among others, treat specific literary instances of the silencing of women.

More germane to children's literature, Lissa Paul draws some literary parallels between the silencing of women and the silencing of children: "Children, like women, are lumped together as helpless and dependent; creatures to be kept away from the scene of the action, and who otherwise ought not to be seen or heard. But women make up more than half of the population of the world—and all of us once were children. It is almost inconceivable that women and children have been invisible and voiceless so long" (187).

4. Carolyn Heilbrun theorizes that women have not only been traditionally silenced by the patriarchy, but also that we have lacked our own stories to tell because we have served as objects in male plots ("Silence and Women's Voices" 4–5). Heilbrun proposes that women learn to tell new stories by connecting with the experiences of other women: "Our new fictions must come from our friendships, from the narratives we discover in encouraging each other and sharing our lives" (Heilbrun, "Silence and Women's Voices" 10). Brown and Gilligan also suggest that connections between women and girls are necessary for the psychological health of both groups (216–17).

5. Marianne Hirsch suggests specifically that women connect with the narratives of their mothers as a way to recover their voices (167). Brenda O. Daly and Maureen T. Reddy also advocate adherence to maternal narratives for much the same reason (8–12).

6. Many feminists equate the traditional silencing of women with the suppression of feminine sexuality. In *The Second Sex*, Simone de Beauvoir says that women are "Other" based solely on their biological difference from men (xvii–xix). Hélène Cixous rearticulates the idea in "Castration or Decapitation": "Women have no

choice other than to be decapitated, and in any case the moral is that if they don't actually lose their heads by the sword, *they only keep them on condition that they lose them*—lose them, that is, to complete silence, turned into automatons" (42–43). According to Cixous, the patriarchy is invested in silencing women because it fears their sexuality (45–47). Cixous implies that the articulation of the *jouissance* of feminine sexuality leads to a recovery of voice.

7. MacLachlan's preadolescents seem to be enacting a movement from the Piagetian stage of concrete operations to the stage of formal operations. According to Piaget, this shift, which occurs when the child is eleven or twelve, is marked by the child's ability to understand theoretical concepts that have before eluded him or her (Cohen 29). For more elaborate definitions of concrete and abstract operations see, for example, Cohen (44–49).

8. Definitions of the term *aporia* abound. In the new *Johns Hopkins Guide to Literary Theory and Criticism* alone, two different definitions of the term appear in almost as many pages. J. Douglas Kneale in his entry on "Deconstruction" first defines aporia as "the hierarchical opposition of surface and depth, in which depth is valorized over surface, the ground over the figure" (187) and later as "textual doubt, involving the mutual assertion and negation of opposing systems of logic or rhetoric" (189). For my purposes, I am employing *aporia* as a rhetorical device that results from the undecidability created by another rhetorical device: the rhetorical question. Aporia is not meant to be a synonym for silence—or aphasia—instead, aporia is the experience of uncertainty that leads to aphasia.

9. Mary Field Belenky et al. might describe these characters' growth as a move from the stage wherein a female defines reality by listening to authoritarian voices to the stage wherein she develops a capacity for determining reality by listening to her own inner, subjective voice (54–55). Unlike many psychologists who set up age-driven paradigms, Belenky et al. note that a female's development from living according to "received knowledge" to living according to "subjective knowledge" can occur at any age (55). Certainly not the pinnacle of female development, a reliance on subjective knowledge represents at least a stage of intellectual autonomy on the path to a stage where the female can integrate the voices of many people in constructing her own perceptions (133–35). Belenky et al., as well as Brown and Gilligan, demonstrate the primacy of language and voice to the female's developing sense of self (Belenky et al., 3–20; Brown and Gilligan 216–18).

10. Belenky et al. note that dichotomous thinking is endemic to the stage wherein females turn to authoritarian voices for answers: women in this stage "assume that there is only one right answer to each question, and that all other answers and all contrary views are automatically wrong" (37).

11. Janice M. Alberghene notes how MacLachlan deals with the traditional Cartesian split between mind and body: "For MacLachlan, mind and body are no more opposites than are fact and fiction (or for that matter, reason and imagination); they are complements. Thought and imagination extend the body's knowing" (4–5).

12. According to Bakhtin, the meaning of language emerges from the dialogue (hence the term *dialogic*) between an individual's use of language and an utterance's socio-ideological context. Meaning cannot exist without being influenced by multiple forces; hence, language is inevitably dialogic (Bakhtin 269–75).

13. This passage seems especially evocative of Brown and Gilligan's recognition that girls aged ten or eleven are likely to feel disconnected from their own knowledge and experiences (93–94, 107–08).

14. Brown and Gilligan note that one of the most significant ways that society silences girls is by teaching them to sacrifice having relationships with other females and with themselves in order to maintain a relationship with a significant male other (216–17). Willa and Minna, however, are both capable of mending their relation-

ships with their mothers while they also develop relationships with boyfriends and maintain relationships with their brothers.

15. A slightly modified version of this passage appears on page 5 of Heilbrun's "Silence and Women's Voices."

In Carolyn Steedman's analysis of her mother's and her own narratives, Steedman also discusses narrative as a primary form of meaning making: "Once a story is told, it ceases to be a story: it becomes a piece of history, an interpretative device" (143). She says, "Narratives are a means of exchange" (132); they are how people shape their own identities and their interactions with other people.

Works Cited

Alberghene, Janice M. "The Stories of Patricia MacLachlan, Plain and Tall: A Paper in Two Parts." Presented at the 19th Annual Children's Literature Association International Conference. Trinity College, Hartford, Connecticut. June 5, 1992.

Bakhtin, Mikhail. *The Dialogic Imagination: Four Essays.* Ed. Michael Holquist. Trans. Caryl Emerson and Michael Holquist. Austin: U. of Texas P., 1981.

Belenky, Mary Field, Blythe McVicker Clinchy, Nancy Rule Goldberger, and Jill Mattuck Tarule. *Women's Ways of Knowing: The Development of Self, Voice, and Mind.* New York: Basic, 1986.

Brown, Lyn Mikel, and Carol Gilligan. *Meeting at the Crossroads: Women's Psychology and Girls' Development.* Cambridge: Harvard U.P., 1992.

Cixous, Hélène. "Castration or Decapitation?" *Signs* 7.1 (1981): 41–55.

Cohen, David. *Piaget: Critique and Reassessment.* New York: St. Martin's, 1983.

Daly, Brenda O., and Maureen T. Reddy. *Narrating Mothers: Theorizing Maternal Subjectivities.* Knoxville: U. of Tennessee P., 1991.

De Beauvoir, Simone. *The Second Sex.* 1949. Trans. H. M. Parshley. New York: Knopf, 1974.

De Man, Paul. *Allegories of Reading.* New Haven: Yale U.P., 1979.

Heilbrun, Carolyn G. "Silence and Women's Voices." In *Women's Voices.* Ed. Lorna Duphiney Edmundson, Judith P. Saunders, and Ellen S. Silber. Littleton, CO: Copley, 1987. 4–12.

———. *Writing a Woman's Life.* New York: Norton, 1988.

Hirsch, Marianne. *The Mother/Daughter Plot: Narrative, Psychoanalysis, Feminism.* Bloomington: Indiana U.P., 1989.

Kerferd, G. B. *The Sophistic Movement.* Cambridge: Cambridge U.P., 1981.

Kitch, Sally L. "Gender and Language: Dialect, Silence and the Disruption of Discourse." *Women's Studies* 14 (1987): 65–78.

Kneale, J. Douglas. "Deconstruction." *Johns Hopkins Guide to Literary Theory and Criticism.* Ed. Michael Groden and Martin Kreiswirth. Baltimore: Johns Hopkins U.P., 1993. 185–91.

MacLachlan, Patricia. *Arthur, for the Very First Time.* New York: Harper and Row, 1980.

———. *Baby.* New York: Delacorte, 1993.

———. *Cassie Binegar.* New York: Harper and Row, 1982.

———. *The Facts and Fictions of Minna Pratt.* New York: Harper and Row, 1988.

———. *Journey.* New York: Delacorte, 1991.

———. *Sarah, Plain and Tall.* New York: Harper and Row, 1985.

———. *Unclaimed Treasures.* New York: Harper and Row, 1984.

Moss, Anita. "Varieties of Children's Metafiction." *Studies in the Literary Imagination* 18 (1985): 79–92.

Paul, Lissa. "Enigma Variations: What Feminist Theory Knows About Children's Literature." *Signal* 54 (1987): 186–201.

Showalter, Elaine. "Feminist Criticism in the Wilderness." *Critical Inquiry* 8 (1981): 243–70.

Steedman, Carolyn. *Landscape for a Good Woman.* New Brunswick: Rutgers U.P., 1987.

Stout, Janis P. *Strategies of Reticence: Silence and Meaning in the Works of Jane Austen, Willa Cather, Katherine Anne Porter, and Joan Didion.* Charlottesville: U.P. of Virginia, 1990.

Waugh, Patricia. *Metafictions: The Theory and Practice of Self-Conscious Fiction.* New York: Methuen, 1984.

Remembering Always to Come Back:
The Child's Wished-For Escape
and the Adult's Self-Empowered Return in
Sandra Cisneros's House on Mango Street

Reuben Sánchez

In an essay on "home" and "homelessness" in children's literature, Virginia L. Wolf suggests that one distinction between literature for children and literature for adults may be that the former tends to embrace myth while the latter tends to embrace reality: "Whereas much adult literature laments our homelessness and reflects the fragmentation or loss of myth, most children's literature celebrates home and affirms belief in myth" (54). In doing so, however, children's literature might very well offer an unrealistic view of the world: "Even though I celebrate all those wonderful mythic houses in children's literature as an invaluable legacy of comfort, I worry that they deny too much of reality. Certainly, if children are to reach their potential and make their contribution to humanity, they must eventually move beyond a perception of the world as they desire it to be and accept it as it is—enormously destructive, turbulent, and chaotic as well as creative and peaceful" (66). Though children find myth attractive, they might nonetheless acquire a distorted "perception of reality" should the book emphasize myth—or if myth and reality are irreconcilable. Wolf's distinctions between myth and reality and between literature for children and literature for adults are crucial to scholars who wish to fashion a hermeneutics of discourse concerning children's literature. But as one might expect, the practice of literary interpretation could render such distinctions problematic in certain texts.

The foremost proponent of archetypal criticism, Northrop Frye, describes the structure of the monomyth in historical terms as a movement in Western literature from primitive myth to modern irony, a schema that does much to subordinate myth to irony. Frye's rigorous schema has since been critiqued by historicists, structuralists, post-structuralists, and feminists, but there nonetheless remains

Children's Literature 23, ed. Francelia Butler, R. H. W. Dillard, and Elizabeth Lennox Keyser (Yale University Press, © 1995 Hollins College).

a tendency in literary studies to view myth as the opposite of reality. Such a tendency might limit the appeal, perhaps the usefulness, of texts that are said to be mythic. For the purposes of this essay, however, I should like to consider myth in the sense that Joseph Campbell defines it in *The Hero with a Thousand Faces:* "It would not be too much to say that myth is the secret opening through which the inexhaustible energies of the cosmos pour into human cultural manifestation. Religions, philosophies, arts, the social forms of primitive and historic man, prime discoveries in science and technology, the very dreams that blister sleep, boil up from the basic, magic ring of myth" (3). Campbell's definition blurs the distinction between myth and irony, which allows us to recognize how and why myth moves us and is useful to us, adults and children alike. Through story telling the writer's perception of the world is manifested. We might think of myth, therefore, as cultural story telling, a way by which the writer who belongs to and identifies with a particular community explains why the world is the way it is, from the point of view of that particular community. The writer either validates a myth, or modifies a myth without rejecting it, or rejects a myth and creates a new myth based on his or her own experience. In *The House on Mango Street,* Sandra Cisneros participates in the third type of story telling by combining myth (home) and irony (homelessness) in her depiction of life in the barrio as seen through the eyes of a girl.

Cisneros addresses the theme of home versus homelessness in a series of forty-four vignettes—some as short as a few paragraphs, others as long as four or five pages—written in a language that is easily accessible and in a style that is sophisticated in its presentation of voice and theme. There is no single narrative strand, though the vignettes are loosely connected to each other in that they concern a brief period in which Esperanza, the book's protagonist, lives on Mango Street. We are never told her age, but she seems to be about ten or eleven years old. She wishes to find a house of her own:

> Not a flat. Not an apartment in back. Not a man's house. Not a daddy's. A house all my own. With my porch and my pillow, my pretty purple petunias. My books and my stories. My two shoes waiting beside the bed. Nobody to shake a stick at. Nobody's garbage to pick up after.
>
> Only a house quiet as snow, a space for myself to go, clean as paper before the poem. (108)

This type of story telling incorporates both extremes—home contrasted with homelessness, the ideal house contrasted with the realistic, harsh surroundings—into a larger myth concerning the child's perception of her world and her rejection of the patriarchal myth that would prevent her from finding a house of her own. To free her protagonist of one myth, Cisneros must create another myth.

Esperanza recognizes the reality of her own homelessness, for she points out that until they move into the house on Mango Street her family has lived in several different houses; on Mango Street she continues to wish for her ideal house, a wish that initiates and concludes the narrative, the narrative thus ending with a type of return, a tradition in children's literature. There is closure to the narrative in the repetition of a specific passage at the end of *The House on Mango Street.* At the beginning Esperanza states, "We didn't always live on Mango Street. Before that we lived on Loomis on the third floor, and before that we lived on Keeler. Before Keeler it was Paulina, and before that I can't remember. But what I remember most is moving a lot" (3). Near the end she reiterates, "We didn't always live on Mango Street. Before that we lived on Loomis on the third floor, and before that we lived on Keeler. Before Keeler it was Paulina, but what I remember most is Mango Street, sad red house, the house I belong but do not belong to" (109–110). What Esperanza adds to the second passage evinces her discovery that although what she remembers *initially* is moving often, what she remembers *finally* is Mango Street. The addition to the second passage suggests that there has been a change in Esperanza from the beginning to the end of her story telling, where her concern is with a particular neighborhood and a particular house, to which she vows she will return.

The closure resulting from the narrative circling back on itself by means of repetition can also be described as an example of Freud's *fort da* idea, *fort* meaning "gone away" and *da* meaning "here." [1] Once the reading process has been completed, the reader recognizes how and why the beginning and the end depend upon one another. As Terry Eagleton points out: "*Fort* has meaning only in relation to *da*" (186). Although repetition suggests closure, the narrative, in fact, is not self-enclosed; rather, it is open-ended and encourages the reader to consider what will become of Esperanza after the book has ended.

Margaret Higonnet has suggested that in "its ideological functions of social control" children's literature is an "imperialist form," but that the form is artistic as well as ideological (37–38). Because children's literature is often characterized by repetition and a firm sense of closure, even predictability in that closure, any deviation from that form results in a narrative fragment or rupture—an artistic deviation that involves the child reader in the process of giving meaning to the text. Higonnet describes two types of fragments: the *mosaic* is a gap within the story, which the child reader must fill in; the *sherd* is a gap at the end of the story, which compels the child reader to supply an ending for the (incomplete) story after the narrative itself has concluded. Higonnet argues, "A somewhat older audience permits an author to use the sherdlike fragment not only to evoke threatening subjects but to provoke the reader's conscious activity. The most interesting type of fragment, then, may be that which deliberately propels the reader into responsibility for the *unwritten* narrative conclusion" (49). The sherdlike fragment applies to the ending of *The House on Mango Street.* Although the book has closure, it is also open-ended in that it does not tell us whether Esperanza finds her ideal house. Essential to the didactic quality of the text, however, is the lesson that if Esperanza does indeed escape Mango Street, and we cannot help but believe she will, she must return "for the others." In her depiction of the reality of homelessness and the myth of home, Cisneros shows how and why dialectic—homelessness/home, irony/myth, escape/return—influences Esperanza's growing awareness of who she is and what her ideal house means to her. But the unique fort da quality of the narrative leaves the outcome of that search for the ideal house unresolved for the child/adult reader.

By the end of the narrative, Esperanza recognizes that she must someday "return" to Mango Street empowered as a writer. Cisneros was raised in Chicago and, like Esperanza, in her writing returns to the barrio. Although Cisneros is writing fiction, there are nonetheless parallels between Cisneros and Esperanza. In her autobiographical essay "Ghosts and Voices: Writing from Obsession," Cisneros tells that hers was a large family (six brothers and her parents) living in small apartments, the family traveling often between Chicago and Mexico (69). Like her protagonist (who also comes from a large family—three brothers, a sister, and parents), Cisneros has learned to write about "the ones who cannot out" (110), which implies a tie not only between narrator Esperanza and the characters within the fictional narrative but also between writer Cisneros and the readers of the text. In writing about Esperanza's childhood, Cisneros, as Aidan Chambers would say, writes "on behalf of adolescence" (199). Chambers argues that writers who reject "the adult exploitation of youth" instead write "on behalf of a state of life that still lives inside you, even though you are past the age when it is the socially evident and psychologically pertinent expression of your existence" (199).

The return of the writer—Esperanza and Cisneros—to her childhood is symbolized by the mythic image of the circle, a symbol both of the circular journey she as a writer must take when remembering and writing about her childhood, and of the circle that binds "las Mujeres/the Women," to whom the book is dedicated, *within* and *outside* the narrative. The child's wished-for escape and the adult's self-empowered return comprise the fort da quality of a narrative that is, in its sherdlike conclusion, incomplete.

In the vignette "The Three Sisters," which comes near the end of the book, Esperanza is instructed about what leaving and returning means. At the wake of a child, "Lucy and Rachel's sister," Esperanza meets "las comadres," three old women whom she finds very mysterious. The Spanish word *comadre* is a term that mother and godmother use to refer to each other; it could also be the term women friends who are not related use to address each other. But the word possesses other connotations as well. In New Mexico, for example, La Comadre Sebastiana (or Doña Sebastiana, as she is also known) is the skeletal image of Death seated on *la carreta de la Muerte* (the death cart) in Penitente processions. Penitentes (penitents) are a lay brotherhood of Roman Catholics who observe rituals associated with the passion of Christ. Since the image of La Comadre Sebastiana seems exclusive to New Mexico, Cisneros may not have this specific image in mind in her presentation of las comadres. Yet, the aura of death surrounds these three women; one might say that, like La Comadre Sebastiana, the three sisters are intended to remind us of death:

> They came with the wind that blows in August, thin as a spider web and barely noticed. Three who did not seem to be related to anything but the moon. One with laughter like tin and one with eyes of a cat and one with hands like porcelain. The aunts, the three sisters, *las comadres,* they said.

The baby died. Lucy and Rachel's sister. One night a dog cried, and the next day a yellow bird flew in through an open window. Before the week was over, the baby's fever was worse. Then Jesus came and took the baby with him far away. That's what their mother said. (103)

The vignette is about death, but it is also about life. It concerns the beginning—or, in mythic terms, the birth—of Esperanza's recognition of what it will mean to return to her past.

The three sisters sense that Esperanza wants to leave Mango Street, wants to leave the barrio. "When you leave you must remember always to come back," one of las comadres tells her. But la comadre emphasizes that there is more to it than simply coming back:

When you leave you must remember to come back for the others. A circle, understand? You will always be Esperanza. You will always be Mango Street. You can't erase what you know. You can't forget who you are.

Then I didn't know what to say. It was as if she could read my mind, as if she knew what I had wished for, and I felt ashamed for having made such a selfish wish.

You must remember to come back. For the ones who cannot leave as easily as you. You will remember? She asked as if she was telling me. Yes, yes, I said a little confused. (105)

The thrice-repeated injunction to come back for the others emphasizes for the child the lesson to be learned, but it also focuses the reader's attention on the central issues in *The House on Mango Street:* why Esperanza must leave, and how and why she must return. Esperanza feels "ashamed for having made such a selfish wish," although the injunction does not imply that her wish to escape Mango Street is selfish. Rather, la comadre instructs Esperanza to "return," instructs her to "remember." The return will not necessarily be literal but rather symbolic, described as a circle. As of yet Esperanza is "a little confused," but the implications of this injunction will soon be clear to her.

In "Alicia & I Talking on Edna's Steps," the vignette following "The Three Sisters," Alicia repeats la comadre's injunction to Esperanza, though more emphatically: "Like it or not you are Mango Street, and one day you'll come back too" (107). Esperanza is identified with, is bound to, her neighborhood. Indeed, she *is* Mango

Street, as the young woman (Alicia) and the old woman (la comadre) point out to her. Esperanza finds little if any comfort in the recognition that she is bound to Mango Street. Nor can she find comfort in the prospect of returning. She declares that she will not return, "Not until somebody makes it better." "Who's going to do it?" asks Alicia. "The mayor?" (107). The very thought of the mayor making it better seems funny to Esperanza. She must learn that *she* will have to make it better—by remembering her past and writing about it.

Esperanza learns that she must not leave simply to find a house on a hill in another part of town. She must "remember to come back for the others," and thereby come back for herself. The path she will take as writer is circular: Leaving to come back to leave again, and so on.

Lissa Paul suggests that the restriction of the child or the woman to the home is a common theme in literature, but that the significance of that restriction is only now being recognized: "Because women and children generally have to stay at home without the affairs of state to worry about, their stories tend to focus on the contents of their traps, the minute and mundane features of everyday life around which their lives revolve: household effects, food, clothes, sewing, interior decorating, and nuances of social relationships. These homely details have been redeemed by feminist critics . . . as having interest; as being as worthy for critical attention as descriptions of battles or card games or beer drinking" (151). By focusing on such details and recognizing their significance for the protagonist, feminist critics articulate the "physical, economic, and linguistic entrapment" in which the heroine finds herself. Paul argues that whereas the hero traditionally relies upon *forza* (violence) in his quest, the "survival tactic" the heroine traditionally relies upon to free herself is *froda* (fraud): "Though deceit is the traditional tactic of the heroine, it is most visible in the tactics of defenceless child protagonists in children's literature" (154). This survival tactic is one way that the "difference" or "otherness" can be seen between the male and the female, the adult and the child. That difference is also being recognized as relevant to all readers: "The quickening of academic interest in women's and children's literature testifies that something in their stories is in touch with the temper of our time. Trickster stories express a contemporary reality; powerlessness is no longer a condition experienced primarily by women, children and other oppressed people. It is a condition we all recognize" (153). Powerlessness is of course Esperanza's condition, and she is in danger of remaining powerless. Showing why the female is powerless enables Cisneros to offer a way by which her protagonist may empower herself. Esperanza learns that she can empower herself through "books and paper"—a form of "deceit" in that books and paper enable her to "subvert" the "physical, economic and linguistic traps in women's and children's literature" (Paul 155).

Why Esperanza wishes to escape Mango Street and how and why she must return are the issues Cisneros addresses by means of the home versus homelessness theme. In doing so, she has created a narrative account of "a condition we all recognize"—a narrative, further, accessible to both the adult reader and the child reader. Esperanza wants to escape Mango Street, wants a house of her own, but unlike her male counterparts in other works she does not escape to the pastoral world. Chicanas usually choose to write about female characters in urban settings, whereas Chicanos usually choose to write about male characters in pastoral settings or in either pastoral or urban settings (sometimes moving freely between both settings). Although the choice of setting may not strictly depend upon gender, there does seem to be a tendency among Chicanos to allow their male characters the freedom to move about in the city or in the country or both, whereas there seems to be a tendency among Chicanas to restrict their female characters to movement within the neighborhood, or the house.

The pastoral traditionally concerns the urban poet's praise of nature and the simple life of the shepherd, in contrast with the complicated life of the city dweller. Though seemingly unaffected by the problems typically found in the city, the pastoral is not always and simply utopian, for there are conflicts the protagonist must face. In American literature one might even consider why the writer uses a particular version of the pastoral as a setting: uncontrolled nature (forests, rivers, plains), or controlled nature (fields, pastures, gardens, orchards). These two versions of the pastoral are found in, for example, Rudolfo Anaya's *Bless Me, Ultima*, where the young protagonist Antonio is torn between the *llano* (the plain, representing his father's side of the family) and *Las Pasturas* (the pastures, representing his mother's side of the family). Although his family lives outside the small town, the town is nonetheless a significant factor in that it represents sources of conflict for Antonio.

Often, the male protagonist's movement from the urban to the pastoral may serve only as a momentary escape from the harshness of the urban, the protagonist eventually returning to face his troubles in the city. Or the pastoral itself may be threatening to the protagonist. In works by Chicanos, the pastoral is apropos as well to the search for the mythical Aztlan, the search for what Aztlan symbolizes.[2]

The Chicana's concern with "place"—a house, or a room of one's own—is a reaction against the patriarchal myth that denies the Chicana a place of her own. Whereas the Chicano is free to journey through the mountains or the cities, the Chicana's movement has often been restricted by the Chicana writers themselves.[3] The reality the Chicana addresses, then, is the reality of her restriction to the urban setting—particularly the house or the room. That setting is Esperanza's past and her present in *The House on Mango Street;* she recognizes that it might very well be her future as well.

Instead of wishing to escape to the pastoral, Esperanza wants her house to be in another part of town:

> One day I'll own my own house, but I won't forget who I am or where I came from. Passing bums will ask, Can I come in? I'll offer them the attic, ask them to stay, because I know how it is to be without a house.
>
> Some days after dinner, guests and I will sit in front of a fire. Floorboards will squeak upstairs. The attic grumble.
>
> Rats? they'll ask.
>
> Bums, I'll say, and I'll be happy. (87)

Her vision of an escape is to a house on a hill, far away from Mango Street but still in the city. Some of the visitors she will receive will not be from the utopian world of the pastoral but from the realistic world of the barrio. The passage is a poignant and gently humorous reminder of the significance of the home versus homelessness theme in this book.

Yet, the passage has also drawn criticism. Ramon Saldivar states, for example: "Incapable of imagining a house without rats in the attic, and naively accepting the derogatory epithet 'bums' for all street people, the child innocently combines the features of a cognac advertisement with a scene from a shelter for the homeless" (184). Saldivar might be distinguishing between Esperanza's naivete and Cisneros's maturity, might not be criticizing Cisneros per se. Although a concern with the protagonist's naivete might be relevant to children's literature, Saldivar's concern seems more ideological than literary. In many children's books the young protagonist seems naive, but can also seem sophisticated for her years. Recall Alice, Dorothy, Bobbie (Roberta from *The Railway Children*), Jo March, Mary Lennox, Meg Murray, Lucy Pevensie, and a host of princesses from fairy tales.

Esperanza's use of the word *bums* is derogatory only from the adult reader's perspective—perhaps an example of "the adult exploitation of youth." The negative implication of the word is not indicative of Esperanza's attitude toward the homeless. That is, if she "naively" uses a derogatory term, she certainly does not have a derogatory attitude toward the homeless. (On the other hand, her use of the term "Bum man" in the vignette "The Family of Little Feet" is intended to be derogatory because of the sexual threat the man poses to Rachel and to the others.) Esperanza declares that she will give the homeless shelter and will care for them because she identifies with their plight: "I know how it is to be without a house." If they are homeless, she implies, then so is she. The word *bums* should perhaps be understood more properly in its specific context in the story and by means of criteria appropriate to the literary text.

A much harsher view of Esperanza—and, by extension, Cisneros—is expressed by Juan Rodriguez in his review of *The House on Mango Street*. Like Saldivar, Rodriguez faults Esperanza for wanting a particular type of house: "That Esperanza chooses to leave Mango St., chooses to move away from her social/cultural base to become more 'Anglicized,' more individualistic; that she chooses to move from the real to the fantasy plane of the world as the only means of accepting and surviving the limited and limiting social conditions of her barrio becomes problematic to the more serious reader" (quoted in Olivares 168). The literary value of *The House on Mango Street* is thus suspect for Rodriguez, but his conclusions seem based on whether Cisneros espouses a particular political ideology. Rodriguez does not recognize that Cisneros's text is political *and* serious in that she writes about oppression (political, economic, sexual) and the way her protagonist might free herself from that oppression. Her politics just do not happen to be his politics. Of the significant distinctions to be made between Chicano narrative and Chicana narrative, one might thus distinguish in terms of politics. The intention, however, should be to understand as fully and clearly as possible both the politics and the manner in which the politics is presented. Even Saldivar's critique of Esperanza's politically incorrect use of the word *bums*—Esperanza's politics, if you will—does little to clarify this distinction, since his overall treatment of Chicana narratives is rather brief (one twenty-eight-page chapter, six pages of which are devoted to Cisneros's book) in comparison to his overall treatment of Chicano narratives (six chapters).

Conclusions that the word *bums* is derogatory and indicative of Esperanza's naivete and that Esperanza's desire to escape her environment shows that she (with Cisneros) lacks political commitment serve as examples of what can happen when one does not evaluate a literary text on its own terms and on the terms appropriate to the genre, when one complains instead of analyzes. If we prefer complaint to analysis, we may miss the significant points made in the vignette "Bums in the Attic": Esperanza will not give up her dream; she will not forget "those who cannot out"; she will not forget who she is; she will find a house of her own.

The dangers critics like Saldivar and Rodriguez risk when they evaluate the work of a writer like Cisneros are similar to the dangers adults risk when they attempt to evaluate children's literature according to criteria they may bring with them from their work in other genres or other disciplines. The criteria by which one evaluates literature for children is often, and perhaps unavoidably, at least in part the same criteria by which one evaluates literature for adults. "Whatever the topic to be studied," Margaret Meek argues,

in literature, as elsewhere, we inherit the theories of our predecessors, willy nilly: and in making our own we are bound to represent not only their earlier methods of inquiry, but also the pattern of associated constructs already existent in our own minds. Thus, I cannot speculate about children's literature without incorporating the tissues of ideas that inform my everyday thinking about literature, children, reading, writing, language, linguistics, politics, ideology, sociology, history, education, sex, psychology, art, or a combination of some or all of these, to say nothing of joy or sadness, pleasure or pain. This is a lengthy way of saying that those who would theorize do so initially about themselves. (166–167)

We cannot, therefore, help but evaluate children's literature according to what we have learned from our predecessors and according to our personal tastes. Yet as Meek reminds us: "In the past 20 years, we have outgrown the need to establish children's books as a legitimate area of study, but we are still looking through the lorgnettes of critical models now outworn in adult literature" (167). Theorizing of course enables us to articulate the value of children's literature or of Chicana literature; but as we have seen, theorizing that is not based on close literary analysis or that is not based on an appreciation of genre can lead to the subordination of these literatures for political reasons.

Cisneros addresses the home versus homelessness theme in an urban rather than pastoral setting. In the vignette "The Monkey Garden," she shows why the pastoral must be rejected—a rejection, certainly, of the pastoral image of Eden, perhaps a postlapsarian vision of Eden, for this garden is overgrown *and* decaying. The urban world has overtaken the pastoral world in that the garden becomes a junk yard where "Dead cars appeared overnight like mushrooms" (95).[4] In the garden, too, Esperanza, brick in hand, realizes that Sally does not want to be "saved" from "Tito's buddies." This realization results in a form of self-expulsion in that Esperanza now feels she no longer belongs in the garden: "I looked at my feet in their white socks and ugly round shoes. They seemed far away. They didn't seem to be my feet anymore. And the garden that had been such a good place to play didn't seem mine either" (98). It is time, she senses, for her to leave the garden and what it represents. She is changing, outgrowing that which kept her in the garden until now, and she expresses that awareness through a reference to her feet and shoes—one of many references to feet and shoes in Cisneros's book. Others may be found, for example, in "The Family of Little Feet" and "Chanclas" (a *chancla* is a type of slipper or old shoe), vignettes concerned with the confusion involved in the transition from childhood to adolescence.

Cisneros presents the image of the garden in order to reject it. Any attempt to return to an edenic past would be ironic for the female who seeks freedom from the patriarchal Genesis myth. Though Esperanza may not fully understand why, she nonetheless feels that she no longer belongs in the garden: "Who was it that said I was getting too old to play the games?" (96). Nor does she require a deity to evict her. The theme of exile from the garden—the recognition and rejection of what the garden represents—is specifically related to the home versus homelessness theme: the home Cisneros rejects is the patriarchal, edenic home.

The rejection of the patriarchal home has become an important theme in Chicana literature. For example, Estela Portillo Trambley also critiques the patriarchal myth in her short story "The Trees." Nina, "a confident city girl," marries the youngest of four sons of Don Teofilo Ayala, the head of a family that owns a large and very productive apple orchard. When the old patriarch dies, Nina worries about how the orchard will be divided among the brothers. She wishes to acquire the inheritance for herself and for her husband, Ismael (a name reminiscent of exile). By turning the brothers against each other, Nina eventually brings about the destruction of *that* garden—because she is greedy, to be sure, but also because she is opposed to the patriarchal world of which she is a victim. She was raped when she was a child; and as an adult she is expected to play the role of submissive housewife: "The family, with its elementary tie to the earth, had established a working patriarchal order. The father and sons lived for a fraternal cause, the apple orchards. Their women followed in silent steps, fulfilled in their women ways. If ambition or a sense of power touched the feminine heart, it was a silent touch. The lives were well patterned like the rows of apple trees and the trenches that fed them. Men and women had a separate given image until Nina came" (13). Although Portillo Trambley does not justify Nina's destructive behavior or encourage the reader to sympathize with Nina, she nonetheless shows how the patriarchal order can, through its obsessive adherence to a "fraternal cause," bring about its own destruction. After all, Nina is "an avenging angel come to the Garden of Eden" (16). In her critique of the Eden myth Portillo Trambley makes her protagonist, as Hamlet would say, both "scourge and minister." Like Cisneros, Portillo Trambley presents the patriarchal image of the garden to show why it must not only be rejected but also destroyed. This metaphorical significance of rejection/destruction is fundamental to Cisneros's handling of the home versus homelessness theme: Esperanza understands that she must assert her independence if she is to find "A house all my own" (108).

In the vignette "Beautiful & Cruel," Esperanza declares that she will rebel against the traditional role expected of her by acting like a man: "I have begun my own quiet war. Simple. Sure. I am one who leaves the table like a man, without putting back the chair or picking up the plate" (89). Yet, only three vignettes later in "Red Clowns," which immediately follows "The Monkey Garden," Esperanza becomes a victim. She goes with Sally to the carnival, where Sally goes off with a boy and leaves Esperanza alone. What happens next is not clear, but it appears that Esperanza is raped, or if she is not, the experience is just as traumatic:

> Sally Sally a hundred times. Why didn't you hear me when I called? Why didn't you tell them to leave me alone? The one who grabbed me by the arm, he wouldn't let me go. He said I love you, Spanish girl, I love you, and pressed his sour mouth to mine.
>
> Sally, make him stop. I couldn't make them go away. I couldn't do anything but cry. I don't remember. It was dark. I don't remember. I don't remember. Please don't make me tell it all. (100)

The pattern seems similar to what happens to Nina; however, Esperanza will diverge from that pattern, we assume, for only two vignettes after "Red Clowns" Esperanza meets las comadres in the vignette "The Three Sisters." Esperanza will destroy the male myth, not by literally destroying the garden as Nina does, but by becoming a writer and writing about her past.

Cisneros's critique of patriarchal society—the forms of power through which it protects its "fraternal cause"—and her reaction against that society are evident through much of the book. The critique and the reaction are examples of what Gloria Anzaldúa refers to as "writing" that is "dangerous": "Writing is dangerous because we are afraid of what the writing reveals: the fears, the angers, the strengths of a woman under a triple or quadruple oppression. Yet in that very act lies our survival because a woman who writes has power. And a woman with power is feared" (171). Esperanza seeks to possess this kind of power. In the vignette "My Name" she declares that "the Chinese, like the Mexicans, don't like their women strong" (10). Although she has inherited her grandmother's name, Esperanza will not "inherit her place by the window" (11). Instead, she will "baptize" herself "something like Zeze the X," a name whose very sound conjures resistance, a cacophonous name that she feels will help her assert her power to avoid her grandmother's fate. Esperanza decides "not to grow up tame like the others who lay their necks on the threshold waiting for the ball and chain" ("Beautiful & Cruel" 88). Vowing to break away from what confines her makes Esperanza "dangerous" (a word Cisneros uses often in the book): "'Them are dangerous,'" Mr. Benny points out to Esperanza and her friends. "'You girls too young to be wearing shoes like that. Take them shoes off before I call the cops, but we just run'" ("The Family of Little Feet" 41). Sally, too, is considered dangerous because of the type of clothes and shoes she wears, as Esperanza says to her: "I like your black coat and those shoes you wear, where did you get them? My mother says to wear black so young is dangerous, but I want to buy shoes just like yours, like your black ones made out of suede, just like those" ("Sally" 82). Esperanza is fascinated by what is deemed dangerous.

Throughout *The House on Mango Street*, the many references to children's literature are evidence of that genre's impact on Cisneros. In "Ghosts and Voices: Writing from Obsession," Cisneros tells of books and fairy tales that were especially significant to her as a child. One such book was Virginia Lee Burton's *The Little House*, which "was my own dream. And I was to dream myself over again in several books, to reinvent my world according to my own vision" (71). She mentions such favorite fairy tales as "Six Swans" and "Ugly Duckling," as well as the *Doctor Dolittle* series, *The Island of Blue Dolphins* series, the Alice books, and *Hitty: Her First 100 Years,* this last book being "a century account of a wooden doll who is whisked through different homes and owners but perseveres" (71). One can easily see, then, how the adult writer indeed writes "on behalf of adolescence."

In certain instances in *The House on Mango Street,* the references to children's literature also serve as metonyms through which Cisneros develops the home versus homelessness theme and the rejection of the patriarchal myth theme. For example, in the vignette "Edna's Ruthie," Esperanza tells how she had memorized "The Walrus and the Carpenter" from *Through the Looking-Glass,* and one day recited it to Ruthie, a friend, "because I wanted Ruthie to hear me" (69). In Tweedledee's poem the unsuspecting oysters are tricked and then eaten by the walrus and the carpenter. Esperanza's selection of this story is not accidental, as it bears special relevance to her vow not to be overpowered by the society in which she lives—her vow, that is, "not to grow up tame like the others who lay their necks on the threshold waiting for the ball and chain" (88).

Besides the Alice books, there is another text that Cisneros uses in her characterization of Ruthie. Esperanza describes Ruthie's whistling as "beautiful like the Emperor's nightingale" (68). This fairy tale serves as a metonym of the world in which Ruthie and Esperanza live. In Andersen's "The Nightingale," the emperor, one of the last people in his realm to know about the nightingale, finally recognizes and appreciates the beauty of its song. He cages the nightingale, however, so that it can sing only for the court. An artificial nightingale is later manufactured and brought to the court, which results in the loss of interest in the live nightingale; no one notices when the nightingale escapes back to the forest. But when the artificial nightingale breaks and the music is gone, the emperor begins to grow weak. With Death sitting on his chest and the demons of his past surrounding the emperor, the nightingale returns from the forest and rescues him through the beauty of its song. The nightingale then agrees to come and sing for him from time to time, though the emperor must promise not to tell anyone.

According to Esperanza—who perhaps got it from Ruthie herself—Ruthie was married and left Mango Street only to be forced to return and live with her mother: "She had lots of job offers when she was young, but she never took them. She got married instead and moved away to a pretty house outside the city. Only thing I can't understand is why Ruthie is living on Mango Street if she doesn't have to, why is she sleeping on a couch in her mother's living room when she has a real house all her own, but she says she's just visiting and next weekend her husband's going to take her home. But the weekends come and go and Ruthie stays" (69). Of course, Ruthie does not have "a real house all her own," and that is Cisneros's point. Like Andersen's nightingale, Ruthie is caged and ignored. For example, if she was indeed married, then she is ignored by her husband. Nor does her mother seem to show much affection for her: "Once some friends of Edna's came to visit and asked Ruthie if she wanted to go with them to play bingo. The car motor was running, and Ruthie stood on the steps wondering whether to go. Should I go, Ma? she asked the grey shadow behind the second-floor screen. I don't care, says the screen, go if you want. Ruthie looked at the ground. What do you think, Ma? Do what you want, how should I know? Ruthie looked at the ground some more. The car with the motor running waited fifteen minutes and then they left" (68). The image of Ruthie is of a female literally trapped and unable to escape Mango Street, to escape "her mother's living room," for that matter. Ruthie is only one of many symbols in *The House on Mango Street* of the trapped female.

For Esperanza, there is something at once sad and beautiful about Ruthie. Like Andersen's nightingale, Ruth is much admired and loved because she is undemanding and unselfish. She "sees" beauty and, for Esperanza, she possesses beauty: "Ruthie sees lovely things everywhere. . . . When we brought out the deck of cards that night, we let Ruthie deal. . . . We are glad because she is our friend" (68–69). Interpreting the allusions to stories by Dodgson and Andersen enables us to understand the themes Cisneros addresses through the characterization of Ruthie: the homelessness and the victimization of the female.

Ruthie loves books and says she "used to write children's books once," although now she seems unable to read (69), which suggests the possibility of losing the empowerment that comes through reading and writing. Books and paper give Esperanza the power to be dangerous and (possibly) to avoid Ruthie's fate.[5] She recognizes that through the power of books and paper she will make the prophecies of the old woman (la comadre) and of the young woman (Alicia) come true:

> One day I will pack my bags of books and paper. One day I will say goodbye to Mango. I am too strong for her to keep me here forever. One day I will go away.
>
> Friends and neighbors will say, What happened to that Esperanza? Where did she go with all those books and paper? Why did she march so far away?
>
> They will not know I have gone away to come back. For the ones I left behind. For the ones who cannot out. (110)

She says that she will leave and that she will come back. But these actions are beyond the confines of the narrative—a narrative fragment, that is, to be resolved by the reader.

Perhaps most important, the power Esperanza acquires through books and paper will give her the strength to return. This is the world of myth, but it is also the world of irony. Wolf makes a compelling argument for the distinction between children's literature and adult literature in terms of the myth/home–irony/homelessness dichotomies. But she also argues that in five books—Jarrell's *The Animal Family,* Norton's *The Borrowers,* Lively's *The House in Norham Gardens,* Fox's *One-Eyed Cat,* and Schlee's *Ask Me No Questions*—we can trace the movement from myth to irony. The five books "range in their portraits of houses from the romantic to the ironic" (Wolf 56). I suggest that this range may be seen specifically in *The House on Mango Street.*

Mango Street is a place where Esperanza may have at times felt joy and a sense of belonging, but it is also a place where she realizes that women are locked in their rooms by jealous and insecure husbands, a world in which there is violence, incest, and rape. She describes a harsh world from which she seeks escape, but a world to which she must return empowered as writer.

At the end of *The House on Mango Street* Esperanza recognizes, and Cisneros validates, the empowerment that comes through writing and remembering. Hence, the writer can find her freedom, can find her voice as writer, though she can only find that freedom and voice by honoring an injunction: You *will* come back, she is told. She may or may not go far away, but she will come back for herself and "for the others." Here, then, is yet another circle in the book that includes those outside the fictional narrative, those to whom the book is dedicated, and those who will read the book, thereby perpetuating the circular journey of the child/adult each time the text is read. There is indeed a circle that binds, that extends beyond the confines of the narrative to bind las mujeres. Dedicating her book "A las Mujeres / To the Women," *Cisneros* has come back "For the ones who cannot out." The book's dedication and the very last line of the book form a circle symbolic of remembering always to come back.

Notes

1. For a discussion of Freud's fort da theory, see Terry Eagleton (185–186).
2. For example, though urban settings are significant in Rudolfo Anaya's *Heart of Aztlan* and in Miguel Mendez's *Peregrinos De Aztlan,* the pastoral remains the symbolic

goal. That is, the pastoral image of Aztlan symbolizes the spiritual or psychological return to the place of origin, a paradise lost.

Though some works may not refer specifically to Aztlan, they nonetheless partici-pate in a literary tradition concerning the protagonist's quest through the world of nature as symbolic of the struggle to find the self. Oscar Zeta Acosta's *Autobiogra-phy of a Brown Buffalo* involves Zeta's movement away from a city in California to the mountains of Idaho, to a city in Mexico, and finally back to a city in California (one finds a similar movement in Acosta's *The Revolt of the Cockroach People,* in the movement from Los Angeles to Acapulco and the mountains of Guerrero then back to Los Angeles). Ron Arias's *The Road to Tamazunchale* involves Fausto's fantasy of a movement away from Los Angeles to the mountains of Peru. Tomas Rivera's *Y No Se Lo Trago La Tierra* involves a year in the life of a young boy in the world of the migrant workers, a setting that occurs as well in Raymond Barrio's *The Plum Plum Pickers.* Anaya's *Bless Me, Ultima* involves Antonio's movement through the sometimes dangerous and destructive pastoral of northern New Mexico. By no means exhaus-tive, this list is intended to suggest the tendency Chicano writers have of giving their male protagonists freedom of movement.

There are of course exceptions to the emphasis on the protagonist's journey through the pastoral. For example, Nash Candelaria's *Memories of the Alhambra* is set mainly in Los Angeles. Alejandro Morales' *The Brick People* and *Casas viejas y vino nuevo* are set in the barrios of large cities. Rolando Hinojosa's Klail City books are set in a small town along the Mexico-Texas border. Gary Soto's *Living up the Street* and Danny Santiago's/Daniel James's *Famous all over Town* are narratives set in cities, although some of Soto's stories have rural settings, and Santiago's/James's story in-volves Chato's journey from Los Angeles to rural/pastoral Mexico then back to Los Angeles.

3. One need only think of Denise Chavez's *The Last of the Menu Girls,* Lucha Corpi's *Delia's Song,* Mary Helen Ponce's *Taking Control,* Helen Viramontes' *The Moth and Other Stories,* and Estela Portillo Trambley's *Trini,* a work that traces the protagonist's movement from rural/pastoral to urban. These and other examples are narratives that in one way or another place the protagonists in realistic urban environments. Anna Castillo's epistolary novel, *The Mixquiahuala Letters,* does present protagonists who venture away from the city, though usually to other cities—from New York to San Francisco, or to the pyramids in Mexico, for example.

This concern with the urban experience is expressed not only in prose narratives but in Chicana poetry: For example, Lorna Dee Cervantes' *Emplumada,* Evangelina Vigil's *Thirty an' Seen a Lot,* Alma Villanueva's *Bloodroot* and *Mother, May I?,* Pat Mora's *Borders* and *Chants,* and the poetry of Corpi (*Palabras de mediodia/Noon Words*), Cas-tillo (*Women Are Not Roses*), and Cisneros (*My Wicked, Wicked Ways*). Of course, the setting is not always as significant in poetry as it is in prose narratives, but when it is significant to a particular poem, it is often (though not always) an urban setting. For example, perhaps one of the most significant Chicana poems in recent years is Lorna Dee Cervantes' "Beneath the Shadow of the Freeway," a poem about three women—the grandmother, mother, and granddaughter—who live in a house next to a California freeway.

4. Elements of the pastoral might be seen as well in the vignette "Four Skinny Trees"—trees surrounded by concrete, trees that cling to the soil, trees that symbol-ize Esperanza's struggle to survive.

5. For two insightful discussions concerning Esperanza's empowerment as writer, see Yvonne Yarbro-Bejarano, "Chicana Literature from a Chicana Feminist Per-spective," and Julian Olivares, "Sandra Cisneros' *The House on Mango Street* and the Poetics of Space."

Works Cited

Acosta, Oscar Zeta. *The Autobiography of a Brown Buffalo*. San Francisco: Straight Arrow Books, 1972.

———. *The Revolt of the Cockroach People*. New York: Bantam Books, 1974.

Anaya, Rudolfo. *Bless Me, Ultima*. Berkeley: Tonatiuh-Quinto Sol International, 1972.

———. *Heart of Aztlan*. Berkeley: Editorial Justa, Publications, 1976.

Andersen, Hans Christian. *Tales*. "The Emperor's Nightingale." Ed. Charles W. Eliot. Danbury, CT: Grolier, 1980.

Anzaldúa, Gloria. "Speaking in Tongues: A Letter to Third World Women Writers." In *This Bridge Called My Back*. Ed. Cherrie Moraga and Gloria Anzaldúa. New York: Kitchen Table/Women of Color Press, 1981, pp. 165–174.

Arias, Ron. *The Road to Tamazunchale*. Albuquerque: Pajarito Publications, 1978.

Barrio, Raymond. *The Plum Plum Pickers*. Sunnyvale, CA: Ventura Press, 1969.

Campbell, Joseph. *The Hero with a Thousand Faces*. Princeton: Princeton University Press, 1949.

Candelaria, Nash. *Memories of the Alhambra*. Palo Alto, CA: Cibola Press, 1977.

Castillo, Ana. *The Mixquiahuala Letters*. Binghamton, NY: Bilingual Press, 1986.

———. *Women Are Not Roses*. Houston: Arte Publico Press, 1984.

Cervantes, Lorna Dee. *Emplumada*. Pittsburgh: University of Pittsburgh Press, 1981.

Chambers, Aidan. "All of a Tremble to See His Danger." *Signal: Approaches to Children's Books*, 51 (September 1986), 193–212.

Chavez, Denise. *The Last of the Menu Girls*. Houston: Arte Publico Press, 1986.

Cisneros, Sandra. "Ghosts and Voices: Writing from Obsession." *The Americas Review*, 15, no. 1 (Spring 1987), 69–73.

———. *The House on Mango Street*. New York: Vintage Books, 1989.

———. *My Wicked, Wicked Ways*. Berkeley: Third Woman Press, 1987.

Corpi, Lucha. *Delia's Song*. Houston: Arte Publico Press, 1988.

———. *Palabras de mediodia / Noon Words*. Berkeley: El Fuego de Aztlan Publications, 1980.

Eagleton, Terry. *Literary Theory: An Introduction*. Minneapolis: University of Minnesota Press, 1983.

Fox, Paula. *One-Eyed Cat*. Scarsdale, NY: Bradbury, 1984.

Frye, Northrop. *Anatomy of Criticism*. Princeton: Princeton University Press, 1957.

Higonnet, Margaret R. "Narrative Fractures and Fragments." *Children's Literature*, 15 (1987), 37–54.

Hinojosa, Rolando. *Kail City*. Houston: Arte Publico Press, 1987.

———. *This Migrant Earth*. Houston: Arte Publico Press, 1987.

———. *Dear Rafe*. Houston: Arte Publico Press, 1990.

Jarrell, Randall. *The Animal Family*. New York: Pantheon, 1965.

Lively, Penelope. *The House in Norham Gardens*. New York: E. P. Dutton, 1974.

Meek, Margaret. "What Counts as Evidence in Theories of Children's Literature?" In *Children's Literature: The Development of Criticism*. Ed. Peter Hunt. New York: Routledge, 1990, pp. 166–182.

Mora, Pat. *Borders*. Houston: Arte Publico Press, 1984.

———. *Chants*. Houston: Arte Publico Press, 1984.

Morales, Alejandro. *The Brick People*. Houston: Arte Publico Press, 1992.

———. *Casas viejas y vino nuevo*. San Diego: Maize Press, 1981.

Norton, Mary. *The Borrowers*. New York: Harcourt, 1953.

Olivares, Julian. "Sandra Cisneros' *The House on Mango Street* and the Poetics of Space." In *Chicana Creativity and Criticism*. Ed. Maria Hererra-Sobek and Helena Maria Viramontes. Houston: Arte Publico Press, 1988, pp. 160–170.

Ponce, Mary Helen. *Taking Control.* Houston: Arte Publico Press, 1987.

Portillo Trambley, Estela. *Rain of Scorpions.* Berkeley: Tonatiuh International, 1975.

————. *Trini.* Binghamton, NY: Bilingual Press, 1986.

Rivera, Tomas. *Y No Se lo Trago La Tierra.* Houston: Arte Publico Press, 1987.

Rodriguez, Juan. "*The House on Mango Street,* by Sandra Cisneros." *Austin Chronicle* (10 August 1984). Cited in Olivares, "Sandra Cisneros' *The House on Mango Street,* and the Poetics of Space." In *Chicana Creativity and Criticism.* Ed. Maria Hererra-Sobek and Helena Maria Viramontes. Houston: Arte Publico Press, 1988, pp. 160–171.

Saldivar, Ramon. *Chicano Narrative: The Dialectics of Difference.* Madison: University of Wisconsin Press, 1990.

Santiago, Danny. *Famous all over Town.* New York: New American Library, 1983.

Schlee, Ann. *Ask Me No Questions.* New York: Holt, Rinehart and Winston, 1976.

Soto, Gary. *Living up the Street.* San Francisco: Strawberry Hill Press, 1985.

Vigil, Evangelina. *Thirty an' Seen a Lot.* Houston: Arte Publico Press, 1982.

Villanueva, Alma Luz. *Bloodroot.* Austin: Place of Herons Press, 1982.

————. *Mother, May I?* Pittsburgh: Motheroot, 1978.

Viramontes, Helena Maria. *The Moths and Other Stories.* Houston: Arte Publico Press, 1985.

Wolf, Virginia L. "From the Myth to the Wake of Home: Literary Houses." *Children's Literature,* 18 (1990), 53–67.

Yarbo-Bejarano, Yvonne. "Chicana Literature from a Chicana Feminist Perspective." In *Chicana Creativity and Criticism.* Ed. Maria Hererra-Sobek and Helena Maria Viramontes. Houston: Arte Publico Press, 1988, pp. 139–145.

Reviews

Children's Literature and Considered Bravado

Gary D. Schmidt

Teaching Children's Literature: Issues, Pedagogy, Resources, edited by
  Glenn Edward Sadler. Options for Teaching, 11. New York: Modern Language Association, 1992.

It is the universal assumption of Glenn Sadler's essayists that the
battle to legitimate children's literature in the academy has been
won. Such optimism is generally a popular thing, even when the
optimism verges on bravado. Yet it is more often than not true that
children's literature is a kind of weird sister in the English Department. Even with the recent push to open the canon toward a wider
understanding of what constitutes literature, we do not seem to
know quite what to do with this stuff whose primary audience is,
after all, merely children.

The ambivalence of the academy is mirrored, unconsciously I
think, in U. C. Knoepflmacher's introduction to this collection. This
volume, Knoepflmacher asserts, "only helps to confirm the serious
place that the study of children's literature now holds in college
courses across the United States and Canada" (1). And yet, only
one page later, he points out that children's literature does not yet
receive "the same serious attention academia expends on so-called
adult texts" (2). The paradox is unresolved in the essay because the
paradox is unresolved in the academy. This volume and the other
small gains in the past ten years—and they are still small—show
some successful battles, but we're still at Bull Run, not Appomattox
courthouse.

Nevertheless, the publication of this volume is to be celebrated
because it does so well precisely what it seeks to encourage: it seriously considers children's literature not as the domain of the edu-

Children's Literature 23, ed. Francelia Butler, R. H. W. Dillard, and Elizabeth Lennox
Keyser (Yale University Press, © 1995 Hollins College).

cationists, but rather as a subject for literary studies. This is something that textbook publishers, the academy at large, and even some
children's book authors have not worked toward with great assidu-
ousness, yet Sadler does. Having assembled some of the top critical
writers in the discipline—John Daniel Stahl, Mitzi Myers, Jon Stott,
Mark West, Susan Gannon, John Cech, Ruth Bottigheimer, Norma
Bagnall, Francelia Butler, Alethea Helbig, M. Sarah Smedman (to
name just some of the most prominent critics)—Sadler divides his
collection into five distinct sections. His first, longest, and most insightful section deals with critical issues such as the definition of
the field, the nature of its canon, the role of theory, genre issues,
feminist issues. This is followed by shorter sections of course descriptions, descriptions of advanced programs and collections in
children's literature, and a short listing of resources.

Certainly one of the goals of a collection like this is to encourage
the reader to rethink his or her own approaches to a course or its
components. One cannot read through the opening two sections of
this book without a pencil in hand, ready to crib the fertile ideas.
The first three essays focus on canon formation, and though one
wishes that they would engage more with the discussions initiated
by the *Touchstone* volumes of the Children's Literature Association,
and that critics could sound less like ideologues when dealing with
canonical issues, John Stahl's encouragement to expand the canon
through internationalization, John Griffith and Charles Frey's exploration of the role of the canon in establishing a forum for cultural questions, and Bruce Ronda's articulation of an American
canon in terms of family, self, and place are pointed expressions of
the issues involved in forming—and re-forming—a canon in this
discipline. In this same section, Jon Stott's article on Native American pieces—the best in the collection—centers on the difficulties of
a writer from one culture attempting to retell the tales of another
culture by focusing on authors such as Paul Goble, Gerald McDer-
mott, Jean George, and Armstrong Sperry.

Mark I. West, the author of *Children, Culture, and Controversy*
(Archon, 1988), contributes an article on teaching the censored
book that is an unfortunate instance of considered bravado. Issues
surrounding censorship will never be resolved so long as censors
are stereotyped by the academy and the academy is stereotyped by
censors, for arrogance extends to both sides. West presents a brief
history of censorship and suggests some reasons for its unfortunate

health in our own time, but an essay in a collection like this should pose questions that allow both sides to be considered seriously, rather than villify and trivialize those who would censor. Although it is true that a library collection cannot develop under the watchful eye of a small but potent group with very narrow definitions, it is equally true that libraries should in some measure consider community standards (however those may be defined). Though it is true that access should be encouraged, it is equally true that most people would argue that there are some kinds of books and journals that do not belong in a children's collection—and the objections do not have to be, as West implies, religious in nature. (Though even if they were, they should still not be dismissed out of hand.) West would have better served his cause by following Griffith and Frey's lead and examining the way that censorship cases can provide cultural frameworks.

Essays by Susan Gannon, George Bodmer, and John Cech provide fruitful avenues of thought for how one might improve and vary an approach to a children's literature course. One does not have to be a Jungian to follow Cech's proposal that children's literature courses should probe beyond students' desire to preserve "what they believe to be the 'innocence' of 'kiddie lit'" (81), and that a psychological reading might be a way of doing this. Bodmer's article on "reading" an illustrated book attempts to do in a very short space what Perry Nodelman attempts in his *Words About Pictures: The Narrative Art of Children's Picture Books* (University of Georgia Press, 1988), and though he goes over familiar ground, he does pose a set of very practical questions that will be useful for students. And Gannon's summary of the outlines and boundaries of children's literature will pose an evocative starting point for any course, undergraduate or graduate, that tries to understand how children's literature does what it does.

While the first section of this volume suggests the ways in which children's literature courses are stretching and expanding our understanding of the nature of children's literature, the section of course descriptions suggests that the stretching and expansion is not entering the university classroom. The overwhelming impression from these descriptions is that instructors are teaching the canonical works—here using canon in its most conservative meaning. *Where the Wild Things Are, Goodnight Moon, Charlotte's Web, Bridge to Terabithia, The Lion, the Witch, and the Wardrobe, Alice in*

Wonderland, The Wizard of Oz, Treasure Island, Tom Sawyer, The Jungle Books, The Just-So Stories, The Tales of Uncle Remus, Pinocchio, At the Back of the North Wind, Sylvester and the Magic Pebble, Little Women, and *The Secret Garden* come up again and again. Are there any surprises here? These are all important texts and say much about how the field has developed, but it does not strike me that any of these works asks probing canonical questions.

Having said this, it must also be said that the course descriptions—like the opening section—encourage one to rethink how one does one's own courses. While the works remain surprisingly consistent, the approaches vary wonderfully. Some take a traditional or "great books" approach. Others focus on the child audience, on the folklore tradition, on the historical underpinnings of the field, on social history, on children's literature and composition, and even on the writing of children's literature.

The final section on readings and resources is most disappointing. It is perhaps too much to ask that these be annotated, but many of these books are dated, and the list seems surprisingly incomplete. Books as basic as the *Touchstone* volumes are missing, as is Nodelman's *Words about Pictures.* Selma Lanes's *The Art of Maurice Sendak* (Abrams, 1980) is not mentioned, though it is a model for works of its type. Peter Hunt's most important contributions are missing, as are many of the recent studies about significant authors. I do not see the usefulness of this list to someone other than a novice.

The accompanying list of periodicals and annuals is poorly conceived. While listing the title and year in which the journal began publication, it gives no information about the focus of the journal, the frequency of its publication, or even an address. It would not have taken much work to develop this list into a useful tool; as it stands, it is virtually useless. There are similar difficulties with the list of special collections. It does little good to list the Bodleian Library (is this truly the only special collection in children's literature in all of the United Kingdom?) without saying what the collection houses. How would a reader of this volume know that Robert McCloskey's materials are housed in the May Massee Collection of Emporia State University? This list is frustrating in its brevity and incompleteness and suggests a haste not typical of the rest of this volume.

This volume does call for some considered bravado. It is a testimony to the multiple ways in which this field may be approached, as well as a paean to the vigor of the discipline. The publication of the volume is a small battle won, and its call to rigorous application of literary methodology to the field and to one's courses suggests the possibility of more battles to be won in the future. But even the need to address the issue of whether children's literature is accepted in the academy suggests that Appomattox courthouse is still a long way off.

Toward the Definition of a Canon

Darwin L. Henderson

JACYL: Journal of African Children's and Youth Literature, edited by Osayimwense Osa. Volume 3. Benin City, Nigeria: Paramount Publishers, 1991–92.

Osayimwense Osa has skillfully gathered essays for this special issue of JACYL on African-American children's literature. These essays trace the growth and emergence of this literature, as Osa puts it in his introduction, by exploring "the life and character of the African-American community, its ideals and dreams and its idiosyncrasies and predilections . . . revealed by its literature" (viii). The idea of exploration which seriously addresses African-American literature was prompted by the editor's perception of cultural links between children's literature of African America and Africa.

The essays in this special issue are organized thematically. Nancy Larrick's landmark article of 1965, "The All White World of Children's Books," begins the volume and provides an ethnic sensitivity and focus by which to measure the growth of literature to which American children are exposed.

Mary Thompson Williams and Helen Bush Caver's "African-Americans in Children's Literature—From Stereotype to Positive Representation" concerns the stereotypic depiction of African-Americans from the early 1800s to the 1900s, as they evolved into the more positive representation of the 1970s, 1980s, and 1990s. This essay is concise and highly informative. Williams and Caver trace the development of an "ethnocultural identity" (11) through literature, from the early slave narratives of Solomon Northrup and Gustaus Vassa to the present with a rich variety of stories by writers such as Walter Dean Myers and Virginia Hamilton. They conclude that "the quality of writing . . . is providing better mirrors from which African-American children can find themselves" (21). Frances Smith Foster's article, "Since the Sixties: Literature for Children by African-American Writers," adds to this background by discussing works that were produced for children by African-

Children's Literature 23, ed. Francelia Butler, R. H. W. Dillard, and Elizabeth Lennox Keyser (Yale University Press, © 1995 Hollins College).

American writers and illustrators since the 1960s. Significant to Foster's thesis is the overwhelming evidence of the pride and passion in the development of this literature that occurred before the Civil Rights and Black Power movements. She calls attention to Amelia E. Johnson's *Joy* magazine (1887), Ellen Watkins Harper's *Iola Leroy* (1892), and W. E. B. DuBois and Augustus Dill *The Brownies' Book* magazine (1920) as milestones.

While the Williams and Caver and Foster essays are placed with Larrick's, and offer a historical perspective, they do not extend the indictment of society and the publishing world for the lack of significant representation of African-Americans in the pages of picture books or lack of significant change in the publishing industry. Foster states that "since the eighties, the stream of books for children by African-Americans has slowed to a mere trickle. . . . Only about 1% of children's books published in the first half of the 1980s focus upon African-Americans" (34). Although publishers have allowed the "delicate shadow" (2), the lack of full representation still exists. If providing a historical context was the editor's intention, then Jeanne S. Chall's "Blacks in the World of Children's Books" (1985) would have been worthy of inclusion in this volume, because it extends Larrick's work and would add depth to this historical cluster.

In addition to this historical perspective, several essays examine the importance of the visual image in this literature. Theme, tone, and style of both text and illustrations focus the reader's attention on the necessity of African-American images that are not distorted and that authentically reflect Black life, as Judith V. Lechner maintains in "Images of African-Americans in Picture Books for Children." She provides insightful descriptions of the work of various well-known contemporary illustrators like Jerry Pinkney, Pat Cummings, John Steptoe, Carole Byard, Floyd Cooper, Jan Spivey Gilchrist, and Leo and Diane Dillon. Lechner discusses the visual image in the context of African-American life and genre, family, community, heroes, fantasy, and poetry. This discussion allows the reader to use context and genre as criteria. However, Tom Feelings's more personal essay, "Illustration Is My Form, The Black Experience, My Stories and My Content," is an impassioned and impressive explanation of the influences of an African cultural rootedness and the "experience of being Black in America" (38). Feelings eloquently speaks of the "rhythmic energy . . . emotional power . . .

way of turning all knowledge into a living experience" (39). He explains how this experience is clearly expressed in Black music, is both spiritual and political, and is evident in the writing, as well as the illustrating, of children's books. Feelings defines his art through the context of music, speaking of framework, change, and, as John Henrik Clark states, "the ability to improvise within a restrictive form dictated by mood" (40). These two articles do not represent the number of artists who have persevered over the years or the new generation of artists who illustrate the diversity of subject matter of African-American children's literature. The art of the picture book has gathered enormous attention from the popular press, scholarly assessment, and museum exhibitions. The voices of artists who represent a variety of styles, art critics, and scholars would have strengthened the discussion on illustrations.

That Feelings defines himself as a storyteller through pictures provides an exciting bridge to the three essays on the oral tradition and storytelling. The section begins with an essay by Madge Gill Willis which details the lengthy history of the oral and written African and African-American literary traditions. Both modes of expression are examined to illuminate their similarly complex cognitive functions. Willis later combines historical and current research in literacy to illustrate the importance of the relationship between oral and written forms in the development of language in African-American children. Finally, Willis discusses the research of Health, Holt, and White, who suggest the use of metaphor and proverbs with African-American children in the school curricula to enhance children's development in oral and written discourse. Willis has woven together both modes of communication through a unified view, thus avoiding stereotypical thinking about African-American oral and literate traditions.

The "legacy of orators, singers, and musicians" (55), which Willis's essay documents, is discussed further by Cynthia Watts in "My Calling as a Storyteller." Watts recalls the richness and beauty of the voices of her family—their songs and prayers during revivals—and describes how the rhythms, rhymes, cadences, and inflections of their language "called" her into the world of storytelling. Kemie Nix's "The Pied Piper of Islesford: Ashley Bryan" is a warm tribute and sketch of the master storyteller, writer, and illustrator. Nix concisely captures Bryan's rootedness in poetry, music, and oral traditions of African America which contribute to his work. The three articles in this cluster provide a brief glimpse of the breadth of the oral and literate traditions associated with the African-American experience. Collectively, however, the cluster lacks depth of knowledge about these traditions. The discussions which inform the reader's understanding of what Toni Morrison describes as "those recognized and verifiable principles of Black art" (389) are essential because they shape the Black Aesthetic.

In "African-American Women Writers of Adolescent Literature," Rosalie Black Kiah characterizes the literature written for a contemporary adolescent audience: "There are several components that comprise the African-American experience, and these have been found in whole or in part in just about all of the offerings of the [women] writers" (82). She characterizes this literature as the patrimony of Africa, of dominance and dependency, and of survival. These various themes are carried out in the literature written by African-American women writers such as Rosa Guy, Mildred Pitts Walter, Sharon Bell Mathis, Mildred Taylor, and Virginia Hamilton. Kiah concludes her essay with a brief discussion that draws a parallel between the decline in published African-American writers and the decrease of political activity in the Black community: "The number of African-American writers being published appeared to decrease when African-American political activity decreased. . . . This occurs when manuscripts are selected for publication based not necessarily on the truth of their messages, but on how much they conform to the philosophy of the publishing firms" (85–86).

Donnarae MacCann's essay, "The Family Chronicles of Mildred D. Taylor and Mary E. Mebane," notes the use of separate schema which an autobiographical stance can present in the exploration of societal history in the writing of Taylor and Mebane. Taylor creates stories that highlight family and community solidarity in often pastoral settings, combined with the conventions often characteristic of the protest novel. In contrast, Mebane focuses on issues of race, gender, and the intricate relationships of bigotry and economic exploitation. MacCann's insightful use of Martin Luther King's *Why We Can't Wait* (1964) further enlightens the reader's understanding of the cultural context of Taylor and Mebane's writing. MacCann concludes by quoting King's question: "How can we make freedom real and substantial?" (148). The answer, she contends, lies in the writing of Taylor and Mebane.

Joan Nist's "Master of Nonfiction: James Haskins," the sole discussion of nonfiction, is a brief introduction to the author of such well-known works as *The Day Martin Luther King, Jr., Was Shot* (Scholastic, 1992), *Black Dance in America: A History Through Its People* (Crowell, 1987), *Black Music in America: A History Through Its People* (Crowell, 1990), *The Autobiography of Rosa Parks* (with Rosa Parks) (Dial, 1990). No attention is given in the discussion to Haskins's interests in historical, sports, and entertainment figures, as well as in the sociological aspects of African-American culture. It would have been more effective to secure an additional article, written perhaps by Patricia and Frederick McKissack, as contrast, balance, or extension of the discussion.

In the brief article on the Coretta Scott King Award, Lee Bernd discusses the history of the now-famous award, which was established in 1969 by Glyndon Greer. Bernd notes the various authors and illustrators who were past recipients of the award and, through her discussion, distinguishes each winner's contribution in fulfilling the goals of the award.

Finally, this special issue concludes with Dianne Johnson's "The International Context of African-American Children's Literature." Johnson examines the international and diasporic manifestations of African-American literature for children through analysis of DuBois and Dill's *The Brownies' Book* magazine, noting the "acculturating, socializing, and educating [of] African-American children as United States and world citizens" (112) through the discussion of serious social and psychological issues in the magazine. This discussion reflected the publishers' concern with world affairs and the need to inform African-American children with detailed and complex reporting about issues and interconnections of decision making and action. Johnson continues her discussion of the international context by focusing on works from the 1970s and 1980s by such authors as Rosa Guy, Lucille Clifton, Walter Dean Myers, and Tom and Muriel Feelings, who have reached an international audience with their books. Johnson concludes, "African-American children's literature is an international literature not solely by force of definition, but because of the conscious and deliberate visions of a succession of writers and artists who from the emerging stages of this canon saw . . . the world as a place in which word and images together can help people to be honest about who they are in both a personal and social/political, and thus, international context" (116).

This special issue of JACYL will introduce the reader with an interest in African-American children's literature to both the historical linkages which this canon shares with Africa and also to the continuing development of this literature within children's literature in general. Collectively, these essays extend the knowledge base and call for, even as they contribute to, a definition of this canon.

Work Cited

Morrison, Toni. "Memory, Creation and Writing." *Thought* 59 (1984): 385–90.

The Drama of the Erotic Child

Naomi J. Wood

Child-Loving: The Erotic Child and Victorian Culture, by James Kincaid. New York: Routledge, 1992.

As plenary speaker at the most recent Cultural Studies Symposium at Kansas State University, James Kincaid described the negative press his book *Child-Loving: The Erotic Child and Victorian Culture* received in England. He attributed these negative reviews to critics' dislike of either his book's mode (irony), its method (a home-grown deconstruction), or its argument. As he told the story, the book received universal opprobrium from the press—from *The Daily Mail* to *The Times*. Scotland Yard, Lord Brain, and other leading child advocates soundly denounced the book for offering consolation and support to pedophiles. The response made in Kincaid's defense by his British publicist: "I haven't read the book, as I have other interests, but I'm sure it doesn't support child molesting."

Child-Loving is a provocative and far-ranging study of the image and role of the child—and of the pedophile—in Victorian literature and culture. Kincaid argues that we have constructed the role of child molester out of our own desire and that what, in fact, we desire in our culture is to continue talking about (and thus participating voyeuristically in) the very child-loving we say that we abhor. What is at stake is our relation to both desire and power. Following Foucault, Kincaid sees power as diffused through systems: discursive systems, social systems, and political systems.[1] Power is not something we can stand "outside." As Paul Bové writes, "all intellectuals, all teachers and students within the disciplines, are to some extent incorporated within these systems of control based upon the mode of knowledge and truth production that defines much of our social world" (54). Key here is the idea that power controls in its very process: it forecloses the terms in which we may consider nature, nations, the sexes, adults and children. In contemporary critical theory, power has become our epistemological ground—it is the way we have come to understand "all human ventures" (Kincaid

Children's Literature 23, ed. Francelia Butler, R. H. W. Dillard, and Elizabeth Lennox Keyser (Yale University Press, © 1995 Hollins College).

17). As such, it is not owned or controlled by any one agency, but is the thing that controls by structuring discourses, relationships, and knowledge itself. Childhood is also a power effect—a product of the discourse of power—not a natural state. Kincaid argues that child-loving is our culture's ritualized test for separating the innocent "sheep" (us) from the guilty "goats" (them—the awful child molesters); its execration, writes Kincaid, is our "pledge of allegiance to power" (378).

> What we think of as "the child" has been assembled in reference to desire, built up in erotic manufactories, and . . . we have been laboring ever since, for at least two centuries, both to deny that horrible and lovely product and to maintain it. Pedophilia, by this reckoning, is located at the cultural center, since it describes the response to the child we have made necessary. If the child is desirable, then to desire it can hardly be freakish. To maintain otherwise is to put into operation pretty hefty engines of denial and self-deception. And that is what we have done. By insisting so loudly on the innocence, purity, and asexuality of the child, we have created a subversive echo: experience, corruption, eroticism. More than that, by attributing to the child the central features of desirability in our culture—purity, innocence, emptiness, Otherness—we have made absolutely essential figures who would enact this desire. Such figures are certainly not us, we insist, insist so violently because we must, so violently that we come to think that what we are is what these figures are not. (4–5)

The only strategic response to this totalizing discourse of power, Kincaid argues, is to refuse to follow the script and the roles we have been assigned. In this, he diverges from many appropriations of Foucault, which affirm that as there is no place outside power from which to critique it, there is nothing to be done. Kincaid asserts that rather than taking power as seriously as it takes itself, we need to transform the seriousness of our critical discourse into irony and even slapstick. By opening up the discourse about child-loving to play, to inconsequence, he writes, we can "squirm" past, "wriggle around," and deconstruct the discourses power has in place and perhaps thereby deconstruct the binary adult/child whose focus on sexuality has proved to be so hurtful to both children and adults within the paradigm of power. "If writing on sex has tended to be trapped in the tragic and the tragic-romantic (or melodramatic), we might do something to free not simply the tone but the whole discourse by switching the center to something like sentimental comedy or even vaudeville. We might find in this process an alternative to the totalitarian protections of power. We might find in this deconstruction of power not freedom but a new set of possibilities" (30). If we simply mirror power discourse, thereby perpetuating it, we miss out on the opportunity to subvert it by refusing to play by the rules.

Kincaid's mode, then, asks us to rethink the seriousness of academic, legal, and institutional discourse in general not simply by revealing its pomposity and emptiness, but also by enacting the critique in his own writing. The result is a demanding but also entertaining book, a book in which Rousseau is linked with Tarzan, and Power and Desire interact like Wile E. Coyote and the Roadrunner: "Desire places the banana peel and then hides around the corner" in order to discomfit power, which "tends to be hostile to deconstructing desire, to place under arrest the desire which scurries across the border only to execute annoying pranks" (32). Kincaid's mode (and method) is a flexible, witty, and ironic deconstruction of such binarisms as child/adult, pure/corrupt, asexual/sexual, and so on that have made the discourse on child-loving so fixated on the monstrous. We need pedophiles in order to distinguish our "good" child-loving in all its voyeurism and exploitation from the "bad" child-loving of those who actually enact what the rest of us only feel: one thinks of the national obsessions with Shirley Temple and Macaulay Culkin, the widespread fascination with the McMartin daycare center child molestation trials, which Kincaid compares with the trials in *Alice in Wonderland* and in Kafka (383). Kincaid asks us to rethink our need to scapegoat people like Raymond Buckey (who may have been innocent, as many close watchers of the McMartin trials concluded). The monster turns out more often than not to be . . . us.

The book is not an easy read, but it is an entertaining one. Because Kincaid does not fulfill our expectations of what a scholarly book on the controversial issue of pedophilia ought to sound like, because he refuses to follow the standard argumentative structure, because he is humorous where we think he ought to be solemn, reading this book is like entering a funhouse where nothing looks normal, requiring us to rethink the normal. Many may find Kincaid's style obnoxious and irritating, but it is entirely consistent with the project he has outlined. In its relentless exhibitionism, its bad puns, and its coy reversals, *Child-Loving* delightedly violates every hallowed model for scholarly decorum—which is precisely the point.

Kincaid organizes his book around Victorian conceptions of childhood because, as he says, we can use the Victorians most truthfully when we use them to read ourselves. The book is divided into four parts: "Preliminaries," in which Kincaid self-reflexively positions himself in relation to contemporary discussions in critical theory about the child, gender, power, and the past; "Victorian Constructions of Children and Eros," in which he outlines the bewildering variety of ways that Victorians talked about the child and their own relation to it; "Figures of the Child," in which he takes the three chief modes of child-loving (the Gentle Child, the Naughty Child, and the Wonder Child in Neverland) and discusses the ways in which children are seen to be instrumental in their own erotic projects, in literature and in life; and "Reading, Watching, Loving the Child," in which Kincaid analyzes both literary and mass culture from nineteenth- and twentieth-century England and America in terms of our own investment in talk, and in the discourses of power, victims, and victimizers.

The Victorians are useful in this regard because of the dizzying variety of their strangeness. Rejecting the idea that we "know" what "the Victorians" "thought" about children and sexuality, Kincaid goes on to show how little we know of what the Victorians thought about anything. In a dazzling discussion of the difficulties inherent in trying to interpret the past, Kincaid argues that silence, for example, can mean any number of things. Although we have tended to interpret it as "repression," it could also mean unthinking acceptance or even indifference. After demonstrating the impossibility of constructing a totalizing picture even of the Victorian discourse on childhood, Kincaid pursues strangeness and variety, arguing that we can better understand the constructedness of the ostensibly "natural" category of child by acknowledging that we may not be as distant from the Victorians as we like to think. Kincaid's extensive work in the child-rearing and sexuality manuals of the period allows us to see just how contradictory and wondrously strange the Victorians could be—and by extension, how strange we are ourselves. In the introductory section he introduces us to four Victorian commentators on sex who fracture most stereotypes about what Victorians thought about the subject: Charles Knowlton advocated birth control and sexual pleasure without the worry about unwanted pregnancy; John Davenport thought that celibacy would atrophy sexual organs and that women were far more sexually alive than men ("at the feast of Love, women are *gourmandes par excellence*" [41]); George Drysdale also opposed celibacy; Richard Burton advocated the practice of pedophilia. Later in the book, Havelock Ellis takes it for granted that pain and sexual pleasure are linked in his commentary on flagellation. Certainly these examples force us to reexamine our received notions about what "the Victorians" thought. As Kincaid points out in his section on "the past," it is extremely difficult to interpret what silence—or talk—means in terms of an entire culture:

> Silence can operate not as an opposite of what is said and done but in complex cooperation with them. It is just as possible that silence indicates indifference, ease, or an unwillingness to be drawn into arenas defined by others. It is in the nature of cranks to hog almost all of the discourse, when no one cares to issue rebuttals. Those who loudly claim that Elvis lives or that millions are worshipping Satan go largely unanswered; will future historians suppose that we were consumed with such things and thought alike on them? Similarly, the silent may have been seeing differently from the vocal (and from us). Perhaps many Victorians felt that the truth was not only disconnected from language but also from the self, even if there were such things as truths and selves. . . . Silence may be figured as the desire to communicate fully. (37)

Most important to his discussion is his treatment of the Victorian construction of the empty child. This child is embodied by being disembodied: it is pure negativity, and thus allows adults full access to the pleasures their own status denies them, by virtue of their "experience." However, this action, according to the logic of desire, is not enough, because it does not extend the game. Therefore the Victorians invented the Gentle Child and the Naughty Child in order to prolong the spectacle and enjoy the play. In countless texts from the period we see images of both these kinds of children playing the roles they have been assigned, and joyously participating in the results—either caresses or beatings, depending on the pleasure of the voyeurs. In his chapter "The Pedophile Reader: Texts," Kincaid suggests that a major part of the pleasure we derive from stories about children is precisely this kind of extended voyeurism—not without its risks, but deeply implicated in the structures of desire that power has constructed.

Most disturbing, Kincaid argues, is the way power has defined beating as an act of love and the caress as an act of violation. These definitions have persisted and form an essential part of the discourse about pedophilia today. He asks us to consider whether child-lovers are really the monsters we have made them by quoting the desperate and honorable love T. H. White had for a young boy and citing the "stiff courage" of *Dream Child*'s Lewis Carroll.

If we begin to question the ways we talk of monstrous child-lovers, he argues, we must begin to confront our own investments in child love. This is a risky process, but, as Kincaid presents it, we are not protecting children particularly well, anyway. In fact, it seems evident that many of the power structures set up to "protect" children actually ensure that the child will be traumatized—he uses as one example a vignette of a child who has been "molested" by a family friend: the child " 'was quiet and alert, answering questions briefly. He showed interest in the hospital equipment and was cooperative during the physical examination, which was primarily visual. His parents, in contrast, were crying, chain-smoking, and talking obsessively about the event and their fears of the aftereffects on their young son.' . . . John's parents have simply been responsive to an explanatory model that leaves them with nothing to do but express their terrors about the damage done to their young son and thereby assure that the damage will take hold" (207).

In addition to the three reasons mentioned at the beginning, Kincaid identified still another reason for the negative reviews in England: that those English critics might just have been correct, that the book was a mean, nasty, and dangerous one. Quite to the contrary, the book provokes us to reexamine our most sacred assumptions about adults and children, and about sexuality. As such, it reveals the stage on which power stands not only to be shaky, but even untenable. We need to ask the questions *Child-Loving* asks in order to increase our knowledge of the Victorians, and to increase our knowledge of ourselves. The book poses important questions for critics of children's literature in particular, questions which, while they cannot be answered easily, promise to enlarge the scope of what we do. *Child-Loving* requires us to rethink what we think we know about how Victorians read themselves and their children, pushing forward the valuable work already done by Jacqueline Rose, Nina Auerbach, Claudia Nelson, and others. It also may require us to rethink the texts being produced so assiduously to "help" children enter into the discourse that power has made so hazardous for them—the texts that insist that all touching is rape, that the stranger-Other who loves is bad, and that the familiar adult who beats is good.

Note

1. "We should admit . . . that power produces knowledge (and not simply by encouraging it because it serves power or by applying it because it is useful); that power and knowledge directly imply one another; that there is no power relation without the correlative constitution of a field of knowledge, nor any knowledge that does not presuppose and constitute at the same time power relations" (Foucault 27).

Works Cited

Paul Bové, "Discourse," in *Critical Terms for Literary Study*. Ed. Frank Lentricchia and Thomas McLaughlin. Chicago and London: University of Chicago Press, 1990.

Michel Foucault, *Discipline and Punish: The Birth of the Prison*. Trans. Alan Sheridan. New York: Vintage Books, 1979. Originally published as *Surveiller et Punir: Naissance de la prison* (Paris: Editions Gallimard, 1975).

Speaking As a Child/Hearing As an Adult

Elizabeth N. Goodenough

*The Voice of the Child in American Literature: Linguistic Approaches to
Fictional Child Language,* by Mary Jane Hurst. Lexington: University Press of Kentucky, 1990.

A twelve-year-old is awarded a $5,000 advance for the daily record
of her first year at a Bronx junior high school; media hype promotes
The Diary of Latoya Hunter (1992) with interviews of the seventh-
grader on the *Today* show. *Paddy Clarke Ha Ha Ha* (1993), narrated
by a fictional ten-year-old, wins Britain's Booker Prize. The Modern Language Association approves a special session on child authors for the 1993 convention. A story on Zlata Filipovic, "Bosnia's
Anne Frank," appears on the cover of *Newsweek* (Feb. 28, 1994). The
novelty of a child's vision is compelling in our society, especially if
this life force can be captured and recorded in a child's own words.

But what is the language of a child? And why, if children so
rarely become authors, have writers over the last two hundred years
chosen to include their speech in fiction? What special problems
does sounding the voice of a pre-verbal or rhetorically unsophisti-
cated young self present a literary artist? The history of childhood
indicates that any simple, uncluttered notion of "the child" is an
invention of adults, a social construction of Western educational
and ideological systems, or as James R. Kincaid puts it for late
twentieth-century readers in *Child-Loving* (1992), a romantic fiction
"assembled in reference to desire" (4). The French word *enfant,* and
its Latin cognate *infans,* define the essential nature of childhood as
unspeaking, reminding us that although actual children are rarely
seen but not heard, adults have an inevitable author-ity in the literary rendering of what children say.

In seeking "to understand the voice of the child and the role
of the child in American fiction" (3), Mary Jane Hurst raises two
related and significant questions: Why have children been so popu-
lous in American fiction over the last two centuries? Why has their
presence been largely overlooked in critical scholarship? Although

Children's Literature 23, ed. Francelia Butler, R. H. W. Dillard, and Elizabeth Lennox
Keyser (Yale University Press, © 1995 Hollins College).

she never fully answers these questions, Hurst draws attention to some of the complex issues raised when adults create or analyze a language for children in literature. Like the burgeoning theories that try to explain how young humans acquire language, this subject is fraught with controversy. For instance, Brian McHale in "Speaking as a Child in *U.S.A.: A Problem in the Mimesis of Speech*" (*Language and Style* 17.4 (1984): 352–70) has challenged the notion that a simple translation of children's speech ever occurs or that objective descriptions of their language can be usefully correlated to literary representation. Such an enterprise, besides its failure to consider the role of contextualization, only conceals the repertoire-based nature of literary stereotyping on which all writers depend when they devise a dialect or child's language (361).

Hurst's investigation is undeterred by such theoretical nuances, but it rightfully distinguishes its contribution from such previous work in the field as Horace Scudder's *Childhood in Literature and Art* (1895), Peter Coveney's *The Image of Childhood* (1967), Robert Pattison's *The Child Figure in English Literature* (1978), Reinhard Kuhn's *Corruption in Paradise: The Child in Western Literature* (1982), and Richard Coe's *When the Grass Was Taller* (1984). These important works are broadly thematic rather than focused on literary children's language, and they all lack Hurst's exclusively American orientation. Laurie Ricou's *Everyday Magic: Child Languages in Canadian Literature* (1987) is Hurst's only real precursor, although his work does not center, like hers, on the direct application of linguistic methodologies to dialogue.

Sorting and assessing the speech patterns of child characters of writers as diverse as J. D. Salinger, Henry Roth, Vladimir Nabokov, Stephen King, Toni Morrison, Richard Brautigan, Betty Smith, and Paule Marshall, as well as Nathaniel Hawthorne, Mark Twain, Harriet Beecher Stowe, and Henry James is an ambitious undertaking. Age-graded talk, intonation patterns, orthographic idiosyncrasies, and speech sounds are given concrete illustration. Hurst also provides samples of dialogue from a wide range of nineteenth- and twentieth-century texts, rigorously classifying them by categories drawn from speech function analysis, as well as speech act and narrative theory, and related to speech characteristics associated with current notions of gender and class and parent/child discourse analysis. Hurst's concluding chapter is organized to apply all the linguistic topics introduced in the body of the book to Faulkner's "That Evening Sun."

Although pioneering aspects of this book include the linguistic study of children's gender differences in a literary context, the value of this study as literary criticism seems limited. Comparing the case roles in *What Maisie Knew* and *Lolita* does not yield new insights into the girls' sense of victimization even if it raises a reader's consciousness about characters' verbal self-presentation. The fact that Maisie "places herself in an experiencer role in 50 percent of her self-references, much more often than she places adults in that role" (37) would demonstrate the special value, if not the powerful ambiguity, James ascribes to what the child feels, observes, and knows—only if one had not picked up the idea from the title of the novel.

When carried beyond categorizations and classifications, the book is sometimes unsound in describing historical speech or the ways narrative voice works in literary texts. The discussion of Huck Finn's impersonation of a girl, for example, tells us something about the late nineteenth-century view of female stereotypes but misses the irony that Huck's overly polite and helpless pretenses are unmasked by a shrewd shanty woman: "Don't go about women in that old calico. You do a girl tolerable poor, but you might fool men maybe." Like Aunt Sallie, who asks why Tom Sawyer had to engage in intrigues to free Jim (to which Tom replies "Well, that is a question, I must say; and just like women!"), the tart women who comment on boys' shenanigans in *Huckleberry Finn* are far from helpless petitioners. Hurst has discovered that Twain sees questioning as an aspect of stereotypical female speech (119), but the real target of his humor is the boys' too ready appropriation of gender stereotypes, not the female speech itself.

Other problems arise from blurring the boundaries between literary speech and actual language use. For example, the language of Faulkner's fictional boys and girls is taken as historical evidence of pre–Civil War speech patterns. The use of Pip's utterance at the conclusion of *Moby Dick*'s Doubloon chapter as an example of the poetic speech function seems reductive: asserting that Pip, whose role is analogous to Lear's fool, is too young and psychologically wounded to understand his own words beyond the level of sound play (46) overlooks the mythical implications of this character and his power to speak. Because Hurst does not examine the philosophical dimensions of such child figures, she does not add insight into larger cultural trends, the subtleties of what "voice" can mean, or the fundamental problems a writer faces in gaining access to the consciousness of the relatively inarticulate child. Tony Tanner's *The Reign of Wonder* (1965), cited in Hurst's bibliography, is more useful in the first regard, relating "the innocent eye" of child figures to the American search for a new vision. Naomi Sokoloff addresses the latter issues effectively in the opening discussion of *Imagining the Child in Modern Jewish Fiction* (1992). Although Hurst notes that in 1927, after his third novel was rejected, Faulkner decided to write for himself rather than change careers, and thus created three young Compson characters (137), it would have been interesting to pursue this point with other failed or flagging writers who also unblocked themselves by writing for or about children.

Nevertheless this book is useful for the nonlinguist because it clearly explains basic concepts and technical terms, alludes to controversies, and provides numerous charts illustrating how language can be examined from a variety of approaches. Another asset of the volume is its comprehensive bibliography, which includes unpublished dissertations. One also gains a startling realization of how much fresh child talk is out there—un-cutesy dialogue, exuberant sounds, funny reflections, and inscrutable outbursts waiting to be heard, read aloud, and pondered. As current linguistic theory becomes more accessible through works like Steven Pinker's *The Language Instinct* (1994) and adults grow accustomed to Chomsky's notion of the three-year-old as a "linguistic genius," the power of children's literature to model young speech is evident. Coming out of the mouths of adults, fictional child language becomes authorized as it is read aloud. Because Hurst's book shows some of the potential problems and uses of applying linguistic principles to literary texts, it could serve as a starting point for other scholars who wish to build a bridge between linguistic study and fictional child language. This approach could be used to investigate boys' and girls' talk in recent children's books, for example, as these works have the potential of social engineering and may well affect speech patterns of the young.

A Varied and Useful Text

Evelyn Butler

Culture, texte et jeune lecteur (*Culture, Text and Young Reader*) Edited by Jean Perrot. Nancy: Presses Universitaires de Nancy, 1993.

This attractive volume of essays (in French) by selected participants in the Tenth Congress of the International Research Society for Children's Literature (Paris, September 16–19, 1991), reminds us of how important children's literature has become in our world. *Culture, Text and Young Reader* presents 38 writers from 17 countries with a range of approaches, from semiotic and feminist to pedagogical and reader response. They raise questions about the "logic" of children's literature, the possibility of integrating new ways of thinking about childhood into discussions of this literature, and whether we can avoid jargon and confusion while employing the new language of criticism.

This volume reflects the sense of a world unified by networks of interest—in this case, the interests of children, and the interest of adults *in* children. Several essays illustrate the international emphasis of the anthology. Gloria Pondé's "The Feminist Vision of the Literature of Youth of the 1980's in Brazil" concentrates on national issues as she links education and progress with industrialization in modern Brazil (135). As women have become workers, she points out, the media and schools have supplanted family influence on children. In industrialized zones, the society of consumption breaks up old social groups and replaces them with movements (consumer, ecological, and feminist) and activities (sports, spectacles, and leisure pursuits) (136). Still, more and more women are writing children's literature in a Brazil that is experiencing cultural crisis, and Ponté hopes the new interest in and discourse about children's texts may help to resolve this crisis (139). Torben Weinreich states in "The Principal Theories of Children's Literature in Industrial Countries" that in Denmark children's literature is directly under the control of schools because it is sold to the schools. This is significant because in Denmark there are more

Children's Literature 23, ed. Francelia Butler, R. H. W. Dillard, and Elizabeth Lennox Keyser (Yale University Press, © 1995 Hollins College).

books in school libraries than in public libraries (98). The positive democratic effects of this power of the education system are offset, he argues, by a prevailing unartistic didacticism (99), and "empty spaces" that have the potential to stimulate the imagination have instead been "occupied" by social propaganda (100). Jerome Griswold points out the power of themes which are tied into national identity in "The Foe Histories of Democracies: The Anguish of the Impostor in Mark Twain's *The Prince and the Pauper*." He introduces us to the psychological concept of "the impostor syndrome" (65) and holds that this syndrome reveals the other side of the Cinderella story: fear of exposure of one's hidden self (66). Griswold shows that Twain's oedipal, antipatriarchal theme ties in with America's image as rebellious child of Europe, exposing another aspect of American self-determination—the insecurity of the son who usurps his father's place instead of inheriting it (68)—and that this insecurity extends to many who rise in class and public notice, like Twain himself (70). P. Osazee Fayose, on the other hand, describes the growth of a new national literature in "Structures and Techniques of Narration in Nigerian Children's Novels." He shows how oral techniques of rhythm, onomotopoeia, contrasting narrative voices, and historical and topical themes are employed to catch the interest of Nigerian children accustomed to recitation (163).

A second important aspect of *Culture, Text and Young Reader* is that it reveals how certain powerful works of children's literature continue to command the attention of adults as both readers and analysts. Some stories achieve such powerful cultural meaning that they become a myth and model for other works, as Elisabeth Stambor of Israel points out in "The Birth of the Myth of Robinson Crusoe in Children's Literature." This enormously popular tale of a man adventuring alone in the wild was praised in Rousseau's *Emile,* and adults since the late eighteenth century have used it to champion the imagination of children, seeing society as corrupt, the individual as unhappy, and nature as a source of instruction and inspiration (260). Lena Käreland claims almost as great mythic potential for Tove Jansson's *The Dangerous Journey,* in "Modernism, Faust, and Children's Literature." Käreland sees the main character, Susanna, as "a feminine Faust" who represents the expanding ego, never satisfied, seeking "adventure, power, development" (268). The intensity of this work, she argues, comes both from the emotional risks taken by its main character and from its rich paradoxes: here the pastoral becomes its reverse, serenity turns into chaos, and ethical and philosophical questions are raised within a fairy-tale structure (266).

Other stories, while not seeming to achieve mythic status, draw the reader into the experiences of young characters through their journeys through landscapes symbolic of their inner turmoil. Michel Defourny and Jean-Marie Jacquemin of Belgium concentrate on *"The Garden of Abdul Gasazi* of Chris Van Allsburg." Analyzing the extraordinary artistic composition of this complex story as well as its narrative content, they see it as a visionary tale of a boy's penetration into a secret magical garden that combines themes of illusion, transgression, and identity. As the protagonist becomes lost in the garden while chasing his dog, Defourny and Jacquemin claim, what is dramatized is a boy's conflict between the demands of instinct (symbolized in part by the dog) and of an adult world, which triumphs in the end when his parents return and he is restored to their domain (224). The power of symbolic journeys is also discussed by Francine Dugust-Portes of France in "J.-M. G. Le Clézio and the Literature of the Young." She calls his novels parables of young autonomous prophetic characters who travel outside daily life and are initiated into experiences of nature with cosmic resonance (145). Many of Le Clézio's stories are pessimistic; Dugust-Portes explains the popularity of such stories by showing that, through adventures which take them from ecstacy to despair amid sordid, strange, disillusioned worlds, Le Clézio's characters stir the child reader to semiphilosophic thought (151).

In contrast to these stories of internal/external adventure is Roald Dahl's serio-comic moral tale, *Charlie and the Chocolate Factory.* Rose-May Pham Dinh (France) questions the moral basis of Dahl's story, pointing to racism in the original color of the Umpa Lumpas, as well as to their exploitation by Willie Wonka in his factory (185). Pham Dinh also stresses Charlie's character flaws; although the story rests on an opposition between vice/wealth and virtue/poverty, she sees no strong indication that Charlie himself will be virtuous when rich (190). Such focus on the moral implications of stories that are enjoyed by many children leads us into the next (and by far the greatest) preoccupation of the essays in *Culture, Text and Young Reader:* the interest of many adults in shaping and controlling what children read, and a sincere opposition by other adults to such control.

On the one hand, some writers in this text stress the need for adult moral surveillance over, and even participation in, the production of books, so that these books will be sure to have a proper influence on children. Roderick McGillis of Canada points out that an author may have hidden political or psychological motives which operate subtly within the story. In "The Reliability of the Narration in Books for Children," he examines two of Mordecai Richler's *Jacob Two-Two* stories, which were criticized in Egoff and Saltman's *New Republic of Childhood* as "caustic" satire inappropriate for children (29). Comparing and contrasting a story from 1975 with one from 1987, McGillis finds disturbing elements in both text and pictures in the later story, and relates this to the fact that Richler published a somewhat pornographic adult book (entitled *Cocksure*) in 1992 (32). He argues that the narrator in children's stories should be trustworthy, with a warm reliable voice, and that we must believe the narrator will not mislead us or—more to the point—mislead the child reader (36). Similarly, in "Culture and Materialism: Does Literature Still Have a Role to Play?" Anne Taylor poses the question of a writer's responsibility in portraying society and helping the child reader to deal with life in a sometimes hard and frightening world (102). Instead of subjecting children to utilitarian "programs" or creating illusions of happy worlds, she maintains, writers should oppose the forces of materialism and robotism, offer relief to psychological suffering, and encourage racial and religious tolerance (106). Dianne Johnson gives a more historical view of how black writers have educated and encouraged black children, in "The International Context of Afro-American Children's Literature." She traces a movement that began in 1920 with *The Brownies' Book* and continues today as writers educate children of the African diaspora to study their origins and think of themselves as citizens of the world (86).

Also concerned with correcting unacceptable subtexts and cultural influences in children's books is Margaret Higgonet's "Politics in the Course of Re-creation: The Feminist Critic and Children's Literature." Higgonet outlines the motives for and background of feminist criticism in children's literature. She states that although women authors were once discouraged from writing or publishing, women were allowed to write for children. Pseudonyms are of special interest to feminists, she points out, as they indicate the emotionally charged nature of gender and voice—whether it is a woman assuming a male name, or a man assuming a female name

(115). Higgonet believes that gender stereotyping and restriction can be changed in (and by means of) children's literature, and urges readers to be open to the rich and varied points of view which feminist criticism can offer (123).

Other critics de-emphasize adult control over children's reading, stressing the freedom of artistic creation and of children's responses to literature. Kari Skjønsberg of Norway, for example, wants us to realize (with Dahl and Eco) how extremely unpredictable children's responses to books can be. In "Memories of Reading: Childhood Reading in Biographies, Memoirs, and Similar Documents," she reports what books well-known authors (of both adult and children's stories) enjoyed and were inspired by as children (285). Proust refused to reread his favorite childhood book, she tells us, whereas others who did so were disillusioned about the quality of those loved works. Skjønsberg's conclusion is that it is impossible to guess what the influence of any given book will be on a child, but that many authors look back with uncritical delight to their early readings. Anna-Maria Bernardinis of Italy also considers the free and artistic element of literature important for writer and child reader alike. She argues that too much stress has been placed on control of children's literature for social ends. Many new theories of literature resemble the old didactic treatment, she feels, but lack its coherent purpose (276). Bernardinis' contention is that pedagogy—which she defines as critical reflection on the act of teaching, to make it better (271)—can and should envision nonutilitarian literature as valuable in itself, and should accept that its world of discourse must run parallel to literature, without converging (277). Francis Marcoin of France concludes the anthology by trying to pull together both streams of criticism in "Reading Without End." Although, in the context of a continuous creation of literature, adults try to control what children think, he observes, children often resist this attempt. Marcoin holds that many adults invent the idea of the child, pushing to an extreme a fictionalization of the reader (303), whereas others who consider themselves on the side of children may consign children to a place outside of reality, to dreams, or to the role of rebel. He also questions whether psychology has provided insights about the child reader; in rejecting fairies, poetry, enchantment, and the idealized image of childhood, he says, psychology may not really be "on the side of children" (304). Nevertheless, reading always expands, Marcoin concludes, and those who are truly learned about culture and childhood affect us with what they discover in literature, and with what they help to tell the world.

Culture, Text and Young Reader is stimulating and informative, a text useful to anyone struck by the explosion of interest in the field of children's literature and puzzled with questions raised by its many facets, only one of which is the relation of adults to children in the creation and dissemination of children's literature, and the discourse about it. For those who do not read French, Perrot plans a future edition in English.

Dissertations of Note

Compiled and Annotated by Rachel Fordyce

Albert, Susan B. "Once Upon a Conflict: A Psychodynamic Exploration of the Meaning and Value of Fairy Tales." Psy.D. diss. Widener University, Institute for Graduate Clinical Psychology, 1992. 112 pp. DAI 53:4360B.

Albert believes that fairy tales may be as valuable as they are popular. By examining their "therapeutic value in the context of a psychodynamic developmental framework" she shows the ways in which fairy tales change children's attitudes and behavior. Defines fairy tales, gives a history of "Little Red Cap" and its "preoedipal issues," and includes an analysis of "oedipal conflict and its prevalence" in fairy tales.

Arthur, Joe. "Hardly Boys: An Analysis of Behaviors, Social Changes and Class Awareness Hidden in the Old Text of *The Hardy Boys Stories*, 1927–1991." Ph.D. diss. Ohio State University, 1991. 362 pp. DAI 52:2963A.

While analyzing the changes in emphasis and the uses of stereotyping, logic, and vocabulary in the Hardy boys series from its inception to 1991, Arthur observes that these "independent" boys, products of passive parents, "left their safe house behind and, not unlike lower class youth and the very criminals they pursued . . . , came and went as they chose, all in the name of law and order." He makes equally pithy observations about gangs, aunts, mothers, children as products of nature, children as products of nurture, and career police officers.

Bown, Roger. "Children and Popular Television." Ph.D. diss. University of Wales College of Cardiff (United Kingdom), 1988. 262 pp. DAI 51:1583C.

Focuses on British popular television, both at home and in school. "Children's understanding of television is considered in the framework for the development of classroom activity" and offers "a substantial amount of material which has important theoretical and conceptual bearings, both on the broad area of media education and on specific aspects of Media Studies in the primary school."

Bristow, Margaret Bernice Smith. "An Analysis of Myth in Selected Fiction of Virginia Hamilton." Ed.D. diss. University of Virginia, 1992. 313 pp. DAI 53:3463A.

Bristow analyzes *Zeely, The Time-Ago Tales of Jahdu, Time Ago Lost: More Tales of Jahdu, The Magical Adventures of Pretty Pearl*, and Hamilton's use of myth and concludes that she "adheres to classic traditions in myth . . . , mythic heroes, traditional archetypes [such] as the great mother, the trickster, the child archetype and [the use] of traditional mythologies [such] as the circle, the snake, the tree, [and] the forest." She believes Hamilton becomes progressively more afrocentric in her novels, that she has created "the first modern Afro-American trickster as well as the first modern mythic black heroine, Pretty Pearl."

Burdan, Judith Hope. "Managing Character: The Child and the Novel in the Eighteenth Century." Ph.D. diss. University of North Carolina at Chapel Hill, 1992. 225 pp. DAI 53:3208A.

Burdan searched child-rearing manuals, eighteenth-century novels for adults, children's books, and educational treatises to further explain the "familiar lyrical treatment of childhood in Romantic poetry." Exemplary works are

Children's Literature 23, ed. Francelia Butler, R. H. W. Dillard, and Elizabeth Lennox Keyser (Yale University Press, © 1995 Hollins College).

Rousseau's *Emile*, Locke's *Some Thoughts on Education*, and Maria and Richard Edgeworth's *Practical Thoughts on Education*. She stresses that "children's literature helped to naturalize and codify the 'childlike' characteristics promoted by educational treatises."

Byrnes, Alice E. "The Archetypal Symbol of the Child in Literature for Children and Adults." D.A. diss. St. John's University, 1992. 191 pp. DAI 53:2802A.

Byrnes deals with the concepts of the child as symbol and archetype in a Jungian approach to literature. She observes that "the symbiotic relationship of the child and adult in literature is a metaphor of the integration of childlike innocence and adult wisdom." The dissertation stresses the significance of the protégé-mentor relationship, e.g., adolescents may read to learn about the passage from childhood to adulthood, while adults may "look to literature that helps them to re-capture the joys of childhood. Literature of the archetypal child . . . helps students of all ages to recognize the mutual benefits that may emanate from the nurturing influence of a protégé-mentor relationship." She discusses *Anne of Green Gables* and *Silas Marner*, among other works.

Caltabiano, Francis Bernard. "Characteristics and Concepts of Italian-Americans as Portrayed in Children's Books." Ed.D. diss. Temple University, 1992. 202 pp. DAI 53:63A.

Caltabiano discusses 50 Italian-American characters in American children's literature and concludes that while stereotypes exist, they are minimal, and that most of them "exemplify and dignify ethnic differences. The behaviors, attitudes, and goals portrayed in [the books] are commendatory in nature."

Cherland, Meredith Rogers. "Girls and Reading: Children, Culture, and Literary Experience." Ed.D. diss. Arizona State University, 1990. 463 pp. DAI 52:120A.

In an intensive exploration of what reading fiction really meant to a group of eleven-year-old girls, both through their school and home reading, Cherland concludes that the girls were "enacting three themes, three sets of cultural beliefs, through their reading of fiction. These themes are time, gender and individualism." She also notes that reading is "a social practice for them," one in which they both "enacted and resisted their culture."

Clarke, Amy Michaela. "A Woman Writing: Feminist Awareness in the Work of Ursula K. Le Guin." Ph.D. diss. University of California, Davis, 1992. 290 pp. DAI 54:176A.

Clarke believes that Le Guin's work is "traditionally conceived despite her experimentation with unconventional social, political, and literary ideas. [Her] increasingly feminist sensibility has led her to explore female characters and the possibility of a women's literature, to question academic standards . . . , and to discover alternatives to the linear, hero-oriented narrative focused on conflict."

Cobb, Jeanne Beck. "Images and Characteristics of African Americans and Hispanic Americans in Contemporary Children's Fiction." Ed.D. diss. University of Tennessee, 1992. 294 pp. DAI 53:4262A.

Cobb demonstrates that research on minority issues in children's literature and textbooks has declined recently. She focuses on "image, characterization, and stereotyping" in 10 Hispanic and 31 African American works of fiction for elementary children published between 1989 and 1991. While the works were "generally favorable in their treatment of minority groups" their number is "appallingly limited"; moreover, women are more typically stereotyped than men, and the "economic status and social class" of each group are "less favorable and positive than [are] the descriptions of physical appearance, attitudes, and interpersonal relationships."

Cooper, Susan Annette. "A Content Analysis of Selected World War II–Related Juvenile Fiction by American and British Authors." Ed.D. diss. 1991. 140 pp. DAI 52:4130A.

Through 845 scenes in 19 children's novels that take place during World War II, Cooper points out significant differences between British and American authors. She also found that American authors were generally more supportive of World War II, and the juvenile fiction by British writers reflected a greater degree of "conditional support for the war effort." Anti-war sentiment is widespread.

Costello, Jane Hunt. "An Inquiry into the Attitudes of a Selected Group of African Americans Towards the Portrayal of African Americans in Contemporary Children's Literature." Ed.D. diss. University of North Carolina at Greensboro, 1992. 230 pp. DAI 54:176A.

Using a team of five adults (teacher, parent, grandparent, minister, and practice participant) to analyze five works of children's literature about and by African Americans, Costello concludes that there are four main themes that must be addressed in contemporary children's literature: "life experiences as African Americans; the concept of beauty; racism, discrimination, and stereotypes; and morals, values, and life lessons."

Creany, Anne Drolett. "The Effect of Sex Role Stereotypes on the Gender Labels Children Apply to Picture Book Characters." D.Ed. diss. Indiana University of Pennsylvania, 1990. 218 pp. DAI 51:2980A.

Creany believes literature is "one of the factors which influences the development of children's sex-role stereotypes." She analyzes the relationships of age, gender, and self-perception to "the rationale which children provide for their choice of gender labels and their . . . knowledge of sex-role stereotypes."

Day, Karen S. "Teachers of Children's Literature: Voices of Interpretation." Ph.D. diss. University of Alberta (Canada), 1991. 240 pp. DAI 53:2679A.

Day describes the classic dichotomy between teachers who believe that children's literature serves the needs of the curriculum and those who believe it fulfills the needs of readers. Teachers who are able to bring rich life experiences and "multiple perspectives" to the classroom and the interpretation of literature perceive literature "as comfort and therapy"; it nourishes and provides "space" for their thinking.

Deijenberg, Margot. "Paedagogics and the View of Man in Fiction and Reality. On Children's Literature and Educational Ambitions in Sweden in the 1860s." Fil.Dr. diss. Lunds Universitet (Sweden), 1992. 240 pp. DAI 54:656C.

Deijenberg discovered that it is possible to characterize the late nineteenth-century Swedish attitudes toward children and class by determining the cost of books. Cheap books, intended for lower-class children, stressed the "emotional engagement [which] lead to religious faith" and more expensive books stressed an "interest in the surrounding world [through] appeals to reason." These patterns exemplify "marked educational differences" among classes.

Devlin, Jean Theresa. "The Caldecott Books: Values and Visions." Ph.D. diss. Southern Illinois University at Carbondale, 1991. 900 pp. DAI 53:1517A.

Devlin analyzes Caldecott Award books by decade, from 1938 on, and applies "every known technique and medium [to] analyze the symbiotic relationship between visual and printed matter, one of the criteria for this coveted award." She indexes and annotates 205 award-winning books and 1,300 additional picture books, focusing on Marcia Brown and Maurice Sendak.

Fillmore, Roxanne Marchant. "A Comparison of Certain Literary Elements Found in the Children's and Teachers' Choices Awards for the Middle Grades for the Years 1985, 1986, and 1987." Ph.D. diss. University of Iowa, 1991. 175 pp. DAI 53:63A.

"The purpose of this study was to determine whether . . . literary elements found in fictional books chosen by children in the third, fourth, and fifth grades . . . for leisure reading were the same as in the fictional books chosen for the children by teachers of the same grades." She finds that teachers preferred books set in the past with rural settings; children preferred contemporary settings, usually with an urban flavor. Moreover, children are "more flexible in their preferences . . . and chose longer books more often." Children also seem to like humor, exaggeration, and slapstick more than teachers and will read a book on a subject to which they were not normally attracted if the comedy is broad. She also notes that children select works of fantasy most commonly if the "setting (time, country, norms) [are] familiar."

Fowler, Rachel Brown. "A Study of the Communication Between Artist and Child through the Use of Toys in the Illustration of Caldecott Medal Books, 1938–1990." Ph.D. diss. University of Alabama at Birmingham, 1991. 139 pp. DAI 52:2016A.

Because children focus on pictures while adults read the texts of picture books to them, Fowler observes that adults often miss the details that children perceive. She notes that seventy percent of the Caldecott award books have illustrations of toys, and that illustrators use toys to relay "secrets," to convey subplots, and "to provide clues to advance the story pictorially."

Frank, Perry June. "*The Adventures of Tom Sawyer* on Film: The Evolution of an American Icon." Ph.D. diss. George Washington University, 1991. 464 pp. DAI 52:971A.

Frank explores the 1917, 1918, 1930, 1938, and 1973 film versions of *Tom Sawyer* in terms of popular culture. She believes that in an attempt to reproduce Twain's satire and "celebration of [an] authentic American experience" "the films locate the true sources of conflict outside the central character, in contemporary anxieties about family instability, child rearing and welfare, [and in] the growing tension between individualism and community, racial and cultural conflict, and success in twentieth-century America." She concludes that while each of the films demonstrates the "evolution of social issues" each also exhibits "a deep need to see Twain as an icon of conservative values."

Gibbons, Frances Vargas. "Isaac Bashevis Singer in Search of Love and God in His Writings for Adults and Children." Ph.D. diss. University of Florida, 1992. 258 pp. DAI 54:173A.

Gibbons's thesis is that "Singer used his work as an aid to his own growth, and that, through his novels and children's stories, he searched for a benevolent God and an idealistic relationship between men and women."

Greenlee, Adele Ann. "A Comparison of Sixth-Graders' Responses to Well-Reviewed and Formula Series Books." Ph.D. diss. University of Minnesota, 1992. 198 pp. DAI 53:430A.

Greenlee found that the children she surveyed could not distinguish between "good" literature and formula books; that they made judgments about literature based on emotion or personal involvement; that, in retelling a story, they had trouble distinguishing between reality and fiction; that children tended to buy formula books and take well-reviewed books out of the library; and that they selected formula books because they could identify a series or an author, whereas they selected well-reviewed books on the basis of recommendation—presumably from an adult.

Hausfeld, Sandra Kay. "An Analysis of Native American Environmental Attitudes

Reflected in Children's Literature." Ph.D. diss. University of Akron, 1993. 327 pp. DAI 54:807A.

Hausfeld poses three questions: what are Native American attitudes toward the earth and the environment? do books by and about Native Americans reflect these attitudes? and can these attitudes be holistically integrated into curriculum? She examines forty books, notes some stereotyping, and analyzes nine major environmental attitudes: earth as mother/grandmother; "all things are related and possess a spirit"; life is the gift of a creator or Earth Mother; life means respect and communication; land and resources should not be destructed; animals are totems, helpers, and teachers; one must have a spiritual and ceremonial connection to the land; and ideas must pass from generation to generation.

Hill, Lynette Joy Hehn. "Children's Response to Story in Illustrated and Non-Illustrated Text at Three Grade Levels." Ed.D. diss. Washington State University, 1991. 207 pp. DAI 52:3524A.

Hill finds that "pictures may enrich the interpretations of stories [but] they may also direct interpretations and limit the extent to which readers create their own images," particularly with first graders. Rich, imagistic language appears to be more crucial to creative response than visual media. She recommends that children occasionally be allowed to listen to books without looking at the illustrations, and that readers of picture books chose works that are abundant in figural and imginative language.

Johnson, Deidre Ann. "Continued Success: The Early Boys' Fiction of Edward Stratemeyer and the Stratemeyer Syndicate." (Volumes I and II). Ph.D. diss. University of Minnesota, 1991. 401 pp. DAI 52:197A.

Johnson covers a variety of topics: librarians' changing attitudes toward children's popular literature in the nineteenth and twentieth centuries; biographies of Edward Stratemeyer and his daughter Harriet Stratemeyer Adams; the history and critical reception of the Stratemeyer books and the Syndicate's boys' fiction in a variety of genres; and "a discussion of prevalent traits and themes" in the boys' fiction. She dwells on the dime novels, career stories, travel fiction, historical fiction, outdoor stories, contemporary Westerns, and school stories.

Karnes-Duggan, Melinda. "An Analysis of Economic Values in Selected Children's Literature, 1974–1987." Ph.D. diss. Saint Louis University, 1991. 187 pp. DAI 52:1662A.

Karnes-Duggan addresses "the projection of commercialism and materialism" in 52 easy-to-read children's Choice books. Principles she deals with are "greed, cultural implications, occupational and natural concerns, industrial wealth, criminal wealth, exploitation of individuals and groups, and anti-commercialist themes." Because children identify with characters, she believes that less savory characters need to be explained well, and that "when negative aspects of capitalism are subliminally projected through children's stories they should be confronted and discussed in an honest, open fashion."

Lundin, Anne Hutchison. "The Critical Reception of Kate Greenaway in England and America, 1879–1901." Ph.D. diss. University of Alabama, 1992. 384 pp. DAI 54:14A.

This dissertation, in library science, examines the considerable critical reception of Greenaway's works in the late 1800s, and uses the reception to generalize about some "common denominators of criticism [in] contemporary periodicals and other related sources." She notes that children's books were often treated as a "commodity"; that artwork, illustrations, and pictorial effects sometimes took precedence over text; that there was "a lack of rigid demarcation between adult and children's literature"; that the literature emphasized "a growing gender division . . . , romantic idealism . . . , [and] historiography"; that "a diversification of the didactic tradition" may be reflected in an "anxiety about the changing character of children's reading."

Marschall, Amy Horning. "Oral Traditions, Written Collections: Johann Gottfried Herder and the Brothers Grimm." Ph.D. diss. Johns Hopkins University, 1992. 461 pp. DAI 53:166A.

Marschall discusses Herder's concern with the relationship of oral and written literature, particularly with the expression of wonder, which he defines as "human reactions to the unknown, encompassing admiration, amazement, and astonishment, in contrast to fear and instinctual responses." He interprets *Märchen,* an oral tradition, as children's literature, addressed to a child's innocent nature, as opposed to the Grimms' definition of it as folk literature. "Herder's vision of a renewal of creativity inspired by the collection of Germany's indigenous literatures is replaced, in the work of the Grimms, by an understanding of the 'folk' as a conservative rather than creative force, and their literature, accordingly, as historical record."

Mitchell, Diana Dawson. "Gendered Constructions in Twenty-Five Recent Young Adult Novels: A Content Analysis of the Cultural Codes of Identity and Position." Ph.D. diss. Michigan State University, 1992. 207 pp. DAI 53:2355A.

Because "reading can influence the attitudes, behavior, and self image of students" Mitchell examines the portrayal of 25 female characters in contemporary young adult novels. She finds that women are "no longer tied to the traditional character codes" although the break with tradition is hardly complete. She also discusses how teachers can deal with gender issues.

Myatt, Rosalind. "The Child and the Story: The Search for Identity." Ph.D. diss. University of California, Los Angeles, 1990. 733 pp. DAI 51:466A.

Using literary analysis and psychoanalytic theory Myatt provides "a developmental description of personal meanings children constructed from their favorite stories throughout childhood . . . to describe the individual child's response as an active reader." Children from six through twelve years of age exhibit a wide range of differences but all were concerned with "separation from parents, identification with the parent of the same sex, and achievement in a dangerous, exciting world."

Nosworthy, Sylvia Byington. "The Role of Religion in Children's Realistic Fiction." Ph.D. diss. University of Minnesota, 1991. 199 pp. DAI 52:2810A.

Of the 93 works of realistic fiction for children that Nosworthy examined, 59 contained at least one significant religious reference. She analyzes the types of religions referred to, their settings, and the correlation between age and attitude toward religion, and found that "religion is not being eliminated from children's realistic fiction, nor does the presence of religion mean automatic exclusion by award committees."

Oliver-Vazquez, Marlen. "Portrayal of the Elderly and Old Age in Elementary School Textbooks Used by the Department of Education of Puerto Rico." Ed.D. diss. Inter-America University of Puerto Rico, 1991. 213 pp. DAI 53:58A.

Most significantly, Oliver-Vazquez's study shows a "low number of portrayal[s] of elderly characters," most of whom are white males who work "in agricultural trades and passive activities." Their portrayal is "homogenous and superficial." She concludes that school textbooks portray an ambiguous, indistinct, and often stereotyped image of the elderly. She strongly suggests that teachers examine their own attitudes toward the elderly and incorporate "gerontologic contents" into their curriculum.

Peters, Jefferson Marlowe. "Art, Artists, and Artistry in Science Fiction." Ph.D. diss. University of Michigan, 1992. 290 pp. DAI 53:3904A.

While Peters's dissertation is an attempt "to define the ideology of the aesthetic in science fiction," he also examines other genre: fantasy, horror, and children's literature, film, poetry, and comic books. He concludes that the study of art is vital to the study of science fiction, even though the genre is too often viewed as scientific, and that "science fiction crucially unites the humanities and sciences in our increasingly technological world."

Piret, Michael John. "Charles Dickens's *Children's New Testament:* An Introduction, Annotated Edition, and Critical Discussion." Ph.D. diss. University of Michigan, 1991. 261 pp. DAI 52:3613A.

Dickens wrote the *Children's New Testament* in 1846 but it remained in the family until its publication in 1934—probably because of the alterations, omissions, and personal biases in the work. Piret provides a scholarly edition of the work, an exploration of Dickens's emendations, and a discussion of his deletion of the Devil from the text, "his liberal attitudes towards Hell and Judgement . . . his radical championship of the New Testament at the expense of the Old," and his predilection for Unitarian theology.

Sanders, Kathleen Cultron. "An Evaluation of Basal Reader Adaptations of an Original Text." Ph.D. diss. Kansas State University, 1991. 223 pp. DAI 52:3571A.

Sanders's primary concern is to determine whether edited versions of original children's literature, adapted to textbook use, are as well written as the original story. The answer is a resounding no.

Sigler, Carolyn. "Wee Folk, Good Folk: Subversive Children's Literature and British Social Reform, 1700–1900." Ph.D. diss. Florida State University, 1992. 182 pp. DAI 53:822A.

Sigler argues that "early writings for children reflect . . . a radical social redirection, since the valuation of children and the state of childhood was the result of cultural upheavals in the late seventeenth and eighteenth centuries which led to the development of a powerful, literate and progressive working class." She deals with educational reform, the industrial age, religious movements, early feminism, and socioeconomic issues, particularly poverty and repression. She sees children's literature of the period as an embodiment of reformers' hopes for the future and deals with the work of John Newbery, Nathaniel Crouch, John Bunyan, Samuel Johnson, Anna Barbauld, Mary Wollstonecraft, Sarah Trimmer, Catherine Sinclair, John Ruskin, Christina Rossetti, Oscar Wilde, J. M. Barrie, and others.

Su, I-Wen. "A Content Analysis of Cross-Cultural Interaction Patterns of Chinese-Americans in Selected Realistic Fiction for Children Ages 8 through 12." Ph.D. diss. University of Florida, 1991. 242 pp. DAI 53:429A.

Su analyzes six aspects of children's fiction that deals with Chinese-Americans: frequency of cross-cultural interaction; demographic information; basic stylistic attributes; values and behaviors of Chinese-Americans and "problems they encounter in their interactions within their own culture and interactions with other ethnic characters"; and incidences of real and stereotyped portrayal. Analysis shows that integration was emphasized in the books and that "positive influences" affected both Chinese-Americans and non–Chinese-Americans even though race and culture are still obstacles to the portrayal of sound realistic fiction. "While not all of the stereotypes were negative, their overpresentation might convey inaccurate messages about Chinese-Americans."

Swan, Ann M. "An Analysis of Selected Pseudoscientific Phenomena in Children's Literature." Ph.D. diss. University of Akron, 1991. 224 pp. DAI 51:3656A.

Swan focuses on ghosts and poltergeists in forty books to determine whether they are described as fantasy or as "serious representations of reality." She concludes that most authors treat these phenomena as fantasy and have no intention to encourage belief in them, but not all.

Tarr, Carol Anita. "Transformations of Fact Into Fiction: The Making of Marjorie Kinnan Rawlings's *The Yearling*." D.A. diss. Illinois State University, 1992. 283 pp. DAI 53:1521A.

Tarr demonstrates that "Marjorie Kinnan Rawlings was especially interested in how fact is used in fiction, insisting that writing was the result of research and reporting that was transformed through the writer's creative fire." She shows how Rawlings methodically collected information for *The Yearling* and carefully compares Rawlings's notes for the novel with her finished product. Tarr also suggests that Rawlings's process "can be used as a model for middle school students who are beginning to come to grips with fiction. They can begin to see how Rawlings used her own experiences and the experiences of others as a factual skeleton which she fleshed out into her own story."

Vandell, Kathy Scales. "The Everlasting If: American National Identity in Children's Historical Fiction, 1865–1965." Ph.D. diss. University of Maryland College Park, 1991. 584 pp. DAI 52:2186A.

Vandell examines children's fictional and nonfictional books, popular periodicals, and historical fiction to determine "the connections between the social locations, experiences, and professional conventions of the writers and the definitions of national identity they created," particularly in terms of "gender, political, ethnic, and racial variations." She sees "a trend toward social (rather than political) history and the trend toward greater representational authenticity in children's books."

White, Donna Rae. "The Mabinogi in Children's Literature: Welsh Legends in English-Language Children's Books." Ph.D. diss. University of Minnesota, 1991. 250 pp. DAI 52:2938A.

White traces the treatment of the Mabinogi from 1881, when Sidney Lanier published *The Boys' Mabinogion*, through the work of Gwyn Thomas and Kevin Crossley-Holland (1984) and Rhiannon Ifans (1988). She notes that contemporary writers "continue to base editorial decisions on conceptions of what is morally acceptable for children." She also analyzes original children's fantasies by Joan Aiken, Susan Cooper, Kenneth Morris, Alan Garner, Lloyd Alexander, and Jenny Nimmo to determine what aspects of their works are related to the Mabinogi and how the authors deal with the original Welsh tales.

Wood, Naomi J. "Better Than Life: Death as a Developmental Trope in Nineteenth-Century British Children's Fiction." Ph.D. diss. Duke University, 1991. 238 pp. DAI 53:1930A.

Beginning with James Janeway's *A Token for Children* (1671–72) and covering works by Charles Dickens, Charles Kingsley, Charlotte Yonge, Margaret Gatty, and George MacDonald, Wood examines how both realistic and fantastic nineteenth-century literature invested the tropic figure of death and dying children "with new intensity." She applies Gilles Deleuze's theories of masochism to MacDonald's *At the Back of the North Wind*, and concludes that "the death-scene in children's literature typifies the problems of negotiating between the terms 'children' and 'literature' in that the categories tend to deconstruct when analyzed, and so the very objects desired evade comprehension."

Also of Note

The dissertations are not annotated if the title is sufficiently descriptive.

Arrowsmith, Deborah K. Masterson. "Informational Books: Their Instructional Impact Upon Young Children's Writing." Ph.D. diss. Ohio State University, 1993. 224 pp. DAI 54:83A.

Barlup, Jacqueline Hovis. "Whole Language, The Librarian, and Children's Literature Beyond the Basal Reader: A Case Study of the Attitudes of Students, Teachers, and Librarians with Literature-Based Reading." Ph.D. diss. University of Pittsburgh, 1991, 163 pp. DAI 53:336.

Bergen, Anne Killelea. "The Effect of a Training Strategy on Changes in Parents' Perceptions of Their Role and Responsibility and of Their Knowledge of Children's Literature in Promoting the Literacy of Their Children in Grades Three, Four and Five." D.Ed. diss. Boston College, 1991. 115 pp. DAI 52:2871A.

Borden, Marjorie L. "The Preschool Teacher's Use of Children's Books to Introduce and Enhance the Teaching of Mathematical Concepts." Ed.D. diss. Temple University, 1993. 147 pp. DAI 54:417A.

Bramwell, Roberta J. T. "The Effect of Drama Education on Children's Attitudes to the Elderly and to Ageing." Ph.D. diss. University of British Columbia (Canada), 1990. 382 pp. DAI 53:3165A.

A serious attempt to show that drama education is not a "mere frill."

Burbank, Lucille. "Children's Television: An Historical Inquiry on Three Selected, Prominent, Long-Running, Early Childhood TV Programs." Ph.D. diss. Temple University, 1992. 326 pp. DAI 53:3028A.

Focuses on *Mister Rogers' Neighborhood, Captain Kangaroo,* and *Sesame Street,* and discusses interviews with their creators, writers, directors, actors, producers, and researchers.

Cooper, Kenneth Dean. "Fables of the Nuclear Age: Fifty Years of World War III." Ph.D. diss. Vanderbilt University, 1992. 352 pp. DAI 54:176A.

"Nuclear criticism" with significant references to Le Guin.

Darigan, Daniel Lee. "The Effects of Teachers Reading Aloud on Elementary Children's Attitudes Toward African Americans." Ph.D. diss. University of Oregon, 1991. 138 pp. DAI 52:2481A.

Dezolt, Denise Elizabeth Mott. "Themes, Age, and Gender Differences in Children's Stories about Caring." Ph.D. diss. Kent State University, 1992. 164 pp. DAI 53:2741A.

Donnelly, Amy Josephine. "Child as Curricular Informant: An Inquiry Into the Learning Processes and Potential of Literature Response Journals." Ph.D. diss. University of South Carolina, 1991. 429 pp. DAI 52:2442A.

Dougherty, James Francis. "A Study of the Experiences of Principals in Dealing with the Sudden Deaths of Students." Ph.D. diss. New York University, 1992. 181 pp. DAI 53:2617A.

Includes children's literature about death and dying.

Dudko, Mary Ann K. "Young Children's Perceptions of a Pretend Television Character." Ph.D. diss. Texas Woman's University, 1992. 71 pp. DAI 54:81A.

Focuses on the "pretend television character" Barney.

Feehan, Patricia Ellen. "State Library Agency Youth Services Consultants: Their Potential as Agents of Change." Ph.D. diss. University of North Carolina at Chapel Hill, 1991. 260 pp. DAI 52:3466A.

Librarians should be agents for change in public library youth services.

Gagne, Kathleen Dunne. "'Kids & Books': A Model for Television as a Medium to Lead Children to Literature." Ed.D. diss. University of Massachusetts, 1992. 218 pp. DAI 53:453A.

Gero-John, Judith. "Commands and Whispers: Renaissance Parental Advice Books, Their Tradition, and Their Value in Literary Studies." Ph.D. diss. Kansas State University, 1992. 138 pp. DAI 53:3536A.

Girous, Dorothy. "Using Children's Trade Books to Enhance the Mathematics Curriculum in the Elementary School." Ph.D. diss. Loyola University of Chicago, 1992. 136 pp. DAI 52:4218A.

    Suggests children's trade books as an alternative to mathematics textbooks.

Guinta, Edvige. "A Raven Like a Writing-Desk: Lewis Carroll Through James Joyce's Looking Glass." Ph.D. diss. University of Miami, 1991. 233 pp. DAI 52:2561A.

Hathaway, Milton Gifford. "Science-Related Gender Roles in the Illustrations of Contemporary Outstanding Science Information Books for the Middle School Student." Ph.D. diss. Indiana University, 1992. 368 pp. DAI 53:4116A.

    Illustrations of males dominate trade book illustrations in the sciences.

Heisterkamp, Jo Anne. "The Effects of Various Questioning Strategies on Creative Thinking and Listening Comprehension Using Selected Orally Presented Children's Literature in Fifth Grade." Ed.D. diss. Delta State University, 1991. 235 pp. DAI 52:1193A.

Innes, Marie Cecile. "Six Children's Responses to Literature." Ph.D. diss. University of Alberta (Canada), 1991. 195 pp. DAI 53:2681A.

    Correlation between listening and comprehension.

Jenkins, Lisa Shamburger. "The Children's Literature Curriculum of an Elementary School: A Microethnography." Ph.D. diss. Florida State University, 1991. 303 pp. DAI 52:3525A.

    Analyzes the influence of teachers' values on children's interpretations of social interaction.

Kaplan, Mindy Lee. "Does Psychology Live on Sesame Street?" Psy. D. Hahnemann University Graduate School, 1989. 99 pp. DAI 50:2627B.

Kerlavage, Marianne Sykes. "Artworks and Young Children: An Historical Analysis of the Paradigm Governing the Use of Art Appreciation in Early Childhood." Ph.D. diss. University of Wisconsin-Milwaukee, 1992. 332 pp. DAI 53:1770A.

Klassen, Charlene Ruth. "Teacher Education That Is Multicultural: Expanding Preservice Teachers' Orientation Toward Learning Through Children's Literature." Ph.D. diss. University of Arizona, 1993. 331 pp. DAI 54:1266A.

Klatt, Beverly Anne. "Elementary Students' Responses to the Genre of Biography and to *Lincoln: A Photobiography*." Ph.D. diss. Texas A&M University, 1992. 224 pp. DAI 53:1854A.

Lagrone, Susan B. "The Influence of African-American Children's Literature on the Academic Self-Concept and Ethnic/Racial Pride of African-American Third-Grade Students." Ed.D. diss. Southern Illinois University at Edwardsville, 1992. 93 pp. DAI 53:3788A.

Lefever-Davis, Shirley Anne. "The Effects of Story Structure and Reader Response Questioning Strategies on Second Graders' Oral and Written Responses to Literature." Ph.D. diss. Kansas State University, 1991. 176 pp. DAI 52:3177A.

Lewicke, Catherine P. Cryan. "Storytelling for the Elementary Classroom Teacher." Ed.D. diss. University of Lowell, 1991. 120 pp. DAI 52:1240A.

    Includes a handbook for teachers who wish to be storytellers.

Litteral, Linda Lambert. "Writing and Designing Science Trade Books for Young Adolescents: Model Development and Application." Ed.D. diss. University of Illinois at Urbana-Champaign, 1993. 434 pp. DAI 54:1748A.

Madigan, Mark John. "Flint and Fire: Selected Letters of Dorothy Canfield Fisher." Ph.D. diss. University of Massachusetts, 1991. 809 pp. DAI 52:2144A.

Manhart, Mary Frances. "Analysis of Affixed Words: Ten Selected Trade Books." Ph.D. diss. University of Nebraska-Lincoln, 1991. 104 pp. DAI 52:2088A.

McKenna, Linda Marie. "The Relationship Between Attributes of a Children's Radio Program and Appeal." Ph.D. diss. University of Pennsylvania, 1991. 122 pp. DAI 52:3866A.

Michaelsen, Scott. "Mark Twain's Capitalism. Gilded Age Capitalists and Aspirants, 1862–1909." Ph.D. diss. State University of New York at Buffalo, 1992. 558 pp. DAI 53:3214A.
    Discusses *Tom Sawyer Abroad, Tom Sawyer, Detective, Tom Sawyer's Conspiracy,* and "The International Lightning Trust."

Mohler, Linda Sue. "The Use of Authentic Literature in the Elementary Classroom." Ph.D. diss. Pennsylvania State University, 1993. 138 pp. 54:1743A.

Morgan, Jeffrey Alan. "Educating the Emotions." Ph.D. diss. Simon Fraser University (Canada), 1991. 173 pp. DAI 54:1292A.

Moriarty, Terry Elizabeth Eusey. "Using Children's Literature: How Literature-Based Writing Influences the Development of Phonological Awareness." Ph.D. diss. Oakland University, 1990. 126 pp. DAI 52:487A.

Morris, David Othniel. "An Analysis of the Critical Standards Adolescents Use to Evaluate the Television Programs They Watch." Ph.D. diss. New York University, 1991. 251 pp. DAI 52:1932A.

Mosley, Alana Jo. "Exploring Whole Language: Incorporating Genuine Reading and Writing Opportunities in a First-Grade Classroom." Ed.D. diss. Boston University, 1993. 180 pp. DAI 54:420A.

Olson, Lorelie. "Using Folk Tale Activities to Develop Cooperative Social Skills in Young Children." (Volumes I and II). Ed.D. diss. Seattle University, 1991. 238 pp. DAI 52:2403A.

Oroms, Lilly J. "A Content Analysis Approach to the Depiction of the Elderly in Literature Books for Children Published Between 1950–1966 and 1970–1985 for Grades Five Through Eight." Ed.D. diss. Temple University, 1992. 119 pp. DAI 53:1393A.

Ouellette, Glenda Dubay. "The Relationship of Children's Expectations for Structure in Story to Their Knowledge of Literature and Their Reading Ability." Ed.D. diss. University of Lowell, 1991. 119 pp. DAI 53:455A.

Ponder, John Mark. "Fourth-Grade Children's Thematic Interpretations of Literary Works Within the Genres of Fantasy, Realistic Fiction and Folktale." Ph.D. diss. University of Georgia, 1992. 184 pp. DAI 53:3156A.

Ramirez, Gonzalo, Jr. "The Effects of Hispanic Children's Literature on the Self-Esteem of Lower Socioeconomic Mexican-American Kindergarten Children." Ed.D. diss. Texas Tech University, 1991. 127 pp. DAI 52:2394A.

Rasool, Mulazimuddin Shareef. "Animated Cartoon: A Pedagogy for the Reinforcement of a Particular World View in Child Viewers." Ed.D. diss. University of Massachusetts, 1991. 133 pp. DAI 52:2107A.

Reimer, Kathryn Meyer. "Literature as the Core of the Reading Curriculum: Multiple Perspectives." Ph.D. diss. University of Illinois at Urbana-Champaign, 1991. 297 pp. DAI 52:2446A.

Rosman, Steven Michael. "Children's Verbal and Nonverbal Responses to Fairy Tales: A Description and Analysis of Storytelling Events with First and Second-Graders." Ph.D. diss. New York University, 1992. 199 pp. DAI 53:765A.

Rosolowski, Tacey A. "Shapes of Indeterminacy: Analogy and Sequence in Vico's *New Science* and Rousseau's *Reveries* and *Emile.*" Ph.D. diss. State University of New York at Buffalo, 1991. 235 pp. DAI 52:2545A.

Saraiva-Mendes, Maria Regina. "The Educational Role of Comic Strips: A Study of Sexual Stereotypes." Public.D. diss. Universitat Autonoma de Barcelona (Spain), 1991. 424 pp. DAI 54:651C.

Shen, Wenju. "Synthetic Texts or Authentic Literature: An Examination of Basal

Reading Series." D.Ed. Indiana University of Pennsylvania, 1991. 131 pp. DAI 52:866A.

Basal readers from MacMillan, Heath, Silver Burdett & Ginn, Scott Fores-man, and Houghton Mifflin show that publishers don't acknowledge cuts from original works.

Shoultz, Elzora Stephens. "A Content Analysis of the Black Author's Portrayal of Black Americans in Children's Fiction for Grades Kindergarten through Six Pub-lished in the United States from 1970 to 1985." Ed.D. diss. Temple University, 1992. 124 pp. DAI 53:3102A.

Smith, Barbara Desrosier. "A Descriptive Analysis of the Content in Three Basal Readers." Ph.D. diss. University of Arizona, 1991. 129 pp. DAI 52:2484A.

Smith, Cleta Gaile Price. "A Content Analysis of Trade Books Selected as Children's Choices to Examine Reading Experiences." Ed.D. diss. Texas Woman's University, 1992. 150 pp. DAI 54:134A.

Highlights the uneven quality of material adapted from original, well-written children's literature.

Stevens-Marchigiani, Deborah Ann. "A Study on Encouraging Parents to Read Aloud Nonfiction Literature to Their Children." Ph.D. diss. Loyola University of Chicago, 1992. 144 pp. DAI 53:1111A.

Stouten, Jack Wilfred. "Literature-Based Reading Program: An Examination of Basal Reading Series." Ph.D. diss. Walden University, 1993. 145 pp. DAI 54:1303A.

Tasdad, Shirley Sisco. "The Effect of a Planned Fantasy Reading Program on the Imagination Development of Children." Ph.D. diss. University of Wyoming, 1992. 105 pp. DAI 53:1710A.

Notes no significant difference in students' ability to read or appreciate literature.

Taylor, Ronald Lee. "Family Support of Children's Reading Development in a Highly Literate Society [Iceland]." Ph.D. diss. University of Missouri–Kansas City, 1992. 173 pp. DAI 53:1024A.

Tejerina-Lobo, Isabel. "Study of Children's Drama in Its Psycho-Pedagogical and Expressive Dimensions." Public.D. diss. Universidad de Cantabria (Spain), 1992. 386 pp. DAI 54:657C.

Walker, Frederick Arthur. "Fictive Diction: Fantasy in Exotic Words." Ph.D. diss. Queen's University at Kingston (Canada), 1991. 305 pp. DAI 54:538A.

Fantasies of C. S. Lewis, J. R. R. Tolkien, and Charles Williams.

Walworth, Margaret Ellen. "Second Grade Pupils' and Teachers' Expressed Percep-tions of Text and Illustrations in Selected Picture Books." Ph.D. diss. University of Georgia, 1991. 172 pp. DAI 52:2090A.

Wilhelm, S. Lynn. "A Study of the Content of Biographical Material Found in Selected Textbooks and Collective Biographies Compared with Students' Stated Preferences." Ph.D. diss. Michigan State University, 1991. 297 pp. DAI 52:3518A.

Young, Ethel Ruth. "Can Children Be Critics? A Participant Observational Study of Children's Responses to Literature." Ph.D. diss. Claremont Graduate School, 1991. 101 pp. DAI 52:832A.

Tries to validate further the reader response research that shows that child-as-critic is a viable concept.

Contributors and Editors

EVELYN BUTLER is co-editor of *Recovering Literature: A Journal of Contextual Criticism,* teaches children's literature at San Diego State University, and has taught at the University of Paris. She writes criticism and fiction.

FRANCELIA BUTLER, founding editor of *Children's Literature,* has published many books on children's literature, including *Skipping Around the World: The Ritual Nature of Folk Rhymes.*

JOHN CECH, book review editor of *Children's Literature,* teaches in the English Department at the University of Florida. He is the author of a book for children, *My Grandfather's Journey* (1991), and recently completed a book on the works of Maurice Sendak.

R. H. W. DILLARD, editor-in-chief of *Children's Literature* and professor of English at Hollins College, is the longtime chair of the Hollins Creative Writing Program and is adviser to the director of the Hollins Graduate Program in Children's Literature. A novelist and poet, he is also the author of two critical monographs, *Horror Films* and *Understanding George Garrett,* as well as articles on Ellen Glasgow, Vladimir Nabokov, Federico Fellini, Robert Coover, Fred Chappell, and others.

RACHEL FORDYCE, former executive secretary of the Children's Literature Association, has written five books, most recently, with Carla Marello, *Semiotics and Linguistics in Alice's Worlds.* She is a professor of English and the dean of humanities and social sciences at Montclair State University.

J. KARL FRANSON, professor of English at the University of Maine at Farmington, has published essays on Milton (his primary research interest), Shakespeare, Blake, Wordsworth, and Coleridge. He is completing a book on numerical structures in the Renaissance elegy.

ELIZABETH N. GOODENOUGH, who teaches Victorian writers and children's literature at Claremont McKenna College, has written articles on Nathaniel Hawthorne, Virginia Woolf, Laura Ingalls Wilder, and Carl Jung. She is co-editor of *Infant Tongues: The Voice of the Child in Literature.*

DARWIN L. HENDERSON is an associate professor of literacy and language at Purdue University. His research interests are twentieth-century African-American writers and illustrators for children and young adults. The co-editor of a forthcoming collection of Caribbean, African, and African-American poetry (Scholastic), he regularly reviews for *Quarterly Black Review.*

CAROLINE C. HUNT teaches Milton, the later Renaissance, young adult, and children's literature at the College of Charleston. She has published a number of essays in these areas as well as articles in reference works, including "The Year in Children's Books" for the *Dictionary of Literary Biography Yearbook.*

ELIZABETH LENNOX KEYSER, editor of *Children's Literature* 22 and 23, is an associate professor of English at Hollins College, where she teaches children's literature, American literature, and American studies. She is the author of *Whispers in the Dark: the Fiction of Louisa May Alcott* and numerous articles on American women writers.

JEAN I. MARSDEN is an associate professor of English at the University of Connecticut and co-editor of *Children's Literature* 19. She is the author of *The Re-Imagined Text: Shakespeare, Adaptation and Eighteenth-Century Literary Theory* and editor of *The Appropriation of Shakespeare: Post-Renaissance Reconstructions of the Works and the*

284 CONTRIBUTORS AND EDITORS

Myth. Her research includes, in addition to Mary Lamb, work on representations of women on the eighteenth-century stage.

EVA-MARIA METCALF teaches German and Swedish at the University of Minnesota. Her area of research is German and Northern European children's literature. She is completing a book on Astrid Lindgren in the Twayne World Authors Series and is working on a book on Christine Nostlinger.

MIRIAM YOUNGERMAN MILLER is an associate professor of English at the University of New Orleans. She is the co-editor of *Approaches to Teaching Sir Gawain and the Green Knight* and of a collection of critical essays on the poems of MS Cotton Nero A.x. Most recently she has published on Old English prosody. Other publication interests include science fiction, fantasy, Tolkien, and Updike. In the field of children's literature, she has published articles on the Middle Ages in nonfiction, illustrations in juvenile editions of *The Canterbury Tales,* and literary dialect in the novels of Rosemary Sutcliff. Eventually she hopes to complete a book on views of the Middle Ages in children's literature.

MITZI MYERS, a member of the *Children's Literature* advisory board, teaches at UCLA. She has published widely on Georgian writers for children, including a prize-winning essay on Mary Wollstonecraft in *Children's Literature* 14. She is completing a book on Maria Edgeworth and, with U. C. Knoefplmacher, will serve as guest-editor of *Children's Literature* 25.

PERRY NODELMAN, a professor of English at the University of Winnipeg, is the author of *Words About Pictures* and *The Pleasures of Children's Literature* (Longman) as well as a children's novel, *The Same Place But Different* (Groundwood).

REUBEN SÁNCHEZ teaches English at California State University, Fresno. He has published essays on Milton and Shakespeare, and is the author of two books of fiction, *The Education of Henry Otero* (Arte Publico Press, 1995) and *The Football Game* (Arte Publico Press, 1995).

GARY D. SCHMIDT chairs the Department of English at Calvin College. He is the author of *Katherine Paterson* (Twayne, 1994) and a retelling of John Bunyan's *Pilgrim's Progress,* illustrated by Barry Moser, for children (Eerdmans, 1994). He is currently editing the memoir of Hannah Adams, the eighteenth-century New England historian.

ROBERTA SEELINGER TRITES is an assistant professor of English at Illinois State University at Normal, where she specializes in children's literature. Her research interests include critical theories—especially feminist and narrative theories—as they apply to recent children's texts. She recently published another essay on Patricia MacLachlan in the *Children's Literature Association Quarterly.*

TIM WOLF, assistant professor of children's literature at Middle Tennessee State University, has published two children's novels, *In Search of Perlas Grandes* (1985) and *The Indian's Ruby* (1986), and serves as chair for the Conference on Modern Critical Approaches to Children's Literature.

NAOMI J. WOOD is an assistant professor of English at Kansas State University. She is the author of a recent essay on George MacDonald in the *Children's Literature Association Quarterly* and is working on a book about death and sexuality in Victorian children's literature.

Award Applications

The article award committee of the Children's Literature Association publishes a bibliography of the year's work in children's literature in the *Children's Literature Association Quarterly* and selects the year's best critical articles. For pertinent articles that have appeared in a collection of essays or journal other than one devoted to children's literature, please send a photocopy or offprint with the correct citation and your address written on the first page to Gillian Adams, 5906 Fairlane Drive, Austin, Tex. 78731. Papers will be acknowledged and returned if return postage is enclosed. The annual deadline is May 1.

The Phoenix Award is given for a book first published twenty years earlier that did not win a major award but has passed the test of time and is deemed to be of high literary quality. Send nominations to Alethea Helbig, 3640 Eli Road, Ann Arbor, Mich. 48104.

The Children's Literature Association offers three annual research grants. The Margaret P. Esmonde Memorial Scholarship offers $500 for criticism and original works in the areas of fantasy or science fiction for children or adolescents by beginning scholars, including graduate students, instructors, and assistant professors. Research Fellowships are awards ranging from $250 to $1,000 (the number and amount of awards are based on the number and needs of winning applicants) for criticism or original scholarship leading to a significant publication. Recipients must have postdoctoral or equivalent professional standing. Awards may be used for transportation, living expenses, materials, and supplies but not for obtaining advanced degrees, for creative writing, textbook writing, or pedagogical purposes. The Weston Woods Media Scholarship awards $1,000 and free use of the Weston Woods studios to encourage investigation of the elements and techniques that contribute to successfully adapting children's literature to film or recording or to developing materials for television and video. For full application guidelines on all three grants, write the Children's Literature Association, c/o Marianne Gessner, 22 Harvest Lane, Battle Creek, Mich. 49015. The annual deadline for these awards is February 1.

Order Form   Yale University Press
                   P.O. Box 209040, New Haven, CT 06520-9040
Phone orders 1-800-YUP-READ (U.S. and Canada)

Customers in the United States and Canada may photocopy this form and use it for ordering all volumes of **Children's Literature** available from Yale University Press. Individuals are asked to pay in advance. We honor both MasterCard and VISA. Checks should be made payable to Yale University Press.

The prices given are 1995 list prices for the United States and are subject to change. A shipping charge of $2.75 is to be added to each order, and Connecticut residents must pay a sales tax of 6 percent.

Qty.	Volume	Price	Total amount	Qty.	Volume	Price	Total amount
____	10 (cloth)	$45.00	_____	____	18 (paper)	$16.00	_____
____	11 (cloth)	$45.00	_____	____	19 (cloth)	$45.00	_____
____	12 (cloth)	$45.00	_____	____	19 (paper)	$16.00	_____
____	13 (cloth)	$45.00	_____	____	20 (cloth)	$45.00	_____
____	14 (cloth)	$45.00	_____	____	20 (paper)	$16.00	_____
____	15 (cloth)	$45.00	_____	____	21 (cloth)	$45.00	_____
____	15 (paper)	$16.00	_____	____	21 (paper)	$16.00	_____
____	16 (paper)	$16.00	_____	____	22 (cloth)	$45.00	_____
____	17 (cloth)	$45.00	_____	____	22 (paper)	$16.00	_____
____	17 (paper)	$16.00	_____	____	23 (cloth)	$45.00	_____
____	18 (cloth)	$45.00	_____	____	23 (paper)	$16.00	_____

Payment of $_____ is enclosed (including sales tax if applicable).

MasterCard no. _____

4-digit bank no. _____ Expiration date _____

VISA no. _____ Expiration date _____

Signature_____

SHIP TO: _____

_____

_____

See the next page for ordering issues from Yale University Press, London. Volumes out of stock in New Haven may be available from the London office.

Volumes 1–7 of **Children's Literature** can be obtained directly from John C. Wandell, The Children's Literature Foundation, P.O. Box 370, Windham Center, Conn. 06280.

Order Form Yale University Press, 23 Pond Street, Hampstead, London NW3 2PN, England

Customers in the United Kingdom, Europe, and the British Commonwealth may photocopy this form and use it for ordering all volumes of **Children's Literature** available from Yale University Press. Individuals are asked to pay in advance. We honour Access, VISA, and American Express accounts. Cheques should be made payable to Yale University Press.

The prices given are 1995 list prices for the United Kingdom and are subject to change. A post and packing charge of £1.75 is to be added to each order.

Qty.	Volume	Price	Total amount	Qty.	Volume	Price	Total amount
___	8 (cloth)	£40.00	_____	___	15 (paper)	£14.95	_____
___	8 (paper)	£14.95	_____	___	16 (paper)	£14.95	_____
___	9 (cloth)	£40.00	_____	___	17 (cloth)	£40.00	_____
___	9 (paper)	£14.95	_____	___	17 (paper)	£14.95	_____
___	10 (cloth)	£40.00	_____	___	18 (cloth)	£40.00	_____
___	11 (cloth)	£40.00	_____	___	18 (paper)	£14.95	_____
___	11 (paper)	£14.95	_____	___	19 (cloth)	£40.00	_____
___	12 (cloth)	£40.00	_____	___	19 (paper)	£14.95	_____
___	12 (paper)	£14.95	_____	___	20 (paper)	£14.95	_____
___	13 (cloth)	£40.00	_____	___	21 (paper)	£14.95	_____
___	13 (paper)	£14.95	_____	___	22 (cloth)	£40.00	_____
___	14 (cloth)	£40.00	_____	___	22 (paper)	£14.95	_____
___	14 (paper)	£14.95	_____	___	23 (cloth)	£40.00	_____
___	15 (cloth)	£40.00	_____	___	23 (paper)	£14.95	_____

Payment of £ _____ is enclosed.

Please debit my Access/VISA/American Express account no. _____

Expiry date _____

Signature _____ Name _____

Address _____

See the previous page for ordering issues from Yale University Press, New Haven. Volumes out of stock in London may be available from the New Haven office.

Volumes 1–7 of **Children's Literature** can be obtained directly from John C. Wandell, The Children's Literature Foundation, Box 370, Windham Center, Conn. 06280.

Order Form   Yale University Press
            P.O. Box 209040, New Haven, CT 06520-9040
Phone orders 1-800-YUP-READ (U.S. and Canada)

Customers in the United States and Canada may photocopy this form and use it for ordering all volumes of **Children's Literature** available from Yale University Press. Individuals are asked to pay in advance. We honor both MasterCard and VISA. Checks should be made payable to Yale University Press.

The prices given are 1995 list prices for the United States and are subject to change. A shipping charge of $2.75 is to be added to each order, and Connecticut residents must pay a sales tax of 6 percent.

Qty.	Volume	Price	Total amount	Qty.	Volume	Price	Total amount
___	10 (cloth)	$45.00	_____	___	18 (paper)	$16.00	_____
___	11 (cloth)	$45.00	_____	___	19 (cloth)	$45.00	_____
___	12 (cloth)	$45.00	_____	___	19 (paper)	$16.00	_____
___	13 (cloth)	$45.00	_____	___	20 (cloth)	$45.00	_____
___	14 (cloth)	$45.00	_____	___	20 (paper)	$16.00	_____
___	15 (cloth)	$45.00	_____	___	21 (cloth)	$45.00	_____
___	15 (paper)	$16.00	_____	___	21 (paper)	$16.00	_____
___	16 (paper)	$16.00	_____	___	22 (cloth)	$45.00	_____
___	17 (cloth)	$45.00	_____	___	22 (paper)	$16.00	_____
___	17 (paper)	$16.00	_____	___	23 (cloth)	$45.00	_____
___	18 (cloth)	$45.00	_____	___	23 (paper)	$16.00	_____

Payment of $_____ is enclosed (including sales tax if applicable).

MasterCard no. _____

4-digit bank no. _____ Expiration date _____

VISA no. _____ Expiration date _____

Signature _____

SHIP TO: _____

_____

_____

See the next page for ordering issues from Yale University Press, London. Volumes out of stock in New Haven may be available from the London office.

Volumes 1–7 of **Children's Literature** can be obtained directly from John C. Wandell, The Children's Literature Foundation, P.O. Box 370, Windham Center, Conn. 06280.

Order Form   Yale University Press, 23 Pond Street, Hampstead, London NW3 2PN, England

Customers in the United Kingdom, Europe, and the British Commonwealth may photocopy this form and use it for ordering all volumes of **Children's Literature** available from Yale University Press. Individuals are asked to pay in advance. We honour Access, VISA, and American Express accounts. Cheques should be made payable to Yale University Press.

The prices given are 1995 list prices for the United Kingdom and are subject to change. A post and packing charge of £1.75 is to be added to each order.

Qty.	Volume	Price	Total amount	Qty.	Volume	Price	Total amount
____	8 (cloth)	£40.00	_____	____	15 (paper)	£14.95	_____
____	8 (paper)	£14.95	_____	____	16 (paper)	£14.95	_____
____	9 (cloth)	£40.00	_____	____	17 (cloth)	£40.00	_____
____	9 (paper)	£14.95	_____	____	17 (paper)	£14.95	_____
____	10 (cloth)	£40.00	_____	____	18 (cloth)	£40.00	_____
____	11 (cloth)	£40.00	_____	____	18 (paper)	£14.95	_____
____	11 (paper)	£14.95	_____	____	19 (cloth)	£40.00	_____
____	12 (cloth)	£40.00	_____	____	19 (paper)	£14.95	_____
____	12 (paper)	£14.95	_____	____	20 (paper)	£14.95	_____
____	13 (cloth)	£40.00	_____	____	21 (paper)	£14.95	_____
____	13 (paper)	£14.95	_____	____	22 (cloth)	£40.00	_____
____	14 (cloth)	£40.00	_____	____	22 (paper)	£14.95	_____
____	14 (paper)	£14.95	_____	____	23 (cloth)	£40.00	_____
____	15 (cloth)	£40.00	_____	____	23 (paper)	£14.95	_____

Payment of £ _____ is enclosed.

Please debit my Access/VISA/American Express account no. _____

Expiry date _____

Signature _____ Name _____

Address _____

See the previous page for ordering issues from Yale University Press, New Haven. Volumes out of stock in London may be available from the New Haven office.

Volumes 1–7 of **Children's Literature** can be obtained directly from John C. Wandell, The Children's Literature Foundation, Box 370, Windham Center, Conn. 06280.